EXISTENTIAL PHENOMENOLOGY

Whereof one cannot speak, thereof one must speak....
For thereof man lives, and thereof he dies....

DUQUESNE STUDIES

Philosophical Series

12

EXISTENTIAL PHENOMENOLOGY

William A. Luijpen, Ph.D.

Revised Edition

DUQUESNE UNIVERSITY PRESS, Pittsburgh

Distributed by Humanities Press, Atlantic Highlands

Printing history of *Existential Phenomenology:*

First edition, Spring, 1960
Second impression, Fall, 1962
Third impression, Fall, 1963
Fourth impression, Spring, 1965
Fifth impression, August, 1966
Sixth impression, July, 1967
Seventh impression, August, 1968
Revised edition, August, 1969
Second impression, Fall, 1972
Third impression, January, 1977

Library of Congress Catalog Card Number 69-13437

International Standard Book Number 0-391-00705-X

DUQUESNE STUDIES—PHILOSOPHICAL SERIES
André Schuwer and John Sallis, editors

Titles in Print—

TABLE OF CONTENTS

Abbreviations

Ideen I Edmund Husserl, *Ideen zu einer reinen Phänomenologie und phänomenologischen Philosophie,* Erstes Buch, *Allgemeine Einführung in die reine Phänomenologie,* herausgegeben von Walter Biemel, *Husserliana,* III, The Hague, 1950.

SZ Martin Heidegger, *Sein und Zeit,* 6th ed., Tübingen, 1949.

EN Jean-Paul Sartre, *L'Etre et le Néant,* 29th ed., Paris, 1950.

EH Sartre, *L'Existentialisme est un Humanisme,* Paris, 1950.

PP Maurice Merleau-Ponty, *Phénoménologie de la Perception,* 14th ed., Paris, 1945.

StC Merleau-Ponty, *La Structure du Comportement,* 3rd ed., Paris, 1953.

SNS Merleau-Ponty, *Sens et Non-sens,* Paris, 1948.

EP Merleau-Ponty, *Eloge de la Philosophie,* 12th ed., Paris, 1953.

JM Gabriel Marcel, *Journal métaphysique,* 11th ed., Paris, 1935.

EA Marcel, *Etre et Avoir,* Paris, 1935.

RI Marcel, *Du Refus à l'Invocation,* 11th ed., Paris, 1940.

HCH Marcel, *Les Hommes contre l'Humain,* Paris, 1951.

*ME,*I-II Marcel, *Le Mystere de l'Etre,* I-II, Paris, 1951.

S.Th. Thomas Aquinas, *Summa theologica.*

Acknowledgments

The editor wishes to express his gratitude to the following publishers for permission to quote from the books listed here:

Librairie Gallimard, Paris: Marcel, *Journal métaphysique* and *Du Refus à l'Invocation;* Sartre, *L'Etre et le Néant;* Merleau-Ponty, *Humanisme et Terreur, Eloge de la Philosophie* and *Phénoménologie de la Perception.*

M. Niemeyer Verlag, Tübingen: Heidegger, *Sein und Zeit* and *Einführung in die Metaphysik.*

R. Piper & Co. Verlag, München: Jaspers, *Einführung in die Philosophie.*

New Directions, New York: Sartre, *Nausea.*

TRANSLATOR'S PREFACE

This book is an extensive revision of the author's work EXISTENTIAL PHENOMENOLOGY. Since its first publication—1960 for the Dutch edition, 1961 for the English edition, and 1967 for the Spanish edition—more than 60,000 copies of this book have appeared in print.

The present text has been so thoroughly revised that the reader will realize that he finds here virtually a new book.

Arrangements have been made for the publication of this work in Dutch, German and English. Simultaneously with the English edition of the book in its present form, there will appear a simplified version of it, entitled A FIRST INTRODUCTION TO EXISTENTIAL PHENOMENOLOGY, co-authored by William A. Luijpen and the undersigned, and destined for use in colleges and universities which desire to offer a course to undergraduates for whom the other work would be too difficult or too long.

The text has been newly translated by the undersigned. He has abstained from translating also the German, French and Latin quotations in the footnotes because practically all of them are sufficiently paraphrased in the text.

To prevent confusion, the term "existence" has been printed in italics whenever it is used in its technical sense, except in headings and subheadings.

The translator wishes to thank Miss Barbara Petrich for her kind assistance in the literary revision of the translation.

Henry J. Koren

INTRODUCTION

When a book mentions the terms "phenomenology" or "existentialism," the reader may still expect almost anything on its pages. Such books generally contain studies *about* phenomenology or *about* existentialism. They are fairly numerous and often contain excellent introductions to various aspects and systems of the philosophy known as existentialism or phenomenology. The thoughtful reader, however, would not infrequently come to the conclusion that there seems to be no trace of unity or interconnection in the philosophical thought of different existentialists and phenomenologists.

Nevertheless, today one can no longer make such an assertion without showing that one suffers from a misunderstanding of existentialism and phenomenology. It is true that from a certain viewpoint one can claim that Kierkegaard and Husserl, Heidegger and Sartre, Jaspers and Marcel, Merleau-Ponty and Ricoeur, each have their own world of thought. But this claim does not do justice to the main element of their thinking. The principal point is that the differences between all these authors reveal themselves of little importance, as soon as one realizes that what today is called "existential phenomenology" is primarily a "movement," a "climate" of thinking whose proper character could not at once be discovered and expressed. It was no accident that the names of certain authors were from the very beginning connected with existentialism and phenomenology, while others were not mentioned at all. It was not without reason that only a certain approach to problems pertaining to the positive sciences was called "existential" or "phenomenological." All this indicates a certain *unity* of "movement" or "climate," no matter how great the differences may be between the explicit theses of various existentialists and phenomenologists.

An historian of contemporary thought could render a valuable service by writing a book about existentialism and phenomenology for the principal purpose of showing that these philosophers have a common style of thinking, for hitherto far too little attention has been paid to this point. Such a study, however, would still be a book *about* existentialism and phenomenology. We wish to emphasize this point to make certain that the readers understand the difference between such a work and the study presented to him in this book. It is *not* our intention to write *about* existentialism or phenomenology.

It is not possible to philosophize in an authentic way if our thinking does not consist in a relatively independent rethinking of the eternal problems which have always occupied the thinking man. Authentic philosophy is the aim of this book. The rethinking, however, presented in this book takes place in the "climate" of thought proper to existentialists and phenomenologists because we are convinced that today existential phenomenology, enriched by the most profound insights of tradition, offers, at least provisionally, the most promising prospective for any endeavor to express the ultimate meaning of integral reality. Obviously, it is impossible to justify this conviction in an *introduction*: the very book itself is presented as such a justification.

The relative independence which is the duty of authentic thinking implies also a certain reservation with respect to the systems and theses proposed by various existentialists and phenomenologists. We do not simply follow any one of them. Nevertheless, we have endeavored to situate our study in contemporary thought, in proof of which we have added an extensive apparatus of scholarly footnotes. It is hardly necessary to point out that these quotations or references should never be understood as arguments.

From the foregoing one can easily deduce that existential phenomenology is not *the* philosophy for us. Any philosopher has to realize that, perhaps not far away from his neighborhood, an exceptionally gifted thinker can happen to express the ultimate meaning of reality by means of a "primitive fact"—a unifying principle—which no one else has ever used before, but which proves to be fruitful in a way no other "primitive fact" was ever fruitful before. At such a moment a new and better philosophy will be born, and it will also be the moment when existential phenomenology becomes antiquated. This, however, does not mean that anyone can claim that existential phenomenology had "nothing to say," for a new philosophy always presupposes an "old" philosophy and is made possible by this "old" philosophy.

In our opinion, no phenomenologist protagonizes the "absolutism" of phenomenology. The great representatives of phenomenological thinking keep their thought "open" to the future, as well as to the past. They have written profound studies of nearly all philosophers whose works became "classics." Contemporary phenomenological thinking would not have been possible without traditional thought. "The absolutism of phenomenology," understood as being-closed to the past and the future, is unthinkable. There exists, however, thinkers who absolutely close their minds to phenomenology. For J.F. Staal phenomenology is a "mythology and metaphysics of backwardness." Speaking of phenomenology, he says that he does not wish to dwell on Heidegger because "hardly anything positive can be said about him"; Sartre's BEING AND NOTHINGNESS is for him an "intelligent French version of Heidegger's BEING AND TIME"; Jaspers "writes a lot about almost anything and has developed a style in which all kinds of topics, both ripe and green, are simply strung together"; Gadamar impresses his readers with the feeling that "they are being seduced to enter an insane asylum"; and phenomenology is simply a "cultural catastrophe." Reading such things in Staal, one would expect to hear also that phenomenology is on the verge of collapse and that sensible thinkers will turn to analytic philosophy, the "therapy for their morbid illusions." Staal, however, says that "he cannot be optimistic with respect to his chances to liberate us from meaninglessness."

This lack of optimism is significant. It is not at all certain that the reason Staal gives for his lack of optimism is the true explanation for the vigorous expansion of phenomenology. It is not at all certain that its growth may be ascribed to the fact that the great French and German philosophers "proceed with a lack of expert knowledge which is inconceivable in any other realm of science." It could also happen to be true that those philosophers have experienced that, more than any other philosophy, existential phenomenology enables them to account for the wealth contained in the "saying" of "is" which man himself is. It stands to reason, however, that they cannot communicate this experience to anyone who systematically closes himself to it.

This book is a thorough revision and expansion of a study first offered to the readers in 1959 and, in English translation in 1960, under the title EXISTENTIONAL PHENOMENOLOGY. The revision has been so thorough that it really is a new book. Even in its present and expanded form, however, it remains an introduction and is not a definitive and exhaustive study of the topics considered in its pages.

CHAPTER ONE

MAN AS EXISTENCE

For twenty-five hundred years man has been philosophizing, and the result of his persistent efforts is innumerable contradictory *systems* of philosophy. The philosophical way of thinking is much older than that of modern positive science, but it has not yet managed to formulate even a few *theses* which are unanimously accepted by all philosophers.[1] One could even say that perhaps there exists not a single thesis which is not denied by some philosopher of the past, present, or future. While the men of positive science marvel at the ever-increasing fruitfulness of their field of learning and pity or mock the poor philosopher, every century sees at least one genius come forward with a new philosophy. Man, so it appears, is unable to stop philosophizing, he simply cannot give up philosophy. If only the mockers could understand this, they would realize that to laugh at philosophy itself is a kind of philosophy, albeit a bad kind.[2]

It may be useful to insist on this point. Many of those who reject philosophy, and are therefore bad philosophers, cannot be discounted as "stupid" people. Just the opposite is often true. Philosophy is not infrequently rejected by people who in other respects are very intelligent, who have become leading experts in a particular branch of positive science and who, precisely because of the success of their science, are tempted to absolutize the value of a particular type of *scientific* knowledge. Down with philosophy, long live physical science! For this science at least gives us genuine and reliable knowledge.

It is not difficult to see that such an attitude contains a philosophy which is in principle "complete." For one who, without any further qualification, identifies the knowledge of physical science with genuine and reliable knowledge, decrees in principle a "complete" theory of knowledge: knowledge, pure and simple, is the kind of knowledge offered by physical science. But, we may ask, is it the task of the man who pursues physical science to define what knowledge, pure and simple, is? Of course not; that is the task of the philosopher. A definition of knowledge is out of place in a treatise of physical science; one can even say

---

[1] K. Jaspers, *Einführung in die Philosophie*, München, 1957, p. 9.
[2] A. van Melsen, *Science and Technology*, Pittsburgh, 1961, p. 13.

that such a treatise is not the proper place for a description of the kind of knowledge that is "physical science." [3]

A theory of knowledge is a philosophical conviction. He who proposes a theory of knowledge which is in principle "complete," cannot avoid proposing at the same time also a theory of reality which is in principle "complete." For no matter how one wishes to define knowledge, there is no escape from admitting that knowledge, unlike dreaming, fancying or hallucinating, is a disclosure of reality. [4] Accordingly, one who decrees a theory of knowledge, pure and simple, by absolutizing the knowledge of physical science, cannot avoid imposing, at the same time, a theory of reality, pure and simple: whatever cannot be disclosed by physical science simply is not real. But, we must ask again, is it the task of the physicist to define what reality is without any qualifications? That task belongs to the philosopher. [5]

Scientism is the absolutism of science, understood in a narrow sense—the sense of physical science, for until recently all positive sciences defined themselves as "still imperfect forms of physical science." Scientism is an internal contradiction. It claims that meaningful statements are statements of physical science, and thus implies that other kinds of statements are nonsense. But this claim itself obviously is not a statement of physical science—anyone who fails to see this does not know what physical science is—and therefore must be classified as a nonsense statement. Those who make the claim, however, imply that it is a meaningful statement; hence they are living in a contradiction.

The temptation to scepticism is very alluring to the philosopher, but he cannot reject philosophy or become unfaithful to it without making himself a defender of the worst possible philosophy. Does it perhaps belong to the essence of man to be a philosopher? In that case he should try to execute this task to the best of his ability.

Whenever a new philosophy makes its appearance, bad or inauthentic philosophers turn to the new system to see whether at last it presents *the* philosophy. Their expectation, of course,

---

[3] E. Husserl, "Philosophie als strenge Wissenschaft," *Logos* I (1910-11), pp. 299-300.

[4] C. A. van Peursen, *Feiten, waarden, gebeurtenissen, Een deiktische ontologie*, Hilversum-Amsterdam, 1965, p. 34.

[5] van Peursen, *op. cit.*, p. 40.

meets with disappointment, that is, they remain bad, inauthentic philosophers. The authentic philosopher knows better, for he realizes that there never was and never will be such a thing as *the* philosophy. He is keenly aware of the fact that, if *the* philosophy existed, there would no longer be any philosophers.

1. THE AUTHENTICITY OF PHILOSOPHY

There exist fully constituted philosophies. History knows a few gifted geniuses who managed to lay down their thoughts in grandiose masterpieces.[6] What else, then, one could say, would be more obvious than to conceive philosophizing as an attempt to "learn" a *system*?

Such an attempt, however, can be successful only with people who suffer from great narrowness of mind and fail to realize that the systems and theses of the great philosophers contradict one another. This alone should suffice to reject the view that philosophy is "just another discipline" to be learned. It would simply be impossible to know which philosophy one should "learn," for on what basis would one decide that one system is better than the other?

Philosophizing as a Personal Task

This difficulty, however, is only a minor objection to the view that philosophizing consists in the "learning" of a system. Even if a particular *system* did not contain any false *thesis* whatsoever, the authentic philosopher would have little use for it. For the truth of a system and of theses is not—or at least not yet—*his* truth; and it will never become his truth if he limits himself to simply learning those theses, with or without the proofs. It is simply impossible for the truth of a system ever to become a *personal* truth if the philosopher neglects *personally* to appropriate the reality which finds expression in the system. Authentic philosophy is an attempt to give a personal answer to personal questions. In this sense authentic or genuine philosophy is *per se* original: it is a personal affair, a questioning and answering of man *himself*.[7]

---

[6]"Aber die schaffende Ursprünglichkeit, der wir die grossen philosophischen Gedanken schulden, liegt. . . . bei Einzelnen, die in ihrer Unbefangenschen Gedanken schulden, liegt. . . . bei Einzelnen, die in ihrer Unbefangenheit und Unabhängigkeit als wenige grosse Geister in den Jahrtausenden aufgetreten sind." Jaspers, *op. cit.,* p. 13.

[7]"Das philosophische Denken muss jederzeit ursprünglich sein. Jeder Mensch muss es selber vollziehen." Jaspers, *op. cit.,* p. 11.

It is life itself which raises the philosophical questions.[8] Man has to find a way to consent to life, and there are so many situations in which he does not really manage to do this. My life is mine, however, and I cannot leave it aside as something that does not concern *me*.[9] It is characteristic of man's being that he has a relationship with his own being. Man *himself* is what he is.[10]

Accordingly, it is no mere coincidence that man is called to philosophize in an original and personal way. His entire life only becomes authentically human when he *himself* lives. Philosophy is authentic philosophy only when man *himself* philosophizes, when he *himself* raises questions and he *himself* tries to asnwer, when he *himself* endeavors to clear away the obstacles to insight. The questions and answers of a system are impersonal, and the obstacles which had to be cleared away to make an integral formulation possible are no longer relevant when the system has been constituted. If philosophy were merely a question of "learning" systems and theses, it would be a boring undertaking, whose knowledge would not contribute more to making man human than does the enumeration of the industrial centers of the U.S.A. or the mining regions of Canada.

Unfortunately, it is true that philosophy is often taught and studied in this way. There is no need to be surprised that such a pursuit of philosophy leaves its students dissatisfied. For if the questions of the systems are not *my* questions, then the answers also are not *my* answers, so that I never become *myself* as a philosopher. The whole affair is reduced to "talk," *Gerede* as Heidegger calls it.[11] The philosopher "talks" as "one" is accustomed to do in a certain tradition: the object ultimately is the talk itself, and no longer implies an understanding of reality. Speech is no longer an original appropriation and a personal expression of reality, but merely a continued talking and repeating of what "one" says in a certain tradition. The end result of all this is a situation in which the philosopher no longer knows

---

[8]Jaspers, *op. cit.*, pp. 20-26.

[9]J. Ortega y Gasset, *De mens en de mensen*, Den Haag, 1958, p. 56 (original title: *El hombre y la gente*).

[10]"Dasein ist Seiendes, das sich in seinem Sein verstehend zu diesem Sein verhält. Damit ist der formale Begriff von Existenz angezeigt. Dasein existiert. Dasein ist ferner Seiendes, das je ich selbst bin. Zum existierenden Dasein gehört die Jemeinigkeit als Bedingung der Möglichkeit von Eigentlichkeit und Uneigentlichkeit." Heidegger, *SZ*, p. 168.

[11]"Man versteht nicht mehr so sehr das beredete Seiende, sondern man hört schon nur auf das Geredete als solches." *SZ*, p. 168.

whether he really understands something or is simply the victim of what "everybody always" says. Heidegger refers to this situation as "ambiguity" (*Zweideutigkeit*).[12]

Philosophy as the "Speaking Word"

A constituted philosophy is a "spoken word" (Merleau-Ponty), solidified thought. This solidified thought, however, has its origin in the "speaking word," [13] the personal expression of reality. If philosophy is a personal affair, then as a "speaking word" it can only find its starting point in the personal presence of the philosopher who I am to reality. This presence is called "experience."

It is of particular importance that the term "experience" be understood in the broadest possible sense. For, without explicitly asking here what is meant by experience, we may say that obviously there exist many ways of experiencing which place us in the presence of a particular reality. There is a difference in experiencing a rock, H_2O, a rose, a mountain, a liar, a board of examiners, a police officer, a child, and being as being. One who tries to understand these differences sees that the experiences in question are not what they are without a determined "attitude" (Husserl's *Einstellung*) of the subject. To experience the reality of a board of examiners, I must be able to place myself, at least in my imagination, in the "attitude" of an examinee who can fail. An entirely different "attitude" of the subject is required to experience the reality of a rose: one who assumes an aesthetic "attitude" to experience the beauty of a flower is not attuned to the reality of an angry police officer. In order to experience the reality of an angry police officer, I must, at least in my imagination, be able to place myself in the "attitude" of one who has actually or possibly violated the law.

All this does not indicate when an experience must be called philosophical, but at least this much is certain: to be meaningful, a philosophy must give expression to *reality*. Thus it follows that philosophy must start from an experience, from the subject's immediate presence to a present reality. If the philosopher were to start from theses,[14] he would never know what he

---

[12]*SZ*, pp. 173-175.

[13]Merleau-Ponty, *PP*, p. 229.

[14]"Nicht von den Philosophien sondern von den Sachen und Problemen muss der Antrieb zur Forschung ausgehen." Husserl, "Philosophie als strenge Wissenschaft," *Logos* I (1910-11), p. 340.

should admit as truth. Such a philosopher does not *see* any reality; yet, a philosopher undoubtedly is a philosopher only, at least in the first instance, insofar as he *sees*. And *seeing* is something which he does either in person or not at all.

The same line of thought applies to philosophical formation. This formation cannot consist in drilling the aspirant philosopher in certain theses—not even if from other sources it would be certain that all these theses are true. There can be question of a genuine philosophical formation only insofar as those in charge of this formation aid the aspirant to make him *personally* see reality. It can be useful, of course, that certain people, because of their future activities, are subjected to a simple drill in a system of theses, but such a drill is without any *philosophical* value. Even a real formation, that is, one which does not amount to a kind of mental drill for practical purposes, implies a risk of falsifying the aspirant's philosophical activity, because the aid given to him to make him *personally* see reality consists (and has to consist) of *also* imparting knowledge of "previously philosophized" philosophy. For how often does it not happen that the program does not go beyond this point? What university professors present as philosophy usually looks like philosophy, but far too often is not philosophy.[15]

Philosophy as a Common Task

The preceding thought requires to be complemented and differentiated. Although the philosopher aims at personal thinking, it would be an illusion to imagine that this goal can be reached independently of tradition. As a philosopher, I am a person, an *I*, and my philosophical thought is only authentic if it is *my* philosophical thinking. Every person, however, is inserted in a history which is not personal, which he himself has not made. There is nothing I can do about the fact that I am inserted in a history, that is, I can never begin to think from zero, for others have thought before me and I am carried by their

---

15"Die Missdeutungen, von denen die Philosophie ständig umlagert bleibt, werden nun am meisten gefördert durch das, was unsereiner treibt, also durch die Philosophie-Professoren. Deren gewöhnliches, und auch berechtigtes und sogar nützliches Geschäft ist es, eine gewisse bildungsmässige Kenntnis von der bisher aufgetretenen Philosophie zu vermitteln. Das sieht dann so aus, als sei dies selbst Philosophie, während es höchstenfalls nur Philosophiewissenschaft ist." Heidegger, *Einführung in die Metaphysik,* Tübingen, 1953, p. 9.

thought. I am in the stream of thought established by tradition at least because of the language I speak and because the ideas embodied in this language permeate me. It is impossible to think without language, and it is just as impossible to think without tradition.[16]

Does it follow, therefore, that the philosopher has to abandon any claim to personal thought? The reply is definitely in the negative. Although he is carried by the history of thought, the philosopher is called to infuse new life into this history. He fulfills this task when he makes a profound study of his predecessors' works. The philosophers of the past have important things to say. In their own way they have given expression to their *experience of reality* and laid it down in their works. They speak to us in these works and enter into contact with us. What is the purpose of this contact? Does it mean that we are invited to make ours their conceptual apparatus and to take over their system? In that case the invitation would amount to a seduction to non-authenticity, to a philosophy that is not genuine. The true purpose and value of the works produced by the philosophers of the past are entirely different.

These works are the vehicle in which they have laid down their experience of reality in order to make us sensitive to the meaning of this reality and to give us access to the wealth of being which they have perceived. Philosophizing is always concerned with a *personal* experience and a *personal* expression of the wealth of being. But it is because others preceded us that it is possible for us *personally* to see something to which otherwise we would perhaps have been blind.[17] If there had been no Plato, our conception of reality and its deepest meaning would have been much more trivial and material: in the totality of being we would perhaps not have experienced, seen, and understood the variegated wealth which we now understand when we reflect

---

[16]R. Kwant, *Phenomenology of Social Existence*, Pittsburgh, 1965, pp. 79ff.

[17]"Der Mensch, jeweils in einer geschichtlich geschaffenen Situation erwachend, hat in jeder Generation neue Möglichkeiten doch nur, weil er schon seinen Grund in einer überlieferten Lebenssubstanz hat. Er würde - was nur im Grenzfall zu denken ist - aus dem Nichts seines vitalen Verstandesdaseins existieren müssen, wenn die Situation ihn in die Weltlosigkeit atomisierter Vereinzelung würfe; er würde in schmerzvoller, aber blinder Verzweiflung leben, nicht wissend, was er eigentlich will; er würde zerstreute Dinge ohne Transparenz ergreifen und sich verkrampfen im leeren Aushaltenkönnen des Nichts." Jaspers, *Philosophie*, 1948, p. 263.

philosophically upon reality. Without Augustine, we would perhaps not have been sensitive to the meaning of restlessness in our being-in-the-world. To Darwin, Marx and Freud we owe our victory over exaggerated spiritualism. The philosophers of the past speak to us in order to make it possible for us to have a personal experience of reality, to make us sensitive to the wealth contained in the totality of all that is.[18]

Some philosophers are "classical"—that is, no one takes them literally; but anyone who really thinks in a personal fashion is obliged to study them because what they "saw" proved fruitful and remains a source of inspiration.[19] Occasionally one is asked, "Are you a Cartesian or not?" This question, strictly speaking, is meaningless, for who could permit himself not to be a Cartesian? The total rejection of Descartes would mean that Descartes did not "see" anything at all and that, therefore, one need not take him into account in the pursuit of philosophy. On the other hand, no one today is Cartesian in the same way as Descartes himself was Cartesian. The reason why Descartes is a "classical" philosopher lies precisely in the fact that we can permit ourselves not to be Cartesians because of a "better seeing" which Descartes himself made possible for us.[20] Plato, Aquinas, Descartes, Marx, etc., all great philosophers are still alive among us.[21] They continue to "speak" to us and inspire us over and beyond their explicit statements.

Once this view is accepted, there is no reason to be scandalized by the existence of many contradictory systems.[22] What matters is not the system but reality. And in every system some aspect of reality finds expression. Every truly great philosopher was struck by a certain aspect of reality. A certain aspect of the wealth of being was perhaps unduly elevated by him to the rank of reality pure and simple; a certain experience may have

---

[18]A. Dondeyne, *Contemporary European Thought and Christian Faith*, Pittsburgh, 1958, p. 41.

[19]"Ce sont là les *classiques*. On les reconnaît à ceci que personne ne les prend à la lettre, et que pourtant les faits nouveaux ne sont jamais absolument hors de leur compétence, qu'ils tirent d'eux de nouveaux échos, et qu'ils revèlent en eux de nouveaux reliefs." Merleau-Ponty, *Signes*, Paris, 1960, pp. 16-17.

[20]Merleau-Ponty, *ibid*.

[21]Merleau-Ponty, *SNS*, p. 189.

[22]A. Dondeyne, "Dieu et le materialisme contemporain," *Essai sur Dieu, l'homme et l'univers*, publié sous la direction et avec une introduction de Jacques de Bivort de la Saudée, Paris, 1957, pp. 22-32.

been proclaimed as the only experience. For this reason the resulting system may be antiquated; nevertheless, we cannot do without it.[23]

Accordingly, the fact of being inserted in a history which is not of his own making does not make it impossible for the authentic philosopher to think in an autonomous, independent, and personal fashion. There is one condition, however: he must take up the past in a creative way, he must endow it with a new life.[24] *He himself*, evidently, has to do this. He does not sign a contract with any school of thought and does not swear by any formula.[25] He does not "accumulate" knowledge, but listens to reality, no matter from where it speaks to him.[26] When he studies the works of the past, he begins with an attitude of trust in and love for those who speak to him, because he realizes that they do not demand anything of him other than that *he himself* accept or reject their insights. For ultimately only that is recognized as true which can become a conviction in independent thought.[27]

It is precisely because a constituted philosophy can exist, and continue to exist, only in assertions and explicitly formulated

---

[23]"Man sieht so eine grosse Reihe von Weltanschauungen, die man mit dem Namen Materialismus (alles ist Stoff und naturmechanisches Geschehen), Spiritualismus (alles ist Geist), Hylozoismus (das All ist eine seelisch lebendige Materie) und unter anderen Gesichtspunkten benannt hat. In allen Fällen wurde die Antwort auf die Frage, was eigentlich das Sein sei, gegeben durch Hinweis auf ein in der Welt vorkommendes Seiendes, das den besonderen Charakter haben sollte, aus ihm sei alles andere. Aber was ist denn richtig? Die Begründung im Kampfe der Schulen haben in Jahrtausenden nicht vermocht, einen dieser Standpunkte als den wahren zu erweisen. Für jeden zeigt sich etwas Wahres, nämlich eine Anschauung und eine Forschungsweise, die in der Welt etwas zu sehen lehrt. Aber jeder wird falsch, wenn er sich zum einzigen macht und alles, was ist, durch seine Grundauffassung erklären will." Jaspers, *Einführung in die Philosophie*, pp. 28-29.

[24]Heidegger, *SZ*, p. 339.

[25]"The fact that a number of 'definitive truths' have been discovered previously does not mean that we do not have a task of our own to fulfill. These truths still have to become ours, they remain to be discovered by us *as truths*, they remain to be seen in their evidence through our own eyes. Although the pursuit of philosophy is an intersubjective undertaking, it is also and especially an adventure each one has to undertake on his own—all philosophy has a moment of solipsism. Even those who adhere to a 'school' will not *a priori* believe the truth of this or that thesis, but at most suspect that it is true. A tradition is not a creed, but each one for himself has to travel the road to insight, the discovery or rediscovery of truth." G. Van Riet, "Geschiedenis van de wijsbegeerte en waarheid," *Tijdschrift voor Philosophie*, XIX (1957), p. 177.

[26]Jaspers, *op. cit.*, p. 115.

[27]Jaspers, *op. cit.*, pp. 143-145.

judgments, that there is an obvious temptation to stop with these judgments. Just as ethics, however, does not consist in the existence of general laws but in life itself as guided by personally experienced and personally accepted moral demands, so also philosophy does not exist in statements and theses but in the personal expression of reality on the basis of a personal presence to reality.[28]

The same applies to the principles of philosophy. These principles are not the most general judgments, but rather are experience itself in its most fundamental and decisive dimension. In systematized philosophies these fundamental experiences are laid down in explicit judgments. To be really meaningful, however, they must be given life again by philosophy conceived as a "speaking word," a personal expression of reality.

"Back to reality itself" was the watchword of Edmund Husserl, the founder of phenomenology. This imperative is valid for all authentic philosophical thinking. While studying systematized philosophies, the philosopher must attempt to return to the reality intended by any statement whatsoever. Only in the presence to reality, in experience, is it possible to arrive at the incontrovertible and to accept it personally. Only in this way does truth really become *my* truth, and are "talk" and "ambiguity" overcome.

The Intersubjectivity of Philosophical Truth

The statement that philosophical truth, to be authentically philosophical, must be truth-for-me is sometimes given a greatly exaggerated sense. Following Kierkegaard, some say that philosophical truth is *per se not* truth-for-all, generally valid or intersubjective. In Karl Jaspers one can find texts which, with the best will in the world, can be interpreted only as the denial of the essential intersubjectivity of philosophical truth. (There are, however, also texts which seem to affirm the opposite.) In this way the *de facto* existing divergence of opinions is changed into an essential characteristic of philosophy.[29] Where philosophers

---

28J. Plat, "Geschiedenis van de filosofie en waarheid," *Handelingen van het XXIIe Vlaams Filologencongres,* Leuven, 1957, pp. 68-74.

29"Dass jede Gestalt der Philosophie, unterschieden von den Wissenschaften, der einmütigen Anerkennung aller entbehrt, das muss in der Natur ihrer Sache liegen." Jaspers, *op. cit.,* p. 10.

reach agreement, philosophy would cease to be philosophy.[30] Intersubjectivity would be an exclusive characteristic of "scientific" truth. The philosopher would have to limit himself to a kind of monologue expressing his strictly personal truth.[31]

This standpoint, defended by a few philosophers of existence, is now antiquated and abandoned because it implies a hidden contradiction.[32] For, how could anyone seriously endeavor to maintain such a philosophical view of philosophical truth unless he presupposes that this view, as true, is in principle valid for all?[33] And without this presupposition it does not make sense to assert that no philosophical truth is valid for all. If I defend against anyone the statement that no truth is valid for all, and, consequently, that *this* truth is not valid for all, I am not making any statement. For the defense of a view which I hold to be true contains *per se* the "claim" that no one can rightly deny this truth. In the denial itself of truth-for-all, then, one must recognize that which it denies, and without this implicit affirmation the denial cannot have any conceivable meaning. In Jaspers the contradiction does not even remain hidden and merely implicit. He first asserts that it pertains to the very nature of philosophy that philosophers do *not* agree; and then he claims that penetration into the history of philosophy finds its meaning and apex in the "moments of communion in the source."[34]

Jaspers would be right, of course, if he merely wished to say that philosophical truth differs from the truth disclosed by the positive sciences. This difference, however, does not mean that, unlike the latter, the former is not intersubjective. It may be true that intersubjectively to undertake research in a positive science and to verify the results of this research are easier than the intersubjective examination of a philosophical question, so

---

[30]"Was aus zwingenden Gründen von jedermann anerkannt wird, das ist damit eine wissenschaftliche Erkenntnis geworden, ist nicht mehr Philosophie." Jaspers, *op. cit.*, p. 9.

[31]"Et encore, remarquons-le bien, ce monologue ne peut qu'*éclaircir*, il ne saurait prétendre *expliquer*, car on n'explique que des situations *objectivables*, et les situations de l'existence ne sont objectivables à aucun degré." A. De Waelhens, *La philosophie de Martin Heidegger*, Louvain, 1948, p. 299.

[32]De Waelhens, *op. cit.*, pp. 295-302.

[33]"La volonté de parler est une même chose avec la volonté d'être compris." Merleau-Ponty, *EP*, p. 74.

[34]"Aber Sinn und Gipfel historischen Eindringens sind die Augenblicke des Einverständnisses im Ursprung." Jaspers, *op. cit.*, p. 138.

that *de facto* there exists more agreement in the realm of positive science than in that of philosophy.[35] *In principle*, however, any truth is intersubjective because truth is truth.

Sartre very explicitly affirms the essential intersubjectivity of truth, albeit that he does this in a context different from ours, viz., that of man's absolute freedom. All people who depreciate their absolute freedom by looking for heavenly signs to guarantee their deeds or by pointing to their passions as excuses for what they have done, are, according to Sartre, "in bad faith," they live inauthentically, immorally. They fail to recognize what they are, viz., absolutely free; they are cowards and rascals! [36] Sartre then asks himself whether, in his absolute freedom, man may not choose to live in bad faith. His answer is unconditionally in the negative. "Here one cannot escape a judgment of truth." [37]   One who chooses to live in bad faith, says Sartre, disregards the *truth* of his essence. If the essence of man is absolute freedom, no one may deny this essence in his deeds. Certain ways of choosing are based on error; others, on the truth about man.[38]   But every man must recognize the truth about man's essence.[39]

Here also, according to Sartre, lies the source of "anxiety." [40] I am anxious, he says, because of the responsibility which I incur because of my choice. For when I choose, I choose not only for myself but for all mankind. If as a laborer I decided to join a Christian union instead of a Communist one, I do this, says Sartre, because I am convinced that man must be resigned to his fate and should not attempt to establish the kingdom of man on earth, as the Communists want. I choose, therefore, because I am convinced of a certain truth. This being-convinced means that I *personally* have come to the insight that something is true, but also that no one else can rightly deny this truth. For this reason Sartre can say: when I choose, I choose for the

---

35"Philosophy is not science. This does not mean, however, that, contrary to science, philosophy does not possess any acquired truth, but only that its truths are not subject to verification as facts and to precise controls." G. Van Riet, *art. cit.* (footnote 25), p. 177.

36Sartre, *EH,* pp. 84-85.

37*Op. cit.,* p. 81.

38"Certains choix sont fondés sur l'erreur, et d'autres sur la vérité." *Op. cit.,* p. 80.

39"Ainsi, bien que le contenu de la morale soit variable, une certaine forme de cette morale est universelle." *Op. cit.,* p. 85.

40*Op. cit.,* pp 25-30.

whole of mankind.[41] In principle, then, there is nothing arbitrary about truth, in principle there is no chaos in life.

De facto, however, truth is not recognized by all. This fact should not become an inducement to profess a relativistic "pacifism," an attitude of indifference, which leaves to everyone his truth or error without any attempt to arrive at a mutual agreement. A society which is truly worthy of man demands a common acceptance of truth. The essential intersubjectivity of truth reveals itself as an impossibility to barter with truth. Although truth has to be unveiled by man, it transcends *us* human beings: *we* are subjected to truth. Truth as truth is disowned when tolerance is interpreted as relativism. In such a case it is impossible still to speak of truth.[42]

The true philosopher's consciousness of the absolute right to recognition which is implied by truth makes him to some extent intransigent. Truth is truth and therefore must be recognized as such. Anyone who for any reason is interested in doing violence to truth will find the philosophers against him. In a certain sense the philosophers speak as representatives of mankind: they protect one of mankind's most precious possibilities. When a society bases itself upon lies, the philosophers will either fall as martyrs,[43] or begin to function as puppets: i.e., they will cease to be philosophers.[44]

The "Usefulness" of Philosophy

For the positive scientist philosophy is a joke. In self-defense the philosopher could perhaps be tempted to demonstrate the usefulness of philosophy.[45] Such an effort, however, would be in vain.[46] How would it be possible for those who do

---

[41]*Op. cit.,* p. 27.

[42]Dondeyne, "L'idée de tolérance," *Les Etudes Philosophiques XII* (1957), *Actes du IXe Congrès des Sociétés de philosophie de langue française,* pp. 398-399.

[43]G. Verbeke, "Apologia Philosophiae," *Tijdschrift voor Philosophie,* XIX (1957), pp. 580-583.

[44]H. L. van Breda, "Les entretiens de Varsovie," *Tijdschrift voor Philosophie,* XIX (1957), pp. 713-721.

[45]"On ne pourra jamais dire à quel degré l'image de l'atelier d'usine et celle du laboratoire auront obsédé les philosophes. Et ici il y aurait à creuser profondément. Complexe d'infériorité du philosophe en face du savant - mais du philosophe qui a trahi. Le philosophe fidèle, ne cédera jamais." Marcel, *RI,* p. 86.

[46]"Die Philosophie soll sich also rechtfertigen. Das ist unmöglich. Sie kann sich nicht rechtfertigen aus einem anderen, für das sie infolge ihrer Brauchbarkeit Berechtigung habe. Sie kann sich nur wenden an die Kräfte,

not see the value of philosophy to attribute any other meaning to the term "useful" than the usefulness which they experience in the pursuit of their own science? Nuclear physics, biology, economics, psychometrics and such sciences are useful, they serve the workaday world in which they are integrated, but *with respect to this world* philosophy is wholly useless.[47] As Josef Pieper expressed it in a splendid address about philosophy and the world of work: a first description of philosophy is "an act through which we pass beyond the world of work." [48] The philosophical act leaves far behind itself "usefulness" as it is pursued in the world of work. Philosophy is characterized by a "uselessness" which it cannot abandon under penalty of ceasing to be philosophy.[49] But it is precisely because our society tends more and more to become a technocratic organization of work [50] that philosophy is not only "useful"—albeit in a totally different sense than its technocratic meaning—but even necessary, at least for many.

This assertion cannot be proved outside the pursuit of philosophical thinking. The understanding of the usefulness and the necessity of philosophy presupposes presence to the reality known as "philosophy," to the experience of actual philosophizing. Because of the fact that this reality is absent from one who is totally absorbed by a technocratic mentality, it must be admitted that what the philosopher says about the act of philosophizing can at most be accepted in good faith by the non-philosopher. There exists, moreover, the above-mentioned difficulty that such an acceptance is non-philosophical. As a rule, therefore, the plea for the usefulness of philosophy fails to convince the non-philosopher. Philosophers, on the other hand, do not need such a plea, because the value of philosophy clearly reveals itself in philosophical thinking itself.[51]

Existentialism, Phenomenology, and Existential Phenomenology

From what was said above about the authenticity of philoso-

---

die in jedem Menschen in der Tat zum Philosophieren drängen." Jaspers, *op. cit.,* p. 16.

[47]Josef Pieper, *Was heisst Philosophieren?*, München, 1956, pp. 23-34.

[48]"Philosophieren ist ein Akt, in welchem die Arbeitswelt überschritten wird." Josef Pieper, *op. cit.,* p. 12.

[49]Verbeke, *art. cit.,* p. 598.

[50]Kwant, *Philosophy of Labor,* Pittsburgh, 1960.

[51]"Jede Philosophie definiert sich selbst durch ihre Verwirklichung. Was

phy it should be evident that existential phenomenology itself may not simply be called *the* philosophy. It also will be transcended, for it always remains possible to express the ultimate meaning of life and reality in a better way.[52] Guesses, however, as to the future of philosophy are a waste of time. On the other hand, it makes sense to pay some attention to the recent past of existential phenomonology, for it offers the reader a measure of historical orientation.

Soren Kierkegaard is the founder of existentialism,[53] but one could hardly call him a phenomenologist. Husserl launched phenomenology, but was not an existentialist. These facts imply that there was a time when a distinction needed to be made between existentialism and phenomenology. Today, however, we also speak of existential phenomenology or phenomenological existentialism. So the question may be asked: what is the difference between existentialism and phenomenology, and how did the unified movement of existential-phenomenological thinking arise?

Despite the differences, there exists also a certain harmony between Husserl's way of thinking and that of Kierkegaard. Their agreement manifests itself perhaps best in their common resistance to the atomistic or elementaristic way of looking at man and things human. Man is not more or less like an atom. The way, however, in which this resistance is executed differs: Kierkegaard speaks of man, while Husserl practically limits himself to consciousness or knowledge.

Kierkegaard conceives man as *"existence,"* as a subject-in-relationship-to-God. Man is not a self-sufficient spiritual "atom," but as a subject is only authentically himself in his relationship to the God of Revelation. In Kierkegaard's view, however, *existenc*e is absolutely original and irrepeatable, radically

---

Philosophie sei, das muss man versuchen. Dann ist Philosophie in eine der Vollzug des lebendigen Gedankens und die Besinnung auf diesen Gedanken (die Reflexion) oder das Tun und das Darüberreden. Aus dem eigenen Versuch heraus erst kann man wahrnehmen, was in der Welt als Philosophie uns begegnet." Jaspers, *op. cit.,* p. 14.

[52]"Es war die falsche Auffassung, die durch das bessere Spätere das Frühere erledigt sein lässt, das als Stufe zu weiterem Fortschritt für ein bloss historisches interesse übrig bleibt. Das Neue als solches gilt dann fälschlich als das Wahre. Man fühlt sich durch die Entdeckung dieses Neuen auf dem Gipfel der Geschichte." Jaspers, *Der philosophische Glaube,* München, 1948, p. 129.

[53]We disregard here the distinction which some have made between existentialism and the philosophy of existence after Sartre's claim that existentialism and atheism could and should be identified.

personal and unique. This view is loaded with consequences.
Kierkegaard's emphasis on the uniqueness of *existence* makes
it impossible to do justice to the aspect of universality when
there is question of thinking about man. Yet this aspect is implied by any "science." (We do not use the term here in the
narrow sense of "positive science.") The *exclusive* emphasis on
the uniqueness and the "exceptional" character of *existence* implies as a consequence that a thinker's assertions about *existence*
are, as a matter of principle, applicable only to the thinker's
own *existence*: in principle they do not possess any validity beyond the thinker himself. Kierkegaard's thinking is consciously
and deliberately anti-"scientific." [54] As a matter of principle, it
cannot go beyond the monologue, the "solitary meditation." [55]

Undoubtedly, such a conception of philosophy has something seductive. When in the past the reproach was addressed
to existentialism that it was not a "science" and unable to become one, Kierkegaard's followers resolutely countered the reproach by saying that existentialism *may not* be a "science."
Usually, however, the rejection of the predicate "scientific" appeared to be based on an aversion to a *particular conception*
of the "scientific" character proper to thinking about man. In the
philosophy of Hegel—the black sheep in Kierkegaard's works—
and in scientism man was "scientifically" discussed in such a
way that the original, irrepeatable, unique and "exceptional"
character of human subjectivity simply disappeared under verbiage.[56] Yet this kind of speaking about man was supposed to
be "scientific" *par excellence*. All this readily indicates why the
reaction against that kind of speech did not wish to be called
"scientific."

This explanation leaves the difficult unsolved, however. If
a *particular* conception of "scientific" thinking about man must
be rejected, it is not yet beyond dispute that philosophizing about
man cannot and must not be "scientific" in any sense whatsoever. Anyone who philosophizes about man can hardly avoid
the use of universal and necessary judgments to indicate the universal and necessary structures of man. The realization of this

[54]De Waelhens, "Kierkegaard en de hedendaagse existentialisten," *Tijd-schrift voor Philosophie*, I(1939), pp. 827-851.

[55]"Il s'agit de savoir si l'existence n'est pas quelque chose qui doit être réservé à la méditation solitaire." J. Wahl, *Petite histoire de l'existentialisme*, Paris, 1947, p. 61.

[56]J. Peters, *Hedendaagse visies op den Mens*, Gesprekken op Draken-burgh, Heerlen, n.d., pp. 228-230.

truth has led some people to claim that perhaps a choice has to be made between authentic *existence* and existentialism.[57]   Those who opt for existentialism would have to resign themselves to speaking about the *universal* structures of being-man, while those who opt for authentic *existence* would have to give up existentialism as a *general* theory of man.[58]

These difficulties hardly exist for those who orientate themselves by Husserl's thought.   Originally a mathematician and physicist, Husserl, like Descartes, was disturbed by the confusion of language and the differences of opinion existing in the realm of philosophy.[59]   For Husserl philosophy was "not yet a science."[60]   This situation induced him to launch his phenomonology as an attempt to make philosophy also a "rigorous science." However, he did not fall into the trap of wishing to ascribe the same scientific character to philosophy as belongs to the positive sciences.[61] Philosophy cannot allow physics or any other science to dictate its methods nor can it take its cue from physics in order to safeguard its own scientific character.[62]   Philosophy is not a positive science.

For Husserl this does not mean, however, that philosophy cannot, and must not, be called "scientific" in any sense whatsoever.   Although philosophy is excluded from pursuing a "scientific" character in the sense positive science is scientific, it can still be "scientific" in its own way.   For philosophy also tends to truth which is in principle intersubjective and objectively general.

To realize his ambitious plan for philosophy, Husserl investigated the character of human consciousness or knowledge.   He conceived consciousness (knowledge) as intentionality—as

---

[57]"Peut-être faut-il choisir entre l'existentialisme et l'existence." J. Wahl, *op. cit.*, p. 61.

[58]"Il restera à se demander si la recherche des existentiaux et la recherche de l'être est compatible avec l'affirmation de l'existence." J. Wahl, *op cit.*, p. 43.

[59]"(Die Philosophie) verfügt nicht bloss über ein unvollständiges und nur im einzelnen unvollkommenes Lehrsystem, sondern schlechthin über keines. Alles und jedes ist hier strittig, jede Stellungnahme ist Sache der individuellen Ueberzeugung, der Schulauffassung, des 'Standpunktes'." Husserl, "Philosophie als strenge Wissenschaft," *Logos* I(1910-11), p. 291.

[60]E. Husserl, *art. cit.*, p. 290.

[61]"Die Philosophie aber liegt in einer völlig neuen Dimension.   Sie bedarf völlig neuer Ausgangspunkte und einer völlig neuen Methode, die sie von jeder 'natürlichen' Wissenschaft prinzipiell unterscheidet." Husserl, *Die Idee der Phänomenologie*, Husserliana II, p. 24.

[62]E. Husserl, *Die Idee der Phänomenologie*, pp. 24-26.

orientation to that which is not consciousness itself. Husserl's view of consciousness or knowledge shows a striking resemblance to Kierkegaard's concept of man as *existence*. Both go against an atomistic conception of man and his consciousness; but for Husserl the emphasis falls on problems of the theory of knowledge, while for Kierkegaard the accent lies on theological-anthropological questions. In this way existentialism and phenomenology were distinct.

This situation did not last very long, however. In Martin Heidegger's BEING AND TIME, Kierkegaard's existentialism and Husserl's phenomenology merged, as it were, to serve as the foundation of the philosophy which today is known to many as "existential phenomenology" or "phenomenological existentialism." Heidegger offers us a philosophy of man, one which does not lapse into the illusions of idealism or positivism. Influenced by the phenomenological theory of knowledge and the phenomenological ideal of "science," existentialism gave up its anti-scientific attitude. Epistemological phenomenology, on the other hand, enriched itself and developed into a philosophy of man by borrowing many topics from Kierkegaard's existentialism.[63] In this way there arose the unified movement of existential-phenomenological thinking of which Heidegger, Sartre—though not in every respect—Merleau-Ponty, and the Higher Institute of Philosophy of Louvain are the principal exponents.

The anti-scientific attitude of existentialism, however, is continued by Karl Jaspers and Gabriel Marcel.[64] These two thinkers thereby place themselves more or less outside the unified movement of existential phenomenology, but there remain numerous points of contact.

In this work we wish to make the reader experience the value of philosophizing in a "true to life" fashion. By actuating philosophical thinking itself, it is possible to "say" what philosophy is and how enormous the value is of the philosopher's "useless" thinking. We are convinced that philosophy cannot be dispensed with in the development of modern society. Modern man is more and more in danger of becoming the victim of a technocratic mentality. The more this process advances and

---

[63]Obviously, we do not deny that Heidegger did more than this. In particular, in Heidegger himself phenomenology took the road to metaphysics and later to the "transcendence" of metaphysics.
[64]Marcel, RI, p. 193.

extends itself, the more difficult it becomes for man to consent to his existence. But—what is man? That is the first question which imposes itself here.

2. MATERIALISTIC AND SPIRITUALISTIC MONISM

Anyone who tries to penetrate into the history of thought will notice that the endeavor to describe what man is amounts to the search for a difficult equilibrium. The materialistic systems, on the one hand, and the spiritualistic systems, on the other, bear witness to the difficulties which thought encounters when it wishes to express what man is. At the same time, these systems are the result of a certain lack of balance in man's thinking. This imbalance does not make them useless, for there is no philosophy which is not concerned with anything. Moments of equilibrium, however, are relatively rare in the history of philosophy.

Such a moment of equilibrium is present in the contemporary philosophy known as existential phenomenology. This philosophy knows how to retain the values perceived by both the materialists and the spiritualists, without falling into the one-sidedness of either system.[65] It is in the use of the term *"existence,"* which expresses one of the most fundamental essential characteristics of man, that this balanced vision of man is, as it were, crystallized.[66]

Materialism

All materialistic systems agree in considering man as the result of processes and forces, just as things are results of processes and forces. A materialist, therefore, would say that the being of man is a being-in-the-world in the sense that, just as all things, man is a thing in the midst of other things of the world, a fragment of nature, a moment in the endless evolution of the cosmos.[67]

---

[65]This point may be found more extensively in almost any study of existential philosophy. For a very clear explanation of the critique which the philosophers of existence address to the materialists and the idealists see Dondeyne, "Beschouwingen bij het atheïstisch existentialisme," *Tijdschrift voor Philosophie*, XIII(1951), pp. 1-41.

[66]Merleau-Ponty, *SNS*, pp. 142-143.

[67]"Il y a. . . . deux vues classiques. L'une consiste à traiter l'homme comme le résultat des influences physiques, physiologiques et sociologiques qui le détermineraient du dehors et feraient de lui une chose entre les choses." *SNS*, p. 142.

This idea is not so foolish that it can be dismissed as wholly impertinent. It expresses a valuable vision; it accounts for a reality which may never be disregarded; it takes seriously the irrefutable fact that man is whatever he is "on the basis of materiality." [68] Sooner or later any philosopher must experience the temptation of agreeing with materialism if he does not wish to depreciate the value of matter. For it is only a small step from the view that man is whatever he is on the basis of materiality [69] to the conviction that man is nothing but a fragment of nature or a passing phase in the endless evolution of the cosmos.[70] After all, there is no spiritual knowledge without sense perceptible objects, without brains, without physiological processes, without sense images or without words. There is no spiritual love without sensitive love, no personal conscience without biological substructures, no artistic act without expression in matter. Thus it is possible to speak, for instance, as a biologist about knowledge, love or conscience, and what the biologist says in these matters is concerned with reality.

This example shows how a certain way of thinking can be materialistic, even though the thinker does not explicitly state that man is a thing. Materialism is often camouflaged. Most of the time it parades as scientism, as an overvaluation of the physical sciences. These sciences are *ex professo* concerned with things and make use of categories and schemata which are exclusively applicable to things. Esteem for the sciences becomes scientism when one asserts that there are no other realities than those disclosed by the physical sciences. Precisely because man only is whatever he is on the basis of materiality, the sciences *also* can say something about everything man is. In principle, for instance, it is possible that there exists a physiological difference between a saint and a criminal, and that an operation can create in the criminal the material conditions for a virtuous life. In principle it is not absurd to claim that there is a material

---

[68]Dondeyne, "Dieu et le matérialisme contemporain," *Essai sur Dieu, l'homme et l'univers,* publié sous la direction et avec une introduction de Jacques de Bivort de la Saudée, Paris, 1957, p. 24.

[69]"Unsere wissenschaftliche Erfahrung hat uns noch keine Kräfte kennen gelehrt, welche der materiellen Grundlage entbehren, und keine 'geistige Welt', welche ausser der Natur und über der Natur stünde." E. Haeckel, *Die Welträtsel,* Leipzig, 10th ed., 1909, p. 259.

[70]"Auch wir Menschen sind nur vorübergehende Entwicklungszustände der ewigen Substanz, individuelle Erscheinungsformen der Materie und Energie, deren Nichtigkeit wir begreifen gegenüber dem unendlichen Raum und der ewigen Zeit." Haeckel, *op. cit.* p. 259.

difference between the conscience of a Christian and that of a Mohammedan. Many alcoholics and prostitutes are not primarily—sometimes not all—"transgressors of God's law," but human beings suffering from bodily deficiencies, for which a cure is more appropriate than is punishment.

One who understands all this must be greatly tempted to claim that the sciences can say all there is to say about any reality. If man is whatever he is only on the *basis* of his materiality, then there is nothing about which the sciences have nothing to say. Why, then, should we not go one fatal step further and assert that, when the scientist has spoken, there is nothing else to be said? The philosopher must have experienced this temptation if he is not to minimize the value of materialism. That fatal step, however, makes esteem for the sciences degenerate into scientism. Scientism is a materialistic theory: apart from the material things with which the sciences are concerned, there exists nothing else worth mentioning.

Materialism as a "Detotalization of Reality"

Materialism attempts to explain man—to express what man is—but fails because it indicates only one aspect of the totality of man, albeit an essential one. In the words of René Le Senne, materialism is a "detotalization of reality." [71] Materialism is a kind of monism which in the totality of reality leaves room only for one type of being, viz., the being of the material thing. Man, therefore, also is a thing, and human life is a chain of processes.

What exactly is involved in this "detotalization"? Generally speaking, one can say that a philosophy does not fail by what it says but by what it disregards or eliminates from reality. This principle applies very clearly to materialism. The materialist disregards the fact that man exists for himself *as* man: i.e., that being-man has *meaning* and *significance* for man, and that things do not have meaning and significance for themselves, or for other things, but only for man. If there were only things, nothing would have any meaning. Materialism disregards the fact that only with and through man there can be question of things and processes.

What is implied by the statement that "there is question of things"? It implies a "speaking" of things, a "saying" that they

---

[71]Quoted by Dondeyne, *art. cit.* (footnote 68), pp. 24-25.

are and what they are. This explicit "speaking" refers to an original saying" of "is," and it is *man* who does this "speaking" and "saying" with respect to both himself and things. No matter, then, how thing-like man may be, it will never be possible to think away the "dimension" of man which makes it possible for him to speak of both himself and things. This "dimension," however, is not the "thing-like" character of man—at least, if with all materialists we are justified in assuming that geological layers and rainstorms do not speak of anything. Man distinguishes himself from the thing by his ability to "speak of . . . ," to "say" his "is." This is what makes man transcend the "thing-like" aspect of his essence,[72] and it is this which all non-materialists call man's subjectivity.

Accordingly, it is the subjectivity of man which the materialist simply disregards.[73] The being of man on the proper level of his manhood is a being-conscious, by virtue of which man exists for himself [74] and can name himself. He calls himself *"I."* Through the "light" of subjectivity, of the conscious *I* who man is, man exists for himself and, at the same time, there is a "light" in the world of things: these now appear to man as meanings, they are-for-man, they are spoken of by man.

Materialism, then, neglects an essential aspect of man's being because ultimately it fails to recognize that being-man is a being-conscious. The materialist cannot defend himself against this reproach by saying that, like all processes belonging to the material order, man's acts of consciousness also can be reduced to an interplay of atoms and molecules. For he would then have to admit that not only do some "atoms" distinguish themselves from the others by the fact that they exist for themselves as atoms, but that other atoms exist for them as atoms, as well as the fact that they can philosophize about themselves and about other atoms or formulate an atomic theory. Now, those special "atoms" we call "men." One who reduces man to a conglomer-

---

72Sartre, *EH,* p. 65.

73"Je ne suis pas le résultat ou l'entrecroisement des multiples causalités qui déterminent mon corps ou mon 'psychisme', je ne puis pas me penser comme une partie du monde, comme le simple objet de la biologie, de la psychologie et de la sociologie, ni fermer sur moi l'univers de la science. Tout ce que je sais du monde, même par science, je le sais à partir d'une vue mienne ou d'une expérience du monde sans laquelle les symboles de la science ne voudraient rien dire." Merleau-Ponty, *PP,* Avant-propos, p. II.

74"En aucun cas, ma conscience ne saurait être une chose, parce que sa façon d'être en soi est précisément un *être pour soi.*" Sartre, *L'Imagination,* Paris, 1948, p. 1.

ation of atoms eliminates the "is" spoken by physical science and consequently the possibility of formulating an atomic theory.

Materialism lives by virtue of a hidden contradiction.[75] It is entirely impossible for the materialist, as a materialistic philosopher, to account for his own being if he continues to hold fast to the view that there exists only one type of being, viz., the being of a thing. The contradiction consists in this: the materialistic philosopher, on the one hand, admits that geological layers and rainstorms, plants and animals, are incapable of creating a philosophy, even a materialistic philosophy; on the other, as a materialistic philosopher, he wishes to explain his own being by means of the same categories through which he expresses the being of geological layers and rainstorms, plants and animals.[76] In materialism we find not only the material world but also the materialistic philosopher,[77] whose existence remains not understood.

The fact that things and processes have a meaning for man as a conscious subject justifies us in attributing a certain priority to subjectivity over things. One who thinks away the subject who man is also removes all meaning, so that the term "is" becomes meaningless. For what could "is" possibly mean without the *affirmation* of *being* by a subject? Which human meanings and significations in the world of things could still be accepted as *real* when, in the absence of a subject, being could only be being-for-no-one? Moreover, the supposition of the subject's absence can only be made because, and to the extent, that this supposition is *de facto* not made. I can formulate this supposition merely in a purely verbal fashion. The subject, then, is

---

[75]"Les vues scientifiques selon lesquelles je suis un moment du monde sont toujours naïves et hypocrites, parce qu'elles sous-entendent, sans la mentionner, cette autre vue, celle de la conscience, par laquelle d'abord un monde se dispose autour de moi et commence à exister pour moi." Merleau-Ponty, *PP*, Avant-propos, p. III.

[76]Merleau-Ponty, *SNS*, p. 143.

[77]"Materialism, which wants to reduce the totality of being to an interplay of moving particles of matter to be explained only in a causal way, cannot be refuted through *a priori* concepts. It does not contain a contradiction in terms but a practical contradiction, that is, in materialism we find, in addition to the system of the material world with its causal laws, the affirmation of the world and the conscious appeal to causal explanations. This appeal is an act of consciousness which, considered in its essential structure, transcends causal determinism." Dondeyne, "Belang voor de metaphysica van een accurate bestaansbeschrijving van de mens als kennend wezen," *Kenleer en metaphysiek (Verslag v.d. 12de alg, verg. der Vereniging v. thomistische wijsbegeerte en v.d. 3de studiedagen v.h. Wijsgerig gezelschap te Leuven),* Nijmegen, 1947, p. 39.

beyond dispute and reveals itself endowed with a certain priority over the world of things.

"No-thingness" as the Being of the Subject

The same conclusion is reached through the analysis of what Heidegger calls "no-thingness," or "non-being" (*Nichts*). The sciences, says Heidegger are interested in being—and "nothing" besides.[78] From a freely chosen "standpoint" they question being; being has the first and the final word; and precisely in this way man secures his mastery over being.[79] They are interested in being, not in "nothing" ("no-thing"). The sciences do not wish to have anything to do with "no-thing," but is such an attitude possible? [80] Can one express the proper character of the sciences without making an appeal to "no-thing"? The answer is in the negative, but what is the reason?

The task of the sciences is to offer explanations, which means that the sciences try to reduce cosmic being to its antecedents, to the cosmic forces and processes which make the cosmic being be. But how is it possible to make such explanations? If man himself also is a being like all the other beings which are scientifically explained by man, there would be nothing but darkness. The light of scientific explanations would not shine anywhere; being would not be "unveiled"—it would not say anything to man or make him think. But the cosmic being *is* "unveiled," it says something to man and makes him think. This is possible only because man (*Dasein*) himself is not just a (cosmic) being. If the latter is to appear and to have a relation to man as *Dasein*, then *Dasein* must transcend the "cosmic-being-in-*Dasein*." Otherwise *Dasein* cannot have a relationship to (cosmic) being and to itself,[81] for cosmic beings do not relate to themselves or to one another.

78"Erforscht werden soll nur das Seiende und sonst - nichts; das Seiende allein und weiter - nichts; das Seiende einzig und darüber hinaus - nichts." Heidegger, *Was ist Metaphysik?*, p. 26.

79Heidegger, *op. cit.*, p. 25.

80"Die Wissenschaft will vom Nichts nichts wissen. Aber ebenso gewiss bleibt bestehen: dort, wo sie ihr eigenes Wesen auszusprechen versucht, ruft sie das Nichts zu Hilfe. Was sie verwirft, nimmt sie in Anspruch." Heidegger, *op. cit.*, p. 27.

81"Würde das Dasein im Grunde seines Wesens nicht transzendieren. . . . . dann könnte es sich nie zu Seiendem verhalten, also auch nicht zu sich selbst." Heidegger, *op. cit.* p. 35.

Now, what is it in *Dasein* that makes *Dasein* transcend
(cosmic) being in itself? This can only be the other-than-being,
which is non-being, no-thingness. "*Dasein* means being projected into 'no-thingness.' " [82] Non-being, no-thingness, makes
it possible for being to dis-close itself and for *Dasein* to be open
for itself.[83] Non-being, obviously, is not simply the negation of
the concept "being," [84] for beings dis-close themselves through
the "nihilating" of non-being, no-thingness.[85] This non-being,
then, is very definitely something positive. The sciences which
are interested in the explanation of (cosmic) being, and in
"nothing" else, cannot understand themselves if they do not understand the nothing of non-thingness. For it is precisely
through "being projected into 'no-thingness' " that the sciences
are possible.[86]

Heidegger presents man here as the oppositional unity of
"being" and "nothingness." By "being" he obviously means the
cosmic being which the sciences can explain. Their explanations are made possible by the fact that in *Dasein* itself the "being" which man *also* is, is transcended. Heidegger calls this
transcendent aspect of man "nothingness," i.e., no-thingness,
because it cannot be like the being explained by the sciences:
the objects of the sciences do not pursue science. Heidegger's
other-than-being, then, clearly refers to the subject, who makes
wonder, asking about the "why" of beings, i.e., science, possible.[87] He calls the subject "non-being" because the subject is
not like what he has called (cosmic) being. This non-being,

---

[82]Heidegger, *ibid.*

[83]"Ohne ursprüngliche Offenbarkeit des Nichts kein Selbstsein und keine
Freiheit." Heidegger, *ibid.*

[84]"Das Nichts ist die Ermöglichung der Offenbarkeit des Seienden als
eines solchen für das menschliche Dasein. Das Nichts gibt nicht erst den
Gegenbegriff zum Seienden her, sondern gehört ursprünglich zum Wesen
selbst." Heidegger, *ibid.*

[85]"Im Sein des Seienden geschieht das Nichten des Nichts." Heidegger,
ibid.

[86]"Jetzt aber wird im Fragen nach dem Nichts offenbar, dass dieses wissenschaftliche Dasein nur möglich ist, wenn es sich im Vorhinein in das
Nichts hineinhält." Heidegger, *op. cit.*, p. 40.

[87]"Einzig weil das Nichts des Daseins offenbar ist, kann die volle Be-
fremdlichkeit des Seienden über uns kommen. Nur wenn die Be-
fremdlichkeit des Seienden uns bedrängt, weckt es und zieht es auf sich die
Verwunderung. Nur auf dem Grunde der Verwunderung - d.h. der Offenbarkeit des Nichts - entspringt das 'Warum'. Nur weil das Warum als solches
möglich ist, können wir in bestimmter Weise nach Gründen fragen und begründen. Nur weil wir fragen und begründen können, ist unserer Existenz
das Schicksal des Forschers in die Hand gegeben." Heidegger, *op. cit.*, p. 41.

however, is not simply nothing, but something positive, no-thing; a positivity which "lets be" (cosmic) being.[88]

Toward an Absolute Priority: Spiritualism

The subject's relative priority can also be explicitated in the following way. The world of things reveals itself always and of necessity as the *non-I*. *Not-being-I* belongs to the *reality* of the world of things. Things in the world of things which are not different from the *I*—which do not reveal themselves as *non-I*— are not real things. One who wishes to express the *reality* of things will, therefore, always be obliged implicitly to affirm this non-identity with the subject. Thus it is impossible to deny or eliminate the *I* in speaking of the reality of things, for such a denial would make it impossible to affirm any longer the world of things as *non-I*. This *not-being-I*, however, belongs to the *reality of* things.

Accordingly, there is no escape from assigning a certain priority to the *I* over things, and for this reason it is impossible to consider the *I* as nothing but the result of cosmic processes and forces. For without the *I* these processes and forces in the cosmos are not what they *really* are, viz., *not-I*. Now, how could that which without the *I* simply is not what it *really* is make the *I* be? Can one who is sinking away in the quicksand pull himself up by the hair of his head?

It should be clear now what direction will be taken by those who wish to exploit the weakness of materialism. In the eyes of the materialist, the conscious subject is not a reality worth mentioning; but for the spiritualist, reflection on reality begins with the affirmation of the subject. As we emphasized before, it is absolutely necessary to experience the power of materialistic thinking if one wishes to understand the gross assertion that man is a thing. By the same token, however, it is also necessary to plunge deeply into the sphere of spiritualistic thinking in order to prevent the results of this way of thinking from being ir- responsibly rejected.

---

[88]In this way one should also understand the seemingly nonsensical state- ment that *"ex nihilo omne ens qua ens fit"* (*op. cit.*, p. 40). There is mean- ing through the "no-thing" of *Dasein*, i.e., through the positivity of subjectivity, by which man transcends in himself the being of cosmic being. "Im Nichts des Daseins kommt erst das Seiende im Ganzen seiner eigensten Möglichkeit nach, d.h. in endlicher Weise, zu sich selbst." Heidegger, *op. cit.*, p. 40.

As soon as one really sees the priority of the subject, there is a danger that the importance of the subject will be exaggerated. Without the *I* the world of things is not what it *really* is, viz., *not-I*. Without the *I* the world of things cannot be spoken of and the term "is" loses all meaning. A slight exaggeration of this point is all that is needed to make one consider things as the result of a kind of creative activity exercised by the subject, or as contents of the subject's consciousness.

In spiritualistic monism this way of absolutizing the importance of the subject becomes a reduction of the being of material things to the subject's being. In other words, the "detotalization of reality" goes here in exactly the opposite direction than that taken by materialism. While materialism disregards the importance of subjectivity or considers the latter not worth mentioning, in spiritualistic monism the density of material things evaporates into the "thin air" of contents of consciousness.[89]

Spiritualistic monism, then, takes seriously the element neglected by materialism—namely, the originality of subjectivity. As a subject, man cannot be the result of material processes; hence, the subject is original. If this originality is exaggerated, however, one eliminates not only the subject's receptivity with respect to the density of material things, but also the possibility of recognizing other subjects as subjects. For how could a self-absolutizing subject recognize and accept the fact that another subject is an *other* subject, possessing an identity of his own with respect to the self-absolutizing subject? The self-absolutizing subject per force must reduce to his own identity the proper and distinct identity of the other subject: he cannot avoid sacrificing the proper identity of the other subject. As soon, however, as the *I* conceives itself as if it contained all other *I*'s within itself, it can no longer conceive itself as the "little," finite *I*, distinct from the other *I*'s, which any real *I de facto* is. The *I* which is the author of this book, for example, does not include all *I*'s.

Spiritualistic monism, then, cannot avoid sacrificing the distinct identity of the "little" *I* to the Absolute Subject. The place of the "little" subject which any real subject is, is taken by the "great" impersonal Subject, and the many distinct sub-

---

89"L'idéalisme transcendental lui aussi 'réduit' le monde, puisque, s'il le rend certain, c'est à titre de pensée ou conscience du monde et comme le simple corrélatif de notre connaissance de sorte qu'il devient immanent à la conscience et que l'aséité des choses est par là supprimée." Merleau-Ponty, *PP*, Avant-propos, p. X.

jects are viewed as particularizations, dialectic moments or functions of that impersonal Subject. The consequences of this way
of thinking are typically illustrated by Fichte's Absolute Ego and
Hegel's Absolute Spirit.[90] The qualifications of the Absolute
Subject will obviously become so fantastic that ultimately they
are identical with the traditional "names" affirmed of God.
Thus spiritualistic monism terminates in the deification of the
subject.[91]

The *reality*, however, of the "little" subject is that it is a
little subject, one which is and remains unmistakably relative.
But the Absolute Subject is assumed to think and act in and
through the "little" subject; hence, at first, the claim is made
that it is *really the Absolute* which acts and thinks, and not the
"little" subject. Since in reality only the "little" subject exists,
the assertion that the Absolute thinks and acts in and through
the "little" subject *actually* amounts to the claim that the thinking and acting of the "little" subject has an Absolute weight.[92]

In this way it can happen that man thinks that he can speak
with "divine" authority and act with a "divine" guarantee. He
assigns to his convictions and assertions so much importance that
in principle he cannot listen to anyone else, and looks upon any
attack on his "truth" as lese-majesty.[93] He fancies that he can
speak in the name of the Absolute, he considers his "truth" as
the design of "God" for the world and man, and holds that his
actions execute this design with a "divine" guarantee.[94]

One who has experienced the power of spiritualistic thinking
can understand that this trend of thought has never been completely overcome in the history of philosophy. Let us add that
it ought not even ever to be fully overcome, in the sense that

---

[90]Dondeyne, "Beschouwingen bij het atheïstisch existentialisme," *Tijdschrift voor Philosophie*, XIII(1951), pp. 27-28.

[91]*PP*, p. 428; J. Ortega y Gasset, *De mens en de mensen*, pp. 57-58.

[92]"Nevertheless, we should not forget that this absolute self-consciousness
ultimately is the consciousness of *no one* although it only comes to itself in
and through the history of mankind. This implies that there will always be
someone—or some people—willing to identify himself with the absolute *Ego*,
ready to proclaim, in a particular historical situation, that he is the authentic
incarnation, the bearer or the herald of the absolute. One may think here
of Fichte's famous "Address to the German Nation." Dondeyne, "Inleiding
tot het denken van E. Levinas," *Tijdschrift voor Philosophie*, XXV(1963),
p. 562.

[93]"Qui se réclame de l'absolu ne voudra écouter personne; il doit se persuader que toute contestation est un crime de lèse-majesté envers l'autorité
qui cautionne son attitude." G. Gusdorf, *Traité de Métaphysique*, Paris,
1956, p. 131.

[94]Gusdorf, *op. cit.*, p. 107.

the original inspiration of spiritualistic thinking should simply disappear entirely from actual thought. On the other hand, however, if one considers the ultimate achievements of spiritualism, he has to acknowledge that in spiritualism hardly anything remains of the original inspiration which gave rise to materialism. In an irresponsible fashion spiritualism buries under verbiage the fact that man only is whatever he is on the basis of his materiality.

Accordingly, there is every reason to try to find an intermediary view, a position which takes into account the valuable insights of both materialism and spiritualism and which, at the same time, endeavors to avoid the extremes of both. As was pointed out before, existential phenomenology wishes to make this attempt. Before describing man as *existence,* however, we would like to speak of Descartes. The reason is that, historically speaking, existential phenomenology is continually in opposition to philosophies which somehow arose directly or indirectly from Descartes' ideas. The latter, moreover, exemplifies how it is possible to be a spiritualist without ever recognizing this fact "officially," just as it is possible to be a materialist without ever explicitly stating that one wishes to reduce man to a mere thing.

3. DESCARTES

Descartes (1596–1650) lived at a time when scholastic philosophy had sadly degenerated into inauthentic thinking. At the end of his studies at the famous Jesuit College of La Flèche, Descartes came to the conclusion that his endeavor to acquire knowledge had had only one beneficial result: a clear knowledge of his own ignorance.[95] He had experienced that in philosophy there was nothing at all about which philosophers did not disagree. On the other hand, the various opinions were represented by ingenious minds; hence, argued Descartes, it will not be possible for me to be more successful in philosophy if I keep pursuing the same paths as those great thinkers. As soon as he could escape from the influence of his masters, he decided to pursue no other knowledge than that which he could find in himself and in the "great book" of the world.[96]

---

[95]René Descartes, *Discours de la méthode,* Texte et commentaire par Etienne Gilson, Paris, 3rd ed., 1962, pp. 4-5.
[96]*Discours,* p. 9.

After spending some years in trying to acquire experience, Descartes decided to use his mental power for an investigation of the *way* by which truth and certainty could be reached. He had never given up hope of finding this way, for he could not forget the example of mathematics. It surprised him that nothing higher had ever been built on the solid foundation of mathematics.[97] Descartes would have liked to join those who are less able to distinguish truth from untruth, and who, on the basis of their lack of abilities, can justify themselves in simply following the opinions of others. For what else can the less gifted do? [98] "Unfortunately," however, Descartes had been taught by more than one master, and these masters contradicted one another. Thus he saw himself obliged to take the initiative.[99]

This initiative led him to suspect that perhaps it would be possible to utilize the method of mathematics, with its inherent certainty, for the whole of human knowledge.[100] The tradition in which Descartes was educated relied on the deductive method. He agreed that this method was useful for the orderly arrangement of acquired knowledge, but denied its usefulness in the acquisition of new knowledge.[101] Now, mathematics gives us new knowledge, its method is not deductive but analytic. Starting from a few very simple axioms, mathematics analytically proceeds to give us understanding of the theses implied in those axioms. Descartes suspected that it would be possible to build the entire edifice of human knowledge in a similar fashion, provided the work was done by one man.[102] He thought that he owed this view to a supernatural inspiration, and devoted his entire life to the construction of that "wonderful science" of a *mathesis universalis,* a universal mathematics.

The "Cogito"

The path to an incontrovertible starting point for the "won-

---

[97]*Discours,* p. 7.

[98]*Discours,* p. 15.

[99]"—et je me trouvai comme contraint d'entreprendre moi-même de me conduire." *Discours,* p. 16.

[100]"Ces longues chaînes de raisons, toutes simples et faciles, dont les géomètres ont coutume de se servir, pour parvenir à leurs plus difficiles démonstrations, m'avaient donné occasion de m'imaginer que toutes les choses, qui peuvent tomber sous la connaissance des hommes, s'entre-suivent en même façon, et que . . . il n'y en peut avoir de si éloignées auxquelles enfin on ne parvienne, ni de si cachées qu'on ne découvre." *Discours,* p. 19.

[101]Descartes, *Regulae ad directionem ingenii,* Texte revu et traduit par Georges Le Roy, Paris, n.d., p. 97.

[102]*Discours,* pp. 11-14.

derful science" with its certainty and truth made it necessary for
Descartes to have recourse to methodic doubt. Anything which
in any way is subject to doubt must be "placed between brackets," i.e., judgment is suspended with respect to it. This does
not mean that Descartes is a sceptic or an agnostic. He wishes
to find the truth and certainty of the "wonderful science," and
therefore is obliged first to demolish his "old opinions" down to
their very foundations because he has experienced how doubtful
everything is that he has learned from his youth.[103]

What, then, falls under Descartes' methodic doubt? If we
may be permitted to systematize the enumeration of the things
Descartes placed betweeen brackets, we can say that it covers
everything which is not the subject himself. God, the world and
the body are included in the list. For methodic reasons Descartes suspends every past judgment with respect to these three
and provisionally wishes to abstain from any judgment about
them. The reason is not that he really doubts the existence of
God, the world and the body, but that in his eyes everything
he has ever learned about them still lacks a foundation, even if
it is something that is true. He does not intend, however, to
examine all opinions one by one.[104] That would not only be impossible but also superfluous. For once the foundation of all
"old opinions" is undermined, the entire edifice of former truths
and certainties will collapse.[105]

With respect to the world and the body Descartes indicates
two reasons why their reality must be doubted: the unreliability
of the senses and the possibility of dreaming. It should be
obvious that our senses *sometimes* deceive us when we try to
derive certain knowledge about the body and the world from the
senses. But if the senses *sometimes* deceive us, they could *always* deceive us.[106] Moreover, in our dreams we have images of
our body and the world of which, upon awakening, we must
deny that they agree with our real body and our real world.
While we are dreaming that we have a more robust or more

---

[103]Descartes, *Meditationes de prima philosophia*, Introduction et notes
par Geneviève Lewis, Paris, 1946, p. 18.
[104]*Meditationes*, pp. 18-19.
[105]"Et pour cela il n'est pas besoin que je les examine chacune en
particulier, ce qui serait d'un travail infini: mais parce que la ruine des fonde-
ments entraîne nécessairement avec soi tout le reste de l'édifice, je m'atta-
querai d'abord aux principes sur lesquelles toutes mes anciennes opinions
étaient appuyées." *Meditationes*, p. 19.
[106]*Ibid.*

beautiful body or dwell in an entirely different world, we are firmly convinced that our dream-body and out dream-world are real—just as we are convinced that a pen, a book, a piece of paper on the table, in a room, in a house standing in a street are real. If, then, we are convinced of the reality of a pen, a book, a piece of paper, a room, a house, and a street, this conviction is just as unfounded as the certainty we have of a dream-body and a dream-world while we are dreaming. For there exists no criterion by which I can determine that I do not dream when I think that I perceive a real pen, book, or piece of paper.[107]

Descartes realizes, of course, that radical methodic doubt cannot be utilized in everyday life. Doubts may sometimes arise there, but people will try to suppress them in order to continue living in a false security. A prisoner who dreams that he is free is unwilling to give up his dream.[108] Everyday life is like a dream, but the search for truth and certainty demands that this dream be disturbed.

For Descartes radical methodic doubt is the path leading to the indubitable certainty of the *cogito*. When man has "placed between brackets" everything which is in any way subject to doubt, then the fact of his doubting itself remains as indubitable and certain. His doubting thought, his thinking doubt, his *cogito* remains indubitable in all his doubt. But, says Descartes, if the *cogito* is indubitable and certain, then it is also beyond doubt and certain that I, who think, *am* something.[109] This certainty remains even if an evil spirit would deceive me in everything I think, for if this spirit deceives me, I *am*. He can deceive me as much as he likes, but he can never make me *not* be as long as I think.[110] *Cogito, ergo sum*—"I think, therefore, I am"—thus constitutes the incontrovertible starting point of the "wonderful science" which Descartes wished to build.

107"Et m'arrêtant sur cette pensée je vois si manifestement qu'il n'y a point d'indices concluants, ni de marques assez certaines par où l'on puisse distinguer nettement la veille d'avec le sommeil, que j'en suis tout étonné." *Meditationes,* p. 20.

108*Meditationes,* pp. 23-24.

109"Mais, aussitôt après, je pris garde que, pendant que je voulais ainsi penser que tout était faux, il fallait nécessairement que moi, qui le pensait, fusse quelque chose. Et remarquant que cette vérité: *je pense, donc je suis,* était si ferme et si assurée, que toutes les plus extravagantes suppositions des sceptiques n'étaient pas capables de l'ebranler, je jugeai que je pouvais la recevoir, sans scrupule, pour le premier principe de la philosophie, que je cherchais." *Discours,* p. 32.

110*Meditationes,* p. 25.

Consequences of the Cogito's Primacy

The radicalism of Descartes' critical procedure in his search for an incontrovertible starting point of philosophy begins to show it consequences in the very first truth of his philosophy. The subject-as-*cogito* is beyond doubt; but what is this subject? Descartes cannot answer: the subject is embodied or involved in the world, for his methodic doubt has placed the reality of the body and the world "between brackets." His answer to the question "What am I?" can only refer to that which has not been "bracketed," viz., thinking: I am thinking. Descartes explicitly accepts this consequence. He thinks that the subject, the "I," the "thinking substance," which he calls "soul," simply is what it is, even without the body and the world, of which it is wholly independent.[111]

The method of radical doubt also decides on the *object* of thinking, of knowledge, or of consciousness. I am thinking, but *what* do I think? Descartes cannot answer that the subject-as-*cogito* thinks of the reality of God, the world, or the body, for their *reality* has been placed "between brackets." His answer, again, can refer only to that which was not "bracketed," viz., thinking itself: I am thinking my own thoughts, I am conscious of the contents of my consciousness, I know my own cognitive images, and this is what I *am*.

The radicalism of the methodic doubt did not remove God, the world and the body from *thought*; it merely affected them with the qualifier "thought of."[112] It is from this qualification that the *cogito*-with-its-contents derives its incontrovertible certainty. For, even if the pen I use, the paper on which I write, the chair on which I sit and the room in which I work are not real— even if I am merely dreaming all this—it still remains incontrovertible that I have the pen-idea, the paper-idea, the chair-idea, and the room-idea.[113] The *cogito*-with-contents is beyond doubt, and this is what I *am*.

The Criterion of Truth and Certainty

The incontrovertible certainty of his "I think, therefore, I

---

[111]*Discours*, pp. 32-33.

[112]Merleau-Ponty, *PP*, avant-propos, III.

[113]"Puis, outre cela, j'avais des idées de plusieurs choses sensibles et corporelles: car, quoique je supposasse que je rêvais, et que tout ce que je voyais ou imaginais était faux, je ne pouvais nier toutefois que les idées n'en fussent véritablement en ma pensée." *Discours*, p. 35.

am," led Descartes to investigate in what this certainty consists. This point was of the greatest importance for the building of his "wonderful science," because the latter had to contain indisputable truth and certainty in all its phases. Having discovered that one thesis—the thesis "I think, therefore, I am"—was characterized by truth and certainty,[114] Descartes investigated the reason for this truth and certainty, and came to the conclusion that his only ground was that he *clearly and distinctly* saw its truth: in order to think, one must exist. In this way "clarity" and "distinctness" of thought revealed themselves to Descartes as the criterion of truth and certainty. He, therefore, decided that in the building of his "wonderful science" he would ascribe truth and certainty only to things of which he had "clear" and "distinct" ideas.[115]

According to Descartes, God's veracity guarantees that "clear and distinct ideas" express things which are really true. The clear and distinct concept is the criterion of truth, but this criterion needs a guarantee.[116] Descartes proves the existence of God [117] in order to be able to affirm that our clear and distinct ideas come from the Creator God. But if our clear and distinct ideas come from God, and if—on the basis of the "clarity" and "distinctness" of those ideas—God forces us to affirm that their content is really true, then God would deceive us if the affirmed were not really true. God's veracity, however, precludes that he deceives man. God, then, guarantees the truth and reality of anything that is conceived in clear and distinct ideas.[118] Our task, therefore, is to determine which ideas are "clear" and "distinct." [119]

Man

Regarding matter, Descartes thinks that only one idea satisfies

---

[114]*Discours,* p. 33.

[115]"Je jugeai que je pouvais prendre pour règle générale, que les choses que nous concevons fort clairement et fort distinctement sont toutes vraies." *Discours,* p. 33.

[116]"Cela même que j'ai tantôt pris pour une règle, à savoir que les choses que nous concevons très clairement et très distinctement sont toutes vraies, n'est assuré qu'à cause que Dieu est ou existe, et qu'il est un être parfait, et que tout ce qui est en nous vient de lui." *Discours,* p. 38.

[117]*Discours,* p. 36; *Meditationes,* pp. 34-52, 62-70.

[118]"Mais si nous ne savions point que tout ce qui est en nous de réel et de vrai, vient d'un être parfait et infini, pour claires et distinctes que fussent nos idées, nous n'aurions aucune raison qui nous assurât qu'elles eussent la perfection d'être vraies." *Discours,* p. 39.

[119]*Discours,* p. 33.

the criterion of "clarity" and "distinctness"—the idea of extension. This statement applies both to the body and to worldly things. Whatever is material, Descartes holds, is essentially extended, quantitative, and nothing else. Now, only the physical sciences study nature by means of the idea of quantity. Thus we see that Descartes holds a scientistic view of the body and the worldly thing. Affirmations which cannot be made by the sciences of nature may perhaps be useful for practical purposes in daily life, but they remain meaningless in the "wonderful science" which is concerned with incontrovertible certainty about truth and reality.

Descartes' standpoint in this matter is loaded with heavy consequences for his view of man. On the one hand, man is a *res cogitans*, a self-thinking substance; but on the other, he is also a *res extensa*, an extended substance. Because material reality is nothing but quantitative for Descartes, every change or movement is *per se* and of necessity a spatial change or movement. The "human" body, therefore, is nothing but "spatially moving quantity," a machine,[120] the object of mechanics. Man, then, consists of two substances which are in principle and essentially separate and independent of each other.[121]

Of course, it did not escape Descartes that soul and body constitute a certain unity. This is obvious from our feelings of hunger, thirst, and pain. When a wound hurts me, my thinking substance does not perceive an injury in the same way as a pilot on a ship notices that something is broken on his ship.[122] Such feelings indicate that there is a "mixture of the spirit with the body"[123] which is much more intimate than the unity of a pilot with his ship.[124] Descartes is thus forced to admit that soul and body exercise a certain influence on each other. Strictly speaking, this should not be possible, but the fact cannot be denied. Descartes tried to solve the difficulty by locating the soul in the pineal gland. Through "animal spirits,"[125] the soul, he argued,

---

[120]*Discours*, pp. 55-56.
[121]*Discours*, pp. 59-60.
[122]"Car si cela n'était lorsque mon corps est blessé, je ne sentirais pas pour cela de la douleur, moi qui ne suis qu'une chose qui pense, mais j'apercevrais cette blessure par le seul entendement, comme un pilote aperçoit par la vue si quelque chose se rompt dans son vaisseau." *Meditationes*, p. 79.
[123]*Meditationes*, p. 79.
[124]*Discours*, p. 59.
[125]*Discours*, p. 54.

could influence the movements of the body. Descartes himself, however, was not very happy with this "solution." This is not surprising: he was attempting to answer the question of how two substances which are *essentially* not a unity can constitute an *essential* unity.

Observations

As was previously mentioned, a way of thinking can be materialistic even if it does not explicitly affirm that man is a thing. Scientism is a camouflaged form of materialism, for in scientism the subject simply does not count. Materialism evokes spiritualism as a reaction: the failure of materialism leads to a spiritualistic way of thinking which takes its starting point in the priority of the subject. Those who affirm the priority of the subject, however, run the risk of letting this correct insight degenerate by reducing the density of things to the "thin air" of subjective contents of consciousness. Nothing then remains of the undeniable fact that man is whatever he is on the basis of materiality.

One of the reasons for the preceding explanation of Descartes' view was to show that, strictly speaking, such a degeneration occurred even in Descartes' thought itself. He only managed to escape from it by being illogical, by filling the subject-as-*cogito* with "clear" and "distinct" ideas of the body and worldly things. Through an unjustifiable appeal to God's veracity as a guarantee for the truth of those "clear" and "distinct" ideas, Descartes gave man again a grip on the reality of the body and of worldly things. Thus one can call Descartes' theory a mitigated form of spiritualism. But the absolute spiritualism of Spinoza, Fichte, and Hegel is a more consistent form of Cartesianism than is Descartes' own theory.

Thus no one needs be surprised that the existential phenomenologist's denial of the Absolute Ego or the Absolute Spirit aims also at Descartes' theory. Descartes is present in very many of the denials made by existential phenomenology.

Let us now point out another important aspect of this Cartesian presence. As we mentioned, the radical methodic doubt about the reality of the world did not let the world perish with respect to man's thinking: the things of the world were merely affected by the qualifier "thought of." Naturally Descartes never really doubted the reality of worldly things. Doubt was for him the *method* by which he hoped to gain truth and certainty: through his doubt he wished to reach the critical affirmation of the reality of worldly things. The effect of the first critical step implied that worldly things were affected by the qualifier "thought of," but Descartes obviously realized that in this way he had not done full justice to the *reality* of the world. The pen I use, the paper on which I write, the chair in which I sit, and the room in which I live are more than the pen-*idea,* the paper-*idea*, the chair-*idea* and the room-*idea*. But what could this "more" be? That the being of all worldly things reveals itself as a being-for-the-subject had already been taken into account by Descartes when he conceived the *cogito* as filled with ideas. In other words, he had reduced the *human* aspect of things to their being the content of the subject. Now, if the being of things is more than being ideas in a subject, this "more" cannot again be the *human* aspect, because the human "dimension" of things has already been accounted for. Because this "more" cannot be a being-for-the-subject, it has to be "brute" reality, the "inhuman" dimension of reality, i.e., reality divorced from the subject.

In this way the reality of things was, as it were, split by Descartes into a human side—being-for-us—and an inhuman side—being in itself. The human side was located "inside" the *cogito,* and the inhuman side "outside" it. The obvious question to arise here was: to what extent does the "inner world" agree with the "outer world"? Is there any "objectivity" corresponding to the ideas "inside" the *cogito*? Objectivity in this question means "brute" reality, of course, for once the subject is divorced from the world, the latter can only be conceived as divorced from the subject—as a collection of things-in-themselves, a world-in-itself.

By the roundabout way of God's veracity in His infusion of "clear" and "distinct" ideas, Descartes thought that he could "affirm" the "reality" of things-in-themselves, of a world-in-itself. We put the term "affirm" between quotation marks because it no longer refers to a real affirmation: the "object" of this "affirmation" is the world-in-itself—that is, the brute reality of the "non-affirmed world." What possible sense can anyone attach to the "affirmation" of a "non-affirmed world"?

In spite of all the difficulties inherent in Cartesianism, the "spirit" of Descartes became part and parcel of both philosophy and everyday life. The subject was divorced from the world, and the world was put out "there" as separate from the subject. Existential phenomenology denies both the extremes of materialism and spiritualism. Its actual resistance to these extremes, however, implies also the denial of Descartes' "spirit."

4. EXISTENCE AS CONSCIOUS-BEING-IN-THE-WORLD

As was mentioned, it would be useless to "refute" materialism and spiritualism if this expression is taken to mean that one wishes to eliminate the inclination to think materialistically or spiritualistically from oneself. Such an attempt would amount to the claim that neither the materialist nor the spiritualist have discerned any truth worth mentioning. Existential phenomenology therefore deliberately tries to walk a middle road, preserving what materialism and spiritualism did "really" see, but avoiding the extreme tendencies of both.

With spiritualism existential phenomenology affirms that man is a subject. The subject who man is, however, is not an Absolute Subject but an *"existent"* subject. Man as subject is *"existence."* [126] This term is taken in a technical and literal sense: man "ec-sists," he puts himself outside himself." [127]

What is meant by this "outside" of human subjectivity? Provisionally this question can only be answered within the present framework of the struggle between materialism and spiritualism. For this reason the answer shows the influence of materialism: the "outside" of human subjectivity is the "thing." The "thing" should be understood as the reality of the human body and the human world. The body and the world are called —albeit in very different ways—the "outside" of the subject because there is an invincible non-identity of subject and "thing." This non-identity, however, can be misunderstood. For the claim that human subjectivity is an *existent* subjectivity means precisely that the subject simply is not what he is without

---

[126]"Le mérite de la philosophie nouvelle est justement de chercher dans la notion d'existence le moyen de penser (la condition humaine). L'existence au sens moderne, c'est le mouvement par lequel l'homme est au monde, s'engage dans une situation physique et sociale qui devient son point de vue sur le monde." Merleau-Ponty, *SNS*, p. 143.

[127]"Le pôle subjectif n'est *rien:* c'est-à-dire qu'il n' 'est' pas à la manière d'une chose, qu'il n'est pas localisable, il n'est pas un être du monde. Il n' 'est' que dans la mesure où il *existe,* et il n'existe ('ek-siste') qu'en se projetant vers: il n'est qu'en étant ailleurs, *hors-de-soi-dans-le-monde."* Francis Jeanson, *La phénoménologie,* Paris, 2nd ed., 1951, p. 75.

being immersed in the body and the world. Without the body and the world the subject is not what he is, viz., a human subject. The subject needs what he himself is *not*—body and world —in order to be a subject.[128] Man as *existence* is neither a thing nor an Absolute Subject. In Heidegger's terms, the being of man is *Da-sein,* and the particle *Da* (there) indicates the "ec-centric" character of human subjectivity.[129]

Because *existence* is *existent subjectivity,* it is not enough to say that the being of man is a being-in-the-world. The materialist could use exactly the same expression and mean by it that man is a little fragment within the evolution of the cosmos. But even if one abstains from such a gross interpretation, the expression "being in the world" does not convey the specific element of man's "being in." Man is not in the world as a cigarette is in a pack or a pencil in the drawer.[130] For there can only be question of a cigarette "in" a pack when the *existent* subject considers the distance of the cigarette to the sides of the pack. The "being in" that is characteristic of man is the "being in" of a subject: the being of man is a being-conscious-in-the-world. In order not to misunderstand the significance of the subject, man's "being in" needs to be expressed by such terms as "dwelling," "being familiar with," "being present to," for these expressions clearly imply the subject.[131]

It would be a mistake, however, to think that man must be called a being dwelling in the world *because* of the fact that there *happens* to be a world. For in that case conscious-being-in-the-world would not constitute the *being* of man; the world would not belong to the *being* of man, conscious-being would also without the world be conscious-being. The idea *existence* wishes to express precisely that human subjectivity is not what it is without the world.[132] It is intended to convey that the world

[128]"La première vérité est bien 'Je pense', mais à condition qu'on entende pas là 'je suis à moi' en étant au monde." Merleau-Ponty, *PP,* p. 466.

[129]Heidegger, *SZ,* p. 11.

[130]*SZ,* p. 54.

[131]"Das In-sein meint so wenig ein räumliches 'Ineinander' Vorhandener, als 'in' ursprünglich gar nicht eine räumliche Beziehung der genannten Art bedeutet; 'in' stammt von innanwohnen, habitare, sich aufhalten; 'an' bedeutet: ich bin gewohnt, vertraut mit, ich pflege etwas; es hat die Bedeutung von colo im Sinne von habito und diligo." *SZ,* p. 54.

[132]"Si le sujet est en situation. . . . c'est qu'il ne réalise son ipséité qu'en étant effectivement corps et en entrant par ce corps dans le monde." Merleau-Ponty, *PP,* p. 467.

belongs to the essence of man: if the world is "thought away," the subject can no longer be affirmed.

The Impossibility of a "Demonstration"

The statement that man is *existence* cannot be *demonstrated* in the strict sense of the term. This means, first of all, that understanding man as *existence* cannot at all be the result of the process of thoughts which is known as "demonstration" in the positive sciences. All positive sciences *presuppose* an understanding of man's essence, if only because of the fact that they consider themselves capable of speaking about man with the aid of certain scientific models. For this fact implies the conviction that man is *essentially* such that it is *possible* to say something about man with the aid of those scientific models. This presupposition has a philosophical character; consequently, it cannot be clarified by the positive sciences themselves.[133] In the positive sciences of man, man occurs as an "ingredient" of the sciences. Man, however, is not called *existence* as an "ingredient" of the sciences but *inter alia* as a pursuer of the sciences.

Secondly, the statement that it is not possible to prove man as *existence* means that his idea cannot be derived from any prior and more fundamental insight. For nothing is prior and more fundamental for man than his own essence, and it is precisely this essence that is said to be *existence*.

On the other hand, the fact that man cannot be *proved* to be *existence* does not mean that the philosopher is powerless with respect to his claim, or that anyone can say about man whatever he fancies. Man's *existent* character cannot be proved, but it can be *pointed out*, albeit with all the risks involved in this.[134] The philosopher can attempt to *let* others *see* the essence of man as *existence*, just as the materialists and the spiritualists attempted to let us see what man is. In his attempt to let others see, however, the philosopher has no absolute guarantee that he will succeed better than others, even though he obviously hopes and desires so.

Before attempting to "point out" *existence*, we must first emphasize how important it is to realize that there is question

---

133Merleau-Ponty, *SNS*, p. 195.

134"Le rapport au monde, tel qu'il se prononce infatigablement en nous, n'est rien qui puisse être rendu plus clair par une analyse: la philosophie ne peut que le replacer sous notre regard, l'offrir à notre constatation." *PP*, Avant-propos, p. XIII.

here of man on the proper level of his being-man. One who is told that man's being is a conscious-being-in-the-world could ask whether new-born children, people who are asleep or under narcosis, imbeciles, idiots, and schizophrenics can still be called human beings. It should be obvious that these examples do not refer to man on the proper level of his being-man. But it is also evident that if such people are called human, this can be done only on the basis of the relationship which being-human on an improper level has to being-human on the proper level. The proper level of being-man, then, is in certain sense "prior" to the improper level, and this is the reason why it is possible to say in what sense even the human being on an improper level of being-human can be called a man. When man is "defined" here as *existence,* we are concerned with man on the proper level of his being-man.

There are several ways in which one can point to man as *existence.* Some authors try to do this through an analysis of *existence,* others prefer the analysis of man's bodily being. Because the first approach will be discussed in Chapter Two, we will limit ourselves here to the analysis of man's bodily being.

Analysis of Man's Bodily Being

One who wishes to speak of the human body must first take certain precautions: he must make certain that he does indeed speak of the *human* body. Otherwise he could easily fall for the temptation to speak of the human body as just another one of the many bodies pertaining to the group of bodies,[135] which, for example, the physicist has in mind when he says: "A body which is wholly or partially immersed in a liquid seems to lose weight. This loss of weight is exactly equal to that of the displaced fluid." One who speaks in such terms of the human body loses sight of the fact that he disregards the *human* aspect of the human body. The human body is *human* because it is "mine," "yours," "his," or "hers," in other words, because it is the body of a subject.[136] The human body is a participation in the sub-

---

[135]Sartre, *EN*, p. 278.

[136]"Si je fais abstraction de l'indice propre à *mon* corps - en tant qu'il est mon corps -, si je le considère comme un corps parmi d'autres corps en nombre illimité, je serai amené à le traiter comme un objet, comme présentant les caractères fondamentaux par lesquels l'objectivité se définit. Il devient dès lors matière à connaissance scientifique; il se problématise, dirai-je - mais seulement à condition que je le regarde comme non-mien." Marcel, *RI*, p. 31.

ject and the subject is immersed in the body. My grasping
hands are "I who grasp," my feet are "I who walk," my eyes are
"I who see," and my ears are "I who hear." My body, then, does
not lie like a thing among other things.[137] My hands do not lie
in the graspable world, my feet do not belong to the world that
can be walked upon, my eyes do not lie in the visible world, and
my ears do not belong to the audible world. The *human* body
lies on the side of the subject. Considered in this way, man, we
must say, *is* his body.[138]

The human body, therefore, does not mean what is asserted
about it in biology, physiology, and anatomy.[139] In books about
these topics the *human* body does not occur because "I," "you,"
"he," and "she" do not occur in those books. Obviously, this
does not mean that biology, physiology, and anatomy do not
speak of anything, but it does imply that they do not express
the *human character* of the human body.[140] These sciences,
moreover, do not know whereof they speak if they disregard the
original "knowing about the body" which the subject as embodied *cogito* himself is.

Once this point is understood, it is easy to see also that "my"
body is the transition from "me" to my world, the place where I
appropriate my world [141]—that it grafts me on the realm of
things and secures for me a solid or shaky standpoint in the
world. My hand with five fingers helps me grasp the world in a
certain way, different from the way I would grasp it if I had only
one finger on each hand; my feet help me walk upon the world
in a certain way, different from the one I would use if I had
wings or webfeet; my ears help me constitute the world for me
as a world of sound; my eyes help me constituting the world as
a visible world; my body helps me occupy the standpoint from
which I say that Mount McKinley is high and the sidewalk low;

137"Mon corps tel qu'il est pour moi, ne m'apparaît pas au milieu du
monde." Sartre, *EN*, p. 365.

138Marcel, *JM*, p. 301.

139"En ce qui concerne le corps, et même le corps d'autrui, il nous faut
apprendre à le distinguer du corps objectif tel que le décrivent les livres de
physiologie." Merleau-Ponty, *PP*, p. 403.

140". . . . le corps objectif n'est pas la vérité du corps phénoménal, c'est-
à-dire la vérité du corps tel que nous le vivons, il n'en est qu'une image
appauvrie, et le problème des relations de l'âme et du corps ne concerne
pas le corps objectif qui n'a qu'une existence conceptuelle, mais le corps
phénoménal." *PP*. p. 493.

141*PP*, p. 180.

that Sirius is far away and my desk nearby; [142] that fire is hot and ice is cold. Anything in the world that is hard, soft, angular, sharp, sticky, red, yellow, purple, spatial, light, heavy, immovable, tasty, nourishing, fragrant, malodorous, small, large, etc. etc. points to the human body. A bicycle points to a posture and movements of the body and the same must be said of a football, a bed, a house, a door, a room, in a word, of all cultural objects.

My body, then, lies on the side of the subject who I am but, at the same time, involves me in the world of things. My body opens me for the world, or rather, opens me toward the world, and signifies my standpoint in this world.[143] My body keeps the visible scene alive, animates and nourishes it.[144] When my body begins to disintegrate, my world also "goes to pieces," and the complete dissolution of my body means a breach with the world, and, at the same time, death—the end of my being as a conscious-being-in-the-world, the end of my being-man.[145]

Accordingly, reflecting upon the human body, we encounter the subject, who is immersed in the body and, through the body, involved in the world. We find the world, which as a "complex of meanings" clings to the body, the body which, as human, points to the subject. We find man as *existence*.

Pact Between Body and World

All this remains unintelligible for one who conceives the human body as a thing like all other things, as just another example of the category "body." The same still holds for one who expresses himself somewhat more subtly and thinks that the human body, as *human*, can be the object of the sciences. As long as one speaks of the human body in the way the sciences speak of it, one has to be resigned to the absolute unintelligibility of the statement that the world has a meaning which clings to the body as the incarnation of the subject, a meaning which the body itself "knows" and "affirms." But in that case one must also be resigned to the unintelligibility of the fact that

---

[142]*PP*, p. 502.

[143]". . . mon corps est aussi ce qui m'ouvre au monde et m'y met en situation." *PP*, p. 192.

[144]*PP*, p. 235.

[145]"Or, si le monde se pulvérise, ou se disloque, c'est parce que le corps propre a cessé d'être corps connaissant, d'envelopper tous les objets dans une prise unique." *PP*, p. 327.

all statements of the positive sciences about the body presuppose a more fundamental and more original "knowing," viz., the kind of "knowing" in which my hands and my feet are not "concealed" from me when I use tools or walk around on the world.[146] In a scientistic conception of the sciences these sciences forget and disregard the origin from which they themselves sprang.

It may be worthwhile to dwell a little longer on the mysterious "knowing" which the human body itself is. The body is human because it is the body of a subject. The subject is "immersed" in the body, and the body participates in the subject. The subject, we said, is *cogito*. But if the body participates in the subject, then the body itself also must be called a kind of *cogito*-in-the-world. This is actually the case. Before I can pronounce any intellectual judgment about space, I have already orientated myself in space: I "have eyes" and "can see." If I wish to develop a science of colors, I must presuppose that my eyes "know" and can "distinguish" the colors. My body "knows" much better than I do what is meant by hard, soft, sharp, sticky, cold, warm, fragrant, and tasty.[147] The arms and legs, or rather the entire body, of a famous football player "know" much more about the field, the ball, the goal, the team, space, and time than the player himself. As long as he can rely on this mysterious "knowledge," he is an excellent player. As soon as he must begin to "reflect," the time has come for him to look for a job as trainer. My feet "know" much better than I myself the stairs which I climb every day, and my body "knows" my car better than I. One who must lead a large congregation in a fixed form of prayer will avoid becoming "mixed up" only if he can rely on it that his lips "know" the prayer better than he himself does. As sexually differentiated, the human body means a bodily *cogito* and *volo* (I will) of the other sex, and every personal sexual initiative is based on this bodily *cogito* and *volo*.

146"Nous avons réappris à sentir notre corps, nous avons retrouvé sous le savoir objectif et distant du corps cet autre savoir que nous en avons parce qu'il est toujours avec nous et que nous sommes corps. Il va falloir de la même manière réveiller l'expérience du monde tel qu'il nous apparaît en tant que nous sommes au monde par notre corps, en tant que nous percevons le monde avec notre corps. Mais en reprenant ainsi contact avec le corps et avec le monde, c'est aussi nous mêmes que nous allons retrouver, puisque, si l'on perçoit avec son corps, le corps est un moi naturel et comme le sujet de la perception." *PP*, p. 239.

147*PP*, pp. 275-276.

A pre-personal subject, then, is at work "underneath" the *personal* subject; [148] this pre-personal subject is presupposed by every personal *cogito* and its prehistory is taken up by the personal *cogito*-in-the-world.[149] This pre-personal—one would almost say "anonymous"—subject is the human body.[150] The human body has already concluded a "pact" with the world before the personal subject accomplishes his personal history,[151] and this pact is not made superfluous in any personal history.[152] It is, however, a pact concluded in semidarkness, a pact, moreover, which becomes wholly unintelligible when it is replaced by the "purely corporeal processes" spoken of by the sciences. This point is the profound truth contained in psychoanalysis, even though Freud himself may not clearly have noticed this truth.[153]

The pact between body and world is also the "place" of many psychical disturbances.[154] The latter are not caused by unilateral, deterministic processes originating in stimuli from the "external world," nor are they to be understood as manifestations of a disorganization in the "inner world." Rather, they are a breach between body and world, usually on an affective level, and this breach cannot be restored by a personal intellectual effort or a personal decision of will: the breach is filled when the body, aided by psychotherapeutic means, again opens itself to the world and to other subjects.[155]

---

[148]"Il y a donc un autre sujet au-dessous de moi, pour qui un monde existe avant que je sois là et qui y marquait ma place. Cet esprit captif ou naturel, c'est mon corps, non pas le corps momenté qui est l'instrument de mes choix personnelles et se fixe sur tel ou tel monde, mais le système de 'fonctions' anonymes, qui enveloppent toute fixation particulière dans un projet général." *PP*, p. 294.

[149]*PP*, p. 293.

[150]"La perception est toujours dans le mode du 'On'. Ce n'est pas un acte personnel par lequel je donnerais moi-même un sens neuf à ma vie." *PP*, p. 277.

[151]". . . il faut que ma première perception et ma première prise sur le monde m'apparaisse comme l'exécution d'un pacte plus ancien conclu entre X et le monde en général . . ." *PP*, p. 293.

[152]Cf. R. C. Kwant, "De geslotenheid van Merleau-Ponty's wijsbegeerte," *Tijdschrift voor Philosophie*, XIX(1957), pp. 217-272.

[153]"Quelles qu'aient pu être les déclarations de principe de Freud, les recherches psychanalytiques aboutissent en fait non pas à expliquer l'homme par l'infrastructure sexuelle, mais à retrouver dans la sexualité les relations et les attitudes qui passaient auparavant pour des relations et des attitudes de *conscience*, et la signification de la psychanalyse n'est pas tant de rendre la psychanalyse biologique que de découvrir dans des fonctions que l'on croyait 'purement corporelles' un mouvement dialectique et de réintégrer la sexualité à l'être humain." *PP*, p. 184.

[154]*PP*, pp. 180-199.

[155]*PP*, p. 192.

The Idea of Essence in Phenomenology

All this shows that much is needed before one can make a competent use of the term *existence*. Actually, however, this competence is often lacking, so that a terminology as technical as that of phenomenology is sometimes used as a kind of jargon designed to give a semblance of truth to nonsense. Existential phenomenology takes up again in a new way all the traditional questions of philosophy: this leads some people to conclude that, as a "phenomenologist" or an "existentialist," one can make almost any assertion as long as it is "personal." Many traditional terms have a new meaning in phenomenology: this meaning escapes some people and induces them to reject phenomenological thinking because of their misunderstanding of the terms.

One of these misunderstandings we will briefly discuss here because it refers to the topic under consideration. It is sometimes said that the emphasis placed on *existence* implies a disregard for the classical idea of essence which is indispensable in any attempt to philosophize. The answer to this objection is very simple. The accent put on *existence* means precisely that the value of the classical idea "essence" is re-emphasized: when the existential philosopher calls man *existence*, he wishes to say that conscious-being-in-the-world is the essence of man [156]—that by which man is man and not a thing, a pure spirit, or a divine Being. Things, pure spirits and God, therefore, do not *exist*,[157] i.e., they are essentially distinct from man.[158] Conscious-being-in-the-world is what man essentially is. Man, then, does not enter a world because there happens to be a world, a world which he could also not enter or from which he could withdraw as he desires. There is only one way for man to withdraw from the world, and that is death. But by death he ceases to be man. One can withdraw, of course, from this or that kind of world, but by the very fact one enters a different world. A definitive with-

---

[156]"Nous sommes donc dans la situation inverse de celle des psychologues puisque nous *partons* de cette totalité synthétique qu'est l'homme et que nous établissons l'essence d'homme *avant* de débuter en psychologie." Sartre, *Esquisse d'une théorie des émotions*, Paris, 1948, p. 9.

[157]"Das Seiende, das in der Weise der Existenz ist, ist der Mensch. Der Mensch allein existiert. Der Fels ist, aber er existiert nicht. Der Baum ist, aber er existiert nicht. Das Pferd ist, aber es existiert nicht. Der Engel ist, aber er existiert nicht. Gott ist, aber er existiert nicht." Heidegger, *Was ist Metaphysik?*, Frankfurt a.M., 7th ed., 1955, p. 15.

[158]A. Dondeyne, "Beschouwingen bij het atheïstisch existentialisme," *Tijdschrift voor Philosophie*, XIII (1951), pp. 6-10.

drawal from the world is possible only for one who ceases to be man.

Accordingly, *existence* is not a quality which man has or does not have, which he assumes or does not assume. Man is not first man and then proceeds, or does not proceed, to enter into a relationship with the world.[159] *Existence* is an *existentiale*, an essential characteristic of man's being.[160] Man is an embodied-subjectivity-in-the-world.[161]

The fact that existential phenomenology conceives man's essence as *existence* does not mean that this philosophy, following Platonism, Aristotelianism, Thomism, and other realistic philosophies, simply "deposits" man's essence among other essences on a congeries of beings-"in-themselves." [162] Such a conception —which can be called "essentialistic"—obscures the true essence of man. It brings us face to face with the question who man is. Is he one who lies on the "congeries of beings" or is he the one for whom the "congeries of beings" is what it is? [163]

The thesis that man is *existence* is accepted by very many thinkers today. Catastrophic historical events have greatly contributed to the fact that today few continue to minimize the importance of this aspect of being-man. The most important consequence of the idea of *existence,* however, is only seen by a few. This consequence is concerned with the ontological status of the world, the mode-of-being of the world, and worldly things.

5. THE MEANING OF THE WORLD

If one takes seriously the assertion that the idea of *existence* expresses an essential aspect of man, there can be no misunderstanding about the ontological status of the world. If man is

---

[159]"Das In-Sein ist nach dem Gesagten keine 'Eigenschaft', die es zuweilen hat, zuweilen auch nicht, ohne die es sein könnte so gut wie mit ihr. Der Mensch 'ist' nicht und hat überdies noch ein Seinsverhältnis zur 'Welt', die er sich gelegentlich zulegt. Dasein ist nie 'zunächst' ein gleichsam in-sein-freies-Seiendes, das zuweilen die Laune hat, eine 'Beziehung' zur Welt aufzunehmen." Heidegger, *SZ*, p. 57.

[160]*SZ*, pp. 42, 54.

[161]". . . nous ne sommes pas esprit *et* corps, conscience *en face du monde*, mais esprit incarné, être-au-monde." Merleau-Ponty, *SNS*, p. 148.

[162]Max Müller, *Existenzphilosophie im geistigen Leben der Gegenwart*, Heidelberg, 1949, pp. 15-22.

[163]"L'objectivisme naturaliste . . . regarde . . . l'omnitudo realitatis, assigne à l'homme son rang . . . et néglige totalement de retenir que l'origine de cette hiérarchie réside dans l'activité législatrice du 'regard' de l'étant illuminateur du spectacle et qui le 'constitue tel.'" De Waelhens, *La philosophie et les expériences naturelles*, La Haye, 1961, pp. 190-191.

fastened to the world,[164] then the world also is fastened to man, so that it is impossible to speak about a world-without-man. In other words, the world is radically human. The idea of *existence* forces us not only to say something about the object-pole whenever we say something about the subject-pole, but also to mention the subject-pole when we speak of the object-pole.

First Step

This thought may sound strange at first and therefore needs to be explained progressively in all its depth and scope. We will endeavor to do this, beginning with a few simple examples. It is necessary, however, to keep in mind that these examples are decidedly insufficient to throw full light on the human character of the world. I enter the vestibule of a stately residence and see there lying on the floor a toy pistol, a torn cap, and two long, dishevelled feathers. These objects are a piece of the world, of a littel boy's world, and I will not understand anything of them if I do not include the child in my understanding. This piece of the world betrays at once the presence of man, and without the little man to whom they refer I cannot understand the true meaning of that world. Similarly, a full ashtray, a well-groomed garden, a bombed-out city cannot be understood without the presence of man.

Accordingly, we should speak of a world-for-the-farmer, a world-for-the-travelling-salesman, a world-for-the-journalist, a world-for-the-politician, a world-for-the-hermit, etc. The essential aspect of all these worlds is that they are world-for-man: without man, or rather without a particular way of being-man, nothing of all those worlds can be understood. What those worlds *are* cannot be stated unless man himself is also named.

The above-mentioned examples are easy to understand, but they do not sufficiently illustrate the significance of the world's human dimension. One could make the remark that all those examples merely describe cultural worlds, in other words, worlds which obviously cannot be understood without man because it is precisely man's intervention which makes the world a cultural

---

[164]We follow here a usage of speech which, strictly speaking, is not correct. Not man, but the subject is attached to the world. Man is the unity of reciprocal implication of subject and world. Because the world belongs to that which constitutes being-man, one cannot, strictly speaking, say that man is attached to the world.

world. But where would there be the human dimension of things which I merely "perceive," such as "earth, water, air, and fire," trees, animals, seas, mountains and continents?

This is the point at which difficulties arise because we have become accustomed to thinking man and world as "divorced" from each other. Descartes, as we saw, had reduced the *human* aspect of the world—the world-for-the-subject—to the content of the subject-as-*cogito*. Realizing that in this way he had not given its due to the authentic reality of the world, Descartes began to seek for something "more" than the content of the *cogito*. This "more," however, could no longer be a human aspect of the world, for otherwise it also would have to be conceived as the content of a *cogito*. Consequently, it had to be conceived as the "inhuman" aspect of the world, the being-in-itself of the world, "brute" reality.

Even those who accept the idea of *existence* as expressing the "ec-centric" character of subjectivity often nullify this victory over spiritualistic monism by conceiving the world as a world which is what it is, without man—in other words, as a "congeries" of "brute" realities. For a world which is conceived as a reality in isolation from man also isolates man as subject from his world, so that the subject is again locked up in himself. If, next, one claims that man knows things and the world, knowledge must per force be conceived as a process occurring "within" man. In this way one faces the impossible task of explaining how it is possible that a subject locked up in himself can, by means of a process occurring "within" him, come into contact "outside" himself with a real world. The existence of the real "external world" must then be proved from the "internal world." This problem is traditionally known as the "problem of knowledge." [165]

We would like to avoid as much as possible all epistemological and gnoseological questions in this chapter because they will be *ex professo* raised in the following chapter. Unfortunately, however, they cannot be completely avoided here: asking

---

[165]"Je eindeutiger man nun festhält, dass das Erkennen zunächst und eigentlich 'drinnen' ist, . . . um so voraussetzungsloser glaubt man in der Frage nach dem Wesen der Erkenntnis und der Aufklärung des Verhältnisses zwischen Subjekt und Objekt vorzugehen. Denn nunmehr erst kann ein Problem entstehen, die Frage nämlich: wie kommt dieses erkennende Subjekt aus seiner inneren 'Sphäre' hinaus in eine 'andere und aussere', wie kann das Erkennen überhaupt einen Gegenstand haben, wie muss der Gegenstand selbst gedacht werden, damit am Ende das Subjekt ihn erkennt, ohne dass es den Sprung in eine andere Sphäre zu wagen braucht?" Heidegger, *SZ*, p. 60.

about the ontological status of the world, one encounters those questions.

The problem, then, is to show that the world, in which man as a subject is involved, is radically human, so that it is impossible to speak of a world-without-man. The matter is evident with respect to cultural worlds, but what must be said about the "natural" world—the world which above was referred to as a world which "man simply perceives"? Does not this world exist in itself, "divorced" from man?

Second Step

The description of man as *existence* compels us to conceive the world in which man as a subject is involved as a *real* world. This statement is almost trivial and it would indeed be trivial if there were no spiritualistic monism which lets the *reality* of the world evaporate into the "thin air" of a content of consciousness. We wish to deny that kind of monism because otherwise nothing remains of the world's *reality*. As a subject, man is involved in things: they are not contents of consciousness, but the solid, immovable massivity and density of reality.[166]

It is useless to object that such an assertion wholly eliminates the problem of knowledge.[167] It must be granted, of course, that there can no longer be question of proving the existence of a real "external world" from our consciousness of an "internal world." Such a proof becomes superfluous as soon as one conceives the subject as *existent*, as involved in the world.[168] It is meaningless to ask whether there really is a world, for without the reality of the world man is not *existence* and therefore not man.[169] If there continues to be a problem of knowledge, the terms in which it is raised will have to come from knowledge as knowledge really is, and not from a constituted philosophy of

---

166"La vérité n' 'habite' pas seulement l' 'homme intérieur', ou plutôt il n'y a pas d'homme intérieur, l'homme est au monde, c'est dans le monde qu'il se connaît. Quand je reviens à moi à partir du dogmatisme de sens commun ou du dogmatisme de la science, je retrouve non pas un foyer de vérité intrinsèque, mais un sujet voué au monde." Merleau-Ponty, *PP*, Avant-propos, p. V.

167Heidegger, *SZ*, p. 61.

168"Je dirais pour mon compte que Heidegger a montré d'une façon probablement définitive qu'il est absurde d'isoler le sujet existant et de se demander à partir de lui si le monde existe ou non. Car en fait ce sujet existant n'est tel que dans sa relation au monde." Marcel, *L'homme problématique*, Paris, 1955, pp. 141-142.

169Sartre, *EN*, pp. 27-29.

knowledge.[170]   But knowledge, as it really is, appears as a mode
of the subject's *existence,* a mode of his being-in-the-real-
world.[171]

The real world, in which man as subject *exists,* however, is
not a world-without-man, not a "brute" reality, a world "in itself." [172]   The idea of *existence,* as expressing man's essence,
makes the thought construct "world-without-man" a contradiction.   Man as *existence* is fastened to the world, so that the world
also is fastened to man.   I can never ask whether there is a world-
without-man or what kind of a world such a world would be: a
world-without-man presupposes that man withdraws from the
world the question addressed to the world which he himself is; or
that man can ask a question "outside" the question which he
himself is.   A world-without-man is simply unthinkable, for to
conceive such a world would have to imply the possibility of
conceiving a world without the thinking presence of an *existent*
subject.

A world-without-man would be a world of which man is not
conscious, which he does not know, of which he has never
heard—briefly, a world which is not affirmed in any way.   Such
a world is simply nothing-for-man.   A world which is not affirmed is a world beyond affirmation: man cannot be conscious of
a world of which he is not conscious; he cannot speak of a world
which is beyond speech.   The thought construct "world-without-
man" is a contradiction.   So-called speaking of such a world is
nothing but stringing together a meaningless combination of
words such as "square circle" or "triangular quadrangle."   Such
a speaking is not *real* speaking, the expression of *reality.*

The strong point of spiritualistic monism manifests itself
here.   A "certain" priority of the subject cannot be eliminated:
the subject-as-*cogito* cannot be disputed.   This subject-as-*cogito,*
however, *is existence,* the "affirming"-of-the-real-world, the "saying"-of-*is* which is involved in the world.   What would "be" if

---

[170]". . . welche Instanz entscheidet denn darüber, ob und in welchem
Sinne ein Erkenntnisproblem bestehen soll, was anderes als das Phänomen
des Erkennens selbst und die Seinsart des Erkennenden?" Heidegger, *SZ,*
p. 61.

[171]"Erkennen ist eine Seinsart des In-der-Welt-seins." *SZ,* p. 61.

[172]"La chose ne peut jamais être séparée de quelqu'un qui la perçoive,
elle ne peut jamais être effectivement en soi parce que ses articulations sont
celles-mêmes de notre existence et qu'elle se pose au bout d'un regard ou au
terme d'une exploration sensorielle qui l'investit d'humanité." Merleau-Ponty,
PP, p. 370.

the world were only composed of things? One who answers "things," does not know what he is saying: he does not see that his affirmation of the being of things *is* the "saying"-of-*is* by his own subjectivity. He does not realize that actually he affirms a being-for-the-subject.

The being of the world must be interpreted neither sub-jectivistically nor objectivistically.[173] Subjectivistically con-ceived, the world would be handed over to the arbitrariness of the subject, it would therefore cease to be objective reality.[174] And if the world is objectivistically conceived, the subject is destroyed as *existent* "affirmation" of the world; hence, the sub-ject would cease being a real subject.[175] A worldly thing is not a "brute" reality, but an "appearing" being, a "phenomenon," [176] a meaning for the subject; and the world is a system of nearby and distant meanings. All "being" therefore, is *per se* "mean-ing," [177] and "meaning arises with man." [178]

The Existent Subject and Speaking

The following objection could be raised: I grant that it is impossible to affirm a world-without-man; nevertheless, *there is such a world without man.* To really understand the term *ex-istence*, it is absolutely necessary to realize that such a statement is meaningless. In a purely verbal way one can, of course, make that statement, but it has no meaning, it does not express any reality. When he uses the term "is," man affirms the "to be" of something. If he uses the term "is" and does not wish to affirm anything, he says nothing. He cannot affirm "to be" outside his own presence as *existent* subject; in other words, man never

---

173"La plus importante acquisition de la phénoménologie est sans doute d'avoir joint l'extrême subjectivisme et l'extrême objectivisme dans sa notion du monde ou de la rationalité." *PP*, Avant-propos, p. XV.

174'Die Bedeutsamkeitsbezüge, welche die Struktur der Welt bestimmen, sind daher kein Netzwerk von Formen, das von einem weltlosen Subjekt einem Material übergestülpt wird.' *SZ*, p. 366.

175Marcel, *L'homme problématique*, pp. 50-51.

176"Der Griechische Ausdruck *phainomenon*, auf den der Terminus 'Phänomen' zurückgeht, leitet sich von dem Verbum *phainesthai* her, das bedeutet: sich zeigen; *phainomenon* besagt daher: das was sich zeigt, das Sichzeigende, das Offenbare." *SZ*, p. 28.

177"Le monde phénoménologique, c'est, non pas de l'être pur, mais le sens qui transparaît à l'intersection de mes expériences et à l'intersection de mes expériences et de celles d'autrui, par l'engrenage des unes sur les autres, il est donc inséparable de la subjectivité et de l'intersubjectivité qui font leur unité par la reprise de mes expériences passées dans mes expériénces présentes, de l'expérience d'autrui dans la mienne." *PP*, Avant-propos, p. XV.

178De Waelhens, *La philosophie et les expériences naturelles*, p. 98.

affirms anything else but being-for-man. The term "to be," then, has no other meaning than "to be"-for-man.[179] Thus I must say that without man there is no world.[180] Because "to be" can have no other meaning than "to be"-for-man, the statement "Without man there is no world," actually says, "Without man no world is-there-for-man." What *else* could I say?

All this necessarily requires that one does not view language solely as an instrument for information or communication,[181] by which thoughts brought to completion in the "interiority" of the subject-as-*cogito* are destined for others, and therefore transferred to "exteriority." The subject-as-*cogito* is an embodied subject, and this implies that there is no thinking without words. Thinking is itself in and through the word; it is accomplished and brought to "perfection" in and through the word.[182] One who cannot say what he is thinking is not yet really thinking; one who wishes to master a problem must write a book about it or teach a course in it.[183] There exists no such thing as a separation between the "interiority" of thinking and the "exteriority" of the word; on the contrary, these two constitute a unity of reciprocal implication. The word is permeated with the "light" of the subject-as-*cogito*, and the subject-as-*cogito* is only a certain "light" through and in the word. Speaking is much more than a contraction of the throat or the movement of the larynx accompanied by the expulsion of air betweeen the tongue and the teeth.[184]

The existent subject-as-*cogito*, however, is the "letting be" of meaning, the dis-closure of meaning, the bringing about of its unconcealedness. But because the *cogito* is equiprimordially "word," one should say that speech lets meaning be, that speech brings about the truth of meaning.[185] In the word the subject

---

[179]Merleau-Ponty, *PP*, Avant-propos, p. III.
[180]"Wenn kein Dasein existiert, ist auch keine Welt 'da.'" *SZ*, p. 365.
[181]"Wir . . . suchen die unzerstörte Nennkraft der Sprache und Worte wieder zu erobern; denn die Worte und Sprache sind keine Hülsen, worin die Dinge nur für den redenden und schreibenden Verkehr verpackt werden." Heidegger, *Einführung in die Metaphysik,* Tübingen, 1953, p. 11.
[182]"La pensée tend vers l'expression comme vers son achèvement." Merleau-Ponty, *PP*, p. 206.
[183]*Ibid.*
[184]*Ibid.*
[185]'Indem die Sprache erstmals das Seiende nennt, bringt solches Nennen das Seiende erst zum Wort und zum Erscheinen. Dieses Nennen ernennt das Seiende erst zu seinem Sein aus diesem. Solches Sagen ist ein Entwerfen des Lichten, darin angesagt wird, als was das Seiende ins Offene kommt.' M. Heidegger, *Holzwege,* Frankfurt a.M., 2nd ed., 1960, pp. 60-61.

lives and dwells in the meaning; through the word, the meaning is called forth and "speaks" to the subject.[186]   There is no meaning without the word; there is no world without language.[187] "Language is the house of Being." [188]

Speech, then, is the original "event" of meaning, of truth, of unconcealedness.   Where there is no language there is also no truth, no unconcealedness, nothing that "speaks" to man.[189]   But the fact that there is something which "speaks" to man means that man is man and not a thing.   Speech therefore is the essence of being-man.[190]   Without language man would not be what he is, and without language meaning would not be what it is.   Speech brings about man's essence [191] and makes meaning be meaning.   The speaking subject "and" meaning, therefore, belong inseparably together, they constitute a unity of reciprocal implication.[192]   As speaking, man is, of course, not the "lord" of meaning but its "shepherd," for genuine speaking is equiprimordially a listening and "letting" reality "speak" to oneself.[193]

The preceding paragraphs obviously attempt to explicitate authentic speaking, the "speaking word," which is much more than a manipulation of terms.   They refer to original speaking, speech which *really* says something, because, as the embodiment of "thoughtful dwelling" in meaning, it tries to put the reality of meaning into words.   The "dwelling" of the subject-as-*cogito* in meaning is always an implicit "affirmation" of the *reality of* meaning.   The word is the embodiment of the *existent* subject-as-*cogito*, it is a word which *really* speaks if it is animated by the "saying"-of-*is* which the subject-as-*cogito* himself is.   Without the subject's implicit "affirmation," the word is an empty shell, which the "speaker" can manipulate in a purely verbal way, without, however, "saying" anything.[194]

It should be clear now why the phenomenologist dares to say

186"Im Wort, in der Sprache werden und sind erst die Dinge."   M. Heidegger, *op. cit.*, p. 11.

187'Etwas ist nur, wo das geeignete und also zuständige Wort etwas als seiend nennt und so das jeweilige Seiende als solches stiftet.'   Heidegger, *Unterwegs zur Sprache*, p. 165.

188Heidegger, *op. cit.*, p. 166.

189"Wo keine Sprache west . . . da ist auch keine Offenheit des Seienden."   Heidegger, *Holzwege*, p. 60.

190Heidegger, *Unterwegs zur Sprache*, p. 11.

191Heidegger, *op. cit.*, p. 241.

192"Ohne das also verhaltende Wort sinkt das Ganze der Dinge, die 'Welt' ins Dunkel weg, samt dem 'Ich'."   Heidegger, *op. cit.*, p. 177.

193Heidegger, *op. cit.*, p. 255.

194"Sagen und Sprechen sind nicht das gleiche.   Einer kann sprechen, spricht endlos, und alles ist nichtssagend. . . . Doch was heisst sagen?   Um

that without the subject there is no world. His assertion takes into account that the particle of speech "is" does not *really* say anything except in an affirmation. In the affirmation being discloses itself as being-for-the-subject. If, then, the philosopher claims that without the subject there *is* no world, he asserts that without the subject there-is-no-world-for-the-subject. This assertion may "sound" trivial, and the statement that without man there is no world may "sound" nonsensical. But words are not things which "sound" but refer to meaning. And the meaning of words can only be understood by one who tries to take part in "real" speech.

Laplace's Primitive Nebula as a "World Without Man"

The assertion that there is no world without man is often attacked as contrary to the findings of the empirical sciences. Geologists, geophysicists, and astrophysicists have determined that the world is much older than man—that before man, and therefore without man, the world was already there. According to Laplace's theory, our earth was formed from a primitive nebula, whose physical conditions were such that no life, and certainly no human life, was possible. The appearance of subjectivity in the endless evolution of the cosmos is of fairly recent origin. What sense does it make, then, to assert that without man there is no world? [195]

No phenomenologist wishes to throw doubt on the results of the physical sciences. Every phenomenologist accepts that the earth is much older than "Adam," i.e., the first man, and no phenomenologist objects to Laplace's primitive nebula. (We may add, however, that today's scientists have their objections to Laplace's hypothesis.) Scientists speak, of course, of a world dating from before man. But, does this mean that the geologists speak of a world-without geologists? This, and nothing else, is the issue. What is the meaning of Laplace's primitive nebula, of Laplace's formulae and calculations without the presence-in-the-world of Laplace's subjectivity or the subjectivity of those who take over the intention with which Laplace stood in the world? [196]

---

dies zu erfahren, sind wir an das gehalten, was unsere Sprache selber uns bei diesem Wort zu denken heisst. 'Sagen' heisst: erscheinen-, sehen-, und hören-lassen." Heidegger, *op. cit.*, p. 252.

[195]Merleau-Ponty, *PP*, pp. 494-495.

[196]"La nébuleuse de Laplace n'est pas derrière nous, à notre origine, elle est devant nous, dans le monde culturel." *PP*, p. 494.

The same conclusion continually imposes itself: the world is radically human, and the truth about this world also is radically human.[197] Without man's subjectivity no affirmation of reality has any meaning, and without the affirmation of reality all words and all assertions are empty shells—an idle playing with words and meaningless combinations of words such as "square circle." The world is not the sum total of "brute" realities which are what they are-without-man in an "absolutely objective" and isolated way. Some of the sharpest minds among those who pursue physical science realize this when they say that the physical sciences do not speak of "nature in itself." [198] Sometimes they use expressions which are not very fortunate; when it is said, for instance, that the physical sciences do not express "objectivity." But what is intended is evident enough: "objectivity" refers to *objectivistically* interpreted objectivity.[199]

The "In Itself" According to Sartre

The fact that it is impossible to speak of "brute" reality is illustrated also by the way in which Sartre attempts to do this. One who limits his attention to Sartre's phenomenological analyses of the human body would not even suspect that Sartre separates subject and world.[200] Yet, this is what he does.[201] Sartre radically opposes two types of beings: the "in itself" and the "for itself." The "in itself" is the material *thing*. The material thing is being in the strict sense—the only being which is rightfully called *being*. It is compact density, full of itself, perfect

---

197"Le monde phénoménologique n'est pas l'explicitation d'un être préalable, mais la fondation de l'être, la philosophie n'est pas le reflet d'une vérité préalable, mais comme l'art la réalisation d'une vérité." *PP*, Avant-propos, p. XV.

198"Auch in der Naturwissenschaft ist also der Gegenstand der Forschung nicht mehr die Natur an sich, sondern die der menschlichen Fragestellung ausgesetzte Natur, und insofern begegnet der Mensch auch hier wieder sich selbst." Werner Heisenberg, *Das Naturbild der heutigen Physik*, Hamburg, 1958, p. 18.

199"Metric numbers, laws, and theories, therefore, do not describe 'objectively' the 'objective' properties of a world-in-itself, but arise only in and through the intentional relationship of the physicist to the world. For this reason they are valid only within the field of meaning proper to this mode of intentionality." Joseph J. Kockelmans, *Phenomenology and Physical Science*, Pittsburgh, 1966, p. 169.

200"On sait qu'il n'y a point, d'une part, un pour-soi et, d'autre part, un monde, comme deux touts fermés, dont il faudrait ensuite chercher comment ils communiquent." Sartre, *EN*, p. 368.

201A. De Waelhens, "De Franse wijsbegeerte tijdens en sedert de oorlog." *Algemeen Nederlands Tijdschrift voor wijsbegeerte en psychologie*, 39(1946), pp. 125-129.

positivity. It is what it is, perfectly identical with itself. It maintains no relations with what it is not, includes no negation, never posits itself as different from anything else. When it disappears, one cannot even say that it is no longer. It cannot be deduced from the possible or reduced to the necessary. It is not created and has no ground of being; it simply *is*, contingent and "too much for eternity." [202]

The sense of these enigmatic expressions becomes somewhat clearer if we keep in mind that Sartre's "in itself" is not a conscious being. Relations, being different, ground of being, being no longer, being deduced from or reduced to, and similar expressions, presuppose consciousness. The "in itself" has no consciousness; therefore, Sartre thinks, it maintains *no* relations, is *not* different, has *no* ground of being, etc.

While the "in itself" is always self-sufficient and simply is what it is, consciousness always needs the "in itself" in order to be able to be consciousness. All consciousness is always conciousness of *something* which is not consciousness itself, and there is no consciousness without that *something*. For Sartre, then, consciousness is essentially relative to the "in itself," it is orientated to the "in itself," it is intentional.[203]

This, however, is not yet the main point Sartre has in mind. What exactly does it mean that I am conscious of something? To clarify this, Sartre invented a new word, to "nihilate" or "noughten" (*néantiser*). When I am conscious of something, I nihilate this something. Let us say that I am conscious of this ashtray. This means, says Sartre, that I am *not* this ashtray, i.e., I am conscious that I am not identical with this ashtray. Consciousness, then, is always consciousness of the "in itself" and, as such, pure nihilation.[204]

Someone could think that this description applies only to the

---

[202]"En fait, l'être est opaque à lui-même précisément parce qu'il est rempli de lui-même. C'est ce que nous exprimons mieux en disant que l'être est ce qu'il est. . . . Il est pleine positivité. Il ne connaît donc pas l'altérité: il ne se pose jamais comme autre qu'un autre être; il ne peut soutenir aucun rapport avec l'autre. . . Il est, et quand il s'effondre on ne peut même pas dire qu'il n'est plus. . . . Incréé, sans raison d'être, sans rapport aucun avec un autre être, l'être-en-soi est de trop pour l'éternité." Sartre, *EN,* pp. 33-34.

[203]"Toute conscience, Husserl l'a montré, est conscience de quelque chose." *EN,* p. 17.

[204]"Le pour-soi est un être pour qui son être est en question dans son être en tant que cet être est essentiellement une certaine manière de ne pas être un être qu'il pose du même coup comme autre que lui." *EN,* p. 222.

consciousness of a worldly object and hold that self-consciousness still implies something positive, and that, therefore, it is not pure nihilation. Do I not *affirm* myself when I am conscious of myself? But Sartre maintains his position in this matter: consciousness is pure nihilation, it expresses only non-identity, even when I am conscious of myself. Let us say that I am conscious of myself as a waiter, as just, or as president of the local yacht club. What does this mean? Nothing but that I am conscious of the fact that I am *not* identical with the waiter, the just man, or the president of the yacht club, for tomorrow I cease being a waiter, just, or president. If, then, I am conscious of myself, I nihilate my own identity. Only the "in itself" is identical with itself, but not consciousness.[205] Consciousness always says *distance*—not being that of which consciousness is conscious. The compact density of the "in itself" thus is broken by consciousness.[206] In the "in itself" there is no room for negativity: because the "in itself" fully coincides with itself, it is the fullness of being.[207] Only where there is question of consciousness can there be question of negativity. Consciousness is nothing but nihilation.

It is worth noting that Sartre explicitates only the negative aspects of consciousness. As a result, nothing remains of the high dignity which is traditionally ascribed to consciousness.[208] As a matter of fact, Sartre thinks, tradition was wrong in this matter. The only being which rightly deserves to be called a being is the "in itself"; the "for itself" is only a "disease of being." One can even say that the being of consciousness is Nothing.[209] The being which makes negativity enter into the world must be its own Nothing.[210]

205". . . l'être de la conscience ne coïncide pas avec lui-même dans une adéquation plénière." *EN*, p. 116.

206"Tout se passe comme si pour libérer l'affirmation *de* soi du sein de l'être il faillait une décompression d'être." *EN*, p. 32.

207"La coïncidence de l'identique est la véritable plénitude d'être, justement parce que dans cette coïncidence il n'est laissé de place à aucune négativité." *EN*, p. 119.

208"Cette présence à soi, on l'a prise souvent pour une plénitude d'existence et un préjugé fort répandu parmi les philosophes fait attribuer à la conscience la plus haute dignité d'être." *EN*, p. 119.

209"L'être de la conscience, et tant que conscience, c'est d'exister à distance de soi comme présence à soi et cette distance nulle que l'être porte dans son être, c'est le Néant." *EN*, p. 120.

210"L'être par qui le Néant arrive dans le monde est un être en qui, dans son Etre, il est question du Néant de son Etre; l'être par qui le Néant vient au monde doit être son propre Néant." *EN*, p. 59.

Sartre is right, of course, when he says that all consciousness is consciousness of *something*. Similarly it is true that all consciousness of something contains a negative aspect. When I am conscious of something, I am indeed conscious of a certain *distance* with respect to this something, of a certain non-identity with this something. I am not identical with this ashtray, this pen, or that wall; I am not identical with the just man, the waiter or the president of the yacht club who I am. But does this mean that consciousness is *nothing but* nihilation?

The affirmative answer to this question simply disregards all positive aspects of consciousness. If consciousness is pure nihilation, I cannot even say that I, when I am conscious of something, affirm this something. Yet the first phenomenological evidence is precisely this affirmation: I affirm the ashtray, the pen, the wall; I affirm the waiter, the just man or the president who I am. I affirm the being, the reality of all this.[211] Is this affirmation a nihilation? Obviously not, but just the opposite.

Nevertheless, a negative aspect is inherent in that affirmation. I affirm that this ashtray is, but this affirmation includes my consciousness that the ashtray is *not* the pen and also that I am *not* the ashtray. But how would this negating be possible, how could I ever say that I am not that ashtray if I did not affirm, in a more primordial way, my own being, i.e., my being-conscious? How could I ever say that this ashtray is not that pen if this negation was not "preceded" by the affirmation of this ashtray as this ashtray and of this pen as this pen? Consciousness is equiprimordially a "saying"-of-*is* and a "saying"-of-*is-not*.

Sartre's theory of Nothingness (*Néant*) means a decline as compared to Heidegger's theory of Nothingness (*Nichts*). Both Heidegger and Sartre saw that human subjectivity has a unique mode of being. Both overcame the temptation to "reify" subjectivity, and both terminologically expressed this victory by refusing to express the uniqueness of subjectivity in terms of "being." Once the term "being" is reserved for the being of things, we can no longer say that subjectivity is a being. To express, then, that subjectivity is not a thing and, nonetheless, not "nothing," it was almost inevitable that the terms *Néant* and *Nichts* would be used for this purpose. In English the hyphenation of

---

211"What Sartre says of knowledge is true, but knowledge is *also* and *primarily* an affirmative act." De Waelhens, "Zijn en niet-zijn," *Tijdschrift voor Philosophie,* VII (1945), p. 113.

"nothing" as "no-thing" is very eloquent. Heidegger added at once that this *Nichts*—this *Nothing*—is something positive.[212] In this way he made it possible to use the term "being" in a sense that is purified of any reification and of materialism. Sartre, on the other hand, expressed all specifically human elements in terms of "non-being." This procedure could be tolerated in order to overcome reification and materialism, but Sartre completely fails to mention that this "non-being" is something positive. For this reason he is not able to discern any affirmative aspect or phase in subjectivity. All positivity is for Sartre *per se* a matter of "thing-like" identity. Thus, he thinks, I can never affirm the waiter, the just man, or the president who I am without ascribing to myself the mode of being proper to a thing, and therefore without being "in bad faith." Even the very attempt to be "sincere" is, he holds, against the very essence of consciousness.[213] To affirm that I have been unjust means only one thing for Sartre, viz., that I conceive my own mode of being just like the mode of being proper to a rotten cauliflower.

In contrast to the negativity of human *existence*, Sartre describes the "in itself" as full positivity. The "in itself" is a thing: the being of a pen and the being of an ashtray are a "being-in-itself." But Sartre conceives this "being-in-itself" as "brute" reality. A pen is something other than an ashtray, but this otherness can obviously only be observed by consciousness. Without my consciousness the ashtray and the pen are nothing-for-me. Sartre, however, claims that the "in itself" is not something other than something else. For otherness presupposes consciousness and the "in itself" does not have any consciousness. "Therefore," the "in itself" is not something other than something else.

Sartre fails here to take into consideration that the being of which he speaks is always phenomenon—appearing being. Otherness presupposes consciousness, but this necessary consciousness is there. *My* consciousness is never, and cannot ever, be "thought away." A pen is something other than an ashtray for *my* consciousness. Although a thing does not have any consciousness, I cannot think the thing without *my* conscious-

---

[212]Heidegger, *Was ist Metaphysik?*, p. 35.
[213]"Que signifie, dans ces conditions, l'idéal de sincérité sinon une tâche impossible à remplir et dont le sens même est en contradiction avec la structure de ma conscience. Etre sincère, disions-nous, c'est être ce qu'on est." *EN*, p. 102.

ness.   Relations, ground of being, otherness, being-no-longer,
being-deduced-from, or being-reduced to—all this obviously
presupposes consciousness.   When Sartre, however, claims that
the "in itself" does not maintain any relations, is not other than
something else, has no ground, etc., he assumes that it is possible
for him to make a judgment, outside the encounter, about the
terminus encountered by consciousness.   He assumes that it is
possible to describe a field of presence while circumventing the
presence of consciousness.   He assumes that it is possible to
know something while "thinking away" knowing itself.

All this clearly violates the fundamental idea of phenomenology.   Consciousness is intentional, says Sartre, but he says
this only when he speaks of the "for itself."   As soon as he deals
with the noematic correlate of consciousness, he withdraws the
intentionality, the orientation-to which consciousness is.   Yet,
he continues to talk.   But what could he possibly talk about?

Everything which Sartre thinks that he can say of the so-
called "in itself" is affirmed of it in opposition to the "in itself
for me."   Sartre realizes, of course, that the appearing thing implies negativity, has relations, is other than other things, comes
to be and passes away, has a ground, is caused, etc.   But then
he artificially withdraws the intentional movement which consciousness is, and imagines that he is no longer dealing with the
"in itself for him" but with the "in itself."   In opposition to the
"in itself for him" he then describes the "in itself" as implying
no negativity, having *no* relations, *not* being other than something else, *not* having a ground or cause.

A reproach addressed to some phenomenologists is that in
their works they continually show themselves influenced by
idealism.   Their phenomenology often deviates from the original
meaning which they themselves had discovered, so that they
lapse into a kind of *idealism of meaning,* mixed with an unmistakable *realism of "brute" reality.*[214]   This reproach is certainly
deserved by Sartre.   He tries to speak of the "in itself" and
therefore is a realist.   On the other hand, he realizes that it is
only through the intentionality of consciousness that the world-

---

[214]De Waelhens, "De la Phénoménologie à l'Existentialisme," *Le Choix,
le Monde, l'Existence* (Cahiers du Collège Philosophique), Grenoble-Paris,
n.d., p. 62.   De Waelhens uses these expressions to characterize Heidegger's
philosophy.   We abstract here from the question whether or not he is right
with respect to Heidegger.

for-man begins to be and have meaning.[215]   But what value do such meanings have?   In his principal novel NAUSEA, which dates from before BEING AND NOTHINGNESS, Sartre had already given à provisional answer to that question.   The meanings of the world are illusory as long as the "in itself" is not laid bare.[216] Soft colors, delicious odors, beautiful weather, the green sea— all this is a matter of meanings which poets and superficial people have thrown over brute reality.[217]   The "in itself" of every- thing is *nauseating*.

"The word 'absurdity' is born here from my pen." [218]   The "in itself" is absurd.   This is Sartre's last word.   But here Sartre, the phenomenologist, ceases to be a phenomenologist.   Not the "in itself" is absurd, but the wish to speak of the "in itself" is absurd.[219]

Not "One" World-in-Itself, But Many Human Worlds

Once it is understood that the world and the truth about the world are radically human, one is also ready to understand the statement that there is not one world-in-itself but many human worlds, corresponding to the many attitudes and standpoints of the *existent* subject.   Man is essentially *existence,* and this im- plies that the meaning of the world is different according as the subject-in-the-world occupies a different standpoint.

Descartes, we saw, split the reality of the world into two by conceiving the human dimension of the world as the content of the *cogito*, and by putting the world as "more"-than-conscious- ness "out there," or as "brute" reality.   But Descartes went even further, and held that, in "brute" reality, only that is objective which can be expressed in quantitative categories.   This amounted to asserting that only one world, the world-for-the- physicist, can be called objective.   Through the influence of Descartes and Locke it has become an unquestioned conviction

---

215". . . la mondanité, la spatialité, la quantité, l'ustensilité, la tempo- ralité ne viennent à l'être que parce que je suis négation de l'être." *EN,* p. 269.

216H. Paissac, *Le Dieu de Sartre,* Paris, 1950, pp. 46-52.

217Sartre, *La Nausée,* Paris, 1938, pp. 161-172.

218J.-P. Sartre, *op. cit.,* p. 164.

219"La chose ne peut jamais être séparée de quelqu'un qui la perçoive, elle ne peut jamais être effectivement en soi parce que ses articulations sont celles mêmes de notre existence et qu'elle se pose au bout d'un regard ou au terme d'une exploration sensorielle qui l'investit d'humanité." Merleau- Ponty, *PP,* p. 370.

in Western thought that we must start from the assumption that the world—the world "in itself"—is the world-for-the-physicist.

As we have sufficiently explained in the preceding pages, a world-in-itself is unintelligible.[220] Even the world-for-the-physicist is a human world, connected with the intentional relationship of the physicist with the world. The world-for-the-physicist is just one of the many possible and actual worlds. The standpoint of the physicist is just one among many other possible and actual standpoints.

What is water for me? It is something I use to wash myself in the morning and for drinking. But if I love to go for a swim, water reveals itself to me under an entirely different aspect: I like to plunge into the "cooling waves." Water is also an extinguisher, but I would never be able to affirm this meaning if I did not know what fire is and what is meant by putting out a fire. For a fisherman water is not an extinguisher or a cooling wave: he faces water with an entirely different attitude, so that water has an entirely different meaning for him. No one goes fishing in an extinguisher or in the cooling waves. One who in the winter falls into a hole and slides underneath the ice sees the most terrifying aspect water can have. No one, however, ever froze to death in the cooling waves. Finally, to end with another arbitrary example, there is one standpoint from which water is H_2O, viz., the standpoint of the chemist. One who, armed with analytic techniques and quantitative categories, asks water what it is hears the answer: H_2O. Outside this standpoint, this attitude of chemical "interest," water is not H_2O, just as water is not the cooling waves for a non-swimmer or for someone who refuses to place himself on the swimmer's standpoint.

What is a church tower? This tower has a particular meaning for the architect, who built it to blend with the city or the countryside where it stands. But this meaning is not necessarily the same for the pastor who had to find the money to pay for the tower. He disagreed with the architect, which is not surprising because the two did not speak of the "same" tower. It was only by explicitly placing themselves on each other's standpoint that they managed to come to an agreement. But the meaning resulting from their agreement was not the one which the tower has for the sacristan, who sees himself forced to

---

220J. Ortega y Gasset, *De mens en de mensen,* pp. 63-64.

climb many steps every day to ring the bells. This meaning, again, differs from the one it has for the altarboys who secretly climb it to play; from the meaning it has for a war-time military pilot, who uses it to orientate himself before unloading his bombs; or for the commercial pilot, who must try to avoid it when making his approach to the airport.

What is the meaning of human nakedness? This depends entirely upon the many possible standpoints of the subject: it may be artistic, medical, sexual, athletic, hygienic, etc.

What is a paint brush? It was not the same for Vincent Van Gogh and for the shopkeeper from whom he regularly bought his brushes. Van Gogh did not wish to part with his old brushes at any price; the shopkeeper did not wish to take them back at any price.[221]

It is not easy to formulate a general theory of man's standpoints or attitudes. At present we must limit ourselves to the following provisional remarks. A first group of attitudes is man's bodily being. The fact that man "has" arms and legs, hands and feet; "has" eyes, ears, a nose and a tongue means that he is involved in many different worlds in many different ways. We say "different" worlds, for in man's visual field there are no sounds, in his world of sound there is nothing to see, and in the graspable world nothing is tasty.

A second group of attitudes is human *praxis*. This *praxis* is connected with many different "pragmatic fields," "realms of affairs." [222] It makes sense, therefore—one can even say that it is necessary—to speak of a world for the farmer, the professor, the revolutionary, the hunter, the commercial traveller, the hermit, the politician, and the artist. These worlds are different from one another, and the things in those worlds refer to one another in *different* ways. For the hunter the gun refers to other things than it does for the revolutionary; for a scholar the book forms part of a different system of meanings than it has for a publisher or a dealer in used paper; the police station has another meaning for the captain of the precinct than for the city's

---

[221]The fact that, in connection with the theme occupying our attention here, we emphasize the difference of the world's meanings does not mean that we deny that they have anything in common. We do not wish to go as far as Francis Jeanson who says: "Seulement, cette objectivité, valable et vraie pour tout le monde, c'est-à-dire pour n'importe qui, *ne 'vaut' précisément* rien et n'est 'réelle' pour personne." Francis Jeanson, *La phénoménologie*, Paris, 2nd ed., 1951, p. 15.

[222]J. Ortega y Gasset, *De mens en de mensen*, p. 91-97.

architect. In every case, however, the particular system of meanings becomes intelligible by way of one's understanding of a particular form of human *praxis*.

In the third place, love could be mentioned as a standpoint. But, until we have presented a phenomenology of love, we cannot say very much about this standpoint. If, however, one is willing to include in the "world" the economic, social, and political structures of our society, then it should be obvious that this "world" offers different aspects according as man is or is not animated by the desire and the will to foster an increasing recognition of man by man. One who lives and breathes humanity lives in another world than one who thinks that other people are there only to cringe as slaves at his feet. Thus it is not surprising that it must be difficult to discuss the world of economic, social and political structures.

Fourthly, the various phases of history need to be mentioned as standpoints or attitudes which co-determine the face presented by the world. This point also can merely be mentioned here. It is important, nevertheless, to realize what the consequences are of this thesis. Only in a *particular* phase of history does it become *possible* to see a *particular* face of the world. One who does not stand in that phase of history simply does not see that aspect of the world. Here, again, one comes inevitably to the conclusion that we should not expect too much from a dialog with *all* men. As a matter of fact, experience can serve to confirm this conclusion.

We are now far removed from the view that a world-in-itself lies over "there," divorced from the subject, and that "here," divorced from the world, stands my subjectivity, knowing the world when the latter is accurately mirrored in consciousness. Yet this view has become almost "second nature" in Western thought; [223] it is simply taken for granted that it is so.[224] For this reason a "reversal" is needed to let man's thinking "be again in its element." [225] In the second chapter of this book we will examine this "reversal" more profoundly in connection with the question of the necessity to abandon the "natural attitude" and to make the phenomenological reduction.

---

[223]G. Noller, *Sein und Existenz*, München, 1962, p. 45.
[224]Heidegger, *SZ*, p. 59.
[225]M. Heidegger, *Über den Humanismus*, Frankfurt a.M., 1947, p. 6.

Is Our View a Kind of Psychologism?

The objection could be raised that our view is a kind of psychologism. Before we reply to this objection, it is necessary to determine what is meant by psychologism when this reproach is made. Generally speaking, the term "psychologism" is used to indicate the tendency to reduce all philosophical problems—all logical, moral, aesthetic, and metaphysical questions—to psychological problems.[226] Those who philosophize with a psychologistic tendency reduce the meaning of all questions and answers to the human psyche, the structure of the thinker's consciousness, or the genesis of his thought, and they explain everything in terms of these psychological factors. In the present context, however, those who address to us the reproach of psychologism wish to say that we take meanings which lie "in" consciousness, project them "outside" on things, and then ascribe these meanings to the things themselves. The special meanings of water for the fisherman, the swimmer, or the drinker, they hold, lie only "in" consciousness and should not be ascribed to water itself.

The answer to this reproach is very simple. The objection presupposes two postulates which are untenable. The first of these implies that the psyche or consciousness is an interiority which is locked up in itself, and contains meanings which we unjustly project upon "things." The second postulate assumes that the "things themselves" are "brute" realities, of which, for instance, the chemist is entitled to speak. There is, however, no consciousness locked up in itself and containing meanings which "belong" to such a consciousness. Being conscious is a mode of *existing*, of being-in-the-world. Secondly, there is no "brute" reality, but there are *existent* subjects and many human worlds. Finally, if the "cooling waves" must be called a psychological meaning, because it obviously cannot be defined independently of human existence, then the same must be affirmed of H_2O. The meaning H_2O clings to the orientation-to-the-world which makes a man a chemist and to the analytic techniques of which the chemist makes use. Without taking into consideration the specific attitude assumed by the chemist when he speaks of water, the formula H_2O offers nothing intelligible and does not say

---

[226]A. Lalande, *Vocabulaire technique et critique de la Philosophie*, Paris, 1947, pp. 836-838.

anything. The "reciprocal implication of subject and world" [227] is the original dimension in which man stands, thinks, and speaks. If he places himself outside this dimension, he no longer stands anywhere and does not speak of anything.

6. THE "PRIMITIVE FACT" OF EXISTENTIAL PHENOMENOLOGY

By calling man the unity of reciprocal implication of subjectivity and world, we indicate that which for some phenomenologists is the "primitive fact" of existential phenomenology.[228] This expression comes from the French philosopher Maine de Biran. The same reality, however, is sometimes also referred to as the "central reference point" (Marcel).[229]

Albert Dondeyne clarifies the meaning of these terms by showing that in every great philosophy there is an original intuition, an all-encompassing light which makes it possible for the philosopher in question to bring clarity to the complexity of reality. Such an intuition can be found in Scholasticism, Descartes, Kant, Hegel, Bergson, etc. No philosophy is satisfied with a disorderly enumeration of the complexity and multiplicity of what is immediately given: philosophy is not a "tale told by an idiot." The philosopher endeavors to find unity in multiplicity, he tries to discover structures, he wishes to com-prehend (Léon Brunschvicg). But he does not *a priori* know how all this is to be done. Every new philosophy, we may perhaps say, begins with the vague suspicion that a certain "approach" will be fruitful, but the philosopher in question does not yet realize what exactly he is doing, by what he is guided, or which "light" or fundamental intuition he uses in his work. Generally speaking, the evident fruitlessness of a certain approach used in the past becomes for him the occasion to try a different way of thinking. What exactly this new way of thinking is, however, remains provisionally obscure. It can happen, for example, that a psychologist comes to the conclusion that a physiological explanation of puberty is insufficient, and he therefore tries a new approach. In the first instance, the intention he has is to explain puberty, and not to reflect upon the light he uses in thinking

---

[227]Kwant, "Menselijke existentie en geschiedenis volgens het wijsgerig denken van Maurice Merleau-Ponty," *Algemeen Nederlands Tijdschrift voor Wijsbegeerte en Psychologie*, 46(1953-1954), p. 234.

[228]Dondeyne, *Contemporary European Thought and Christian Faith*, pp. 25ff.

[229]Marcel, *RI*, p. 18.

about puberty. Only much later does this light become an explicit topic of reflection, and often the man who reflects upon this light is not the one who was the first to make use of it. Thus it could happen that the philosophy of Husserl and Heidegger was much better understood by other thinkers than those two philosophers themselves.

Evidently, a philosophy will be fruitful to the extent that its "primitive fact" can throw light on the complexity and plurality of reality and establish unity in it. The idea "large elephant" is entirely fruitless,[230] but the concept "matter" produces at least some results.

After these remarks one can easily understand that at one time there were existentialists and phenomenologists, but practically no one who could give a definition of either existentialism or phenomenology. On becoming acquainted with what presented itself as existentialism or phenomenology, one could hardly avoid the impression that those terms had as many senses as there were thinkers referring to themselves as existentialists or phenomenologists. If we add to this what in the positive sciences of psychology, psychiatry and sociology was or is called "phenomenological" or "existential," [231] that impression would become even stronger.

All this need not surprise us. Man's entire life runs its course in a kind of semidarkness. As conscious existence, man knows what he does when he lives, but at the same time he also does not know it. He does not escape from his own observation, yet he is not entirely transparent to himself. Philosophizing itself is a way of living and, consequently, shares in that lack of transparency. Thus a new way of philosophizing is also a new way of lacking transparency. Moreover, thinking primarily aims at expressing reality and not at the way in which it reaches expression. This way itself is last in receiving attention. Thus one can understand that a philosophy exists first as a kind of movement or style of thinking and only later becomes conscious of itself.[232] At first, one finds symptoms of this style in various

---

[230]"Ainsi, si quelqu'un venait nous dire que le monde n'est finalement qu'un immense éléphant, dont la multiplicité des existants qui composent le monde ne sont que des aspects ou des manifestations, nous le prendrions pour un insensé et non sans raison." Dondeyne, *Dieu et le matérialisme contemporain*, p. 23, note I.

[231]H. C. Rümke, *Psychiatrie I*, Amsterdam, 1954, pp. 63-71.

[232]"La phénoménologie se laisse pratiquer et reconnaître comme manière ou comme style, elle existe comme mouvement, avant d'être parvenue à une entière conscience philosophique." Merleau-Ponty, *PP*, Avant-propos, p. II.

places, but the "primitive fact," which makes this style of thinking what it is, cannot yet be sharply described.

At present these difficulties have been overcome. The "primitive fact" itself of the new style of thinking became the object of reflection after Kierkegaard's existentialism and Husserl's phenomenology had, as it were, merged in Heidegger's work. It is now agreed that the idea of *existence* or of intentionality—which can be viewed as synonymous with it [233]—is used as the "primitive fact," the fundamental intuition, or the all-pervading "moment" of intelligibility of the new style.[234]

Let us repeat, however, that this "primitive fact" was not pre-selected. It imposed itself in the thinker's reflection itself upon reality and it can be accepted only in an act of faithfulness to reality.[235] This is the reason why we began by presenting a thematic development of the idea of *existence*, or of intentionality, in a discussion with materialistic and spiritualistic monism, letting ourselves be guided by their strong points and avoiding their weaknesses. Only subsequently did we speak about the "primitive fact" of the new style of thinking known as existential phenomenology.

Suitable Terms

A search has been made for terms suitable for expressing as unambiguously as possible the fundamental "moment" of intelligibility proper to existential phenomenology. The *main* purpose of this search was to express that it is impossible to conceive subject and world divorced from each other.[236] The term *encounter* is perhaps one of the best for this purpose, for an encounter is wholly unthinkable as encounter when the two terms of the encounter are not conceived in relationship with each other. An encounter is not an encounter if a subject does not encounter *something*: if he encounters nothing, there is no encounter. Similarly, that which is encountered would not be a term of encounter without the encountering subject. The use of

---

[233]"The term 'to exist' thus becomes synonymous with being-to-the-world, it is ultimately only another way of expressing what Husserl meant by the intentionality of consciousness." Dondeyne, *Contemporary European Thought and Christian Faith*, p. 29.

[234]"Existential phenomenology appears in the history of philosophy as a manner of philosophizing centered round the notion of existence." Dondeyne, *op. cit.*, p. 25.

[235]Dondeyne, *Dieu et le matérialisme contemporain*, p. 23.

[236]"On sait qu'il n'y a point, d'autre part, un pour-soi et, d'autre part, un monde, comme deux touts fermés dont il faudrait ensuite chercher comment ils communiquent." Sartre, *EN*, p. 368.

this term *encounter*, to express the reciprocal implication of subject and world admittedly is not without a serious handicap: in
ordinary speech it refers as a rule to the meeting of a subject
with a subject.[237]   As a technical philosophical term, however,
it is not subject to misunderstanding.   Moreover, the term is
already commonly used for this purpose.

The term *dialog* also is suitable.   Existence is a colloquy to
which both partners contribute their share.   If one of the partners is "thought away," the entire dialog ceases.   Neither partner
can be conceived separately from the other without destroying
the colloquy.   The unity of subject and world is a dialectical
unity, the unity of a dialog.   This dialog is the original, the
primordial *given*, it is that from which all philosophical statements flow as from their source.   The dialog which human
existence is cannot be dissolved in more simple elements without
being reduced to nothing.[238]   Whoever speaks of the subject pole
cannot avoid touching the object pole, and vice versa.   Giving
voice to the dialog which is *existence* is called "dialectics." [239]

There are still other terms to express the "primitive fact" of
existential phenomenology.   Marcel prefers the term *participation*,[240] in the double sense of having part and taking part in the
world.   Merleau-Ponty speaks of *presence*.[241]   This term also
is very clear: presence is not conceivable without "something" to
which the subject is present, and a field of presence does not
make sense without the subject.

Is Man Nothing But Being-Conscious-in-the-World?

One could ask whether the preceding reflections sufficiently
clarify the "primitive fact" of existential phenomenology.   We
are convinced that this is not the case.   Undoubtedly it is true
that all philosophizing about anything whatsoever is always and
of necessity concerned with man as *existence*, as intentionality,
understood as the reciprocal implication of subjectivity and

---

[237]Kwant, "De harmonische uitgroei van een Wijsbegeerte," *Studia
Catholica*, XXX(1955), p. 207, note 9.
[238]Merleau-Ponty, *PP*, pp. 467, 491.
[239]R. C. Kwant, *art. cit.*, pp. 215-219.
[240]"Mais alors cette participation qui est ma présence au monde, je ne
puis l'affirmer, ou la retrouver, la restaurer, qu'en résistant à la tentation de
la nier, c'est-à-dire de me poser comme entité séparée."   Marcel, *RI*, pp.
34-35.
[241]"(L'analyse du temps) éclaire les précédentes analyses parce qu'elle
fait apparaître le sujet et l'objet comme deux moments abstraits d'une structure unique qui est la présence."   Merleau-Ponty, *PP*, p. 492.

world. In love also and even in prayer man is embodied subjectivity in the world. The being of man is a being-conscious-
in-the-world; in other words, this belongs to man's *essence*. As
long as he is man, man can never lay aside or justifiedly deny
his essence.

It would go too far, however, if one were to think that man's
being—as of necessity and essentially a being-conscious-in-the-
world—can be called *exclusively* a being-conscious-in-the-*world*;
i.e., that in man there is *nothing but* the relationship, with all its
modalities, of subjectivity and world. If that were true, love and
hatred, for example, simply could no longer be what they really
are. Although the loving or hating man is *also* related to the
world, one cannot say that love and hatred are *nothing but*
modes of the subject's relationship to a worldly object. It is
intolerable that a philosopher, on the basis of a dogmatic *a priori*
judgment, blocks the road by which it would be *possible* for him
to recognize as reality that which everyone calls reality. He has
the right, or course, to critically investigate what is or is not
tenable in any assertion whatsoever. But he does not have the
right to decide *a priori* through a dogmatic prejudice what the
result of his critique shall be. Only then is the "primitive fact"
of a philosophy not a form of dogmatism, if it is accepted in an
act of faithfulness to reality.

There are forms of existential-phenomenological thinking in
which *existence* or intentionality functions as the "primitive fact,"
but is *exclusively* understood as the unity of reciprocal implication of subject and *world*. This is certainly the case with atheistic existentialism, whose principal exponents are Sartre and
Merleau-Ponty. When Merleau-Ponty says that man as subject
is *nothing but* project of his world [242]—*nothing but* a possibility
to become involved in worldly situations [243]—he arbitrarily en-
capsulates man in a very determined and narrow dimension of
existence: he arbitrarily limits the horizon of *existence* and restricts it to worldly reality.[244] It is evident that such an *a priori*
position at once gives philosophy an atheistic character. For

---

[242]"Le monde est inséparable du sujet, mais d'un sujet qui n'est rien
que projet du monde, et le sujet est inséparable du monde, mais d'un monde
qu'il projette lui-même." *PP*, p. 491.

[243]"Si le sujet est en situation, si même il n'est rien d'autre qu'une
possibilité de situations, c'est qu'il ne réalise son ipséité qu'en étant effectivement corps en entrant par ce corps dans le monde." *PP*, p. 467.

[244]Jean Daniélou, *Le problème de Dieu et l'existentialisme*, Montréal,
1959, p. 14.

what possible sense could still be attached to the statement that man is orientation to God when one has first decreed that man's being is fully encompassed by being in the world—that the horizon of *existence* is exclusively worldly? In such a case the "affirmation" of God can be nothing but the affirmation of a deified, absolutized worldly reality, or of a degraded Transcendence, reduced to a worldly status. In such a case the affirmation of God can never be what it is supposed to be, viz., "affirmation" of the Transcendent. It is intentional that we express ourselves cautiously here. For in this matter also the philosopher has the right and the duty to critically investigate what is tenable in any conviction whatsoever. He has the duty to critically examine what is tenable in an "affirmation" as widely accepted as that of God's existence. But he does not have the right, prior to any critique, to decide, on the basis of a dogmatic prejudice, what the result of his investigation shall be.

For us, the "primitive fact" of existential phenomenology is *existence* or intentionality, conceived as "openness"—the openness of the subject to everything which is not the subject himself. This "everything" certainly includes material things, the world. The unity of reciprocal implication of subject and world is an essential "moment" of *existence*. But nothing gives us the right to limit the subject's openness to the world. Terms such as "encounter," "dialog," "participation," and "presence" can be retained because they possess sufficient flexibility to be used in an enlarged sense if that would become necessary in the progress of philosophy.

CHAPTER TWO

PHENOMENOLOGY OF KNOWLEDGE

In the preceding pages we made use of an insight to which we did not explicitly draw attention and for which no justification was yet presented. We repeatedly spoke of human knowledge and acted as if we knew what knowledge is. This may seem to be an irresponsible procedure, for if I ask myself what knowledge is, I am forced to admit that I cannot at once answer this question. Strange as it seems, the fact that I did not "really" know what knowledge is did not cause me any special difficulties.

Wondering why, I find that the answer is not too difficult: I cannot admit that I do not "really" know what it is to know. True, I cannot express it, but I "know" it. For example, I can distinguish between my knowledge of a person and my love for him; my seeing of a piece of licorice and my dislike of it. I therefore "know" that knowledge is not the same as love or dislike.[1] This implies that I know what knowledge is, and what love and dislike are, for otherwise I would not be able to distinguish one from the other. As soon, however, as I try to express what knowledge is, my tongue is tied and I stammer as if I do not know it. Augustine drew attention to these two forms of "knowing" in connection with the notion of time. He said that he knew what time is, but that, as soon as anyone asked him to express his knowledge, he no longer seemed to know what it is.[2]

1. EXPLICITATION

What, we may ask, is this "really" knowing without being able to express it? This knowing is my being present to the knowing man I am. I know trees, houses, and people, but in this knowing it seems that at first I "omit" my own knowing. When the psychologist tries to know a fellowman who turns to him for help this man is the topic of his knowledge. He will say, for example, that this man is an introvert, emotional and intelligent, or that he suffers from incipient schizophrenia. In these words the psychologist gives expression to the terminus of his knowing encounter, but he "omits" his own knowing and all the inter-

---

[1] I. D. Robert, "Essai d'une description phénoménologique élémentaire du connaître," *Revue philosophique de Louvain,* 58(1960), p. 273.

[2] *Confessions,* bk. 11, ch. 14.

mediary steps leading to his judgment; he does not express them. Nevertheless, the psychologist knows what psychological knowledge is and how he forms his judgment, for he is able to perform these acts of knowing and judging. He is present to the knower he himself is, and for this reason it is possible to make this knowing and judging *themselves* the theme of consideration.[3]

The same can be said with respect to innumerable situations. When I count the number of cigarettes in my pack, I give expression to the terminus encountered by my act of counting by saying: "There are twelve." My counting itself, however, is "omitted"; it does not find expression; it does not become the theme of my consideration. Nevertheless, I know what counting is because I am present to my own act of counting. As soon as anyone asks me what I am doing, I answer: "I am counting." [4] At that very moment, then, the cigarettes are no longer the theme of my knowing, but my counting itself. I am present to my own counting, but as soon as someone asks me what I am doing, I *place* myself explicitly in the presence of my counting and give expression to it.

Pre-reflective Consciousness and the "Unreflected"

The difference between the two above-mentioned forms of consciousness should be clear now. There is an implicit, non-thematic, non-thetic, non-reflective consciousness, which consists of a simple presence to my *existence*. This consciousness is called "counting-consciousness," "delight-consciousness," "love-consciousness," "perception-consciousness," "action-consciousness," etc., which is not a consciousness *of* counting, *of* delight, *of* love, *of* perception or *of* action.[5] Originally there is no consciousness *of* self, but self-consciousness compenetrates consciousness *of* something.[6]

Accordingly, when we speak of, e.g., love-consciousness, there is question of being conscious of something, without the explicitness implied by the term consciousness *of* love.[7] But the

---

[3]P. Bierkens, *Het denken van de psycholoog, Een verkenning van het psychodiagnostisch redeneerproces*, Assen, 1966.

[4]Sartre, *EN*, pp. 19-20.

[5]"Toute conscience positionnelle d'objet est en même temps conscience non positionnelle d'elle-même." *EN*, p. 19.

[6]"C'est la conscience non-thétique de compter qui est la condition même de mon activité additive." *EN*, p. 20.

[7]*Ibid.*

implicit, non-thematic consciousness can also be made thematic and explicit. By my consciousness I *am* originally present to myself; by reflection I *place* myself present to myself, so that that which at first I "omitted"—my love, delight, action, or knowing—become the theme of my consciousness.

It is necessary to be on guard here against a possible misunderstanding. Above we enumerated several ways of *existing*, such as love and perception, of which we are non-thematically conscious. It would be a mistake to think that those ways of *existing* lie outside consciousness or that consciousness lies outside them. On the contrary, loving, taking delight in, perceiving, etc. are not what they are without the presence of consciousness. The perception of a table is equiprimordially a perception-consciousness.[8] This rule applies to all ways of conscious *existence*.[9] In other words, implicit, non-thematic consciousness is not something new superadded to *existence* but innerly constitutes *existence* in what *existence* is.

It would be difficult to overestimate the importance of pre-reflective consciousness. Philosophizing begins in this pre-reflective consciousness, for in the first instance philosophizing is nothing but the expression of what can be called in the most general terms life itself.[10] Life, being knowingly, actively, lovingly, desiringly, emotionally in the world, is a being-conscious-in-the-world. Because life is conscious, it does not escape me;[11] nevertheless, I must still "seize" it if I wish to philosophize, for my non-thematic consciousness of my being-in-the-world is only a "lived experience," life is only an unreflective dealing with things and people. Reflective consciousness, however, is continually being nourished by the unreflective dimension, which it thematizes. If it does not thematize the unreflective, our philosophizing "hangs in the air,"[12] without any support.

Philosophy, then, may never contradict the unreflective dimension: my philosophizing is an attempt to "seize" life and give expression to it. This "seizure" and expression are value-

---

[8]*Ibid.*

[9]"Toute existence consciente existe comme conscience d'exister.' *Ibid.*

[10]Ortega y Gasset, *De mens en de mensen,* pp. 47-48.

[11]"Une conduite irréfléchie n'est pas une conduite inconsciente, elle est consciente d'elle-même non-thétiquement.' J-P. Sartre, *Esquisse d'une théorie des émotions."* Paris, 3rd. ed., 1948, p. 32.

[12]". . . la condition de toute réflexivité est un cogito préréflexif,' *EN,* pp. 116-117.

less unless the philosopher expresses that to which he is present, and "lived experience" supports his reflective expression.[13]

Thus it seems as if the result of the method of explicitation is presupposed as the starting point: the course of thought looks like a circular argument.[14] This impression is correct, but the philosopher need not apologize for it: he may not, and even cannot, try to avoid such a course of thought. The circular character of his thinking, however, is not a vicious circle because he does not proceed after the manner of a syllogism.[15] The so-called circular process of explicitation is the expression of what man himself is in his inner structure: a being for whom, in his being, his being itself is at issue;[16] a being whose being is consciousness of being.[17] It is from this consciousness, which he himself is, that the philosopher must start. There is no other starting point, for, outside the consciousness of his *existence*, there is nothing but *concealedness* with respect to both the subject pole and the object pole.

Above we asked what knowledge is. An answer to this question is possible because I am present to the knower who I myself am. My *existence* is a knowledge-consciousness, which is not consciousness *of* knowledge. The answer to the question will consist in the explicitation of that knowledge-consciousness, so that the latter becomes consciousness *of* knowledge. The answer, then, can never be "reasoned out" or demonstrated in the strict sense of the term in which, e.g., the properties of a sphere are derived or demonstrated from the nature of the sphere.[18] In explicitation nothing is demonstrated: all I can do is "point out." I can merely try to "seize" and express that to which I am present.

The history of thought, however, shows how easily the philosopher can disregard an essential aspect of unreflected life in his explicitations. Yet, even this statement can never be *demonstrated*. If I think that someone failed to see an essential aspect, I can at most, by means of very precise descriptions, try to point

---

[13]Merleau-Ponty, *PP,* Avant-propos, pp. II-V.
[14]Heidegger, *SZ,* p. 152.
[15]*SZ,* pp. 152, 315.
[16]"Der 'Zirkel' im Verstehen gehört zur Struktur des Sinnes, welches Phänomen in der existenzialen Verfassung des Daseins, im auslegenden Verstehen verwurzelt ist. Seiendes, dem es als In-der-Welt-sein um sein Sein selbst geht, hat eine ontologische Zirkelstruktur." *SZ,* p. 153.
[17]*SZ,* p. 14.
[18]*SZ,* p. 315.

out to him that which he has disregarded. Much time may have to pass before such an attempt will succeed. It can happen that an entire generation of thinkers remains totally blind for a particular phenomenon. Through all kinds of conscious or subconscious prejudices—by being wholly immersed in a particular system of views or unquestioned convictions—they may be unable to see certain phenomena.[19]

If a discovery is too far ahead of its time because the general attitude of thinkers is not yet ready to see a certain phenomenon, the ingenious thinker who does see has no other choice than to remain provisionally silent about his discovery and to work first at the "education" which can prepare his contemporaries for seeing what he sees.[20]

Certain insights, then, require a long time of preparation. They are born in the course of history and it can also happen that they disappear again in history. This historical growth of insight is clearly illustrated in the history of the definition man has given of knowledge.

2. REALISM AND IDEALISM

In the first chapter we explained how it came about that, since Descartes, philosophy accepted without question that knowledge was a mirroring of "brute" reality, and that the system of the physical sciences was the system *par excellence* of objective mirror images. The same conception also resulted from John Locke's philosophy of knowledge, although this thinker began with a starting point that was radically different from that of Descartes.

Primary and Secondary Qualities

Descartes accepted innate ideas, but to Locke such ideas were anathema.[21] He held that man's cognitive power is like a piece of paper on which nothing is written [22]: the "writing" on it

---

19"Or, il se peut qu'une période tout entière soit par suite de certains partis pris inconscients, de certaines vues systématiques, imperméable à certains phénomènes. Ce sera plus tard seulement, quand la première attitude aura changé pour faire place à une nouvelle, que ceux-ci pourront s'imposer comme objectifs." A. Brunner, *La personne incarnée*, Paris, 1947, p. 184.

20Brunner, *op. cit.*, pp. 180-184.

21J. Locke, *An essay concerning human understanding*, I, 2-4.

22"Let us suppose the mind to be, as we say, white paper, void of all characters without any ideas; how comes it to be furnished?" Locke, *op. cit.*, II, 1, 2.

has to be done entirely from without and, according to Locke, it is experience alone which does the "writing." [23]

Locke made a distinction between "ideas in the mind" and "qualities in the body." That which consciousness perceives in itself he called "idea"; the idea is produced in consciousness by certain forces in things, called "qualities." [24] Next, Locke distinguished primary and secondary qualities.[25] Primary qualities of things are those characteristics which are open to more than one sense organ; for example, the shape of an apple is open to both the sense of touch and that of sight. Scholastic philosophy used to speak here of "common sensibles." The secondary qualities, which the Scholastics called "proper sensibles," are the proper object of one sense organ only; for instance, the color of an apple is the proper object of the sense of sight, and odor is that object for the sense of smell.

According to Locke, the ideas of the primary qualities are objective, but those of the secondary qualities are subjective. For water having a certain degree of warmth can produce in one hand a perception of heat and, at the same time, in the other hand a feeling of cold; but a particular shape can never produce through one hand the idea of a square and through the other that of a sphere.[26]

At first sight, this distinction does not seem too important, but this impression is not at all correct. Locke's discriminatory distinction in favor of primary qualities and against secondary qualities contains an implicit theory of human knowledge. For, as long as knowledge is conceived as a way of *existing*—i.e., as the immediate presence of the knowing subject to a present reality—one cannot possibly claim that the primary qualities of things are objective and the secondary qualities not objective. In the subject's immediate presence to an apple shape as well as odor and color are given as present realities, as objective. Nevertheless, Locke claims that only the shape is objective. What, then, does this claim imply?

---

[23] "Whence has it all the materials of reason and knowledge? To this I answer in one word, From experience: in that all our knowledge is founded." Locke, *op. cit.*, II, 1, 2.

[24] "Whatsoever the mind perceives in itself, or is the immediate object of perception, thought, or understanding, that I call 'idea'; and the power to produce any idea in our mind I call 'quality' of the subject wherein that power is." Locke, *op. cit.*, II, 8, 8.

[25] Locke, *op. cit.*, II, 8, 9-10.

[26] Locke, *op. cit.*, II, 8, 21.

This claim implies that knowledge is *not* conceived as the knower's immediate presence to a present reality. Thus, from the epistemological standpoint, this claim can hardly avoid considering human knowledge as a purely passive mirroring of a world "divorced" from the subject. In such a view, the knowing subject is not understood as *existence*, but as a passive, worldless subject; and the world is conceived as a collection of things-in-themselves, a "brute" reality, a world in which the knowing subject is not involved, in which he does not live and with which, as a subject, he does not, as a matter of principle, have any dealings. In that case one can say that only the primary qualities are objective, and this statement then means that only the quantitative aspects are "accurately" mirrored. With respect to secondary qualities, accurate mirroring was considered impossible [27] because the knower was judged to spoil their mirroring through his subjective admixtures.[28]

There are, of course, differences between Descartes and Locke; yet, these two are fundamentally in agreement concerning the definition of human knowledge: our knowledge is a mirroring-in-a-worldless-subject of a world-divorced-from-the-subject; and the system *par excellence* of objective mirroring is the system of the physical sciences because only these sciences operate with the categories of quantity. For both Descartes and Locke, ideas are the direct objects of man's knowledge, and this meant that the so-called "critical problem" was formulated as the question about the *reality* in the "outside world" of those things whose ideas were assumed to be present in the "inner world."

A Twofold Possibility

Given the divorce between subjectivity and world, the common starting point of Descartes' and Locke's thought left different directions open according to the emphasis placed on

[27]"What I have said concerning colours and smells may be understood also of tastes and sounds, and other the like sensible qualities; which, whatever reality we by mistake attribute to them, are in truth nothing in the objects themselves, but powers to produce various sensations in us, and depend on those primary qualities, viz. bulk, figure, texture, and motion of parts, as I have said." Locke, *op. cit.,* II, 8, 14.

[28]"From whence I think it is easy to draw this observation, that ideas of primary qualities of bodies are resemblances of them, and their patterns do really exist in the bodies themselves; but the ideas produced in us by those secondary qualities have no resemblance of them at all. There is nothing like our ideas existing in the bodies themselves." Locke, *op. cit.,* II, 8, 15.

either consciousness or the world. Thus we can distinguish idealism and realism.

Idealism puts the main emphasis on consciousness—its priority, spontaneity, and activity. For Descartes, consciousness was still connected with the world, although he could not justify the way in which he claimed there was a connection. Idealism considered that its task was to overcome the bond tying consciousness to the world, to eliminate the world entirely as a source of knowledge. It viewed the perception of the world by consciousness—with the implied darkness and confusion—as an inauthentic form of knowledge, a type of knowledge that should be overcome and replaced by the clarity of the self-sufficient idea. In perception, idealism argued, consciousness is in a state of self-alienation: in the material world, clear and distinct ideas are in a state of estrangement. It is the task of consciousness to revert to itself, to overcome its self-alienation-in-matter. Once it has reverted to itself, consciousness is wholly sufficient unto itself, pure "for itself," capable of perfect reflection.

While idealism isolates consciousness from the world, and explicitates consciousness as pure activity with respect to the content of knowledge, realism does almost exactly the opposite. Just as idealism is struck by a certain aspect of consciousness—viz., its spontaneity—and exaggerates this aspect, so also realism is born from a fundamental intuition, viz., an insight into the "sensitivity," as opposed to spontaneity, the passivity of consciousness. For it is undeniably true that the reality of things *imposes* itself on our perceiving consciousness—that perceiving consciousness finds reality. For this reason the realists have always rejected innate ideas and maintained that all knowledge arises from experience of reality.

The *reality* of the world, however, as well as our experience of it, are explicitated in a very special way. For the realist reality is a world-in-itself, it is "brute" reality, an *inhuman* world, in the sense that man and his perceiving consciousness are "thought away" from the world. The realist totally disregards the spontaneity—the active presence of consciousness—and thinks that he can speak of a world-without-man. Consciousness, therefore, must be conceived as pure passivity, as a *tabula rasa*—a piece of paper on which nothing is written, a kind of photo-sensitive plate, a mirror in which a fully isolated world inscribes or impresses itself.[29] Realism *first* affirms a world which is *not* the terminus of the encounter which knowledge is, and then claims that consciousness undergoes the influence of reality in a purely passive way. The world is "the totality of reality" (*omnitudo realitatis*),[30] purely a spectacle for a consciousness which as a "surveying look" considers the world, without having a standpoint, finding itself in a certain situation, or being involved in the world.

In realism, then, the full emphasis falls on the *reality* of the world, and in this respect it differs from idealism, for which all reality tends to become increasingly more ethereal. Nevertheless, realism did not manage to build a bridge between consciousness and the world. For, following Locke, all realists taught that the proper and immediate object of perceiving consciousness is the perception-impressions themselves. It would have been inconceivable if the realists had not taught this. For in realism consciousness occurs only as divorced and isolated from objectivity although knowledge is said to be objective, i.e., knowledge is in agreement with a reality which is isolated from the knower. This requires that the knowing subject somehow *possesses* reality. But, how can a reality which is divorced from the subject be possessed?[31] Obviously, reality cannot entitatively, in its physical nature, be in the knower. But there is in the knower a mirror image,[32] an "impressed species": physical reality impresses in the knowing subject an image, which, as an imitation or replica of reality-in-itself, is the proper and immediate object of knowledge.[33] Accordingly, I never know a chair, a house or a plant, but only the chair-impression, the house-

---

[29]". . . le réalisme tente de rendre compte de la connaissance par une action du monde sur la substance pensante. . . ." Sartre, *EN*, p. 277.

[30]Merleau-Ponty, *StC*, p. 218.

[31]"C'est d'abord le sensible, le perçu lui-même, qu'on installe dans les fonctions de chose extra-mentale, et le problème est donc de comprendre comment un double ou une imitation du réel est suscité dans le corps, puis dans la pensée." *StC*, p. 205.

[32]"Puisqu'un tableau nous fait penser à ce qu'il représente, on supposera, en se fondant sur le cas privilégié des appareils visuels, que les sens reçoivent des choses réelles de 'petits tableaux' qui excitent l'âme à les percevoir. Les 'simulacres' épicuriens ou les 'espèces intentionnelles', 'toutes ces petites images voltigéantes par l'air' qui apportent dans le corps l'aspect sensible des choses, ne font que transporter en termes d'explication causale et d'opérations réelles la présence idéale de la chose au sujet percevant qui, nous l'avons vu, est une évidence pour la conscience naïve." *StC*, p. 205.

[33]*StC*, pp. 205-206.

impression, the plant-impression. Realism dogmatically and without any foundation accepts that, on the one hand, there is a world and, on the other, a passive and encapsulated consciousness. Thus there is no bridge between consciousness and the world.

A "Scientific" Theory of Perception

Meanwhile the existence of these perception-impressions must be said to be rather problematic. When Descartes asked himself to what extent his knowledge of the world could be called objective, he answered that there is only one clear and distinct concept of the material world, viz., that of quantity. Because this concept obviously refers to the realm in which physical science is interested, Descartes' answer assigned a privileged position to experience as it is known in physical science. The same was done by Locke with his claim that only the primary qualities of things are objective.

To explain the existence of perception-impressions, the psychologists let themselves be guided again by their admiration for the physical sciences: they proceeded to study all contents of consciousness with the same method with which the physicist studies matter. This method consists in the analysis of matter into its ultimate elements. The psychologist, then, was supposed to do the same with the contents of consciousness: [34] a house-impression, a plant-impression was to be reduced to its component elements. These elements, it was thought, could be found in the elementary sensations, caused by physical stimuli possessing a measurable strength, which exercised a unilateral and physically determining influence upon man's sensitivity. A house-impression or a plant-impression could ultimately be constructed by means of the summative connection of innumerable elementary sensations caused by physical stimuli, and this summation was assumed to come about through the mechanism of association.[35]

Other psychologists, however, considered such a way of speaking about perception not sufficiently "scientific." They argued that "scientific" speech should not speak of perceptions but of nerve paths, cerebral processes, etc. Accordingly, a psychology of perception was possible only for one who was willing

---

[34]Merleau-Ponty, *PP*, p. 72.
[35]J. van Dael, *Geschiedenis der empirische psychologie*, Zeist, 1929, pp. 12-20.

to forget that which interested him as a psychologist and be content with the pursuit of physiology.

A Blooming Tree in the Meadow

Since Descartes and Locke only the world-for-the-physicist was thought to be objective. The next step was that also in the act of *perceiving* this world only that was called objective which the physical sciences can say about it.

But what does all this mean? It would appear most trivial that when one speaks of a blooming tree in the meadow, one "claims" to speak of a blooming tree in the meadow. With respect to the perception of a tree, physical science, physiology and psychology can say something both about the tree and about its perception. They register all kinds of physical, physiological and psychological processes. With the aid of instruments they can make the cerebral processes acoustically perceptible and present their course in curves. But what sense does it make to wish to speak *only in this way* about the perception of a blooming tree in the meadow? Must a blooming tree be reduced to a vacuum in which there are here and there scattered electric charges moving to and fro with great velocity? [36] It does not make sense to say that we "naturally" perceive a blooming tree, and then to replace the tree by the "ingredients" of various sciences, in order to let these sciences determine what is real in a blooming tree and what is unreal. Where do the sciences obtain their competency to pronounce judgment upon these matters? [37] When there is question of perceiving a tree, should we not leave the tree standing where it is? The tree is not a series of processes in our brain but a tree-in-the-meadow.[38] What the sciences say is true; nevertheless, "everything here remains subject to question." [39]

What, then, "remains subject to question" here? The an-

---

[36]"Denn unversehens geben wir alles preis, sobald uns die Wissenschaften der Physik, Physiologie und Psychologie samt der wissenschaftlichen Philosophie mit dem ganzen Aufwand ihrer Belege und Beweise erklären, dass wir eigentlich keinen Baum wahrnehmen, sondern in Wirklichkeit eine Leere, in die spärlich hie und da elektrische Ladungen eingestreut sind, die mit grosser Geschwindigkeit hin- und hersausen." Heidegger, *Was heisst Denken?*, Tübingen, 1954, p. 18.

[37]Heidegger, *op. cit.*, p. 18.

[38]"Aber wo bleibt . . . bei den wissenschaftlich registrierbaren Gehirnströmen der blühende Baum? Wo bleibt die Wiese? Wo bleibt der Mensch?" Heidegger, *op. cit.*, p. 17.

[39]Heidegger, *op. cit.*, p. 16.

swer is not difficult: how do the scientists know what they are speaking about? When they make all kinds of cerebral processes acoustically perceptible, and present them in curves; when they speak of electric charges which move to and fro with great velocity, *they do not speak of anything at all* if they do not accept that ultimately they are trying to speak about the perception of a blooming tree in the meadow. As a matter of fact, they do know whereof they speak because surreptitiously they consider the "ordinary" perception of a blooming tree in the meadow more original than the ingredients of their various sciences.[40] But in that case it does not make any sense to *replace* the blooming tree in the meadow by a system of meanings disclosed by those sciences and to *substitute* "ingredients" of the sciences for perception itself.[41]

It should be clear now what Husserl had in mind when he launched his phenomenology as a "method to find ground." His call—"Back to the things themselves" [42]—was an invitation to return to the original experience of the original world. The world—for-the-physicist is not this original world but is built upon the original world.[43] The experience of the physical sciences is not the original experience but is founded on original experience.[44] A phenomenology of knowledge must subject the traditional prejudices concerning the definition of knowledge to a fundamental critique. Knowledge must be explicitated in terms of the integral way in which it occurs.[45] It is a matter of "restoring to experience its ontological weight." [46]

---

[40]Merleau-Ponty, *PP*, Avant-propos, p. III.

[41]"Si éloignée que soit de la perception la physique moderne, celle-ci serait absolument 'en l'air', si, en définitive, elle ne nous expliquait que les pommes tombent des arbres mais n'y remontent jamais, que l'eau des glaciers descend vers la mer sans jamais gravir la pente qui conduit au sommet." De Waelhens, *La philosophie et les expériences naturelles*, La Haye, 1961, p. 52.

[42]"Nicht von den Philosophien sondern von den Sachen und Problemen muss der Antrieb zur Forschung ausgehen." Husserl, "Philosophie als strenge Wissenschaft," *Logos*, I(1910-11), p. 340.

[43]"Le monde 'vrai' pensé et construit par la science ne peut s'édifier qu'en prenant appui sur le monde du 'sens commun' dont la science feint de contester la réalité." De Waelhens, *op. cit.*, p. 51.

[44]"On n'est jamais fondé à interpréter cette expérience spontanée. . . . en fonction de savoir scientifique, et, moins encore, à lui intégrer des éléments ou des réalités qui relèvent de ce savoir." De Waelhens, "Signification de la phénoménologie," *Diogène*, V (1954), p. 59.

[45]"(La phénoménologie) s'efforce de concevoir la philosophie comme l'explicitation de l'expérience humaine intégrale." De Waelhens, *art. cit.*, p. 60.

[46]Marcel, *EA*, p. 149.

3. HUMAN KNOWLEDGE AS INTENTIONALITY

Phenomenology calls the subject-as-*cogito*, or human knowledge, "intentionality." [47] When Husserl used this term for the first time, he explicitly referred to Franz Brentano.[48] It is certain, however, that Husserl merely took over the term itself from Brentano, for he gave it a meaning which is radically different from that attributed to it by Brentano.[50] Scholasticism also used the same term to refer to the "impressed species," the substitute "forms" for "brute" reality. Scholastic philosophy presented reality as divorced from the subject-as-*cogito*, and assigned to the substitute cognitive images the role of building a bridge between the subject and reality.[51] Scholasticism answers the question concerning the mode of being proper to those images by saying that they do not have any entitative being but only intentional being. In other words, their whole being consists in their referring to reality.[52] The subject-as-*cogito*, then, is first separate from reality and then enters into contact with reality by means of those impressed images.

When Husserl, however, uses the term "intentionality," he does not refer to a subject isolated from the world and encapsulated, but he describes the subject-as-*cogito*—knowledge *itself*—as orientation-to and openness-to-the-world. Knowledge is not a matter of "storing cognitive images" in the subject's interiority, but the *immediate* presence of the subject as a kind of "light" to a present reality.[53] As a mode of being-man, human knowledge is a mode of being-*existent,* a mode of being-involved-in-the-world, and this being-involved is the subject him-

---

[47]Husserl, *Ideen* I, pp. 79-80, 203-212, 357-358. "Die Grundeigenschaft der Bewusstseinsweisen, in denen ich als Ich lebe, ist die sogennannte Intentionalität." Husserl, *Cartesianische Meditationen und Pariser Vorträge,* (*Husserliana* I), p. 13.

[48]"Wir werden also. . . . von *intentionalen Erlebnissen* sprechen. 'Erlebnis' ist dabei in dem oben fixierten phänomenologischen Sinne zu nehmen. Das determinierende Beiwort *intentional* nennt den gemeinsamen Wesenscharakter der abzugrenzenden Erlebnisklasse, die Eigenheit der Intention, das sich in der Weise der Vorstellung oder in einer irgend analogen Weise auf ein gegenständliches Beziehen." Husserl, *Logische Untersuchungen,* II Band, 1 Teil, Halle a.d.S, 1928, p. 378.

[49]Husserl, *op. cit.,* p. 380.

[50]Kockelmans, *A First Introduction to Husserl's Phenomenology,* Pittsburgh, 1967, p. 170.

[51]J. Peters, *Metaphysics,* Pittsburgh, 1963, pp. 258 ff.

[52]J. Hoogveld and F. Sassen, *Inleiding tot de Wijsbegeerte,* I, Utrecht-Nijmegen, 1944, p. 22.

[53]Merleau-Ponty, *PP,* Avant-propos, p. V.

self. The subject, then, is not "first" and in himself a kind of "psychical thing" which "subsequently," by means of cognitive images, enters into relationship with physical things. Knowledge is not "something in between two things in themselves"— not a relationship between two different realities—but is the subject himself involved in the world.[54]

Closely considered, the theory of substitute images also is forced to presuppose that which it does not wish to admit. The theory refuses to admit that the subject-as-*cogito* is immediate presence to a present reality; nevertheless, it calls the cognitive images images of *reality*. But how is this possible if the subject is *not* immediately present to reality? If we assume that there really are images of reality in the subject, there must be a reason to assume that those images are really *images*, "forms" representing reality. But this affirmation can only be made when the subject is immediately present to reality and, on the basis of this presence, recognizes that the images are really images. One who again conceives this ever presupposed presence to reality as the "storing of images in the subject," postpones to infinity the possibility of recognizing these images as images. Images can only be called *images* on the basis of the subject's immediate presence to a present reality.[55] But once this immediate presence is admitted, those images are no longer necessary.

Is the "Critical Problem" Talked out of Existence Here?

In the first chapter we pointed out that the critical problem, as it has been formulated since Descartes, is a pseudo-problem. It does not make sense to ask whether the world is real, for this question can be raised only by a constituted philosophy which does not take the terms, in which the critical problem must be raised, from knowledge as knowledge really occurs. Human

---

[54]"Wohl zu beachten ist dabei dass hier nicht die Rede ist von einer Beziehung zwischen irgendeinem psychologischen Vorkommnis - genannt Erlebnis - und einem anderen realen Dasein - genannt Gegenstand - oder von einer psychophysischen und sonstwie realen Verknüpfung, die in objektiver Wirklichkeit zwischen dem einen und anderen statthätte. Vielmehr ist hier und überall von rein phänomenologischen Erlebnissen, bzw. von ihrem Wesen die Rede, und von dem, was in ihrem Wesen 'a priori', in unbedingter Notwendigkeit beschlossen ist." Husserl, *Ideen* I, p. 80.

[55]"Das Raumding, das wir sehen, ist bei all seiner Transzendenz Wahrgenommenes, in seiner Leibhaftigkeit bewusstseinsmässig Gegebenes. Es ist nicht statt seiner ein Bild oder Zeichen gegeben. Man unterschiebe nicht dem Wahrnehmen ein Zeichen- oder Bildbewusstsein." *Ideen I*, pp. 98-99.

knowledge really occurs only as intentionality, and this implies that knowledge simply is not what it is without the real world. The reality of the world cannot and need not be proved,[56] for the subject-as-*cogito* himself is relation-to-the-real-world.[57] The "scandal of philosophy" is not, as Kant still thought, the fact that no one has ever managed to offer a valid proof for the reality of the world, but the fact that, as Heidegger has shown, people continue to look for such a proof.[58]

But, one will argue, do the reasons which made Descartes doubt the reality of the world carry no weight? Can I not dream and, while dreaming, think that I perceive a real world even though I do not really perceive such a world? Can I not hallucinate, fear, and desire, and be, nonetheless, convinced that all kinds of hallucinated, feared, or desired meanings are real while they are as a matter of fact not real?

Obviously I am able to do this. But the fact that Descartes himself distinguished between perceiving and dreaming means that he implicitly recognized the difference between a perceived world and a dreamt world: he implicitly recognized that, while perceiving, he was involved in the real world, and that he was not so involved when we dreamt or hallucinated.[59] Nevertheless, Descartes bracketed the "entire world," including the world of perception which he had already implicitly affirmed as real. By including the world of perception in the "bracketed" world, Descartes wiped out the distinction between perceiving and dreaming, for this distinction exists by virtue of the difference between a perceived world and a dreamt world. Descartes filled the *cogito* with immanent images, but in those images the subject

---

[56]"On voit . . . comment le problème de l'existence du monde extérieur ne présente à la rigueur aucun sens quelconque." Marcel, *JM*, p. 26.

[57]"Je dirais pour mon compte que Heidegger a montré d'une façon probablement définitive qu'il est absurde d'isoler le sujet existant et de se demander à partir de lui si le monde existe ou non. Car en fait ce sujet existant n'est tel que dans sa relation au monde." Marcel, *L'homme problématique*, Paris, 1955, pp. 141-142.

[58]Heidegger, *SZ*, p. 205.

[59]"Car si je peux parler de 'rêves' et de la 'réalité', m'interroger sur la distinction de l'imaginaire et du réel, mettre en doute le 'réel', c'est que cette distinction est déjà faite par moi avant l'analyse, c'est que j'ai une expérience du réel comme de l'imaginaire, et le problème est alors non pas rechercher comment la pensée critique peut se donner des équivalents secondaires de cette distinction, mais d'expliciter notre savoir primordial du 'réel', de décrire la perception du monde comme ce qui fonde pour toujours notre idée de vérité." Merleau-Ponty, *PP*, Avant-propos, p. XI.

can never "see" whether they are dream images or images of reality.[60] One who takes the idea of intentionality seriously no longer asks whether the world which he "sees" is real, but he can ask whether he really "sees" or merely dreams.[61]

Phenomenological Realism

Phenomenology's idea of intentionality excludes idealism. The subject-as-*cogito* is, as intentionality, orientation to that which is *not the subject himself*. By a reflective return to knowledge as it really occurs, the philosopher always comes face to face with the invincible facticity of the "bodily given." The density of this *de facto* givenness can never be overcome, for the subject-as-*cogito* himself is a way of being-in-the-world.[62] Thus the subject-as-*cogito* is never pure activity but always *also* "sensitivity" to a reality which it not the subject himself. Knowing man is merely the "shepherd" of reality.[63]

Realism also, as it was traditionally conceived, is rendered impossible by the idea of intentionality.[64] The world, as conceived by phenomenology, is the *real* world. The correlate of the *existent* subject-as-*cogito* is "that which shows itself, which discloses itself, the disclosed," [65] the "unconcealed," the "phenomenon," in brief, appearing being itself. Phenomenology calls appearing being "meaning." Meaning "speaks" to the subject-as-*cogito* because meaning is unconcealedness. But meaning is unconcealed because the subject is not *pure* passivity: the subject is, despite his passivity, also activity because he is the "letting be" of meaning.[66] Meaning is the unconcealed which

---

[60]"Si je disais avec le sensualisme qu'il n'y a là que des 'états de conscience' et si je cherchais à distinguer mes perceptions de mes rêves par des 'critères', je manquerais le phénomène du monde." *Ibid.*

[61]"Il ne faut donc pas se demander si nous percevons vraiment un monde, il faut dire au contraire: le monde est cela que nous percevons." *Ibid.*

[62]"Mais puisque au contraire nous sommes au monde, puisque même nos réflexions prennent place dans le flux temporel qu'elles cherchent à capter . . . , il n'y a pas de pensée qui embrasse toute notre pensée." *PP*, Avant-propos, p. IX.

[63]"Der Mensch ist der Hirt des Seins." Heidegger, *Ueber den Humanismus*, p. 19.

[64]"Si, au contraire, nous voulions définir sans préjugé le sens philosophique de la psychologie de la Forme, il faudrait dire qu'en rélévant la 'structure' ou la 'forme' comme un ingrédient irréductible de l'être, elle remet en question l'alternative classique de l' 'existence comme chose' et de l' 'existence comme conscience', elle établit une communication et comme un mélange de l'objectif et du subjectif. . . .' Merleau-Ponty, *SNS*, pp. 171-172.

[65]Heidegger, *SZ*, p. 28.

[66]"Heidegger, *Vom Wesen der Wahrheit*, 3rd ed., Frankfurt a.M., 1954, pp. 14-17.

imposes itself on the subject in knowledge: [67] it is the real. But the fact that the real imposes itself does not give anyone the right to conceive the real as an "in itself," for the "in itself" "is" something which in principle and definitively is concealed, i.e., which does not "speak" to the subject. The "real" as it is conceived by traditional realism is not "phenomenon," but one could say that it "has been phenomenon" and was "realized." This expression means that the "in itself" of traditional realism is, in spite of everything, first the "result" of the subject's "letting be" and fused with it; but then this "result" is divorced from this "letting be" and "deposited" outside *existence* as an absolutely original reality.[68] Meaning is inseparately connected with the saying of "is" which the *existent* subject-as-*cogito* himself is; [69] but traditional realism removes this saying of "is" and thinks that, in spite of this removal, it can call being *being*.

The traditional dilemma, then, of either realism or idealism is not a genuine dilemma. For this reason one need not object to calling phenomenology a realistic philosophy, because the term "realistic" cannot be understood here in the objectivistic sense in which it was taken by traditional, representational realism.[70] To distinguish the term "reality," however, as it is understood by phenomenology, from the "brute" reality of representational realism, the terms "in itself for us" and "being for us" are used rather widely: they express the *autonomy of being* proper to worldly meaning *in reference to* the subject.

The World as System of "Nearby" and "Remote" Meanings

We used the term "meaning" to indicate the correlate of the *existent* subject's-as-*cogito* intentionality and we may call the action of the subject-as-*cogito* "perception." If we conceive perception as intentionality and carefully analyze this form of intentionality, we notice several things which, in the traditional

[67]"Das Aussagen ist ein Sein zum seienden Ding selbst. Und was wird durch die Wahrnehmung ausgewiesen? Nichts anders also dass es das Seiende selbst ist, das in der Aussage gemeint war. . . . Das gemeinte Seiende selbst zeigt sich so, wie es an ihm selbst ist, d.h. dass es in Selbigkeit so its, als wie seiend es in der Aussage aufgezeigt, entdeckt wird." *SZ*, p. 218.

[68]"Pour la première fois, la méditation du philosophe est assez consciente pour ne pas réaliser dans le monde et avant elle ses propres résultats." Merleau-Ponty, *PP*, Avant-propos, p. XV.

[69]"C'est par la connaissance . . . que l'être brut accède au niveau de l'existence véritable, et notre conscience d'exister est présupposée dans celle de l'existence du monde." P. Foulquié, *L'existentialisme*, Paris, 1953, p. 38.

[70]*PP*, Avant-propos, p. V; *SNS*, p. 187.

psychologies of perception, have led to very peculiar hypotheses. It is not simple, however, to offer an accurate description of those things. With due apologies, therefore, we will begin by using a terminology which subsequently we will have to correct, because it will become evident that it is wrong.

When I see a house, I do not hesitate to say that I really see a *house* even though it is true that I merely perceive a particular *profile* of the house. I see the front, one of the sides, and a part of the roof, but I do not really see the rear, the other side and the other part of the roof. I could see the unseen parts of the house if I changed my spatial standpoint with respect to the house, but this would mean that I would no longer see the profile I saw first. In principle I can perceive an endless number of profiles because I can occupy innumerable different standpoints with respect to the house.[71] An object of perception, then, shows an *internal horizon.* An endless plurality of evanescing partial acts involve me in an endless plurality of evanescing profiles. This assertion applies to any object whatsoever of perception.[72] In every partial act and with respect to any actually appearing profile however, I am aware of the fact that all profiles are profiles of one and the same house.[73]

How are the different partial acts of the subject and the various appearing profiles of the perception-object connected with one another? It would be a mistake to think that perception, either in its subjective side (*noesis*) or in its objective side (*noema*), consists in a kind of "addition." [74] Perception as totality does not consist of partial acts glued together. For every profile of the perceived house *intrinsically* refers to other pro-

---

[71]"In Wesensnotwendigkeit gehört zu einem 'allseitigen', kontinuierlich einheitlich sich in sich selbst bestätigenden Erfahrungsbewusstsein vom selben Ding ein vielfältiges System von kontinuierlichen Erscheinungs- und Abschattungsmannigfaltigkeiten, in denen, wenn sie aktuell gelten, alle in die Wahrnehmung mit dem Charakter der leibhaften Selbstgegebenheit fallenden gegenständlichen Momente sich im Bewusstsein der Identität in bestimmten Kontinuitäten darstellen bzw. abschatten." Husserl, *Ideen I,* p. 93.

[72]*Ideen I,* pp. 100-101.

[73]"Gehen wir von einem Beispiel aus. Immerfort diesen Tisch sehend, dabei um ihn herumgehend, meine Stellung im Raume wie immer verändernd, habe ich kontinuierlich das Bewusstsein vom leibhaftigen Dasein dieses einen und selben Tisches, und zwar desselben, in sich durchaus unverändert bleibenden. Die Tischwahrnehmung ist aber eine sich beständig verändernde, sie ist eine Kontinuität wechselnder Wahrnehmungen." *Ideen I,* p. 92.

[74]"Die Stücke und Phasen der Wahrnehmung sind nicht äusserlich aneinandergeklebt. . . ." Husserl, *Cartesianische Meditationen und Pariser Vorträge,* (Husserliana I), p. 17.

files,[75] which will appear when I change my standpoint. I can follow the various lines of an actually appearing profile to a point where I can no longer see them. But they refer to the future appearance of another profile which clings to my future perception from a different standpoint. If it were to become evident that those lines do not really refer to another profile—that the front of the house does not really refer to its rear—then I did not actually perceive a real front. If I perceive the back of my friend, and it later becomes "evident" that his body has no front —not merely the front I expected, but no front whatsoever— then I did not perceive a *real* back.

Accordingly, every actually appearing profile *intrinsically* refers to potentially appearing profiles, and this means that, *without* this reference, that which actually appears is not what it is. Similarly, without reference to potential perceptions, the actual perception is not a real perception. Thus so-called perception implies not only pure actuality but also potentiality, and these distinct "moments" of perception are not what they are, independently of each other. Potentiality belongs to the *reality* of the actuality, and actuality belongs to the *reality* of the potentiality.[76] The object, then, of perception is a system of ever evanescent, "nearby" and "distant" meanings, in correlation with the ever evanescent "moments" of perception's actuality and potentiality. Perception shows in both its noetic and its noematic aspects a spatio-temporal, internal horizon, which is accessible only to an intentional analysis.[77]

It is about time to correct the terminology used above: we should not say that the perceiver "really" sees only one particular profile of the house, and that he does *not* see another profile. Similarly, we should not say that a particular profile is present and that another is *not* present. For one who makes such statements begins with the assumption that only the moment of actuality is *real* and disregards that this moment of actuality is

---

[75]Husserl, *Erfahrung und Urteil,* Redigiert und herausgegeben von L. Landgrebe, Hamburg, 1948, pp. 26-27.

[76]"Ebenso wesentlich als Aktualität des Lebens ist auch Potentialität, und diese Potentialität ist nicht eine leer Möglichkeit. Jedes cogito, z.B. eine äussere Wahrnehmung oder eine Wiedererinnerung usw. trägt in sich selbst und enthüllbar eine ihm immanente Potentialität möglicher und auf denselben intentionalen Gegenstand beziehbarer und vom Ich her zu verwirklichender Erlebnisse." Husserl, *Cartesianische Meditationen und Pariser Vorträge,* p. 18.

[77]Husserl, *op. cit.,* p. 19.

not what it is, without the moment of potentiality. He is oblivious to the fact that the present presence of an actually appearing phenomenon is not what it is, without the absent presence of a potentially appearing phenomenon. The perceiver *sees* present and absent presences, and this is possible because perception itself essentially includes moments of both actuality and potentiality.[78]

The object of perception shows not only an internal horizon but also an external one. Emphasis should be given not only to the totality of the perception object, but also to the unity of this totality with the entire *field* of perception. Every object appears as a particular "figure" against an horizon: it appears against an horizon of meanings. The apple which I perceive as a unity and totality in an endless series of profiles, only appears as a real apple against the horizon of the table, the fruit bowl, the book or the buffet on which it lies. An apple which does not lie on a table, a fruit bowl, or in the dealer's basket, which does not hang on a tree or is in a child's hand—in brief, an apple which does not appear against a background—simply is not a real apple, not an object of a real perception, but an imaginary apple, the product of a dream or an hallucination.[79] The very perception of an apple essentially includes the field of perception, the background, the horizon.

Because I direct my attention to the apple and not to the child's hand in which it lies, the apple appears to me as an emphasized figure, as a meaning which is, as it were, cut out and brought forward from the background of meanings. The hand, the arm, and the child's body; the floor on which the child stands, the room, and the house, however, are co-constitutive of the real apple. An apple which does not have an external horizon cannot be perceived and is not real.

Accordingly, perception is always perception of the whole thing, taken up in a more-encompassing field, and this field itself is taken up in an horizon of more distant meanings.[80] The

---

[78]Merleau-Ponty, *StC*, pp. 200-203.

[79]"Quand la Gestalt-théorie nous dit qu'une figure sur un fond est la donnée sensible la plus simple que nous puissions obtenir, ce n'est pas là un caractère contingent de la perception de fait, qui nous laisserait libres, dans une analyse idéale, d'introduire la notion d'impression. C'est la définition même du phénomène perceptif, ce sans quoi un phénomène ne peut être dit perception." Merleau-Ponty, *PP*, p. 10.

[80]"La vision est une *pensée assujettie à un certain champ* et c'est là ce qu'on appelle un sens." *PP*, p. 251.

totality of this complex system of ever-evanescent, "nearby" and "distant" meanings, clinging to the ever-evanscent moments of actuality and potentiality of perception, is called the "world" by phenomenology.

Critique of the Traditional Psychology of Perception

Once the original unity of the figure—horizon structure, given in perception, is understood, it is not difficult to see that the psychological explanation of perception by the proponents of elemental psychology fails to do justice to perception as it occurs in reality. Those psychologists assume that perception is *put together* from elementary, insular, pointlike sensations, caused by physico-chemical stimuli.

This explanation offers no prospects, for the simple reason that those alleged elementary sensations have never actually been found.[81] Moreover, pointing to a constellation of stimuli fails to take into account perception as it occurs in reality, it does not express that which is really given in perception. In perception color is never nothing but color, but is always color of something.[82] There is an enormous difference between the woolly red of a rug, the slippery and sticky red of blood, the fresh and radiant red of a healthy face, and the seductive red of painted lips. These differences are not accounted for by pointing to physico-chemical stimuli.[83] It is the totality of the object that is given in perception; and the object does not appear in perception as an agglomerate of stimuli but as a given *meaning*. An agglomeration of stimuli is something else than the fury or sorrow I see in the face of my fellowman. I perceive fury and sorrow as meanings of a face.[84] To reduce meaning to a particular constellation of stimuli implies that I can no longer perceive

---

[81]*PP*, p. 10.

[82]"Une couleur n'est jamais simplement couleur, mais couleur d'un certain objet, et le bleu d'un tapis ne serait pas le même bleu s'il n'était un bleu laineux." *PP*, p. 361.

[83]The so-called *"Konstanz-Annahme,"* the theory which says that stimuli having a certain strength provoke at least a constant "reaction," is in conflict with facts recognized as such by the psychologists. Cf. *PP*, p. 14.

[84]"Définissant une fois de plus ce que nous percevons par les propriétés physiques et chimiques des stimuli qui peuvent agir sur nos appareils sensoriels, l'empirisme exclut de la perception la colère ou la douleur que je lis pourtant sur un visage, la religion dont je saisis pourtant l'essence dans une hésitation ou dans une réticence, la cité dont je connais pourtant la structure dans une attitude de l'agent de ville ou dans le style d'un monument." *PP*. p. 32.

that a landscape or a face is gay, sad, lively, somber, monotonous, or desolate.[85] A happy or gay face is not defined by the physico-chemical qualities of an agglomeration of stimuli; nevertheless, I know that I have seen happy or gay faces.

From the side of the subject also there are innumerable difficulties against the psychological explanation of perception offered by the elemental theory. The perceiving subject is reduced to an agglomerate of insular, pointlike impressions. The elementarists realized, of course, that it was not feasible to point to a stimulus as the cause for each of those impressions. When I read a book or conduct a conversation, I do not receive a separate impression from each written or spoken letter; nevertheless, I read and hear sentences and words. My sensitive "receiving and registering apparatus" does not receive stimuli "messages" from the other side of the table and from its underside; nevertheless, I know that I am perceiving a table. When I perceive my attic room, I receive only stimuli from the walls in front of me and at my sides, not from the wall behind me and the roof; nevertheless, I know that my room has four sides and that it is an attic room.

These difficulties did not induce the elementarists to abandon their stimuli theory: they thought that they could overcome these objections by the introduction of a new theory, viz., the hypothesis of complements through association, reproduction, or other similar *ad hoc* inventions.

The underlying idea is obvious: perception *may* not be perception of reality's totality, perception of the totality *may* not be primary, but *has to* be built up of psychical elements. In other words, the psyche *has to* be composed as things of nature are composed, the contents of consciousness *have to* be elements and have to be treated in the same way as physical sciences treats its elements. This is the unconditional demand imposed by the "scientific" character of psychology.[86]

Meanwhile the theory of association or reproduction, as the explanation of the "complements" demanded by the theory of stimuli, presupposes what it intends to explain. In the termi-

---

85*PP*, pp. 31-32.
86"Man ist sicher in der Ueberzeugung, dass in prinzipieller Allgemeinheit betrachtet, die Methode aller Erfahrungswissenschaften ein und dieselbe sei, in der Psychologie also dieselbe wie in der Wissenschaft von der physischen Natur." Husserl, "Philosophie als strenge Wissenschaft," *Logos,* I(1910-11), p. 309.

nology of Claparède,[87] association is conceived as a psychical "cord" connecting the pointlike impressions. Because the impressions are connected, a very fragmentary stimulation from without suffices to reproduce the whole, the totality of the perceived. In this way the primacy of the isolated impressions could be maintained, it was thought, over the perception of the totality.

This theory presupposes what it intends to explain. For the impressions are associated in many ways with other impressions. Hence the reproduction of a totality could occur in many ways. How, then, does it happen that precisely *this* totality is reproduced? On the occasion of a fragmentary stimulation, several totalities could be formed: how do the actual impressions "know" which impressions must be called up to complement the whole? If it is merely a matter of chance, and there is no "reason" why *these* and not *those* impressions are called from memory to complement the actual impressions, the theory does not explain perception, for chance is no explanation.[88] If, on the other hand, there is a "reason" to reproduce *this* and not *that* totality, this implies a certain "knowing" of the totality. By the very fact, the explanation through association is made superfluous, for it then presupposes the knowledge of the totality which it wished to explain.[89]

Accordingly, elemental psychology also must affirm the priority of the perceived object, for the theory of association and reproduction presupposes this priority.[90] If we hold fast to perception as it occurs, we must affirm the priority of the totality; and if one does not hold fast to perception as it occurs, one implicitly affirms this priority by presupposing it.

This brings us back to our starting point: it is a contradiction to replace ordinary everyday experience by that of physical science.[91] It is a contradiction to replace the world of everyday experience by a system of meanings disclosed by one or the

---

[87]E. Claparède, *L'association des Idées,* Paris, 1913, p. 7.

[88]Merleau-Ponty, *PP,* p. 22.

[89]"Au moment où l'évocation des souvenirs est rendue possible, elle devient superflue, puisque le travail qu'on en attend est déjà fait." *PP.* p. 27.

[90]"Si nous nous en tenons aux phénomènes, l'unité de la chose dans la perception n'est pas construite par l'association, mais, condition de l'association, elle précède les recoupements qui la vérifient et la déterminent, elle se précède elle-même." *PP.* p. 24.

[91]*PP,* Avant-propos, pp. II-V.

other science.[92]   Philosophical reflection demands a return to original experience and to the original world, stripped of the superstructure of theories which have been added to it by the sciences.   This return is called "phenomenological reduction."

The "Phenomenological Reduction" and the "Lived World"

The aim of Husserl's phenomenology always was to find a ground and foundation for any statement whatsoever of the positive sciences.   This aim implied the conviction that scientific statements are in need of a ground or foundation—in other words, that they do not have that ground in themselves.   For Husserl this conviction did not mean that the sciences should be rejected, but that many questions are implied and, in principle, even answered in the pursuit of the sciences, even though these sciences *themselves* cannot even *ask* those questions.   The physicist *as* physicist does not ask about the essence of his physical knowledge, he does not inquire into the subject and the specific object of physics or the conditions which make their relationship possible.[93]   *As* a physicist, he need *not* ask these questions; thus there is a standpoint from which one can say that the pursuit of physics is a "naive" occupation.[94]   Obviously, this does not mean that the physicist is uncritical, but it does mean that an entirely different way of being critical is possible and necessary.   The physicist is critical with respect to his specialty's scientific experience, but he does not ask himself what this scientific experience itself is and even less what experience *tout court* is.[95]   These questions are philosophical.

Philosophy, then, must disclose the ultimate ground of scientific judgments.   It is the "radical science," [96] or rather it ought to be that science, for Husserl is convinced that *de facto* philosophy is not such a science.[97]   It is the philosopher's task

---

92"Nous l'avons vu: on ne peut pas reconstituer ainsi, en combinant des significations idéales (stimuli, récepteurs, circuits associatifs) la structure de l'expérience perceptive." Merleau-Ponty, *StC*, p. 235.

93E. Husserl, "Philosophie als strenge Wissenschaft," *Logos* I(1910-11), pp. 299-300.

94"Alle Naturwissenschaft ist ihren Ausgangspunkten nach naiv." Husserl, *art. cit.*, p. 298.

95"Aber wie sehr diese Art der Erfahrungskritik uns befriedigen mag, solange wir *in* der Naturwissenschaft stehen und in ihrer Einstellung denken - eine ganz andere Erfahrungskritik ist noch möglich und unerlässlich, eine Kritik, die die gesamte Erfahrung überhaupt und das erfahrungswissenschaftliche Denken zugleich in Frage stellt." Husserl, *art. cit.*, p. 299.

96Husserl, *art. cit.*, p. 340.

97Husserl, *art. cit.*, pp. 289-291.

to express what experience *tout court* is. But philosophy has been side-tracked because it adheres to a view of experience-which *certainly* cannot be held to be the ground and foundation of scientific judgments. Since Descartes and Locke philosophy has been convinced that experience is a kind of mirroring and that *the* system of objective mirroring is to be found in the physical sciences. Philosophy has lapsed into scientism, so that it can no longer be considered to be the "radical science." Authentic philosophizing is entirely different from the way of thinking proper to positive science,[98] but the philosophers have failed to notice this difference. Husserl's call, then, "Back to the things themselves," does not mean that the sciences do not speak of "the things themselves," but was addressed to philosophy: philosophical thinking had turned away from reality.[99]

Husserl's search for an authentic, philosophical conception of the *cogito*, of knowledge and of experience, led him to the idea of intentionality. Some of this idea's implications were described above and they pointed to the answer to be given to the question about the importance of the "phenomenological reduction." Before describing its function, however, we would like to devote a few words to a particular view of this reduction which in phenomenology itself is no longer acceptable.

When Husserl defined the subject-as-*cogito* as intentionality, he "bracketed" the actual existence of the worldly meaning to which the subject is orientated. This is the first sense in which Husserl used the term "reduction": the "bracketing of being." [100] This reduction consists in this: Husserl suspended his judgment about the actual existence of the worldly meaning.[101] What, we may ask, induced him to suspend judgment in this matter?

According to De Waelhens, the nineteenth century theory of knowledge led him to do this. This theory struggled with

---

[98]"Die Philosophie aber liegt in einer völlig neuen Dimension. Sie bedarf völlig neuer Ausgangspunkte und einer völlig neuen Methode, die sie von jeder 'natürlichen' Wissenschaft prinzipiell unterscheidet." Husserl, *Die Idee der Phänomenologie*, Fünf Vorlesungen, *Husserliana*, II, p. 24.

[99]A. De Waelhens, "De la phénoménologie à l'existentialisme," *Le choix, le monde, l'existence*, Grenoble-Paris, n.d., p. 42.

[100]*Ideen I*, p. 65.

[101]"Bei jeder erkenntnistheoretischen Untersuchung . . . ist die erkenntnis-theoretische Reduktion zu vollziehen, d.h. alle dabei mitspielende Transzendenz mit dem Index der Ausschaltung zu behaften, oder mit dem Index der Gleichgiltigkeit, der erkenntnistheoretischen Nullität, mit einem Index der da sagt: die Existenz aller dieser Transzendenzen, ob ich sie glauben mag oder nicht, geht mir hier nichts an, hier ist nicht der Ort, darüber zu urteilen, das bleibt ganz ausser Spiel." Husserl, *Die Idee der Phänomenologie*, p. 39.

the "critical problem," i.e., with the question whether an external
reality corresponds with the contents, representations and concepts of the encapsulated, isolated, and closed *cogito*.[102]   For
idealism meaning is a content of the *cogito,* and this content in
its being is not distinct from the *cogito*; for realism meaning
is totally divorced from the *cogito* and its being is wholly foreign
to the *cogito*.   Husserl did not wish to become involved in the
controversy between idealists and realists because he did not
wish to get caught in this bottomless quagmire.   He thought
that his phenomenology could succeed, that he could perform
his phenomenological analyses, even if he did not choose sides
and did not make any assertion about the being of meaning.
For this reason he "bracketed" the ontological status of meaning.

Husserl himself did not yet see at that time that his definition
of knowledge as intentionality made it impossible to "bracket"
the being of meaning.   Whoever accepts intentionality, however,
has already decided about the being of meaning.   Husserl did
not yet see that the "bracketing" of the being of meaning is possible only if one starts from the supposition that the *cogito* is an
isolated reality, filled with contents.   But it is precisely this supposition which is rejected when one affirms intentionality.[103]
Only gradually did Husserl become aware of this inconsistency
in his own ideas.   As a result, the "bracketing" of the being of
meaning occurred less and less frequently in his work, and finally
it disappeared completely.   Unsurprisingly, therefore, there remains no trace of it in the works of Heidegger and Merleau-
Ponty.

While the "bracketing" of the being of meaning occurred
less and less in Husserl, he increasingly emphasized the necessity of the phenomenological reduction.   This implies that his
views about the nature of the phenomenological reduction underwent a change.   Husserl remained faithful to the aim of his
phenomenology, viz., to find a foundation for any scientific statement whatsoever.   He gradually began to see that all scientific
statements presuppose a much more fundamental experience
than scientific experience: that those statements, without explicitly admitting it, "live" by virtue of this much more fundamental
experience, and that precisely for this reason they know what

---

[102]De Waelhens, *Une philosophie de l'ambiguïté, L'existentialisme de
Maurice Merleau-Ponty,* Louvain, 1951, pp. 89-93.
[103]De Waelhens, *op. cit.,* pp. 89-90.

they are speaking about.[104]   This much more fundamental experience is the subject-as-*cogito* with its many different attitudes, and the correlate of that experience is the "lived world." [105]

Conceived as the return to our most original experience of our most original world, the phenomenological reduction is an essential part of phenomenological philosophy.   This reduction is performed by those who place themselves within *existence* and recognize the implications of this step.   By performing the reduction, one finds indeed a ground for any scientific statement whatsoever.   When there is question of perceiving a blooming tree in the meadow, I can call all kinds of sciences to my assistance, but I only know what the results of all those scientific investigations mean when I know what is meant by the "ordinary" perception of a blooming tree in the meadow.   If the sciences do not ultimately speak of a world in which the sun rises and sets, a world in which there is a difference between a dead man and a murdered man, a world in which girls are pretty and boys handsome, a world in which, by simply going on vacation, I can learn to know what a sea, a river, or a mountain is, then even the most intelligent men of science do not know what they are speaking of.[106]   The sciences do not have a ground in themselves.   They do not know of what they speak unless they accept that ultimately they are merely explicitating "moments" of an experience that is much more original than scientific experience, and of a world that is much more original than the world disclosed by the sciences.[107]   The primarily real and objective world is the world in which the physicist is happily or

---

[104]De Waelhens, *op. cit.,* p. 91.

[105]". . . Allen Zwecken, auch den theoretischen der 'objektiven' Wissenschaften, denn darin liegen ja die 'Selbstverständlichkeiten', die der Wissenschaftler beständig gebraucht - universal gesprochen, die Welt dieser selbstverständlich verständlich seienden und in der Weise der *doxa* als wahr und wirklich auszuweisenden Dinge ist der Boden, auf dem alle objektive Wissenschaft erst sich entfalten kann; mit einem Worte die Lebenswelt, diese 'bloss' subjektive und relative, in ihrem nie stillhaltenden Fluss der Seinsgeltungen, deren Verwandlungen und Korrekturen ist - so paradox das erscheinen mag - der Boden, auf dem die objektive Wissenschaft ihre Gebilde 'endgültiger', 'ewiger' Wahrheiten, der ein für allemal und für jedermann absolut gültigen Urteile aufbaut." Husserl, *Die Krisis der Europäischen Wissenschaften und die transzendentale Phänomenologie, Husserliana,* VI, p. 465.

[106]"Si éloignée que soit de la perception la physique moderne, celle-ci serait absolument 'en l'air', si, en définitive, elle ne nous expliquait que les pommes tombent des arbres mais n'y remontent jamais, que l'eau des glaciers descend vers la mer sans jamais gravir la pente qui conduit au sommet." De Waelhens, *La philosophie et les expériences naturelles,* La Haye, 1961, p. 52.

[107]Husserl, *op. cit.,* pp. 126-129.

unhappily married, in which he has or does not have good friends, in which he is warm or cold, regardless of what the thermometer says, and in which, just before sunset, he managed to buy a copy of a book on astronomy which explains that the sun does not set but stands still.[108]

In the lived world there is a great difference between the soft red of a rug, the sticky red of drying blood, the healthy red of a young and rosy face, and the seductive red of painted lips.[109] If science speaks of "movements of the larynx and sound waves," the man of science does not know that these words refer to speech unless he admits that he knows what speech is because of the fact that previously he has spoken with someone. If science speaks of "certain motions of the nostrils and certain contractions of the corners of the mouth, accompanied by twinkling of the eyes," the man of science only knows that there is question of a smile because of the fact that he has previously experienced what it means that someone smiled at him.

The "return to the things themselves" is the return to the lived world, and this return implies the recognition of the *existent* subject-as-*cogito* with his many standpoints as the most original experience of the world.[110] This recognition is the execution of the phenomenological reduction. The experience of the lived world used to be—and still is—characterized by the sciences as "merely" subjective and relative; in actual fact, however, this experience is the "ultimate foundation." [111] It is thanks to this experience that the men of positive science know what they really talk about. Thus it will not do to replace the meanings of the lived world by a system of meanings disclosed by the sciences and to substitute the experience of positive science for the much more original experience upon which scientific experience is based.[112] Scientism is a philosophy of experience

---

[108]De Waelhens, "Signification de la phénoménologie," *Diogène*, V (1954), p. 59.

[109]Merleau-Ponty, *PP*, p. 361.

[110]"Revenir aux choses mêmes, c'est revenir à ce monde avant la connaissance dont la connaissance parle toujours, et à l'égard duquel toute détermination scientifique est abstraite, signitive et dépendante, comme la géographie à l'égard du paysage où nous avons d'abord appris ce que c'est qu'une forêt, une prairie ou une rivière." *PP*, Avant-propos, p. III.

[111]Husserl, *op. cit.*, p. 127.

[112]"Tout l'univers de la science est construit sur le monde vécu et si nous voulons penser la science elle-même avec rigueur, en apprécier exactement le sens et la portée, il nous faut réveiller d'abord cette expérience du monde dont elle est l'expression seconde." *PP*, Avant-propos, pp. II-III.

which disregards its own origin,[113] and a science without philosophy does not know of what it speaks.[114]

4. SENSITIVE AND SPIRITUAL KNOWING

The reader must have noticed that we have not yet mentioned the distinction between sensitive and spiritual knowing, which is commonplace in treatises devoted to human knowledge. We do not wish to insinuate that there is no ground for making such a distinction, but would like to point out that it is often incorrectly presented. All too often that distinction is, at the very start, simply posited as, e.g., the difference between sensitive seeing, hearing, smelling, etc., on the one hand, and intellectual understanding on the other. Next, the authors simply pass on to a consideration of sensitive knowing, *divorced* from intellectual knowing. In this way the impression is created that the distinct ways of knowing are not only distinguishable but also separable, so that one can speak of seeing without speaking of understanding.[115] Seeing, so it is said, is found only in animals, but not understanding; hence it is by the latter that man is distinct from the animal.

Such a way of representing the matter is contrary to the most immediate phenomenological evidence. It is utterly impossible to isolate certain "moments" of knowing from each other, and for this reason there is no justification for representing them as if they could be isolated.[116] There is no *purely sensitive* seeing in man, a seeing that would not be permeated with spiritual consciousness or understanding. If, then, the term "seeing" is meant to refer to a purely sensitive activity of knowing, man does not have any sight. Thus man and animal are not the same in this respect.[117]

On the other hand, it should be recognized that among an-

---

[113]"La science classique est une perception qui oublie ses origines et se croit achevée." *PP*, p. 69.

[114]"Une science sans philosophie ne saurait pas, à la lettre, de quoi elle parle." Merleau-Ponty, *SNS*, p. 195.

[115]Ch. Boyer, *Cursus philosophiae*, II, pp. 9-64.

[116]Consequently, we may not say: "Manifestum est enim intellectum incipere ubi sensus desinit." *De principio individuationis* (Mandonnet ed. of St. Thomas' *opuscula*, vol. 5, Paris, 1927, p. 194). The authenticity of this work is rejected by Mandonnet. It is rather striking, however, that Johannes Capreolus, the *Princeps Thomistarum*, quotes precisely this text to express the view of the Master. Cf. *Defensiones theologiae in IV Sentent.*, dist. 10, q. 4, *ad* 6 (Paban-Pegués ed., Turin, 1906, p. 212).

[117]Man *as* man does not agree in *any* respect with the animal.

imals there also occurs something which more or less resembles
that which in man is seeing. The behavior of an animal cannot
be understood without certain "shadows of knowledge." [118] But
if this animal seeing is a *purely* sensitive form of knowing, man
does *not* know what it is because he has no experience of such
acts of knowing.[119]

A Difficult Distinction

If the above-mentioned distinction is not posited *a priori*, it
becomes difficult to *find* it in reality. Thus it is not surprising
that many philosophers reject it entirely. Their position, however, is the opposite extreme and, likewise, phenomenologically
unjustifiable. For it cannot escape my attention that my knowing a worldly object reveals different "moments" which are irreducible to one another. To show this, let us return to the
perception of *this* table.

I actually see only one particular profile of this table because I occupy a particular standpoint with respect to the table.
I can also actually perceive a different profile, but I must then
change my standpoint. There is a relationship between the actually appearing profile and my standpoint in space. The perception, then, of this table here is determined by spatial
conditions.

These spatial conditions are, at the same time, temporal
conditions. *Now* I perceive *this* profile, but my perception of
this profile, appearing *now*, intrinsically refers to past perceptions of other profiles from other standpoints which I occupied
and to future perceptions of again other profiles from standpoints which I will occupy. Perceiving consciousness, therefore,
is the synthesis of present, past and future, i.e., of temporality.
Perceiving consciousness, then, is determined by spatio-temporal
conditions, i.e., I see *here and now* something other than I will
see *later there* or saw *earlier yonder*. When the spatio-temporal

---

[118]F.J.J. Buytendijk, "Schaduwen van het kennen," *Tijdschrift voor Philosophie*, I (1939), pp. 5-28.

[119]It is rather striking that authors who divorce sense knowledge from
spiritual knowledge and attribute sense knowledge primarily to animals prove
several of their statements about animal knowledge "from the testimony of
consciousness." On the one hand, they feel that it is impossible to place themselves "inside" animal cognition, but on the other they forget that the "testimony of consciousness" does not refer to animal cognition. See, e.g., Paul
Siwek, *Psychologia metaphysica*, Rome, 1948, pp. 89-214.

conditions of perception change, perception itself also is modified.

This is not all, however, While I *now*, from *this* standpoint, perceive a particular profile of the table, I also *understand what a table is* and I experience that this understanding does not change when the spatial and temporal conditions are modified. With respect to this understanding the phases of temporality and the standpoint of the perceiving subject in space are accidental. Through *every* appearing profile, from *every* standpoint in space, in *every* phase of temporality, I unchangeably *understand* what a table is.

The same can be said with respect to perception itself. I *understand* what perception is, independently of the spatio-temporal conditions of perception: the understanding of perception does not change when the spatio-temporal conditions of perception are modified. It is only because I have a *concept* of perception that a phenomenology of perception is possible. A phenomenology of emotional life, the imagination, the will, etc. presupposes an implicit *concept* of these modes of *existing*.[120]

Knowledge, then, contains at least "two" moments which are not equivalent. On the one hand, my consciousness depends on conditions of time and space, but on the other it does not depend on them. These two moments, therefore, cannot be wholly identical; otherwise one and the same reality would simultaneously, and in the same respect, be characterized by opposite characteristics. Understanding transcends the relativity affecting sense perception. The aspect of the terminus of the encounter, i.e., that which appears to my sensitively perceiving look, has a spatio-temporal relationship to me. The noema of my understanding also has a relationship to me, but it is not affected by the relationship to spatio-temporal standpoints.

A Faulty Conception

It is impossible, therefore, to obliterate the distinction between sense perception and understanding but, at the same time,

---

[120]"Sans toutefois renoncer à l'idée d'expérience (le principe de la phénoménologie est d'aller aux choses elles-mêmes et la base de sa méthode est l'intuition eidétique) au moins faut-il l'assouplir et faire une place à l'expérience des essences et des valeurs; il faut reconnaître même que seules les essences permettent de classer et d'inspecter les faits. Si nous ne recourrions implicitement à l'essence d'émotion, il nous serait impossible de distinguer parmi la masse des faits psychiques, le groupe particulier des faits d'émotivité." Sartre, *Esquisse d'une théorie des émotions*, Paris, 3rd ed., 1948, p. 7.

it is very difficult to understand this distinction correctly. "On the one hand," my consciousness is consciousness of something which is, of that by which a thing is what it is, of the essence, nature or quiddity of something.[121] "On the other hand," my consciousness is consciousness of the "this," the "here and now" of something.[122] Thus one could easily be tempted to isolate these distinct aspects. Being conscious of what something is, is called "to understand" (*intelligere*)[123] or "spiritual consciousness"; while with respect to the "this, here and now," one speaks of seeing, hearing, feeling, or sensitive consciousness. Such a procedure, however, easily is inclined to put the two "moments" of consciousness "side by side" or "one after the other"—as if the spirit were not present to the "this, here and now": the spirit "only" seizes the essence of something, and the "this, here and now" is merely accidental to this essence. Sensitive knowledge, on the other hand, would be limited to the concrete and changeable aspects of the essence. As a matter of fact, however, human knowing is undivided; my seeing, hearing, feeling, etc. are permeated with spiritual consciousness or understanding. If, then, an animal is not a spiritually-living being, I may not ascribe human seeing, hearing or feeling to it. On the other hand, it is also certain that my spiritual understanding is never isolated from sense knowledge.[124]

The Concept

The proper character of what we have called understanding or man's spiritual consciousness manifests itself even more strikingly if we pay attention to its "result" or "terminus." Through my knowing, a particular worldly thing is raised above the nothing-for-me. Through my understanding it is constituted into a certain essence or "whatness"-for-me; it has received an intelligible meaning for me. This is not all, however. The essence of a thing imposes itself upon me: I cannot arbitrarily

---

121"Objectum intellectus nostri, secundum praesentem vitae statum, est quidditas rei materialis quam a phantasmatibus abstrahit." *S.Th.*, I, q. 85, a. 8.

122". . . sensus est singularium, intellectus autem universalium." *S.Th.*, I, q. 85, a. 3.

123". . . nomen intellectus quamdam intimam cognitionem importat: dicitur enim *intelligere*, quasi *intus legere*. Et hoc manifeste patet considerantibus, differentiam intellectus et sensus: nam cognitio sensitiva occupatur circa qualitates sensibiles exteriores; cognitio autem intellectiva penetrat usque ad essentiam rei. Objectum enim intellectus est quod quid est. . . ." *S.Th.*, II-II, q. 8, a. 1.

124*S.Th.*, I, q. 84, a. 7.

give any meaning to the world. A chair represents another intelligible meaning than does a cigar or a plant. My understanding, then, is a dialog between me and the essence of the thing which I understand.

This dialog finds a provisional terminus in the expression I give to what I understand. That which I understand imposes itself upon me, it is interiorized, assimilated in and by my understanding, and it is embodied and expressed in language. This expression—which Scholasticism called "the word" (*verbum*)—results from my understandingly-being-in-the-world, and is known as "idea" or "concept." [125] The result of the understanding of this tree, this chair, or this cigar is the concept "tree," "chair," or "cigar," in which the intelligibility imposing itself upon me is expressed.[126] Through my understanding I dwell in my world as a world of essences, a system of intelligible meanings, but insofar as I express that intelligibility in my ideas and embody it in words, I dwell in a "world of ideas."

We come very close here to Plato's theory: there certainly is a "world of ideas." Plato was right when he saw that the knower is not merely able to absorb the variable impressions of changeable things, that he is not merely open to the mutable and variable shape of things. Plato realized that man also "possesses" immutable ideas. He was puzzled, however, how such ideas could be acquired, because—being influenced by Heraclitus—he could not see anything else in the world than change. From the encounter with the world no unchangeable ideas could ever arise, Plato thought, and for this reason he posited an independent world of ideas, contemplated by the soul in a mysterious pre-existence. By admitting this contemplation of ideal essences, prior to the soul's enclosure in the body, Plato at least safeguarded the possibility of something which *de facto* occurs, viz., man's possession of immutable ideas.

It is obvious today, however, that such a myth is superfluous. There is a world of ideas, but this world is not autonomous. The

---

[125]Sometimes a distinction is made between concept and idea—namely, when the term *idea* is reserved for concepts which guide man's *agere* and *facere*. For instance, an artist works out an "idea." For us here the two terms are synonymous. Regarding other terms to indicate concepts, see J. Maritain, *Formal Logic*, New York, 1937, p. 17, note 3.

[126]"Quicumque autem intelligit, ex hoc ipso quod intelligit, procedit aliquid intra ipsum, quod est conceptio rei intellectae, ex ejus notitia procedens. Quam quidem conceptionem vox significat, et dicitur verbum cordis significatum verbo vocis." *S.Th.*, I, q. 27, a. 1.

world of ideas is produced by me and my world. My subjec-
tivity-as-*cogito* is a dwelling in the world on "two" levels, and
"one" of these "two" levels is a dwelling in the world of essences.
I give expression to this dwelling through and in the immutable
idea, which I embody in language. In this way, I dwell in a
"world of ideas."

While discussing understanding and calling it "spiritual,"
while writing about the concept and calling it "immutable," we,
nevertheless, experience a certain reluctance to use these terms.
The reason is that "spiritual" and "immutable" are terms which
still bear the marks of a long and unfortunate history. One
could object that there is no spiritual knowing because man is
whatever he is solely "on the basis of materiality." This objection, however, can be sustained only if one starts from the conviction that the term "spiritual" necessarily refers only to *"purely*
spiritual." Obviously the author does *not* take the term in this
sense; for this reason he can use it to indicate that the one and
undivided human attitude of knowing implies "two" moments.
The "spiritual" moment cannot be reduced to the cognitive moment which is determined by conditions of space and time. In a
similar way we may also call the concept "immutable." This
term does not deny the historicity of human understanding and of
the concept, but merely expresses that, unlike sensitive knowing,
understanding does not change with the change in spatio-temporal conditions. The perspectivism of man's spatio-temporally
situated sensitive knowing is transcended in and through understanding.[127]

The Abstracting and Universalizing Character of Understanding

Our intellectual, understanding dwelling in the world implies
a special organization of the world. When I really *understand*
what a house, a plant, a court of justice, a stop light, or an island
is, I leave out of consideration the concretely individual, the

---

[127]"En un certain sens, le perspectivisme de l'expérience immédiate est
surmonté. Car si l'expérience perceptive est perspective, le fait qu'elle peut
être regardée indirectement et par l'intermédiarie du moi réfléchi lève déjà
de quelque manière ce perspectivisme. Se voir en situation n'est plus simplement une situation, même si cette vue est inséparable de la vue de la situation
qui en fournit l'occasion. La possibilité de réflexion qui vient d'être posée
comporte donc une certaine *Aufhebung* de la perspective." De Waelhens,
Une philosophie de l'ambiguïté, L'existentialisme de Maurice Merleau-Ponty,
Louvain, 1951, p. 401.

"this, here and now" which, nonetheless, characterizes every object. A certain aspect of the object considered—that which is essential to it—is drawn to the foreground of my *existence's* field of presence, and the concrete and individual characteristics of the object are pushed into the background. In my concept, only that is expressed which in my field of presence figures as the foreground, and the background is left out of consideration. Thus my concept "house," "stop light," or "island" does not say anything about the concrete and individual "this, here and now" of those objects. This means that my understanding is abstractive and my concept abstract.[128]

We have met a similar situation before when we spoke of the "figure—horizon" structure of perception. If I look for the biggest apple in the fruit bowl, the apples come forward as pronounced figures in a field of presence of nearby and distant meanings, consisting of plums, bananas, etc., while one of the apples detaches itself, as it were, and places itself present as the biggest against the horizon of other smaller apples. The figure—horizon structure, then, has already become differentiated on several levels. The same must be said, however, with respect to the biggest apple which I take. Because I looked for the *biggest* apple, other meanings, such as color, juiciness and savor—which are qualities of the same apple—fell into the background of my field of presence: in this field now only size occurs as a figure.

In this matter one could begin to speak of abstraction, for I have "ab-stracted" a certain meaning from the network of nearby and distant meanings which is my field of presence.[129] In the strict sense of the term, however, "abstraction" is used only to characterize understanding. When I understand something, my understanding "ab-stracts" the essence of the thing from the "this, here and now," the individual.[130] In this way the essence is brought forward as a pronounced figure, while the individual

---

[128]Cf. Dondeyne, "L'abstraction," *Revue Néoscolastique de Philosophie*, 1938, pp. 5-20, 330-373; L. B. Geiger, "Abstraction et séparation d'après S. Thomas," *Revue des Sciences philosophiques et théologiques*, 31 (1947), pp. 3-40; G. Van Riet, "La théorie thomiste de l'abstraction," *Revue philosophique de Louvain*, 1952, pp. 353-393.

[129]"Et hoc possumus videre per simile in sensu. Visus enim videt colorem pomi sine ejus odore. Si ergo quaeratur ubi sit color, qui videtur sine odore, manifestum est quod color, qui videtur, non est nisi in pomo. Sed quod sit sine odore perceptus, hoc accidit ei ex parte visus, in quantum in visu est similtudo coloris, et non odoris." *S.Th.*, I, q. 85, a. 2, ad 2.

[130]*S.Th.*, I, q. 85, a. 1.

characteristics of this figure are shifted to the horizon of my field of presence. Thus the result, the terminus of my understanding, i.e., the concept, does not *express* the individual character of the terminus of my encounter. My world of ideas, therefore, contains only one abstract idea "house," "stop light," "island," or "horse." The abstract concept retains only an implicit reference to the individual, in the sense that it connotes that, of necessity, the concept can be realized only in the individual. The abstract concept is an "open" concept.[131]

The fact, however, that my concepts are always abstract does not at all mean that I do not know the individual. I could not even assert my ignorance of the individual without contradicting myself. For I observe that my understanding leaves "this, here and now" out of consideration, which I would be unable to do if I were not conscious of the individual. Whenever I know something, it is *always primarily* an individual something to which I am present. But because I cannot seize the individual's reality in a single concept, I need many conceptual expressions to state what the concrete terminus of my cognitive encounter is. The concept is always an expression of the concrete individual, and, consequently, is essentially a predicate.

The abstract-conceptual expression of the terminus encountered by my act of knowing does not merely divide the original unity of this terminus into fragments. In a certain sense, abstractive understanding also establishes unity in the field of presence of the *existent* subject-as-*cogito*. If I stand in reality "without understanding," this reality is for me a chaotic agglomerate of concrete, individual, and unique things. If I do not *understand* what a house is, every concrete house is an enigma for me. My understanding of a house, however, is such that it brings about a kind of "com-prehending" of "all" houses.[132] "All" houses are com-prehended in my understanding, not as individual concrete things, but as *essentially* in agreement with one another. In and by my understanding, I draw a specific meaning to the foreground of my field of presence, but this implies that a specific *region* of meanings which are essentially in agreement are put together. For one who dwells

---

131G. Van Riet, *art. cit.,* p. 360.
132"Etymologically, to 'comprehend' as Brunschvicg pointed out, means 'to take simultaneously,' to establish relationships, to bring back the diversity of data to the unity of an idea or system of ideas." Dondeyne, *Contemporary European Thought and Christian Faith,* p. 152.

"understandingly" in the world, the world is composed of specific "regions of being," in which things agree with one another by a specific "being such." [133] Thus, "understandingly" standing in the world means that the chaotic character of the world is overcome, that there come unity and interconnection into the world, and that man can move in this world on the basis of a kind of "transparency" of the world.[134]

The fact that understanding is abstractive implies that the subject-as-*cogito* always dwells in specific regions of being. The "result" of understanding is the abstract concept. But this concept is, at the same time, also universal or objectively general.[135] It can be affirmed of many, viz., of all objects pertaining to a specific region of being; for to understand *is* to express the meaning of such a region.

The Abstract Concept is Not a Schematic Image

Have we now perhaps put too much emphasis on man's so-called "spiritual consciousness," as if spiritual consciousness or understanding is isolated from sensitive consciousness? Is there, then, no longer anything of the sensitive consciousness to be found in the terminus of understanding? I see, hear, feel "this, here and now," and *in* my seeing, hearing, and feeling, I understand the essence of something, expressed in a concept that is abstract. But, when matters are presented in this way, what remains of the original assertion that the sensitive and the spiritual consciousness are inseparable "moments" of an undivided cognitive attitude? [136]

We wish to repeat here emphatically that the sensitive and spiritual consciousness are distinct but not separable. In the

---

133Max Müller, *Sein und Geist,* Tübingen, 1940, p. 33.
134"Im Vorstellen, z.B. einer Linde, Buche, Tanne als Baum, wird das je einzelne Angeschaute als das und das bestimmt, aus dem Hinblick auf solches, was 'für viele gilt'. Diese Vielgültigkeit kennzeichnet zwar eine Vorstellung als Begriff, trifft jedoch noch nicht dessen ursprüngliches Wesen. Denn diese Vielgültigkeit gründet ihrerseits als abgeleiteter Charakter darin dass im Begriff je das Eine vorgestellt ist, in dem mehrere Gegenstände übereinkommen. Begriffliches Vorstellen ist Übereinkommenlassen von Mehreren in diesem Einen. Die Einheit dieses Einen muss daher im begrifflichen Vorstellen vorgreifend herausgesehen und allen bestimmenden Aussagen über das Mehrere vorgehalten werden. Das vorgängige Heraussehen des Einen, darin Mehreres soll übereinkommen können, ist der Grundakt der Begriffsbildung." Heidegger, *Kant und das Problem der Metaphysik,* Frankfurt, a.M., 1951, pp. 53-54.
135Heidegger, *op. cit.,* p. 47.
136J. D. Robert, "Essai d'une description phénoménologique élémentaire du connaître," *Revue philosophique de Louvain,* 58 (1960), pp. 286-288.

expression of what I have appropriated in my encounter with things so much of man's sensitive consciousness remains that many philosophers do not even manage to distinguish the two above-mentioned aspects of expression.[137]   If I perceive a box of matches on my desk and then close my eyes, I am able to picture or represent to myself this box in its individuality.   This representation is a way of expression, but it is an individual way, for it is the image of *this* box, lying here and now on my desk. This image is certainly not the concept "box of matches," for it is not the abstract expression of the box's essence.   *In* the seeing of the individual box, and also *in* its individual image, the abstractive understanding of what a box is is realized.   I give expression to the box's essence in my concept, but the abstract expression cannot be isolated from the individual representation; [138] nevertheless, it is not identical with it.[139]

Empiricists such as Hume think that, strictly speaking, there is no difference between the concept and the image.   Every impression from without is wholly individual—an impression of *this* box or *that* box.   Nevertheless, I use only one term to indicate all those impressions, viz., the general term "box of matches."   If one asks by what right, we answer that we do this because, in my experience of this box or that box, I acquire the abstract concept "box of matches," and in my understanding I leave behind the *this* or *that*.[140]

The empiricists, however, cannot agree with this answer. They are convinced that our so-called abstract concept is nothing but an impoverished and debilitated image of individual things, in which all the striking features of individuality have simply faded away.   Some of them, such as Galton, appeal to a kind of merging of superimposed individual impressions: through the overlapping of the individual impressions, the combined result of these impressions becomes a vague kind of schema, a schematic image of the many individual realities.   What we have

---

[137]A. Marc, *Psychologie réflexive,* Paris, 1949, I, p. 167.
[138]*S.Th.* I, q. 84, a. 7.
[139]"Le contenu de la pensée n'est pas l'image qui lui est connexe.   La pensée dépasse l'image, bien qu'elle s'en accompagne nécessairement." Robert, *art. cit.,* p. 286.
[140]"Der Gegenstand einer Anschauung, der je ein Einzelnes ist, bestimmt sich jedoch als 'das und das' in einer 'allgemeinen Vorstellung', d.h. im Begriff." Heidegger, *op. cit.,* p. 53.

called the abstract concept and distinguished from the image is, according to empiricism, merely a vague schematic image.[141]

We encounter here again an insufficient explicitation of unreflected reality. The phenomenologist must give expression to knowledge *as knowledge occurs* in reality. Now, it is undoubtedly true that knowledge contains a schematizing aspect.[142] In very many cases man does not even succeed in going beyond a kind of schematization. But this schematizing representation certainly is not the abstract expression of a thing's essence.[143] The cases in which man does not go beyond a schematic image are obviously cases in which there is no understanding. An anthropology, for example, which would restrict itself to the orderly arrangement of schematic images of individual human beings could produce only trivial statements about man. The schematization of the individual produces only an individual image: although this image is schematized, it is not an *abstract* conceptual expression of what a thing is.[144] Even a theory about the schematizing aspect contained in human knowledge is not possible without a *concept* of schematization.[145] This understanding of schematization itself is not a schematization.[146]

"Surveying the World"

The difference between schematic image and abstract concept is based on the distinction between sense consciousness and

---

[141]R. Jolivet, *Traité de Philosophie* II, *Psychologie*, Lyon, 1945, pp. 435-437.

[142]*S.Th.* II-II, q. 173, a. 2

[143]A. D. Sertillanges, *Saint Thomas d'Aquin*, II, Paris, 1925, p. 141.

[144]Marc, *op. cit.*, p. 253.

[145]The distinction between abstract concept and representation was established by empirical psychology and emphasized especially by the 'School of Wurzburg.' Külpe and his followers Bühler, Messer and Marbe, through the method of experimental introspection, were forced to distinguish between imaginative and non-imaginative consciousness. For a survey of the experiments, see F. Roels, *Handboek der Psychologie*, Utrecht, 1934, pp. 73-93.

[146]To clarify the distinction between concept and schematic representation, an appeal is sometimes made to the fact that man can perfectly understand a figure having 75 angles, without being able to represent this figure schematically in his imagination. Hence, so they conclude, concept and schematic representation are not identical. We do not make use of this argument because we do not think that it is valid. When we speak of the concept, we mean the abstract expression of the essence of a discovered reality. In this sense the "concept" of a figure having 75 angles is not a concept. Nor is that of a simple triangle. The content of such a "concept" is not the expression of the essence of a discovered reality but is, on the basis of perception, simply posited in an unequivocal and indisputable fashion.

spiritual consciousness. Empiricism does not recognize the proper character of spiritual consciousness. Rationalism, on the other hand, exaggerates and absolutizes it. Alarmed by the fact that our senses *sometimes* deceive us, the rationalist starts with the assumption that they could *always* deceive us. For this reason, he does not consider man's sensitivity a reliable source of knowledge. For the rationalist "genuine" knowledge is found in "thinking." That which can be coherently "thought" in necessary and universal concepts has, by that very fact, value for reality in the eyes of the rationalist. Starting from an indubitable principle, then, one can be certain, according to rationalism, that the results of the logical deductions will be in agreement with reality. By simply exploiting the inner, logical power of reason, man could "excogitate" the whole reality. According to rationalism, only thinking in abstract and universal concepts, "divorced" from sense experience, has value for reality.

We are strongly inclined to think that aversion to rationalism makes it difficult—perhaps even impossible—for certain phenomenologists to do justice to the specifically spiritual aspect of *existence* as *cogito*. In our description of perception we showed that the object of perception always reveals itself to the perceiver in ever changing profiles. The profiles of this object refer to the attitudes of the embodied subject who the perceiver is. Husserl, however, has explicitly stated that the perceiver is conscious of the fact that "he has to do with" profiles of *one and the same* object of perception.[147] The recognition of the proper character of spiritual consciousness or understanding contains an answer to the question as to how this is possible. By understanding, I seize the essence of an object, so that a profile can appear *as* a profile. In and through understanding, I transcend the perspectivism which is inherent in my being situated in space and time as a perceiver.[148] I "see" the essence.

One who *limits* himself to pointing out that, in perception, profiles disclose themselves, runs into difficulties when he tries to take into account the perceiver's consciousness that the different profiles are concerned with the same object of perception. Merleau-Ponty, we think, did not manage to overcome this difficulty. He emphasizes the perspectivism of perception and

---

[147]Husserl, *Ideen*, I, p. 92.
[148]Husserl, "Philosophie als strenge Wissenschaft," *Logos*, I(1910-11), p. 317.

shows that every profile of the object of perception intrinsically contains the promise that ever new profiles will appear. The series of profiles in which the object reveals itself is infinite because the possibilities to modify the standpoint of the perceiver in space and time are infinite. It follows, therefore, says Merleau-Ponty, that the perceived object *itself*—the table or the rock *itself*—are never reached.[149]

To reach the object *itself* would imply that I could comprehend all possible standpoints in space and time, i.e., that I could make a synthesis of all these standpoints in space and time, so that I could be "everywhere" and "always" with respect to an object of perception. But the idea of such a synthesis makes a mockery of every *real* standpoint. A real standpoint is a standpoint here and now, and not "everywhere" and "always." One who alleges to be "everywhere" and "always" is *in reality* "nowhere" and "never." As soon, however, as every real standpoint with respect to an object of perception is denied, one denies also the subject's embodied being and the subject's involvement in the world. The subject is then represented as separated from meaning, as a "surveying look"; [150] the being of the thing is no longer a being-for-the-subject, and is consequently no longer a *real* being.[151]

What was said of the *thing*, Merleau-Ponty adds, applies also to the world. In perception, I bring a certain figure forward, and this figure appears against a background of remote and more distant meanings. I can, of course, make a figure of a distant meaning, but in that case other meanings will be put into the background. Remote meanings in the background of my field of perception, however, also have a certain background. But the background of all backgrounds, the horizon of all

---

149"L'ipséité n'est, bien entendu, jamais *atteinte:* chaque aspect de la chose qui tombe sous notre perception n'est encore qu'une invitation à percevoir au delà et qu'un arrêt momentané dans le processus perceptif. Si la chose même était atteinte, elle serait désormais étalée devant nous et sans mystère. Elle cesserait d'exister comme chose au moment même où nous croirions la posséder." Merleau-Ponty, *PP*, pp. 269-270.

150"Si la synthèse pouvait être effective, si mon expérience formait un système clos, si la chose et le monde pouvaient être définis une fois pour toutes, si les horizons spatio-temporels pouvaient, même idéalement, être explicités et le monde pensé sans point de vue, c'est alors que rien n'existerait, je survolerais le monde, et loin que tous les lieux et tous les temps devinssent à la fois réels, ils cesseraient tous de l'être parce que je n'en habiterais aucun et ne serais engagé nulle part. Si je suis toujours et partout, je ne suis jamais et nulle part." *PP*, pp. 382-383.

151*PP*, Avant-propos, p. III.

horizons—in other words, the world itself—is never reached in perception. The thing and the world are only as experienced by me or my other subjects like me, for they are the concatenation of our perspectives. But the thing and the world transcend all perspectives, because that concatenation is temporal and unfinished.[152]

One can ask, of course, what this "transcendence" is. Merleau-Ponty's answer can be presented in this way: "When I say that things are transcendent, this means that I do *not possess* them. They are transcendent to the extent that I do not know what they are and that I blindly affirm their naked existence.[153] The transcendent is the *real*, and it is *real* to the extent that it escapes our possession.[154] The natural world gives itself as existing 'in itself' on the other side of its existence-for-me." [155]

We ask ourselves, however, whether Merleau-Ponty's train of thought is entirely coherent here. On the one hand, he affirms that all reality is always, and of necessity, reality-for-me; on the other, he calls real that which escapes being-for-me; that of which I do not know what it is; that whose existence I blindly affirm; that which exists "in itself" on the other side of its existence-for-me.

It does not seem difficult to find the source of this incoherence. As long as there is question of the profiles of the thing and the world, i.e., as long as there is question of the noematic correlates of man's spatially and temporally situated sense-consciousness, Merleau-Ponty emphasizes reality's being-for-me. The many different profiles of the object of perception "cling" to the subject. The *existent* subject—as the saying of "is"—affirms the being of the object on "two" levels. Insofar as the *existent* subject-as-*cogito* contains an affirmative moment in which the spatio-temporal situation of the subject is transcended (*not* left behind), the subject dwells in a world of essences and

---

152"La chose et le monde n'existent que vécus par moi ou par des sujets tels que moi, puisqu'ils sont l'enchaînement de nos perspectives, mais ils transcendent toutes less perspectives parce que cet enchaînement est temporel et inachevé." *PP*, pp. 384-385.

153"Quand je dis que les choses sont transcendantes, cela signifie que je ne les possède pas, que je n'en fais pas le tour, elles sont transcendantes dans la mesure où j'ignore ce qu'elles sont et où j'en affirme aveuglément l'existence nue." *PP*, p. 423.

154"Ce qui fait la 'réalité' de la chose est donc justement ce qui la dérobe à notre possession." *PP*, p. 270.

155"En effet, le monde naturel se donne comme existant en soi au delà de son existence pour moi." *PP*, p. 180.

attains the table and the rock *themselves* in what they *essentially* are-for-the-subject.   To attain this does not require that the subject be able to make a synthesis of all possible standpoints in space and time and to comprehend all possible profiles.   Such a requirement can be made only if one demands that sense consciousness accomplish something which only a spiritual consciousness can do.   Because Merleau-Ponty did not realize the proper character of spiritual consciousness,[156] he saw himself forced to make that demand.   At the same time, however, he saw that such a demand was impossible: to be "always" and "everywhere" present to an object is to be *in reality* "never" and "nowhere."   The table and the rock *themselves* are "therefore" never reached.   Nevertheless, the noematic correlate of spiritual consciousness imposes itself, for all profiles of the table reveal themselves as profiles of one and the same table.   In Merleau-Ponty this fact remains unexplained.

Hume's identification of the abstract concept with the schematic image implied that he could not do justice to the uniquely proper character of the spiritual "moment" contained in the *cogito*.   Merleau-Ponty's aversion to rationalism led him to the same disregard.   For ultimately it does not make much difference whether one conceives understanding as the schematization of concrete and individual impressions, or tries to represent the essence of a thing as the never-finished series of its spatio-temporal profiles.

The "Eidetic Reduction"

Accordingly, the return to "integral experience" as the gateway to "the things themselves" implies the recognition of an "eidetic moment."   Integral experience contains the possibility to seize the *eidos*, the "general essence" [157] of something, and express it.   This principle applies not only to objects in the strict sense but also to the ways in which man is related to them, such as by perceiving, remembering, and willing.[158]

---

[156]Merleau-Ponty "has neglected to investigate that which in common parlance is called the 'life of the spirit.'   His efforts have been concentrated on understanding the spirit in the light of the body-subject and for this reason he has not paid sufficient attention to the proper character of the human spirit."   Kwant, *The Phenomenological Philosophy of Merleau-Ponty*, Pittsburgh, 1963, p. 242.

[157]Husserl, *Formale und transzendentale Logik*, Halle, 1929, p. 219.

[158]Husserl, "Philosophie als strenge Wissenschaft," *Logos*, I (1910-11), p. 315.

There was a time in Husserl's life when the reduction of that which is "intended" by a statement to its essence occupied a predominant place in his phenomenology. Husserl thought that it was possible and necessary for his phenomenology to be an "intuition of essences." That which shows itself reveals not only a concrete and individual face but also an essential meaning which coincides in all individuals. Husserl thought it possible to seize the essence of something by using the method of fictitious variations. This method consists in this that in the imagination one tries to vary or omit certain characteristics of the intended reality, in order to see whether the reality can then still appear as a reality of a certain species.[159] For instance, is it still possible for a thing to appear as a thing if I think away its extension; or can perception still be called perception if actual perception does not intrinsically refer to potential perceptions? [160] The "ideating abstraction," then gives rise to a "consciousness of generality," in which is seized that which is essentially "intended" in a particular statement.[161]

Husserl's emphasis on the eidetic reduction led some of his first followers to the opinion that phenomenology is, strictly speaking, entirely eidetic. Thus it could happen that phenomenology came to be considered a revival of realism or even of Platonism. When, however, it became evident that a philosophy is not phenomenological by the mere fact of including something eidetic, the eidetic reduction was too hastily relegated to the backstage of phenomenology.[162] In consequence of this, a man like Merleau-Ponty could never have written his PHÉNOMENOLOGIE DE *la* PERCEPTION if he had not implicitly accepted that perception contains much more than he explicitly admitted.[163]

The return to "the things themselves," and to "integral experience" as the gateway to the things themselves, is the return to *existence itself. Existence is* the integral experience, for *existence* is the subject's immediate presence to a present reality "and" to himself as *existence*. This presence, however, contains —both in its noetic aspect and in its noematic aspect—an

159*Ideen* I, pp. 160-164.
160Husserl, *Cartesianische Meditationen und Pariser Vorträge,* pp. 104-105.
161Husserl, *Die Idee der Phänomenologie,* p. 8.
162P. Ricoeur, "Méthodes et tâches d'une phénoménologie de la Volonté," *Problèmes actuelles de la Phénoménologie,* Bruges, 1951, pp. 115-116.
163De Waelhens, *Une philosophie de l'ambiguïté, L'existentialisme de Maurice Merleau-Ponty,* pp. 386-390.

original eidetic moment,[164] by virtue of which the world and the modes of *existing* do not appear to us as pure chaos.[165]

5. PHENOMENOLOGY OF TRUTH

As soon as the implicit "affirmation" of reality—which the *existent* subject-as-*cogito* himself is—is made explicit, the subject pronounces a judgment.[166] The judgment expresses that a certain object "truthfully" and "really" *is* what it is said to *be*; and, at the same time, the judgment implicitly "says" that the object is *not* something else.[167] This intention exists in every way of saying "is," both in everyday speech and in the speaking of positive science and philosophy. The copula "is" is used in every judgment, and in every judgment the subject who says "is" intends to express that what he affirms "truthfully" and "really" *is* this or that, no matter on what level or from which standpoint the affirmation is made. Thus it is not surprising that "truth" is traditionally defined as the agreement of the judgment with reality.[168]

This definition is hardly debatable. All philosophers will be ready to subscribe to it, but the reason for this unanimity lies in the fact that the definition as such does not say anything. As long as nothing is *really* said, unanimity can, of course, prevail in philosophy. As soon, however, as one asks what the terms "agreement" and "reality" mean, the opinions at once differ.[169]

Phenomenology also accepts the traditional definition of the truth of the judgment. But it refuses to separate the explicit saying of "is," accomplished in the judgment, from the implicit saying of "is" which the *existent* subject-as-*cogito* himself is. That which in the judgment is explicitly affirmed to be "truly" and "really" what it is said to be, clings to the original, implicit saying of "is" which *existence* is. The truth of the judgment,

---

[164]"Le rôle de la phénoménologie est le dégagement des structures eidétiques impliquées dans la perception." De Waelhens, *op. cit.*, p. 391.

[165]Sartre, *Esquisse d'une théorie des émotions*, p. 7.

[166]"Chaque concept se présente comme une affirmation en germe, une possibilité de jugement et tout jugement est un mode de concevoir le réel, une manière humaine de se dire à soi comment les choses sont." Dondeyne, "L'abstraction," *Revue Néoscolastique de Philosophie*, 1938, p. 340.

[167]Max Müller, *Sein und Geist*, Tübingen, 1940, p. 40.

[168]Thomas Aquinas, *Quaestiones disputatae de Anima*, Q., un., a. III, *ad* 1.

[169]"They begin to quarrel only after the question is raised as to what may precisely be meant by the term 'agreement', and what by the term 'reality', when reality is taken as something for our ideas to agree with." William James, *Pragmatism, A New Name for Some Old Ways of Thinking*, New York, 1914, p. 198.

then, is preceded by a certain "event"— the "event" in which the
judged meaning becomes meaning-for-the-subject; the "event"
of truth as unconcealedness. One who disregards this "event"
can hardly escape making the judgment the "locus" of truth and
conceiving truth as agreement with "brute" reality.[170] But in
that case, all truth is talked out of existence, for the statement
that there is agreement between judgment and "brute" reality
necessarily presupposes that it is possible to compare the judged
reality with the non-judged reality.[171] The realism of the so-
called "natural attitude" directly and inevitably leads to scepticism. As a matter of fact, this is what happened in the case of
Hume.

Hume's Intelligent Scepticism

Hume never wanted to have anything to do with innate
ideas: all knowledge, for him, is knowledge of sense experience
and begins with simple impressions.[172] Hume was, likewise,
averse to an active *cogito:* the knower is purely passive, a mere
"recipient" of impressions or "messages" from a world in which
the knower does not live.

Regarding the question as to *what* exactly the knower knows,
Hume does not hesitate: the knower knows impressions, i.e.,
contents of consciousness. For Hume, as for all empiricists, this
answer flows from his realism—from the fact that the world is
conceived as divorced from the knowing subject. For, how
could anyone seriously maintain that the knower knows worldly
things *themselves*, if the subject and the world are first posited
as separate realities? Before Hume, Locke had already explicitly stated that what the knower knows is the *ideas* themselves.[173]
Consciousness was conceived as a kind of "locker" in which

170"Je veux réproduire les choses comme elles sont, ou comme elles
seraient, si moi je n'existais pas." Taine, cited by G. Gusdorf, *Traité de
l'existence morale*, Paris, 1949, p. 82.

171Heidegger, *SZ*, pp. 214-219.

172"And therefore we shall here content ourselves with establishing one
general proposition. That all our simple ideas in their first appearance are
deriv'd from simple impressions, which are correspondent to them, and which
they exactly represent." D. Hume, *A Treatise on Human Nature*, I, part I,
sect. I.

173"Every man being conscious to himself, that he thinks, and that which
his mind is applied about, whilst thinking, being the ideas that are there, it is
past doubt that men have in their mind several ideas, such as are those expressed by the words, 'whiteness, hardness, sweetness, thinking, motion, man,
elephant, army, drunkenness' and others." J. Locke, *An Essay Concerning
Human Understanding*, II, 1, 1.

contents of consciousness are stored.[174] The "locker" itself is fully separated from the world from which it receives "messages." Hume took over this view from Locke. Thus he could not escape from considering the "messages" arriving from the world in which the knower does *not* live as the object of knowledge: the knower knows the "phenomena," the subjective impressions in his interiority.[175]

Before Hume other thinkers had tried to make use of the principle of causality in order to transcend the phenomena and reach that which is hidden behind them. But for Hume such an attempt is sheer philosophical nonsense.[176] For the idea of casuality is simply the result of experiencing the regular succession of phenomena: this experience gives rise to the subjective expectation that a particular impression will be followed by another particular impression. All things considered, Hume thinks, one cannot fail to recognize that sense experience produces nothing but the impression that the motion of billiard ball *A* takes place *after* it is struck by billiard ball *B*. If this experience is repeated, it gives rise to the subjective expectation that it will always happen. Finally, the motion of billiard ball *A* is conceived as in reality produced or caused by ball *B*.

The affirmation, however, of the existence of a cause and its operation *in reality* lies beyond the reach of any justified affirmation: justified affirmations can only be concerned with subjective impressions.[177] Any affirmation which tries to reach beyond the subjective impressions is nothing but an expression of a "belief." Such a "belief" may be useful for everyday life,[178] but cannot be maintained in the light of critical reflection. A critical attitude

---

174"The senses at first let in particular ideas, and furnish the yet empty cabinet: and the mind by degrees growing familiar with some of them, they are lodged in the memory, and names got to them." Locke, *op. cit.*, 1, 2, 15.

175"Nur darf bei der Charakteristik der Humeschen Lehre nicht vergessen werden, dass diese absolute gewisse Tatsächlichkeit der Impressionen lediglich diejenige ihres Vorhandenseins als Vorstellungen ist. In dieser Bedeutung und Beschränkung umfasst die intuitive Erkenntnis nicht nur die Tatsachen der inneren, sondern auch diejenigen der äusseren Erfahrung, - aber um den Preis, dass die letzteren eigentlich auch nur eine Art der ersteren sind, ein Wissen nämlich von Vorstellungszuständen." Wilhelm Windelband, *Lehrbuch der Geschichte der Philosophie*, herausgegeben von Heinz Heimsoeth, Tübingen, 1957, p. 405.

176"All unser Wissen beschränkt sich auf die Konstatierung der Impressionen und auf die Verhältnisse dieser Vorstellungen untereinander." Windelband, *op. cit.*, p. 406.

177Windelband, *op. cit.*, p. 407.

178Hume, *op. cit.*, I, part IV, sect. VII.

can only lead to a radical phenomenalism.[179] Hume's own contemporaries realized that his phenomenalism was a radical form
of scepticism and did not hesitate to say so.[180] In Hume, nothing
remains of the possibility to know "reality."

We cannot avoid making the remark that Hume's scepticism
is the inevitable and logical consequence of any mirror theory of
knowledge, which refuses to conceive knowledge as the immediate presence of the knowing subject to a present, real world.
In such a theory the "real" world occurs as a world-without-
subject. But a world-without-subject is a world of which no
subject is conscious, of which no subject really speaks, with
which no subject really deals, in which no subject really lives,
and which is not affirmed by any subject. Such a world can, of
course, never be affirmed. From this Hume concluded that we
can never affirm anything other than our impressions.[181] Before
Hume, there were philosophers who conceived the world as an
"inhuman" world but, nonetheless, "affirmed" the "existence"
of this world. Hume was right when he claimed that a justified
and real affirmation of a non-affirmed-world is impossible. The
only surprising aspect of the matter is that philosophy had to
wait for Hume before it *allegedly* lapsed into scepticism. Hume
was right when he thought that an appeal to the principle of
causality cannot save the world; for the affirmation that "in
reality" there "exist" also causal actions lies beyond the possibilities of any justified affirmation, if "existing in reality" has
to be taken to mean "existing in a non-affirmed world."

Hume was the first thinker to see the ultimate consequences
of the realistic mirror theory of knowledge, which Locke did not
see. For Locke the world of things was separated from the
knowing subject; nevertheless, he called the *ideas* of primary
qualities objective. The objects of knowledge were the ideas
themselves; yet Locke thought it possible to declare that some
ideas reveal themselves as resemblances of the things themselves.

179"Damit ist jede Theorie, jede Erforschung der Ursache, jede Lehre vom
'wahren Sein' hinter den 'Erscheinungen' ausgeschlossen." Windelband, *op.
cit.*, p. 408.

180Windelband, *op. cit.*, pp. 407-408.

181"The idea of existence, then, is the very same with the idea of what
we conceive to be existent. To reflect on any thing simply, and to reflect on
it as existent, are nothing different from each other. Now since nothing is
ever present to the mind but its perceptions and since all ideas are deriv'd
from something antecedently present to the mind; it follows, that it is impossible so much as to conceive or form an idea of any thing specifically different
from ideas and impressions." Hume, *op. cit.*, I, part II, sect. IV.

In Locke's theory, however, the things "themselves" are non-affirmed, non-known things; the affirmed and known things are the ideas. Locke did not at all realize that his assertion that the ideas of primary qualities are accurate mirror images presupposes the possibility of comparing the ideas—the affirmed and known things—with the "bodies themselves," i.e., the non-affirmed and non-known things. Such a comparison, however, is evidently impossible, and for this reason the distinction between primary and secondary qualities is baseless.[182] In the ideas themselves the subject cannot "see" whether or not they mirror the non-known qualities of the "bodies themselves."

In Hume himself nothing remains of this kind of ambiguity. For him, justified affirmations solely refer to subjective impressions in consciousness. "Existing reality," i.e., the non-affirmed and non-known world, is beyond our reach as far as Hume is concerned. Hume's *alleged* scepticism was a very intelligent kind of scepticism.

Very often, however, the consciousness of the sceptic is an "unhappy consciousness." The sceptic is "very sorry" that he has to be a sceptic. But what does this sorrow mean? Does it not betray the fact that the sceptic himself continues to cling to a false ideal of knowledge, viz., that truth *must* be the agreement of the judgment with "brute" reality? Phenomenology rejects both scepticism and the "sorrow" of the sceptic because the sceptic's ideal of truth is a contradiction.

Truth as Unconcealedness

The truth of the judgment—in Heidegger's language, of the *Aussage* [183] or *Satz* [184]—is preceded by a more original truth. The truth of the judgment presupposes that what is expressed in the judgment is "already" meaning, is "already" withdrawn from concealedness; it presupposes *alētheia*—the unconcealedness of the matter judged.[185] This unconcealedness requires a certain

---

182"I assert, that instead of explaining the operations of external objects by its means, we utterly annihilate all these objects, and reduce ourselves to the opinions of the most extravagant scepticism concerning them. If colours, sounds, tastes, and smells be merely perceptions, nothing we can conceive is possest of a real, continu'd, and independent existence; not even motion extension and solidity, which are the primary qualities chiefly insisted on." Hume, *op. cit.,* I, part IV, sect. IV.
183Heidegger, *SZ,* p. 214.
184Heidegger, *Vom Wesen der Wahrheit,* 3rd ed., Frankfurt, a.M., 1954, pp. 6-9.
185Heidegger, *op. cit.,* p. 15.

"light." If there existed nothing but cosmic things, there would be no light and nothing would ever be true. The unconcealedness of things presupposes that man has broken through and transcended thinglike being in himself—that man is a certain "light" for himself. This "light" is a "natural light" (*lumen naturale*), i.e., it is a light which is man's own essence.[186] This "light" is the "light" of man's subjectivity.[187] The "light" of subjectivity, however, is an *existent* "light" and for this reason the unconcealedness of things is included in man's unconcealedness for himself: [188] the *existent* subject is the "letting be" of the meaning of things.[189]   To indicate the light which man is for himself and for the other than himself, the Greek philosophers used the term *logos*.[190]   The *logos* draws beings from their concealedness.[191]

The transcendence of thinglike being in himself—which transcendence man essentially is—is a mysterious "event." [192] The essence of man, then, is a kind of coming-to-presence (*Wesen*, in the verblike sense of the term).   Man's essence "comes to pass" (*gescheht*),[193] because the "light" which constitutes the essence of man "issues forth."   But if the unconcealedness of things and of the world clings to the "coming to pass" of the *existent* subject's "light," then the truth of things and of the world also is a certain "coming to pass" or "issuing forth."   The true is that which comes to presence (*west, anwest*),[194] which discloses or reveals itself.[195]   Primarily "true,"

---

[186]"Die ontisch bildliche Rede vom lumen naturale im Menschen meint nichts anderes als die existenzial-ontologische Struktur dieses Seienden, dass es *ist* in der Weise, sein Da zu sein.   Es ist 'erleuchtet' besagt, an ihm selbst als In-der-Welt-sein gelichtet, nicht durch ein anderes Seiendes, sondern so, dass es selbst die Lichtung *ist.*" Heidegger, *SZ*, p. 133.

[187]"Das Dasein ist seine Erschlossenheit." *Ibid.*

[188]"Erschlossenheit . . . betrifft gleichursprünglich die Welt, das In-Sein und das Selbst." *SZ*, p. 220.

[189]Heidegger, *Vom Wesen der Wahrheit*, p. 14.

[190]"Das Wahrsein des *logos* als *apophansis* ist das *alētheuein* in der Weise des *apophainesthai:* Seiendes - aus der Verborgenheit herausnehmend - in seiner Unverborgenheit (Entdecktheit) sehen lassen.   Die *alētheia*, die von Aristoteles nach den oben angeführten Stellen mit *pragma, phainomena* gleichgesetzt wird, bedeutet die 'Sachen selbst', das was sich zeigt, das Seiende im Wie seiner Entdecktheit." *SZ*, p. 219.

[191]"Also gehört zum *logos* die Unverborgenheit, *a-lētheia.*" *SZ*, p. 219.

[192]"Tout processus de fondement de soi est rupture de l'être-identique de l'en-soi, recul de l'être par rapport à lui-même et apparition de la présence à soi ou conscience." Sartre, *EN*, p. 714.

[193]Heidegger, *Vorträge und Aufsätze*, Pfullingen, 1954, p. 38.

[194]Heidegger, *Identität und Differenz*, Pfullingen, 1957, p. 24.

[195]Heidegger, *Vorträge und Aufsätze*, p. 142.

therefore, is the "coming to pass" of man's essence,[196] because this "coming to pass" implies the truth of things and of the world.[197] The "coming to pass" of man's essence is man's standing in truth-as-unconcealedness.[198] Accordingly, much precedes the truth of the judgment, conceived as agreement with "reality." The "coming to pass" of the subject "and" meaning, as the unity of their reciprocal implication, implies the "letting be" of the agreement which is expressed in the true judgment.

With the necessary changes, the same holds for the untruth of the judgment. The untruth of the judgment presupposes the "uprootedness" of *existence*.[199] This uprootedness consists in this, that the subject no longer stands in truth as unconcealedness but in "semblance." Reality is then not fully concealed: it is dis-closed to some extent but, at the same time, deformed.[200] The untrue judgment is the expression of standing in "semblance."

Objectivity and Objectivism, Subjectivity and Subjectivism, Relativity and Relativism

From the preceding considerations it should be clear that it is impossible simply to take for granted the meaning about which the true judgment makes a statement, i.e., this meaning cannot be conceived as an "in itself," as being what it is said to be, independently of man.[201] Otherwise one disregards the fact that the meaning has been constituted as meaning, that meaning is the "result" of a "coming to pass." This "coming to pass" presupposes a certain "activity," viz., the "letting be" of the *existent* subject. Accordingly, one who conceives the truth of the judgment as the expression of the accuracy with which the "thing in itself" is passively mirrored, first "realizes" the results of knowledge, and then conceives these results as the absolute

---

196"Primär 'wahr', d.h. entdeckend ist das Dasein. Wahrheit im zweiten Sinne besagt nicht entdeckendsein (Entdeckung), sondern entdecktsein (Entdecktheit)." *SZ*, p. 220.

197"Sofern das Dasein seine Erschlossenheit ist, als erschlossenes erschliesst und entdeckt, ist es wesenhaft 'wahr'." *SZ*, p. 221.

198"Dasein ist 'in der Wahrheit'." *SZ*, p. 221.

199"Das Sein zum Seienden ist nicht ausgelöscht, aber entwurzelt." *SZ*, p. 222.

200"Das Seiende ist nicht völlig verborgen, sondern gerade entdeckt, aber zugleich verstellt; es zeigt sich - aber im Modus des Scheins." *SZ*, p. 222.

201"Une évidence c'est une présence." Sartre, *L'Imaginaire*, Paris, 14th ed., 1948, p. 210.

origin of those accurate mirrorings.[202]   The fact that truth needs
to be "originated" is simply lost sight of in this way; yet truth
is an "origination" by man.

All this, however, does not mean that in "originating" truth
man can proceed arbitrarily,[203] for in his saying of "is" man has
bonds.[204]   He is bound to being itself—to that which shows
itself, to that which is open, unconcealed.[205]   Man is not the
lord of what is but only its shepherd and guardian,[206] in order
that meaning may appear as what it is.   The "coming to pass"
of the knowing man's essence is response.[207]

Thus it should be evident that there continues to be a "critical problem," although this problem is not the traditional one.
The critical problem contains the question about the criterion to
determine whether in my saying of "is" I let myself be guided
by unconcealedness; i.e., whether my "seeing" is not merely a
putative seeing.   Before we consider this question, we must first
clarify certain terminological points.

There is no reason why truth as unconcealedness should not
be called "objectivity."   Only for people who defend an objectivistic view of objectivity is the objectivity of phenomenology
not sufficiently objective.   They hold that one may speak of
objectivity only when the subject has been eliminated from the
encounter which knowledge is.[208]   However, the subject's elimi-
nation would destroy the encounter, i.e., knowledge itself, so that
there could no longer be question of objectivity in any sense.

Most men of positive science, and also some philosophers,
reserve the term "objectivity" for that which is connected with
the intentionality of the standpoint assumed by positive science
and which can be *verified* by anyone who assumes this stand-

---

[202]Merleau-Ponty, *PP*, Avant-propos, p. XV.
[203]Heidegger, *Identität und Differenz*, p. 23.
[204]Heidegger, *Der Satz vom Grund*, Pfullingen, 1957, p. 121.
[205]"Das Aussagen ist ein Sein zum seienden Ding selbst.   Und was wird
durch die Wahrnehmung ausgewiesen?   Nichts anderes als dass es das Seiende
selbst ist, das in der Aussage gemeint war. . . .   Das gemeinte Seiende selbst
zeigt sich so, wie es an ihm selbst ist, d.h. dass es in Selbigkeit so ist, als
wie seiend es in der Aussage aufgezeigt, entdeckt wird." *SZ*, p. 218.
[206]Heidegger, *Über den Humanismus*, p. 19.
[207]Heidegger, *Identität und Differenz*, p. 22.
[208]"Plus je mettrai l'accent sur cette objectivité des choses, en coupant le
cordon ombilical qui les relie à mon existence. . . . - plus j'affirmerai l'in-
dépendance du monde par rapport à moi, sa radicale indifférence à ma
destinée, à mes fins propres, - plus ce monde ainsi proclamé seul réel se
convertira en un spectacle senti comme illusoire, un immense film documen-
taire offert à ma curiosité, mais qui en fin de compte se supprime par le
simple fait qu'il m'ignore." Marcel, *RI*, p. 32.

point.[209] Objective is *this* sense obviously is not identical with the unconcealed: it is merely one region or a plurality of regions of the unconcealed; much more is unconcealed than can be verified by these sciences.

It could be very confusing, however, if phenomenology simply resigned itself to being called "subjective" with respect to its theory of truth. For, those who like to call it this far too often surreptitiously intend to say that phenomenology adheres to a *subjectivistic* concept of truth. This accusation certainly is false: phenomenology does not deliver truth to the subject's arbitrary choice.[210] The subject-as-*cogito* is a "seeing" on many levels, but on every level of seeing the subject remains bound. The phenomenologist's statement, then, that all truth is subjective means nothing but that truth expresses objectivity-*for-a-subject*. Objectivity-for-a-subject is, of course, much more "objective" than objectivistically interpreted "objectivity." [211]

What has been said here with respect to the use of the term "subjective" applies also to the term "relative." The statement that all truth is relative may not be interpreted in a relativistic way. The relativity of truth solely means that truth *in its relation to* a subject is absolute.[212]

The preceding considerations offer a basis for a correct understanding of the historicity of truth. If the truth of the judgment presupposes truth as unconcealedness, then truth, noetically considered, also presupposes the *historical* act by which man draws truth from concealment.[213] Truth "issues forth" with the "coming to pass" of man's essence. We will develop here somewhat more extensively the historicity of truth, and describe the essentially unfinished character of man-as-history and of his truth-as-history. First, however, we wish to make explicit a con-

---

[209]Poincaré, *La valeur de la science,* Genève n.d., pp. 65-66, 282-283.

[210]"Alle Wahrheit ist gemäss deren wesenhafter daseinsmässiger Seinsart relativ auf das Sein des Daseins. Bedeutet diese Relativität soviel wie: alle Wahrheit ist 'subjektiv'? Wenn man 'subjektiv' interpretiert als 'in das Belieben des Subjekts gestellt', dann gewiss nicht. Denn das Entdecken entzieht seinem eigensten Sinne nach das Aussagen dem 'subjektiven' Belieben und bringt das entdeckende Dasein vor das Seiende selbst." Heidegger, *SZ,* p. 227.

[211]"Wenn das 'Subjekt' ontologisch als existierendes Dasein begriffen wird, dessen Sein in der Zeitlichkeit gründet, dann muss gesagt werden: Welt ist 'subjektiv'. Diese 'subjektive' Welt aber ist dann als zeitlich-transzendente 'objektiver' als jedes mögliche 'Objekt'." *SZ,* p. 366.

[212]*SZ,* pp. 226-227.

[213]Dondeyne, *Contemporary European Thought and Christian Faith,* pp. 49 ff.

sequence implied in our theory, viz., the implication that truth is radically human.[214] The history of truth began with the appearance of man,[215] and the appearance of a new human being means fhe beginning of a new history of truth. Man knows only human truth, and therefore there was no truth before man was: [216] before man was, nothing was unconcealed from man.

At this junction the objection is usually made that, before man appeared, there was truth-for-God. But what can this expression mean? It certainly does *not* mean that the unconcealedness of reality-for-God would be in agreement with the unconcealedness of reality-for-man. Even if one admits that to some extent man can enter into the reality-for-God, it certainly could not have been done before the appearance of man, the one for whom both God and reality-for-God would be unconcealed.[217] We realize, of course, that for many people such statements are indigestible: the entire history of Western thought manifests the hidden or openly avowed pretension to place oneself on the "standpoint" of God in speaking about truth and in this way assign a divine guarantee to human statements. In the first chapter we saw that this pretension is openly present in idealism; [218] in a hidden form it exists also in Scholasticism.

The Essentialism of Scholastic Philosophy

In Scholasticism reality occurs as a collection of essences-in-themselves, stored in a land whose discovery is never commemorated. This view has its roots in the philosophy of Plato. As was mentioned, Heraclitus' heritage forced Plato to accept a separate world of necessary and universal ideas if he was to offer any acceptable explanation for the necessity and universality

---

[214]De Waelhens, *Phénoménologie et Vérité*, Paris, 1953, pp. 165-166.
[215]"Das Dasein ist als konstituiert durch Erschlossenheit wesenhaft in der Wahrheit. Die Erschlossenheit ist eine wesenhafte Seinsart des Daseins. Wahrheit 'gibt es' nur, sofern und solange Dasein ist. Seiendes ist nur dann entdeckt und nur solange erschlossen, als überhaupt Dasein ist." *SZ*, p. 226.
[216]*SZ*, pp. 226-227.
[217]". . . nous dirons qu'il est absolument certain qu'il ne faut pas chercher une autre sorte d'être que l'être-pour-moi, par le fait même qu'il ne peut y avoir d'autre: un être ou une sorte d'être qui ne serait pas pour-moi, serait, par définition, radicalement extérieur et étranger à toute appréhension et à toute connaissance. De ce point de vue, Dieu, s'il est, est nécessairement pour-moi: il entre de quelque façon dans le champ de mon expérience et, à ce titre, il en prend nécessairement la forme." R. Jolivet, "Le problème de l'absolu dans la philosophie de M. Merleau-Ponty," *Tijdschrift voor Philosophie* XIX(1957), p. 59.
[218]G. Gusdorf, *Traité de métaphysique*, Paris, 1956, pp. 102-132.

found in human knowledge. Plato conceived the being of ideas as the only "really real" being and depreciated the being of worldly meaning: the worldly meaning, strictly speaking, "is" not because of the fact that in matter the idea, the "pure appearance," is mis-shaped.[219] Thus ideas became prototypes of worldly realities. They were conceived as necessary and universal norms by which worldly realities, as shadows of the ideas, could be measured and on the basis of which one could determine whether a being had this or that particular essence.[220] In the world of ideas, then, there existed for Plato the pure essence of the state, the work of art, man, virtues, the horse, etc. The ideas were conceived as the norm for the truth of things. Things themselves were not "really" true. "Really" true were the ideas, and for this reason all things occurring in worldly reality had to be guided by the ideas as their prototypes.[221] Concrete living man also had nothing else to do but to realize his necessary, universal, immutable, and eternal essence in the changeability of time.[222]

Plato conceived the world of pure ideas as a world of pure "light." What is pure idea is pure "light." The meaning spoken of by phenomenology is not pure "light" but an admixture of "light" and "darkness," of unconcealedness and concealedness.[223] The unconcealedness of meaning presupposes the "letting be" of meaning by the subject-as-*cogito*. The moment of the subject-as-*cogito*'s emergence is the "moment of vision" at which truth as unconcealedness issues forth. This moment is the beginning

---

219"Das Sein als *idea* wird jetzt zum eigentlich Seienden hinaufgesteigert, und das Seiende selbst, das vormals Waltende, sinkt herab zu dem, was von Plato *mē on* genannt wird, was eigentlich nicht sein sollte und eigentlich auch nicht ist, weil es die Idee, das reine Aussehen, in der Verwirklichung doch immer verunstaltet, indem es dieses in den Stoff hineinbildet." Heidegger, *Einführung in die Metaphysik,* p. 140.

220"Die *idea* ihrerseits wird zum *paradeigma,* zum Musterbild. Die Idee wird zugleich und notwendig zum Ideal. Das nachgebildete 'ist' eigentlich nicht, sondern hat nur Teil am Sein, *methexis.* Der *chōrismos,* die Kluft zwischen der Idee als dem eigentlich Seienden, dem Vor- und Urbild, und dem eigentlich Nichtseienden, dem Nach- und Abbild, ist aufgerissen'. Heidegger, *op. cit.,* pp. 140-141.

221Heidegger, *op. cit.,* p. 141.

222"So ist von vornherein festgelegt und erblickt, was der Mensch sein soll und sein muss. Ihm bleibt nichts anderes übrig als Verwirklicher seines eigenen ewigen Wesens zu sein, seine unveränderliche, ihn ermöglichende innere Möglichkeit ins Dasein überzuführen." M. Müller, *Existenzphilosophie im geistigen Leben der Gegenwart,* p. 17.

223"Die Unverborgenheit braucht die Verborgenheit." Heidegger, *Vorträge und Aufsätze,* p. 221.

of a never-finished history of dis-closure. Meaning is never *pure* "light."

The fact that phenomenology conceives meaning as the semi-darkness of unconcealedness and concealedness, makes it possible to call meaning the *real* terminus of the cognitive encounter. *Real* termini of man's cognitive encounter are an admixture of "light" and "darkness." When Plato represents meaning as pure idea, i.e., as pure "light" he has already ceased to conceive meaning as a real *terminus of encounter*. The Platonic idea, conceived as pure "light," actually is meaning whose "moment of vision"—of dis-closure—is "forgotten," and whose history of dis-closure is considered finished. But for such a finished result there is no room within knowledge as a genuine *encounter*, for in the *real* encounter with meaning the latter reveals itself as the *chiaroscuro* of unconcealedness and concealedness, and, consequently, as a never-ending invitation to dis-closure by the subject-as-*cogito*. Plato, then, had to cut meaning loose from the encounter in order to place it as an "in itself" of a purely ideal kind in a world of pure essence.[224]

Aristotle's philosophy no longer conceived essences as lying in an ideal world, but placed them in the real world. Plato's essences were ideal "in themselves," not termini of encounter. But because Aristotle limited himself to "realizing" the essences, i.e., placing them in "reality," he also implicitly conceived the "reality" of the essences as "in themselves." Aristotle "relocated" the "in itself'" from the ideal world to the real world, but he did not restore it to the encounter. Just as with the Platonic essences, the Aristotelian essences were conceived as an absolute "light," albeit of a real, and not an ideal, character. His essences were represented as in themselves necessarily, universally, immutably, and eternally "true" because, as absolute, real "light," they were held to be the norm of truth for judgmental knowledge. In this way there arose a picture of reality as a collection of essences, stored in a land of supposedly absolute "light," while the history of the birth of "light" failed to receive any attention.

This view underlies Scholasticism's realistic philosophy of order, which gives each essence its proper place in "brute"

---

[224]"Jetzt treten *on* und *phainomenon* auseinander." Heidegger, *Einführung in die Metaphysik*, p. 141.

reality. Man also, with his own essence, was assumed to have, a place of his own in that order: [225] below God, but above animals, plants, and things. In addition, the place of the holy was above the beautiful, the beautiful above the useful, the useful above the agreeable, the common good above the individual good, and the soul above the body.[226] Similarly, the essences of human acts were located as pieces of rocks in the "totality of reality"; they were assumed to be in their essences what they are: necessarily, universally, immutably, and eternally "true" "in themselves." The essence of the marriage act, for example, was conceived as in itself necessarily, universally, and immutably orientated to reproduction. This orientation was the "truth in itself" of the marriage act, the norm for every true judgment about this act. Natural rights and natural duties also were placed as hills and valleys in the "totality of reality"—as necessarily, universally, immutably and eternally "true in themselves," and, consequently, as the norm of all statements.

This state of affairs led to a specific theory of ethical deeds. If immutable and eternal essences are stored in the "totality of reality"; if immutable and eternal relations constitute an immutable and eternal hierarchical order of essences; and if man and his actions occupy an immutable and eternal place in this complex of "truths in themselves," then the concrete and living man will do ethically good if he "reads" the essences and their essential order and conforms his actions to what he reads.[227] By doing this, he will fulfill God's will. For Scholasticism did not merely transfer the Platonic ideas to the "real" world, but also located them, as exemplars of the real essences, in God's intellect: by a command of his will, God realized these exemplars in his act of creation. Scholasticism, then ascribed a "truth in itself" to the essences, which was measured by and

---

[225]"L'objectivisme naturaliste . . . regarde . . . l'omnitudo realitatis, assigne à l'homme son rang . . . dans le spectacle qu'elle s'offre et néglige totalement de retenir que l'origine de cette hiérarchie réside dans l'activité législatrice du 'regard' de l'étant illuminateur du spectacle et qui le 'constitue' tel." De Waelhens, *La philosophie et les expériences naturelles,* pp. 190-191.
[226]Müller, *op. cit.,* pp. 19-20.
[227]"Für die Handlungen gibt es keine anderen Maxime als die: Beobachte den unveränderlichen *Ordo,* schütze ihn, wo er bedroht ist, stelle ihn her, wo er gestört ist, verwirkliche ihn dort, wo sein Gegenteil Wirklichkeit geworden und in die Möglichkeit zurückgesunken ist. Zu diesem *Ordo* gehört auch dass du den Platz einnimmt, der dir auf Grund deines Wesens zukommt." Müller, *op. cit.,* p. 20.

derived from their being "true" in God's intellect: "every being is true." [228]   Insofar as man's true knowledge mirrored the "truth in itself" of the essences, man possessed God's view of things.   In this way the essentialism, objectivism, or realism of Scholastic philosophy terminates in the claim to speak in the name of God.[229]

An objectivistic philosophy emphasizes, more than any other type of philosophy, that man is held by bonds in his speaking about reality.   This point, however, is exaggerated so much that truth is conceived as an absolute "initiative" of "objective" reality.   The subject "humbly" withdraws as an "unprejudiced spectator," in the sense that he thinks that he can isolate himself from the "coming to pass" of truth.   But in this way, the "objective" reality is "objective"-for-no-one, so that no one can can say anything whatsoever.   This conclusion, however, is not acceptable to the objectivist: he continues to speak and the "humble" subject claims to express "objectivity" in spite of everything.   But his "humility" turns into absolutism here, for what the subject says he ascribes to the absolute "initiative" of "objectivity."   "God's created truth" is assumed to have the "initiative," but the subject cannot avoid thinking that he represents this "initiative" if he is to say anything at all about "objective" reality.

It is not difficult to see that an objectivistic philosophy is dangerous because it eliminates all risks from man's search— his "origination" and "letting come to pass" of truth.   In the preceding pages we have strongly emphasized that the *existent* subject-as-*cogito* lets truth as unconcealedness "come to pass." We will see still that, in doing this, the subject has no guarantee whatsoever.   While he thinks that he gives expression to his standing-in-unconcealedness, it can happen that *de facto* he merely expresses his standing-in-semblance.   Objectivism buries this risk under verbiage.   It does not lapse into scepticism, but elevates itself to the absolutism of "God's created truth-in-itself," by means of which it can declare wrong anyone who has at his disposal only his seeking and groping for truth-for-man.   It declares them wrong "in the name of God."   The objectivist

---

[228]L. Landgrebe, *Philosophie der Gegenwart*, Bonn, 1962, p. 157.
[229]". . . comme si la conscience humaine pouvait en quelque sorte se survoler elle-même et son monde, et contempler l'univers du point de vue de Dieu." A. Dondeyne, "La différence ontologique chez M. Heidegger," *Revue philosophique de Louvain*, 56(1958), p. 57.

does not even need to enter into a dialog with anyone else,[230] for "he knows." [231] But, who does not see that the objectivist also does not have God's "seeing" of the truth at his disposal but only his own seeking and groping subjectivity? [232]

The "Agent Intellect"

There exists, however, one topic in Scholastic philosophy which, if fully exploited, could have eliminated radical objectivism: the topic known as the Aristotelian theory of the "agent intellect" (*poiētikos nous*). How *exactly* Aristotle conceived the agent intellect is not likely to be determined by anyone.[233] But the texts of both Aristotle and Thomas Aquinas are sufficiently clear to claim that, if full justice had been done to them in scholastic philosophy, they would have made it impossible to conceive knowledge as the passive mirroring of "brute" reality.

According to Thomas, the intellect is "in potency" with respect to the things to be understood: it is receptive with respect to reality. The intellect lets itself be governed by reality, and in this sense is passive. A certain movement or influence, therefore, has to come from the things to be understood in order to make the intellect pass from potency to act, from potential understanding to actual understanding.

That which is *not*, however, cannot move, cannot influence. One cannot say that the intelligible as intelligible *is*, if one solely pays attention to the intellect insofar as it is in potency and, therefore is passive. The intelligible is not "something existing in the nature of things"; it does not, as intelligible, lie ready for mirroring in "brute" reality: things are not "intelligible in act." [234] If the intelligible is to be able to move or influence, it must *be* as such: it must be constituted as intelligibility. But, insofar as it is passive, the intellect cannot make the intelligible actually intelligible. Therefore, the intellect cannot be solely a "potential intellect," but must also be an active or "agent

---

230"Qui se réclame de l'absolu ne voudra écouter personne; il doit se persuader que toute contestation est un crime de lèse-majesté envers l'autorité qui cautionne son attitude." Gusdorf, *Traité de métaphysique*, p. 131.

231"Comment y aurait-il véritable échange entre celui qui sait et celui qui ne sait pas?" M. Merleau-Ponty, "L'homme et l'adversité," *La connaissance de l'homme au XXe siècle, Rencontres internationales de Genève*, 1950, p. 74.

232Merleau-Ponty, *SNS*, p. 189.

233I.J.M. van den Berg, *Aristoteles' verhandeling over de Ziel*, Utrecht-Nijmegen, 1953, pp. 173-178.

234*S.Th.*, I, q. LXXIX, a. 3.

intellect." The "action" of the intellect consists in this, that it constitutes the intelligible as intelligibility, by means of the "light" which it itself is.[235]

A phenomenologist would say: outside the active presence of consciousness things are nothing-for-man; things must be raised by consciousness from concealedness, from being nothing-for-man. Insofar as consciousness is passive, it cannot do this. But consciousness is also active, for it constitutes being as being-for-man: it lets being be for man what it is.[236] Only as unconcealedness can reality act as a norm of knowledge.[237]

The Historicity of Truth

One who understands that truth-as-unconcealedness is a reference to man's essence—the "coming to pass" of being-man [238] —has implicitly affirmed the first reason for which truth must be called historical. The "coming to pass" of man's essence is the rupturing of the density, the massivity, and darkness of the "thing-in-man." It makes man be a being which exists for itself; a being for which, in its being, its being is at issue; a being whose being is a being-conscious. But this means at the same time that for man there are things and a world; for the being of man as a being-conscious is the "letting be" of things and the

---

235"Respondeo dicendum, quod necesse est ponere intellectum agentem. Ad cujus evidentiam considerandum est, quod cum intellectus possibilis sit in potentia ad intelligibilia, necesse est quod intelligibilia moveant intellectum possibilem. Quod autem non est, non potest aliquid movere. Intelligibile autem per intellectum possibilem non est aliquid in rerum natura existens, in quantum intelligibile est; intelligit enim intellectus possibilis noster aliquid quasi unum in multis et de multis. Tale autem non invenitur in rerum natura subsistens, ut Aristoteles probat in VII Metaphys. Oportet igitur, si intellectus possibilis debet moveri ab intelligibili, quod hujusmodi intelligibile per intellectum fiat. Et cum non possit esse id quod est, in potentia ad aliquid factum ipsius, oportet ponere praeter intellectum possibilem intellectum agentem, qui faciat intelligibilia in actu, quae moveant intellectum possibilem." Thomas Aquinas, *Quaestiones disputatae de Anima,* q. un, a. 4.

236D. De Petter, "De oorsprong van de zijnskennis volgens de H. Thomas van Aquino," *Tijdschrift voor Philosophie,* XVII(1955), pp. 199-254.

237We do not claim that the scholastic theory of the agent intellect wholly agrees with the constitution theory of phenomenology. Neo-scholasticism has reduced the role of consciousness' spontaneity to an abstractive power. The intellect is supposed to be active only insofar as through its illumination it strips the phantasm, resulting from sense knowledge, of individual sensible matter. The above-mentioned text of Thomas Aquinas readily leads to such an interpretation. Cf. Van Riet, "La théorie thomiste de l'abstraction," *Revue philosophique de Louvain,* 1952, pp. 363-366.

238Heidegger, *Was ist Metaphysik?,* p. 13.

world.[239] Thus the "coming to pass" of the unconcealedness of things and the "coming to pass" of man's essence go hand in hand.[240] The "coming to pass" of the standing-in-unconcealedness which man is, is equiprimordially the "coming to pass" of the truth-as-unconcealedness of things. The "moment" of the emergence of man as subject is equiprimordially the "moment of vision" (*Augen-blick*) at which truth is born. In this sense, truth is "historical."

There is also a "second" reason why truth must be called historical: the meaning which clings to the *existent* subject-as-*cogito* clings to the never-finished history which *existence* itself is.[241] Every actual act of "seeing" intrinsically refers to a future of unconcealedness. Meaning, then, is not pure unconcealedness, but the *chiaroscuro* of unconcealedness "and" concealedness, and it is this that makes meaning *real*.

We penetrate here deeper into the "coming to pass" which is the essence of man. This "coming to pass" occurs not only in the breaking through the "thing-in-man," but continues in the transcendence of every facticity. In the "now" the subject reaches beyond the "past" of his "seeing" toward the realization of a future of "seeing." [242] Knowledge, then, as dis-closure of meaning, is history—as the unity of present, past, and future. But this history carries along the history of unconcealedness, i.e., of truth. Emphasis must be put on the synthesis of present, past, and future with respect to both the noetic and the noematic aspects of *existence*-as-*cogito*. This synthesis, however, is never "finished," for every past intrinsically refers to a future, so that

---

[239]"Mit dem Sein des Daseins und seiner Erschlossenheit ist gleichursprünglich Entdecktheit des innerweltlichen Seienden." Heidegger, *SZ*, p. 221.

[240]Heidegger, *Identität und Differenz*, pp. 22, 23.

[241]"Die These von der Geschichtlichkeit des Daseins sagt nicht, das weltlose Subjekt sei geschichtlich, sondern das Seiende, das als In-der-Welt-sein existiert. Geschehen der Geschichte ist Geschehen des In-der-Welt-seins. Geschichtlichkeit des Daseins ist wesenhaft Geschichtlichkeit von Welt, die auf dem Grunde der ekstatisch-horizontalen Zeitlichkeit zu deren Zeitigung gehört. Sofern Dasein faktisch existiert, begegnet auch schon innerweltliches Entdecktes. Mit der Existenz des geschichtlichen In-der-Welt-seins ist Zuhandenes und Vorhandenes je schon in die Geschichte der Welt einbezogen." *SZ*, p. 388.

[242]"La possession effective de l'idée vraie ne nous donne donc aucun droit d'affirmer un lieu intelligible de pensée adéquate et de productivité absolue, elle fonde seulement une 'téléologie' de la conscience qui, avec ce premier instrument, en forgera de plus parfaits, avec ceux-ci de plus parfaits, et ainsi sans fin." Merleau-Ponty, *PP*, p. 453.

without the future the past is not what it is. The future co-
constitutes the reality of the past, so that the history of truth
can never be "finished." [243]

There is still a "third" sense in which truth must be called
historical. Truth is historical, we saw, first, as an "event,"
secondly, as a "never-finished event"; but to these we must add,
in the third place, that the "event" which the birth of unconcealedness is, is possible only in a *particular* phase of the knowing subject's personal history and in a particular phase of the
collective history of mankind's search for truth in which every
personal history is contained. A particular phase of the personal
and collective history of knowledge plays the role of a particular
attitude or standpoint in asking questions, and it is this attitude
alone which makes it possible to *see*. For example, one who
has barely started to think does not yet see the true essence
of society, authority, love, justice, marriage, family, the good,
religion, etc. One who has merely assimilated the first principles
of physics does not yet possess the intellectual attitude needed
to ask meaningfully questions concerning nuclear physics. The
same can be said with respect to the collective history of mankind's search for knowledge or that of a particular society.

All this should make it evident how difficult it must be for
"us men" to engage in dialog. In order to "see" certain truths,
one has to stand in an advanced phase of history so as to have
the required attitude. With a blind man one cannot converse
about the perspective of the human field of vision because the
blind do not have the standpoint required by such a dialog.
Similarly it is meaningless to discuss the truth of the ethical
demand of support for widows and orphans in a society which
has not yet reached the phase of ethical history, in which the
abolition of the practice of burning widows together with their
deceased husbands, and of sacrificing children, is seen as an
ethical demand. Such a society does not have the attitude in
which the truth of a "more profound" ethical demand can
"come to pass." This truth *is* not "there" at "that time."

But, one could say, why ought we to converse and enter
into dialog with one another? This question does not permit
any answer as long as one restricts himself to pointing out that

---

[243]"C'est l'hypothèse d'une conscience sans avenir et d'une fin de l'histoire
qui est pour nous irréprésentable." Merleau-Ponty, *Humanisme et Terreur*,
Paris, 1947, p. 99.

truth has an historical character. Truth, however, is also trans-historical. This point must be discussed now.

The Transhistoricity of Truth

Earlier in this chapter we explained in what sense truth must be called relative: all unconcealedness is only unconcealedness *in relation to* a subject having a certain attitude or standpoint. Among these attitudes belong also the various phases of history. Historicity, then, is an aspect of truth's relativity. Every historical phase of truth's dis-closure, however, is subsequently transcended, and for this reason truth is never "finished." The dis-closure of truth dispels a little darkness, but human knowledge never "possesses" its object in perfect lucidity. Darkness is never dispelled in such a way that nothing remains to be disclosed. There is no truth which does not have a future,[244] for every truth opens up new gaps.[245]

As we also emphasized, however, this relativity of truth must not be interpreted in a relativistic fashion. Our statement that truth is relative means that truth is *absolute in relation to* the subject. Thus the recognition of historicity does not justify historicism, i.e., the view that a truth is true today because today is today, and that tomorrow it will no longer be true because tomorrow will be tomorrow. Such a view would be a vulgar form of relativism, which is not even self-consistent. For whoever accepts this view as true must admit that its truth is today's truth and, for this very reason is not tomorrow's truth. Yet the defender of this view *intends* to express a "definitive" truth.[246] Thus the relativity of truth's historicity does not justify the relativism of historicism.

It happens, nevertheless, that phenomenologists reject "absolute truth" on the basis of truth's historicity. Thus the question arises how this rejection should be understood. In our opinion, it should be viewed as a refusal to accept the absolute

---

[244]*PP*, pp. 452-453.

[245]". . . il sait seulement qu'il n'y a pas de savoir absolu et que c'est par cette lacune que nous sommes ouverts à la vérité." *EP*, p. 55.

[246]"Mais, à ce niveau et sous une forme aussi générale, qui ne voit que déjà cette argumentation dépossède celui qui l'avance? Car cette constatation de l'absolu de la pensée et de la valeur devient elle-même, dans le propre contexte de M. Merleau-Ponty, une 'vérité' définitive et indispensable, bloquant sans recours tout progrès de la pensée, Nous sommes devant un autre absolu." R. Jolivet, "Le problème de l'absolu dans la philosophie de M. Merleau-Ponty," *Tijdschrift voor Philosophie*, XIX (1957), p. 62.

aspect of truth as *isolated* from its relativity. In this sense the denial of "absolute truth" is a rejection of the *absolutism* of truth, in which one is bound to fall if one does not do justice to the relativity inherent in historicity. Both idealism and realism actually fail to do this.

Idealism cannot accept that "genuine" knowledge contains darkness. It conceives genuine knowledge as a situationless self-intuition of Thought, as the perfect transparency of the Idea for the Spirit, as the perfect self-possession of the Subject. Truth as unconcealedness is conceived as perfect unconcealedness, as light without darkness—in other words, as "finished" truth. But such a conception assumes that the history of disclosure is completed, and this implies a denial of the real history, which is not finished.[247] In the sense in which idealism understands the term, one can and must say that there is no "absolute truth." The reason for this statement is that we must recognize historicity, the fact that the subject is situated in a particular historical "attitude," the relation of a particular unconcealedness to the history of the *existent* subject. One who accepts an "absolute truth" in the sense of idealism actually has ceased to continue the history of progressive dis-closure because he holds that this history is finished.[248] The "absolute truth" of idealism is the *denial* of the relationship to history, the denial of *every* relativity and, consequently, is a form of absolutism.[249]

The same applies to realism. According to realism, meaning is "true"-in-itself, an absolute "light"-in-itself. For such a light there is, of course, no room when knowledge is conceived as encounter. Meaning, as the *real* terminus of encounter is the *chiaroscuro* of light and darkness, of unconcealedness and con-

---

247Dondeyne, *Foi chrétienne et pensée contemporaine*, Louvain, 2nd ed., 1952, p. 41.

248"Tout arrêt dans le mouvement de la conscience, toute fixation de l'objet, toute apparition d'un 'quelque chose' ou d'une idée suppose un sujet qui cesse de s'interroger au moins sous ce rapport-là. Voilà pourquoi, comme Descartes le disait, il est à la fois vrai que certaines idées se présentent à moi avec une évidence irrésistible en fait, et que ce fait ne vaut jamais comme droit, ne supprime pas la possibilité de douter dès que nous ne sommes plus en présence de l'idée. Ce n'est pas un hasard si l'évidence même peut être révoquée en doute, c'est que *la certitude est doute,* étant la reprise d'une tradition de pensée qui ne peut se condenser en 'vérité' évidente sans que je renonce à l'expliciter." Merleau-Ponty, *PP,* p. 454.

249". . . cette épreuve de la vérité ne serait savoir absolu que si nous pouvions en thématiser tous les motifs, c'est à dire si nous cessions d'être situés." *PP,* p. 453.

cealedness.[250] Meaning as absolute "light"-in-itself is a meaning which, as finished, is thrown out of the encounter, i.e., "put down" somewhere outside the real history of progressive explicitation. Strictly speaking, such a claim makes all truth impossible; nevertheless, the realist pretends to express truth. Thus he is forced to pretend to speak "absolute truth," "divorced" from the relativity of his historical standpoint. Obviously such a claim is a death blow for the *genuine*, historically situated search of truth. For this reason the "absolute truth" of realism also must be rejected.[251]

The "Moment" of Absoluteness in the Life of Truth

The recognition of the historicity of truth, understood as the "coming to pass" of subject "and" meaning, makes "absolute truth" impossible in the absolutistic sense in which both realism and idealism conceived it.[252] This does not mean, however, that there is no sense in which one can speak of absolute truth. Absolute truth does not lie outside the history of the *existent* subject-as-*cogito* but within this history, and precisely for this reason absolute truth is not a denial of relativity.

Carefully considered, *every* truth, no matter how personal, is absolute.[253] When the subject-as-*cogito* stands before this or that unconcealedness, then this unconcealedness is *indisputable*. When a degenerate mother stands before the corpse of the little child which she herself has killed, the truth of her crime is indisputable. In no phase of the history which this truth will have can the truth of her crime be disputed. It *can* never be not true for her that she did not kill her child. This is not all, however. It could happen that the mother realizes that no one else will ever know what she has done, that no one else can ever

---

[250]"Il y a, plutôt qu'un monde intelligible, des noyaux rayonnants séparés par des pans de nuit." Merleau-Ponty, *SNS*, p. 9.

[251]"La conscience métaphysique et morale meurt au contact de l'absolu." *SNS*, p. 191.

[252]"Quand donc je place hors de l'expérience progressive le fondement de la vérité ou de la moralité, ou bien je continue de m'en tenir aux probabilités qu'elle m'offre, - seulement dévalorisées par l'idéal d'une connaissance absolue, - ou bien je les déguise en certitudes absolues, et alors je lâche le vérifiable pour la vérité, c'est-à-dire la proie pour l'ombre." *SNS*, p. 190.

[253]"Wir sind also - wie könnten wir davon absehen - in unserem Philosophieren Funktionäre der Menschheit." Husserl, *Die Krisis der Europäischen Wissenschaften und die transzendentale Phänomenologie, Husserliana*, VI, p. 15.

affirm what she has to affirm. But, at the same time, she also
knows that she will *never* be able to agree with others if the
latter should deny that she killed her child. Thus she affirms
her truth not only in her own name but also in the name of all
others who would pronounce judgment upon her deed. Her
personal truth has absolute validity. At the historical *moment*
of this truth's birth it acquired a transhistorical validity, and
this transhistorical validity is, in principle, an intersubjective
validity. An unconcealedness born in history can never be disputed by anyone. Accordingly, the statement that a truth is
absolute in its *relativity* to a subject means that this truth is, in
principle, transhistorical and intersubjective. This absoluteness
is more than "the result of our verification," [254] "more" than the
matter-of-fact "agreement" to which Merleau-Ponty, at least in
some of his less fortunate expressions, seems to reduce the *essential* intersubjectivity of truth.[255]

The "moment" of absoluteness can also be expressed in the
traditional terms "immutable" and "eternal," provided one is
willing to understand them properly. We use them only to indicate that those who reject "immutable" and "eternal" truths
must imply, in their very rejection, that it is immutably and
eternally true that there are no "immutable" and "eternal"
truths. Accordingly, we express the "moment" of absoluteness
contained in the absolute rejection of "absolute" truths,[256] but
we do not re-introduce the "immutable" and "eternal" truths of
Plato, Aristotle, and Aquinas, which lie *beyond* history. The
immutability and eternity of truth is "brought about" by man
at an historical moment.

Similarly, the eternity of truth does not imply that there always have been and always will be human beings.[257] One who
thinks that this is implied is mistaken about the *intention* living

----

[254]*SNS*, p. 191.

[255]"L'accord avec moi-même et avec autrui reste aussi difficile à obtenir,
et j'ai beau croire qu'en droit il est toujours réalisable, je n'ai d'autres
raisons d'affirmer ce principe que l'expérience de certaines concordances, si
bien qu'enfin ma croyance à l'absolu, dans ce qu'elle a de solide, n'est rien
que mon expérience d'un accord avec moi-même et avec autrui." *SNS*,
p. 190.

[256]Kwant, *The Phenomenological Philosophy of Merleau-Ponty*, Pittsburgh, 1963, pp. 110 f.

[257]"Dass es 'ewige Wahrheiten' gibt, wird erst dann zureichend bewiesen
sein, wenn der Nachweis gelungen ist, dass in alle Ewigkeit Dasein war und
sein wird. Solange dieser Beweis aussteht, bleibt der Satz eine phantastische
Behauptung, die dadurch nicht an Rechtmässigkeit gewinnt, dass sie von den
Philosophen gemeinhin 'geglaubt' wird." Heidegger, *SZ*, p. 227.

in the affirmation of truth's eternity. He who claims that there is no "eternal" truth because there have not always been human beings also *intends* to say that it is eternally true that there have not always been human beings. The eternity of truth, then, is not merely an illusion arising from language,[258] but lives *in* language. For this reason it is not possible to divorce the eternity of truth from the "coming to pass" of unconcealedness, as if language would merely express once more, as it were, "superabundantly," something that is in-itself already "true" . . . for no one.[259] The eternity of truth "comes to pass" at the historical moment of the "coming to pass" of the language-of-truth. This eternity belongs to the essence of truth's "coming to pass," and therefore is implicity affirmed whenever it is denied.

The immutability of truth, likewise, is not excluded by its historicity. Truth's historicity excludes that truth is "finished," i.e., that all darkness can be driven away from unconcealedness, so that unconcealedness would be perfect transparency. But the historicity of truth does not mean that today's truth will be tomorrow's untruth. It is possible, of course, that tomorrow my "seeing" of today will reveal itself to have been merely putative, and that my "truth" was mere semblance. If, however, I "see" today, my truth is immutable and, nonetheless, unfinished. For in the historical dialog of the *existent* subject-as-*cogito* with reality, the "already" of unconcealedness is taken up into the "now": the truth of "now" does not destroy yesterday's truth but makes it more profound and integrates it.[260] In this sense, all truth is immutable.

The example, given above, of a mother who faces her misdeed referred only to a *de facto* truth. What is true for this mother is not *of necessity* true for her and is not *universally* true for every mother.

There are, however, also truths *de jure*. They are concerned

---

[258]Merleau-Ponty, *PP*, pp. 459-460.

[259]"Qu'est-ce-que ce vrai éternel que personne n'a? Qu'est-ce-que cet exprimé au delà de toute expression, et, si nous avons le droit de le poser, pourquoi notre souci constant est-il d'obtenir une expression plus exacte?" *PP*, p. 452.

[260]"Je pense, et telle ou telle pensée m'apparaît vraie; je sais bien qu'elle n'est pas vraie sans condition et que l'explicitation totale serait une tâche infinie; mais cela n'empêche pas qu'au moment où je pense, je pense quelque chose, et que toute autre vérité, au nom de laquelle je voudrais dévaluer celle-ci, si elle peut pour moi s'appeler vérité, doit s'accorder avec la pensée 'vraie' dont j'ai l'expérience." *PP*, pp. 455-456.

with the *essence* of man and thing.[261]   The truth about the essence of man and thing is necessary and universal.[262]   This statement can easily be misunderstood, for necessary and universal truths about the essence of man and thing are, nonetheless, also "conditional" truths.   If an essence must be called "man," then this essence is necessary and universal; and the same must be said with respect to a thing.[263]   It is not difficult to see how tempting it must be to put the essence of man and thing "somewhere" unconditionally and "in itself," "divorced" from the never-finished "coming to pass" of truth.   But it cannot be done without falling into contradictions.   Necessary and universal truths also are born, they presuppose the historical moment, the "fact" of their "coming to pass," [264] and this fact is not a necessary fact.[265]   *In this sense* truths *de jure* must still be called truths of fact.[266]

6. The Criterion of Truth

"There are things that are indisputable . . . that are true and that are false." [267]   The indisputable, the true, is the unconcealed for the subject-as-*cogito*.   It is that which is "evident." [268] What is traditionally called "evidence" is the "experience" of truth as unconcealedness,[269] the standing in unconcealedness with which certainty is fused.[270]   "Seeing," in the broadest sense of the term, i.e., the immediate presence of the *existent* subject-as-*cogito* to a present reality, decides about truth.[271]

261Sartre, *EH*, pp. 80-85.
262"Ainsi, bien que le contenu de la morale soit variable, une certaine forme de cette morale est universelle." *EH*, p. 85.
263"Il est possible que les hommes cessent d'exister. . . . Il est possible encore que cette structure évolue . . . mais il est certain, par exemple, que l'étant non libre ou non situé cessera de pouvoir être appelé un homme, et qu'en ce sens homme désignera toujours et nécessairement un étant *ex-sistant, libre, qui se projette, est situé*, et est de soi auprès de l'autre."   De Waelhens, *Une philosophie de l'ambiguïté*, p. 389.
264*PP*, p. 455.
265"La contingence ontologique, celle du monde lui-même, étant radicale, est au contraire ce qui fonde une fois pour toutes notre idée de vérité." *PP*, p. 456.
266*PP*, p. 451.
267Merleau-Ponty, *SNS*, p. 191.
268"Evidenz ist . . . nichts anderes als das 'Erlebnis' der Wahrheit. . . . Das evidente Urteil . . . ist ein Bewusstsein originärer Gegebenheit."   Husserl, *Logische Untersuchungen*, I, p. 190.
269"Man nennt die Evidenz ein Sehen, Einsehen, Erfassen des selbst gegebenen ('wahren') Sachverhalts."   Husserl, *ibid.*
270Heidegger, *SZ*, p. 256.
271"Am Prinzip aller Prinzipien: dass jede originär gebende Anschauung

Anyone, however, realizes that such statements do not yet mean very much. For the *existent* subject can not only "see" but also dream, fancy, hallucinate, fear, desire, and get lost in illusions. Nevertheless, the preceding paragraph did say something: it expressed that the recognition of the fact that much "seeing" subsequently proves to have been a purely putative "seeing" is not a ground to reject "seeing" as the justification of truth.[272] For, if we withdraw a judgment because we realize that we were dreaming when we thought that we "saw" something, we cannot avoid assuming that *now*, while withdrawing our judgment, we *really* "see." We know that we sometimes make mistakes and we correct our errors. But we can do this only in the name of truth.[273] Thus we have found a possibility of formulating the "critical problem" in a correct way. Just as it does not make sense to ask whether the wealthiest people have the most money,[274] so also it is meaningless to ask whether that which is "evident"—that which we "see"—is true, for true is that which we "see." [275] We can merely ask where we can find the criterion to determine here and now whether we are really "seeing" or dreaming, fancying, hallucinating, fearing, desiring, or getting lost in illusions.

We are not merely able to ask this question, but we *must* raise it, for we contradict one another. This means that one man thinks that the other lives in illusions, while the latter thinks

---

eine Rechtsquelle der Erkenntnis sei, dass alles, was sich uns in der 'Intuition' originär, (sozusagen in seiner leibhaften Wirklichkeit) darbietet, einfach hinzunehmen sei, als was es gibt, aber auch nur in den Schranken, in denen es sich gibt, kann uns keine erdenkliche Theorie irre machen." Husserl, *Ideen*, I, p. 52.

[272]"Zugestanden, dass es beim phänomenologischen Sehen Täuschungen durch deutende Einlegung gibt; gibt es sie beim äusseren Sehen weniger? Ist die Deskription wertlos, weil es Täuschungen der Deskription gibt?" Husserl, "Entwurf einer 'Vorrede' zu den 'Logischen Untersuchungen'," *Tijdschrift voor Philosophie*, I(1939), p. 335.

[273]"Nous ne savons qu'il y a des erreurs que parce que nous avons des vérités, au nom desquelles nous corrigeons les erreurs et les connaissons comme erreurs." Merleau-Ponty, *PP*, p. 341.

[274]William James, *Pragmatism*, New York, 1914, p. 220.

[275]"Plus généralement, il ne faut pas se demander si nos évidences sont bien des vérités, ou si, par un vice de notre esprit, ce qui est évident pour nous ne serait pas illusoire à l'égard de quelque vérité en soi: car si nous parlons d'illusion, c'est que nous avons reconnu des illusions, et nous n'avons pu le faire qu'au nom de quelque perception qui, dans le même moment, s'attestât comme vraie, de sorte que le doute, ou la crainte de se tromper affirme en même temps notre pouvoir de dévoiler l'erreur et ne saurait donc nous déraciner de la vérité. Nous sommes dans la vérité et l'évidence est l'expérience de la vérité." *PP*, Avant-propos, p. XI.

that the former is blind. Where are we to find a criterion to distinguish the one's illusion from the other's blindness? [276]

The "Fruitfulness" of Truth

Let us begin with an example which, according to William James, lies on a "common sense level of fact." [277] I have a certain instrument in my hands, of which *A* affirms that it is a pen while *B* claims that it is a screwdriver. *A* says that *B* must be dreaming, but *B* argues that *A* must be blind. By what criterion can I determine who is "right"? In ordinary life one would reply: "Let *B* try to use the instrument to fasten the screws of his garden gate; then he will *see*." The philosopher expresses the same idea when he says that the criterion of truth is the *fruitfulness* of the dialogue with reality, which *existence* is. *Existence* is a dialogue of a subjectivity with that which is not that subjectivity. The reality of things reveals itself within this dialogue, if only because at a given moment the dialogue becomes wholly impossible: reality becomes overloaded with fancied or dreamt meanings. A consequence of this overloading is that *reality* ceases to give answers, offers resistance or is destroyed; for the dialogue which human *existence* is continues *as if* those dreamt or fancied meanings were *real*—witness the wrecked fountainpen which was taken to be a screwdriver. If I use the pen as a pen, my action results in writing. The continuation of the dialogue is fruitful: the verification of the pen's meaning as a pen consists in the affirmation of "its leading to no frustration or contradiction." [278] True is that which is "fruitful."

This theory brings us close to the inspiration that lives in pragmatism's theory of truth. It stands to reason, however, that we do not understand this theory in the way it was presented by those critics of pragmatism against whom James himself had to voice his protest. "True" is that which "works," which "gives satisfaction," says James. But this does not mean that anything which "works" or "gives satisfaction" on no matter which level of verification is true on every level of speaking.[279] James

---

276A. Brunner, *La personne incarnée,* Paris, 1947, p. 181.
277James, *op. cit.,* p. 209.
278James, *op. cit.,* p. 207.
279"Schiller says the true is that which 'works'. Thereupon he is treated as one who limits verification to the lowest material utilities. Dewey says truth is what gives 'satisfaction'. He is treated as one who believes in calling everything true which, if it were true, would be pleasant." James, *op. cit.,* p. 234.

wanted to settle the score with representative realism, but he raised the problem of truth in terms of this kind of realism. He asked what it means that there is "agreement" between "ideas" and "reality." To make truth human truth again, however, he proceeded in a way that was bound to horrify the representationalist. James understood "agreement" as "agreeable leading"; he spoke of "the truth's cash-value"—of truth as that which leads to something, that with which something can be done, which eliminates frustrations and inconsistencies.[280] Unsurprisingly, James at once had to defend himself against the accusation that all this implied arbitrariness.[281] The insight that truth is human truth opened James's eyes to the fact that truth has to be "brought about," "made."[282] He was promptly told that truth need not be made but *is*.[283]

James's theory of truth can be integrated into phenomenology. The term "agreement," which James rejected, can be retained, provided reality is not conceived as "brute" reality. In order to prevent that the true be conceived as true-in-itself, and to make sure that the true be understood as true-for-the-subject, one need not define the true as the "useful,"[284] which could easily give rise to misunderstandings. True is that which is unconcealed, which is "seen," and not dreamt or fancied. For this reason, the true makes it possible to continue the dialog, it "leads somewhere," opens a future, and eliminates frustrations and inconsistencies. Truth can be distinguished from untruth by its "fruitfulness."

The sciences make use of the same criterion.[285] The physicist questions reality by means of a certain *a priori* view, an hypothesis. He "thinks" that reality will be such or such, but he does not accept this as true and certain until reality *itself* reveals itself as such. The physicist draws answers from reality, and, before reality *itself* answers his question, he does not speak of

---

[280]James, *op. cit.,* pp. 198, 200, 202.
[281]"Yet in the choice of these man-made formulas we can not be capricious with impunity any more than we can be capricious on the common-sense practical level." James, *op. cit.,* p. 216.
[282]"The truth of an idea is not a stagnant property inherent in it. Truth *happens* to an idea. It *becomes* true, is *made* true by events. Its verity *is* in fact an event, a process: the process namely of its verifying itself, its veri-*fication*. Its validity is in the process of its valid-*ation*." James, *op. cit.,* p. 201.
[283]James, *op. cit.,* p. 218.
[284]"It is true because it is useful." James, *op. cit.,* p. 204.
[285]J. Kockelmans, *Phenomenology and Physical Science,* pp. 169f.

scientific truth.[286] If his hypothesis is wrong, his dialogue with
reality comes to a halt: [287] reality gives no answer, resists his
question, or is destroyed. The physicist then realizes that he
was imagining things when he formulated his hypothesis: his
dialogue with reality became unfruitful.[288]

The same applies to the human sciences, but there is a difference: in these sciences it is much more difficult to question
reality than in the physical sciences, because in many cases it is
not possible to perform experiments. In the realm of the human
sciences truth is discovered only with the greatest difficulty. Entire generations of thinkers sometimes have to pass away before
it becomes evident that a certain view is false. That view is
then said to be no longer "tenable," which means that it "con-
tradicts" the terminus of the encounter: the dialogue has come
to a halt. New views are then needed to re-open the dialogue.
An example is provided by orthodox Freudianism. Psychoanalytic practice showed that there are other dimensions to man
than sex. A fruitful dialogue between the psychotherapist and
his patient often became impossible if the ·therapist held fast to
Freud's narrow framework of ideas.[289]

It may be good to return from the human sciences to "ordinary life." For what these sciences try to express *in a universal
way* the "ordinary man in everyday life" is assumed to "know"
concretely. The human sciences try to capture man's way of
dealing with himself, his fellowmen, society, and God, and formulate general insights about these relationships. In everyday
life, however, man "practices" these relationships, which presupposes concrete insights into them. The more complex the situation is, the more difficult it is to disclose the objective meaning
of reality. Thus there is no escape for man from making mistakes
in religious, social, and political life, education and instruc-
tion, courts of law, mental care, etc. Very often the dialogue
with reality has to continue for a long time before man realizes
his error and sees that he was living in mere "semblance."
Frequently he does not even realize that long ago he got

286"We must find a theory that will *work*." James, *op. cit.,* p. 216.

287R. C. Kwant and J.H.G. v. d. Berk, "Het gesprek van de physicus met
de wereld," *Annalen van het Thijmgenootschap,* 53(1955), pp. 13-15.

288"Truth in science is what gives us the maximum possible sum of satis-
factions." James, *op. cit.,* p. 217.

289J. Nuttin, *Psychanalyse et conception spiritualiste de l'homme,* Louvain, 1955, pp. 98-134.

caught in a no-exit street. Sometimes an entire life, education or even a civilization, has to fail before man recognizes the truth about himself, his fellowmen, society, or God. How often does it not happen that only at the end of his life a husband realizes that his wife is really his wife, or rather, he realizes what it really means that his wife is his wife.

In spite of his conviction that he often errs, man must act. He cannot escape "making a mess of it," and he experiences that others also cause misfortunes. He cannot even abstain from acting and from having an opinion, for not having an opinion is also having an opinion, and not acting is also acting. Man's hands are always stained. There is a kind of material sinfulness in every personal history, as well as in mankind's collective history, a sinfulness of which the superficial man has no inkling. But this sinfulness inspires the philosopher to the greatest prudence and reserve in his thinking, it teaches him to be modest and self-effacing when he forms his opinion. The fruitfulness of his dialogue with reality is based on the condition that he be willing to deny himself. In connection with this, Marcel writes:

> An inexhaustible concreteness lies, I believe, in the center of reality or human destiny. No progress is made in our knowledge of it by stages or by passing on our knowledge to one another, as is done in any of the particular sciences. Each one of us can only penetrate into this inexhaustible concreteness with the most integral and most virginal part of his essence. Let me add that it is enormously difficult. For experience shows that this integrity, which alone can come into touch with being, is at once covered by much contamination and dirt. Only through a long and difficult cleansing or rather purification, a painful asceticism do we succeed in liberating this integrity.[290]

"Fruitfulness" of the dialogue with reality is also the criterion of truth in religion. That a religion is a true religion does not mean that a religious society is in possession of theses expressing the truth-in-itself about God. Religious truths also are truths in relation to man. The statement that truth is truth-for-man holds *in one particular way* for physical truth and *in another particular way* for religious truth. The statement that the "fruitfulness" of the dialogue with reality is the criterion of truth

---

[290]Marcel, *RI,* pp. 91-92.

holds in one particular way for physical science and in another particular way for religious knowledge. The statement that the dialogue of the physicist with the world is fruitful, means that the affirmation of a particular unconcealedness "leads some-where," opens a future, makes new physical questions possible, eliminates the frustrations of "wrongly formulated" physical questions, takes away inconsistencies in previously given answers, in brief, it means that the physicist as physicist can realize him-self. *In this sense* one can say that the true is the "useful." The true is true for a subject with a particular standpoint; con-sequently, the "fruitfulness" or "unfruitfulness" of the dialogue with reality also lies within that region of reality which is cut out for dialogue by the corresponding standpoint. The fact that the affirmation of a particular unconcealedness from an artistic standpoint is not "fruitful" for man's self-realization as a physicist does not disqualify artistic truth. The criterion of truth functions always only within a particular region of *existence*. It would be unthinkable, however, that a truth would be without "fruit" on any level of man's being and, nonetheless, would be a worthwhile truth.

These ideas apply in a specific way to the truth of a religion. Where can the criterion be found to distinguish between the illusion of one and the blindness of the other? The "fruitful-ness" of religion for a specific way of man's self-realization must supply the answer to this question. A religion is not true be-cause it would eliminate the frustrations of a wrongly formulated question of physics. But this does not mean that a religion can be true and, nonetheless, not "fruitful" on any level. If someone wishes to catch a plane and asks me what time it is, and I answer that I live in New York, my reply is "useless," "unfruitful." The fact that I really live in New York is devoid of importance: it would make no difference at all if I did not live there.[291] That fact, however, would be important if the man did not wish to catch a plane but to visit me. He could verify the truth of my answer in New York. Then it would become evident that he had reached his goal, that my answer was "useful," "im-portant" for him, because it enabled him to realize himself as my visitor. The truth of my answer would be evident from

---

[291]James, *op. cit.*, p. 232.

its "fruitfulness" for his self-realization as a visitor. But a statement that is of *no* "importance" to anyone cannot be distinguished as true from untruth.

These remarks are not made with the intention of now proceeding to an enumeration of the "characteristics" of the true religion. On the contrary, they were made in order to explicitate the "dizziness" of the search for the truth about man. A true religion reveals itself "fruitful" for man's self-realization, and an untrue religion is untrue because and to the extent that it does violence to man. In line with the examples given above, which were borrowed from "ordinary" life and the sciences, it is easy to write this. As a matter of fact, however, we tacitly assume that we are in possession of enough truths about man to establish the "fruitfulness" of certain religious views for man's self-realization and the "unfruitfulness" of others. But where do we find the criterion for the truth about man? A religion which leads to sacrificing little children and the burning of widows is inhuman, we say, and therefore untrue. Rightly so. A religion which rejects work, physical science, and technology is dangerous for man's self-realization, we say, and therefore untrue. Right again: such a religion opens no future, does not free man, is "unfruitful."

Who does not see, however, that all this can only be said in the supposition that the truth about man implies man's *duty* of self-realization and the *essential* role that work, science, and technology must play in this self-realization? One who does not make this supposition has no reason whatsoever to say that a religion which makes man's self-realization impossible is untrue. He will call such a religion "fruitful" because he has an entirely different view of man's "having to be." We call a religion which leads to the sacrifice of children and the burning of widows untrue because it is not "fruitful" and even pernicious for man, conceived as destiny for his fellowman—a destiny which is accomplished in love. But such a statement presupposes that the truth about man's "having to be" lies indeed in love: one who does not make this supposition cannot call the religion in question untrue. If certain religious views are the reason why in a particular society nothing is done to prevent nine out of every ten new-born children from dying at an early age, we say that such a religion is a disaster for man and therefore a pseudo-religion. But such a claim can only be made in the supposition that the fate of the one survivor is not worse than that of the prematurely dead.

"Deciding" About the Truth and "Receiving" the Truth

In connection with the examples given above, is it right to speak of presuppositions or assumptions? Are not those alleged assumptions really evidences, truths about man? We have no intention of denying the affirmative answer to the last question, but wish to mention that this answer itself evokes many new difficult questions. For with respect to the truth about man also we must affirm the statement made previously regarding the truth about the world: this truth is historical, i.e., it "originates," "comes to pass," and is "brought about." The truth about man is brought about by man. Man accomplishes the truth about his essence by dis-closing his essence to himself in a never-finished history of becoming conscious of himself. Man is not the "lord," but only the "shepherd" of this history. His becoming conscious of himself is a "letting be" of his essence, not an autonomous and arbitrary deciding about his essence. But what criterion is there for the truth about his essence? How can man distinguish his illusions from his blindness?

The sceptics have a ready answer: "Never." Sometimes the philosopher has great difficulty to resist the temptation of that answer. Obviously, however, giving in to it would mean an end to philosophy. That would not be too bad, one could say, for what is meaningless need not survive. The scepticism, however, which would make philosophy impossible itself is also a philosophy, albeit a bad one. If one takes the sceptic seriously, one must assume that he is convinced of his own statement: "The essence of man is such that he never knows whether a thesis about this essence is objective." But then such a statement is presented as an objective explicitation of that essence— the possibility of which is precisely what the sceptic wishes to deny. His denial, therefore, surreptitiously affirms what he wishes to deny, and only this implicit affirmation makes his denial possible. Scepticism is an internal contradiction.[292]

---

[292]"Aller echte Skeptizismus, welcher Art und Richtung er auch ist, zeigt sich durch den prinzipiellen Widersinn an, dass er in seinen Argumentationen implizite, als Bedingung der Möglichkeit ihrer Geltung, eben das voraussetzt, was er in seinen These leugnet. . . . . Wer auch nur sagt: Ich bezweifle die Erkenntnisbedeutung der Reflexion, behauptet einen Widersinn. Denn über

How seductive and, perhaps we may add, how "strong" is the standpoint of the objectivist! He has simply eliminated every possibility of *arbitrariness* from the history of truth by positing that man *first* is "all kinds of things" and *then* becomes conscious of "a number of things." It does not matter whether one calls this "being" of man "ideal" with Plato or "real" with Aristotle and Aquinas. The essence of man "is" necessarily, universally, immutably, and eternally "true"-in-itself. In becoming conscious of himself man is bound to this essence-in-itself.

The price, however, which the objectivist must pay is too high, and his "advantage" is an illusion.[293] For, whether there is a truth-in-itself about man or not does not matter: "to judge, I can dispose only of my own opinions, which remain subject to error." [294] The objectivist "antedates" a truth which was born in history,[295] and refuses to consider even the possibility that the "moment of truth" could be a "moment of illusion."

The truth about man's essence also must be "brought about," but what does this mean? Hitherto we have always understood this term as the "letting be" and "dis-closing" of reality. It is impossible to "antedate" the unconcealed; therefore, it is also impossible to present matters as if man *first* is "all kinds of things" and *then* becomes conscious of "a number of things." This statement, however, does not exclude the possibility of saying, for example, that the essence of Descartes was intentionality or *existence*, even though he himself was not conscious of it. *We* say this now in terms of *our* phase of becoming conscious of ourselves, just as *we* affirm geological periods before the first man in terms of a particular phase in the geologist's growing consciousness. Understood in this *sense* one can say that man becomes conscious of what he "already" is.

But is this *all* that must be said of man's being, insofar as this being is a "having to be"? One cannot argue that the essence of man *ever* was non-*existence* while, nonetheless man was

---

sein Zweifeln aussagend, reflektiert er, und diese Aussage als gültig hinstellen setzt voraus, dass die Reflexion den bezweifelten Erkenntniswert wirklich und zweifellos (sc. für die vorliegenden Fälle) habe, dass sie die gegenständliche Beziehung nicht ändere, dass das unreflektierte Erlebnis im Übergang in die Reflexion sein Wesen nicht einbüsse." Husserl, *Ideen*, I, pp. 189-190.

[293]"En morale comme en art, il n'y aurait pas de solution pour celui qui veut d'abord assurer sa marche." Merleau-Ponty, *SNS*, p. 9.
[294]*SNS*, p. 189.
[295]James, *op. cit.*, p. 220.

man. Man did not *decide* to be *existence*, corporeal, free, etc.,[296] so that, through this decision, he *became existence*, corporeal, free, etc. But man did *decide* to realize himself as a worker; he did decide to destine himself for his fellowman at least to the extent of not arbitrarily destroying the other's life; [297] he did decide to realize himself as a pursuer of science; he did decide to abolish polyandry; and he did decide that his sexuality would be heterosexuality. With respect to these modes of "having to be," man's becoming conscious of himself, then, was not a becoming conscious of what he "already" was *in the same way* as the affirmation of being-*existence* is the affirmation of what man "already" is. The affirmation of those modes of "having to be" is a *decision* about the *essence* of man by which man has come to be.[298]

No one, however, will claim that this decision is an arbitrary decision.[299] Man is not the "lord of his own being." But it is very difficult to account for that decision. *We* can *now* affirm that by the above-mentioned decisions man opted for the truth of his authentic being. In a certain sense one can even say that "not knowing beforehand" forced man to make a *decision*: that "not knowing" is the origin of "having to will." [300] Now that man has chosen, however, he can never deceive himself into thinking that he would just as well have been standing in the truth if he had decided to deny his actual choice. This means not merely that man cannot go back on his decision, but even more that man would destroy himself by reneging his decision. Man would lose himself if he would no longer realize

---

[296]De Waelhens, *Une philosophie de l'ambiguïté*, p. 389.

[297]"Irgendwann dämmerte dem Menschen zum ersten Mal die Freiheitsidee. Irgendwann entschloss er sich, das Leben der Artgenossen nicht willkürlich zu vernichten." E. Fechner, *Rechtsphilosophie, Soziologie und Metaphysik des Rechts,* Tübingen, 1956, p. 250.

[298]"Wahl ist der Ausdruck für das Bewusstsein, dass ich in freier Entscheidung nicht nur in der Welt handle, sondern mein eignes Wesen in geschichtlicher Kontinuität schaffe. Ich weiss, dass ich nicht nur da bin und so bin und infolgedessen so handle, sondern dass ich im Handeln und Entscheiden Ursprung bin meiner Handlung und meines Wesens zugleich. . . . . . Freiheit ist als die Wahl meines Selbst. . . . . . Was ich selbst sei, ist zwar noch offen, weil ich noch entscheiden werde: insofern bin ich noch nicht. Aber dieses Nichtsein als Nichtendgültigsein in der Daseinserscheinung wird durchleuchtet von der existentiellen Gewissheit meines Seins, dort, wo ich wählend im Entschluss Ursprung werde." Jaspers, *Philosophie,* p. 451.

[299]"Das Ergreifen der Chiffre ist als Wahl aus der Freiheit des sie Lesenden. Darin überzeuge ich mich, dass mein Sein so ist, weil ich so will - obgleich ich darin schlechthin nichts erzeuge, sondern empfange, was ich wähle." Jaspers, *op. cit.,* p. 808.

[300]Jaspers, *op. cit.,* p. 459.

himself as a worker and a pursuer of science; he would lose himself if he were to opt for polyandry and homosexuality, and had not decided to destine himself for his fellowman, at least to the extent of not arbitrarily destroying the other's life.

In the actions which followed his decisions, it became clear that man indeed let the truth of his essence "come to pass": the continuation of man's dialogue with his own essence revealed itself "fruitful"; man's becoming conscious of himself revealed itself a "successful" becoming conscious of himself. *We* who affirm this *today* are convinced that with respect to the truth about man we did *not arbitrarily* proceed—so much so that we simply would not think of saying that others who did not make the above-mentioned decisions are just "as right" as we ourselves are "right." In our eyes, these others live still on a sub-human level. If they wish to find the truth about their own essence, they will have to make the same decisions. At the same time, we know that discussions with them are meaningless, for "one cannot come to an agreement with someone who is unwilling or is unable to see." [301]

Nevertheless, even this is not the last word with respect to the criterion of truth. Granted that only *post factum* man's becoming-conscious-of-himself revealed itself "successful," must not man have also "beforehand" a certain criterion if he is to be *able* to determine what can be called "successful" in the human realm and what not? But how are we to conceive the "coming to pass" of this criterion's truth? Is there perhaps a "resort outside man" which "decides" about the truth of man's essence, so that man is merely called to listen to its decisions in order to be able to find the truth about his own essence? In his later works at least, Heidegger insinuates that this is indeed the case. He describes Western man as immersed in the nihilism of "forgetfulness of Being," [302] which consists in the absolutism of metaphysics and technology.[303] This "forgetfulness" is not an "unfortunate" project of man, however, but must rather be as-

---

301Husserl, "Entwurf einer 'Vorrede' zu den 'Logischen Untersuchungen'," *Tijdschrift voor Philosophie,* I(1939), p. 335.

302"Wir bewegen uns mit dem ganzen Bestand noch innerhalb der Zone des Nihilismus, gesetzt freilich, das Wesen des Nihilismus beruhe in der Seinsvergessenheit." Heidegger, *Zur Seinsfrage,* Frankfurt a.M., 1956, p. 40.

303Cf. the numerous references to Heidegger with respect to this topic in S. IJsseling, *Heidegger, Denken en danken, geven, en zijn,* Utrecht, 1966, and the author's *Phenomenology and Metaphysics,* Pittsburgh, 1965.

cribed to the "tarrying of Being itself." [304] Metaphysics and technology are projects of Being which, as "mission" (*Geschick*), is in a certain sense a "resort over man," [305] an "initiation." [306] The "event" of metaphysics and technology is a form of Being's own "event." [307] The "forgetfulness of Being," in which Being in the past "came to pass" and through which metaphysics and technology are what they are, is, according to Heidegger, not man's "negligence" but, on the contrary, implies that "it is 'no go' with Being, Being itself tarries." [308]

"If the history of the West lies immersed in forgetfulness of Being, what must we do?" Heidegger asks. But he adds at once that this is not the appropriate question. Not what we must do is a problem, but "how must we think?" [309] The proper "action" implies being receptive to the "event" of Being, and this is thinking. Thinking must prepare a "place" for the "event" of Being, a "place" where man is sensitive to the "appeal of Being." Man must first of all recover the scope of his own essence. This will not happen as long as man merely tries to offer morphological, psychological, and historical explanations for the metaphysical order in which he lives; as long as he tries to present his own situation as an "effect" of "causes"; as long as he works with the apparatus of adding explanatory symptoms. The metaphysical-technological order can only be understood as a phase in the history of Being, "in the sense that Being itself sends itself." [310] Whether or not man will succeed in letting the truth of Being come to pass in his own essence is not decided by man himself but depends on the "mission" of Being.[311]

304Heidegger, *Nietzsche*, Pfullingen, 1961, II, p. 353.
305J. v.d. Wiele, *Zijnswaarheid en onverborgenheid, Een vergelijkende studie over de ontologische waarheid in het Thomisme en bij Heidegger*, Leuven, 1964, p. 282.
306W. J. Richardson, *Heidegger, Through Phenomenology to Thought*, The Hague, 1963, p. 435.
307Heidegger, *Die Technik und die Kehre*, Pfullingen, 1962, p. 43.
308"Aus dem Geschick des Seins gedacht, bedeutet das nihil des Nihilismus, dass es mit dem Sein nichts ist. Das Sein kommt nicht an das Licht seines eigenen Wesens. Im Erscheinen des Seienden als solchen bleibt das Sein selbst aus." M. Heidegger, *Holzwege*, 4th ed., Frankfurt a.M., 1963, p. 244.
309Heidegger, *Die Technik und die Kehre*, p. 40.
310Heidegger, *op. cit.*, p. 38.
311"Uberdies aber ist der Entwurf wesenhaft ein geworfener. Das werfende im Entwerfen ist nicht der Mensch, sondern das Sein selbst, das den Menschen in die Ek-sistenz des Da-seins als sein Wesen schickt. Dieses Geschick ereignet sich als die Lichtung des Seins, als welche es ist. Sie gewährt die Nähe zum Sein. In dieser Nähe, in der Lichtung des 'Da' wohnt

The sway of metaphysics and technology is a "danger"; but since man does not autonomously decide about metaphysics and technology, Being itself is "danger." [312] The danger of metaphysics and technology cannot be overcome by man's autonomous decision because man is not "the lord of Being." [313]

"Where there is danger, however, there salvation also develops." [314] When danger *as* danger "is," the danger itself is salvation. For when danger *as* danger "is," then, together with the reversal of "forgetfulness," the truth of Being "comes to pass." In the "coming to pass" of danger, there "comes to pass" and "dwells" a favor, the grace of the reversal from "forgetfulness of Being" to the truth of Being.[315] This reversal comes about without any intermediary whatsoever, for it is Being itself, which does not lie in a causal connection.[316] The coming of Being, then, is not guaranteed. It does not come about without man; at the same time, it does not come about through man's own absolute initiative.[317] In the past history of the West the self-giving of Being assumed the form of metaphysics and technology. This meant the "tarrying of the truth of Being," but it is not necessary that it always remains so.[318] Perhaps we are already living in the shadow which the "reversal" throws ahead of itself.[319] Whether and when the "reversal" will come about nobody knows, but it is not necessary to know this. It

---

der Mensch als der Ek-sistierende, ohne dass er es heute schon vermag, dieses Wohnen eigens zu erfahren und zu übernehmen." Heidegger, *Über den Humanismus*, p. 25.

[312]"Insofern die Gefahr das Sein selber ist . . . ." Heidegger, *Die Technik und die Kehre*, p. 41.

[313]"Wenn das Wesen der Technik, das Gestell als die Gefahr im Sein, das Sein selbst ist, dann lässt sich die Technik niemals durch ein bloss auf sich gestelltes menschliches Tun meistern, weder positiv noch negativ. Die Technik, deren Wesen das Sein selbst ist, lässt sich durch den Mensch niemals überwinden. Das hiesse doch: der Mensch sei der Herr des Seins." Heidegger, *op. cit.*, p. 38.

[314]Heidegger, *op. cit.*, p. 41.

[315]"Wenn die Gefahr als die Gefahr ist, ereignet sich mit der Kehre der Vergessenheit die Wahrnis des Seins." Heidegger, *op. cit.*, p. 42.

[316]Heidegger, *op. cit.*, pp. 42-43.

[317]"Der Mensch ist vielmehr vom Sein selbst in die Wahrheit des Seins 'geworfen', dass er, dergestalt ek-sistierend, die Wahrheit des Seins hüte, damit im Lichte des Seins das Seiende als das Seiende, das es ist, erscheine. Ob und wie es erscheint, ob und wie der Gott und die Götter, die Geschichte und die Natur in die Lichtung des Seins hereinkommen, an- und abwesen, entscheidet nicht der Mensch." Heidegger, *Über den Humanismus*, p. 19.

[318]"Geschick aber ist wesenhaft Geschick des Seins, so zwar, dass das Sein selber sich schickt und je als ein Geschick west und demgemäss sich geschicklich wandelt." Heidegger, *Die Technik und die Kehre*, p. 38.

[319]Heidegger, *op. cit.*, pp. 40-41.

could even be dangerous because it belongs to the essence of man to be "expecting." Man must "expect" the "coming to pass" of Being by thoughtfully guarding Being,[320] and not by trying to master it by his calculations.[321] The "mission of Being" is equiprimordially the "mission of thinking." [322]

We were looking for a criterion of the truth about man's essence, and voiced the idea that perhaps a "resort outside man" "decides" about that truth in such a way that man is merely called to listen to those "decisions" in order to be able to enter into the truth about his own essence. According to Heidegger, this is really the case: "We never come to thoughts, but thoughts come to us." [323] Is this answer satisfactory, however? The "coming to pass" of Being must "send" man the truth about his own essence: man is the one who is "expecting." But in the past Being "came to pass" as "forgetfulness of Being," and thus untruth about his essence was "sent" to him by Being. Where does man find the criterion to determine whether he is given the truth or the untruth about his essence? I cannot give up the "initiative" of my thinking, for "I have only my own opinions at my disposal for judging."

After writing about 150 pages, I have the impression that I have barely started genuinely to philosophize. But at the place where I now have arrived, I see no light whatsoever.

7. REASON AND SCIENCE

When we spoke of the "natural light"—the "light" which the *existent* subject-as-*cogito* himself is—we were actually concerned with what a tradition of long standing always refers to as human "reason." The insight that man is a "light" for himself, and that he illuminates that which is not himself found expression in the "definition" of man as "rational animal."

One certainly does not go too far by claiming that today it

---

[320]"Wann und wie sie sich geschicklich ereignet, weiss niemand. Es ist auch nicht nötig, solches zu wissen. Ein Wissen dieser Art wäre sogar das Verderblichste für den Menschen, weil sein Wesen ist, der Wartende zu sein, der des Wesens des Seins wartet, indem er es denkend hütet. Nur wenn der Mensch als der Hirt des Seins der Wahrheit des Seins wartet, kann er eine Ankunft des Seinsgeschickes erwarten, ohne in das blosse Wissenwollen zu verfallen." Heidegger, *op. cit.*, p. 41.

[321]Heidegger, *op. cit.*, p. 46.

[322]Heidegger, *Über den Humanismus*, p. 46.

[323]Heidegger, *Aus der Erfahrung des Denkens*, Pfullingen, 1954, p. 11.

is difficult to defend this "definition." Is not existentialism characterized precisely by its struggle against reason *tout court*? One can relive the struggle about man's essence in the works of the forerunners of existential phenomenology, such as Pascal, Kierkegaard, Newman, Scheler, and Blondel. But what else was this struggle but a *tour de force* to escape from the clutches of "rational," "scientific," and "objective" knowledge of man, in the hope of thus arriving at an "existential" experience of "concrete" human reality?

This jargon is familiar. It was and is used in season and out of season in connection with all kinds of things, but usually without much competence. Thus the view became widespread that the philosophers of *existence* were in favor of a mysterious type of irrationalism, against which serious philosophers were bound to raise their voices in protest to defend philosophy as the *scientia scientiarum*, the "science *par excellence*."

Now that the smoke of the first battles has cleared and the light by which existential phenomenology thinks itself also has been explicitated at least to some extent, it has become possible to see the matter with greater clarity. It has become evident that existential phenomenology does not object to reason *tout court*, but only to certain conceptions of reason which, in the opinion of the phenomenologists, overestimated or underestimated the true power of reason.

"Enlarged Reason"

It is not our intention to describe here *in extenso* how reason was overestimated or underestimated in the course of history.[324] We will restrict ourselves to investigating to what extent existential-phenomenological thinking can accept the qualifier "irrational" and, above all, to understanding what is meant by so-called "enlarged reason."

Existential phenomenology would have to accept the predicate "irrational" for its way of thinking if this term could not have any other meaning than the one ascribed to it since Descartes. Momentarily abstracting from the idealistic interpretation of reason since Descartes, let us concentrate on the scientism, for which Descartes also laid the foundations. His methodic

---

[324]Dondeyne, *Contemporary European Thought and Christian Faith*, pp. 67-107.

doubt was a sly maneuver designed to give the physical sciences exclusive rights to the qualifiers "rational," "objective," and "scientific," once the real world had been regained by Descartes. Only the clear and distinct ideas of quantity are objective, said Descartes; hence, reason *tout court, the* light which lets objectivity *tout court* appear, must be described as "mathematical and physical reason." [325]

It stands to reason that, once such a view is accepted, one has to speak of irrationalism as soon as one sees that other modes of knowing are possible: they have to be called irrational because "rational" is exclusively reserved for mathematical and physical thinking. Thus one can understand why Pascal could claim that in the realm of metaphysics and morality reason can only lead to errors.[326] Pascal does not mean that man cannot say anything about God or about man's acting according to God's laws. He certainly can, but his words do not come from reason but from the heart, says Pascal. The heart has reasons which reason does not know.[327]

This attention to the so-called irrational moments of knowledge itself was a certain enlargement of the theory of knowledge. Nevertheless, this "irrational" knowledge continued to be considered less "objective" and, especially, less "scientific." This was a tacit admission of the Cartesian prejudice that reason should only refer to mathematical and physical reason. Objectivity is the correlate of reason and is guaranteed in science, as the critically reflective development of reason's achievements. Less objective and less scientific, therefore, meant less "reason."

Phenomenology cannot accept this. Reason is the "locus" where objective meaning appears and is the power to let it appear. *Objective* is that which I "see," in the broadest sense of the term. Objective reason is human *existence* as the "letting be" of any presence whatsoever, even if the latter cannot be expressed in categories of quantity. Reason must be understood existentially, i.e., it must be seen as the "light" of *existence* itself; and this "light" discloses much more objectivity than scientism would have us believe. Scientism adheres to a narrowed view of reason, and it is against this narrowness that those above-

---

[325]Dondeyne, *ibid.*, p. 68.
[326]J. Laporte, *Le coeur et la raison selon Pascal,* Paris, 1950.
[327]"Le coeur a ses raisons que la raison ne connaît point." B. Pascal, *Pensées,* Ed. Brunschwicg, Paris, 1942, no. 277.

mentioned philosophers joined battle. They realized that reason *sees* much more than scientism believes there is to see. "Concrete" reality is much richer than scientism thinks, and this wealth is not less objective than what the sciences discover. There is no justification for considering existentially understood reason—so-called irrational knowledge—less objective; consequently, it is preferable not to speak of irrational knowledge, but of the rational knowledge of "enlarged reason." [328]

The Sciences

The phenomenological view of the character of the positive sciences is in line with its view of reason. Reason is the "locus" where meaning appears and the power to let it appear. The "letting appear" of meaning, however, always takes place from a particular standpoint of the *existent* subject. Because *existence* contains many standpoints, there are also many worlds. There is not one world-in-itself; therefore, there is also not one *scientific* world-in-itself. In principle there are as many specifically different worlds as there are specifically different attitudes or standpoints of asking questions. [329]

The realization of the importance attached to the subject's standpoint has extremely important consequences in the realm of the sciences. For Aristotle, philosophy was an encyclopedia of all sciences and contained both philosophical and non-philosophical questions. With the rise of the modern empirical sciences philosophy was left to its fate, but the scientific ideal of the new sciences did not differ much from that of Aristotle. Under the guidance of Comte, hope continued to persist that ultimately it would be possible to "mirror" the whole of "reality" in one giant system of superadded sciences. [330] Each science was expected to contribute its building block. With in-

---

328"Hegel inaugure la tentative pour explorer l'irrationnel et l'intégrer à une raison élargie." Merleau-Ponty, *SNS*, p. 125.

329"Es gibt kein Weltbild, sondern nur eine Systematik der Wissenschaften. Weltbilder sind immer partikulare Erkenntniswelten, die falschlich zum Weltsein überhaupt verabsolutiert wurden. Aus verschiedenen grundsätzlichen Forschungsideen erwachsen je besondere Perspektiven. Jedes Weltbild ist ein Ausschnitt aus der Welt; die Welt wird nicht zum Bilde. Das 'wissenschaftliche Weltbild' im Unterschied vom mythischen war selber jederzeit ein neues mythisches Weltbild mit wissenschaftlichen Mitteln und dürftigem, mythischem Gehalt." Jaspers, *Einführung in die Philosophie*, p. 75.

330F. J. J. Buytendijk, "Vernieuwing in de wetenschap," *Annalen van het Thijmgenootschap*, 42 (1954), pp. 230-247.

credible optimism it was assumed that all blocks would neatly fit together and constitute a single harmonious whole, a mosaic.[331] To secure this harmony, the demand was made that all sciences adopt the method of physical sciences.

This ideal of science, however, has proved to be idle. First of all, the men of science themselves began to realize that they, too, do not speak of a world-in-itself: [332] the sciences speak of *human* worlds.[333] Secondly, gradually it became evident that the physicist's typical attitude of asking questions is only one among many possible attitudes.

Just as the many attitudes or standpoints of the *existent* subject co-constitute many worlds, so the specific questioning attitudes of specific sciences draw specific regions of being to the foreground of the *existent* subject's field of presence. A science is what it is, this particular science and no other, because it addresses this particular question to reality.[334] Just as only sounds occur in the sonorous world connected with my ears, and only colors and perspectives in the visible world connected with my eyes, so also are the objects of a specific science connected with the specific question asked by this science. Colors are meaningless for my ears and sounds are meaningless for my eyes. But it is nonsense to deny the existence of colors, on the ground that I cannot hear them.

Concretely applied to the sciences, this means that all sciences are ultimately based on *existence* [335] and that, therefore, the specific questions of specific sciences are contained as original

---

[331]R.C. Kwant and J.H.G. van den Berk, "Het gesprek van de physicus met de wereld," *Annalen van het Thijmgenootschap*, 43 (1955), pp. 1-4.

[332]Une réalité complètement indépendante de l'esprit qui la conçoit, la voit ou la sent, c'est une impossibilité. Un monde si extérieur que cela, si même il existait, nous serait à jamais inaccessible." Poincaré, *La valeur de la science*, Genève, n.d., p. 65.

[333]"Das Ziel der Forschung ist also nicht mehr die Erkenntnis der Atome und ihrer Bewegung 'an sich', d.h. abgelöst von unserer experimentellen Fragestellung; vielmehr stehen wir von Anfang an in der Mitte der Auseinandersetzung zwischen Natur und Mensch, von der die Naturwissenschaft ja nur ein Teil ist, so dass die landläufigen Einteilungen der Welt in Subjekt und Objekt, Innenwelt und Aussenwelt, Körper und Seele nicht mehr passen wollen und zu Schwierigkeiten führen. Auch in der Naturwissenschaft ist also der Gegenstand der Forschung nicht mehr die Natur an sich, sondern die der menschlichen Fragestellung ausgesetzte Natur, und insofern begegnet der Mensch auch hier wieder sich selbst." Werner Heisenberg, *Das Naturbild der heutigen Physik*, Hamburg, 1958, p. 18.

[334]J. Kockelmans, *Phenomenology and Physical Science*, pp. 70-91.

[335]"Wissenschaften sind Seinsweisen des Daseins." Heidegger, *SZ*, p. 13.

"interests" in *existence*. A science is born when a particular question, contained as an "interest" in *existence*, is critically, reflectively, and systematically taken up.[336] Let us explain the matter through an example.

Our *co-existence* contains an original psychological "interest." In daily life people deal with one another in ways that are obviously psychological or unpsychological. The behavior of a county judge to a delinquent, of an applicant for a job to his interviewer, a teacher to his pupil, a chaplain to his consultant, a girl to a boy, etc.—all those ways of behaving are obviously either psychological or unpsychological.[337] But, one may ask, what is psychology?

We will not answer this question, but wish to point out one thing. Whatever psychology is, it must undoubtedly cultivate and develop the mysterious psychological "knowing" contained in *co-existence*, by critically, reflectively, and systematically taking up that which "interests" man when he obviously proceeds in a psychological fashion.[338] In psychologically dealing with someone, certain particular questions are unexplicitly and nonthematically asked and answered. A kind of knowing takes place in which the subject assumes a particular attitude, and this attitude at the same time determines the direction in which that knowing develops into a science. If a science does not succeed in taking up the original attitude of questioning, it will not be abel to develop as a science in such a way that its pursuers have the experience of acquiring the knowledge to which, nonetheless, they tend by virtue of their original "interest." In such a case a revision of the fundamental concepts used in that science becomes a necessity.[339]

Through the original "interest" contained in *existence*, a particular region of being, a particular field of presence, is drawn forward and demarcated as a "figure" against an horizon of

---

[336]"Der Ursprung der Wissenschaft aus der eigentlichen Existenz ist hier nicht weiter zu verfolgen. Es gilt jetzt lediglich zu verstehen, dass und wie die Thematisierung des innerweltlichen Seienden die Grundverfassung des Daseins, das In-der-Welt-sein, zur Voraussetzung hat." *SZ*, p. 363.

[337]B.J. Kouwer and J. Linschoten, *Inleiding tot de Psychologie*, Assen, 1951, pp. 7-101.

[338]J.H. v.d. Berg, *Kroniek der Psychologie*, 's-Gravenhage, 1954.

[339]"Die eigentliche 'Bewegung' der Wissenschaften spielt sich ab in der mehr oder minder radikalen und ihr selbst durchsichtigen Revision der Grundbegriffe." *SZ*, p. 9.

distinct meanings.[340] This first demarcation, however, is not at once so sharp that the "landscape" in question is clearly delineated from the rest. The explicitation of a particular question, of a particular way of human *existence* as "natural light," is at first not such that the question is clearly distinct from other questions answered in other sciences.[341] As long as one thinks that the earth is the center of the universe because God became man on earth, one confuses the intention of astronomy with that of theology. As long as the psychologist tries to explain puberty by the maturation of the sex glands, he confuses the intention of psychology with that of physiology. The fact that the various "landscapes" of reality merge, compenetrate one another, and constitute a *Gestalt*, explains why an improperly formulated question can still receive some kind of answer. If a psychologist thinks that he should adopt the ideals and methods of physical science in psychology, he can still say something about a smile. He can then describe it as a "certain contraction of the nostrils and the corners of the mouth, accompanied by a twinkling of the eyes." [342] This is something, but it is not what makes the psychologist interested in the smile. That description tells us what the smile is for a physicist, but a psychologist should be able to say something else about it.[343]

No science can come into its own without experiencing at least once a crisis in its fundamental concepts. The revision of those concepts means a more faithful explicitation of the original "interest," the attitude of asking questions, or the standpoint of that science. At the same time, a particular "landscape" of reality, a region of being is more sharply demarcated. It is in "lived experience" that man vaguely realizes what "really" interests him when, for example, he raises physical or psychological questions. As long as the corresponding science does not fully take over his fundamental interest, the man of science will be dissatisfied with his own science because it does not let him make progress, is not fruitful.

340"Die Ausarbeitung des Gebietes in seinen Grundstrukturen ist in gewisser Weise schon geleistet durch die vorwissenschaftliche Erfahrung und Auslegung des Seinsbezirkes, in dem das Sachgebiet selbst begrenzt wird." *SZ*, p. 9.

341"Wissenschaftliche Forschung vollzieht die Hebung und erste Fixierung der Sachgebiete naiv und roh." *SZ*, p. 9.

342Cf. L. Bigot, Ph. Kohnstamm and B. Palland, *Leerboek der Psychologie*, Groningen, 1950, p. 394.

343B. Kouwer and J. Linschoten, *Inleiding tot de Psychologie*, pp. 13-20.

This leads us to the conclusion that the pursuers of *different* sciences *as such* must be *unable* to speak with one another.. When a particular attitude of asking questions is explicitly taken up, the formal object, method, and language of the science in question is in principle fixed; and over and over again it will become evident that these are distinct from the formal object, method, and language of other sciences.[344] This situation does not exclude an interdisciplinary approach in the scientific enterprise, but it eliminates a false philosophy that could underlie such an approach. One who expects that a single giant scientific system will ever mirror the "one" reality lives in an expectation which the sciences themselves expose as an illusion. For the pursuers of the various sciences have already experienced that, according as a science more faithfully takes up a particular attitude of questioning, that science moves away from the other sciences.[345] This fact does not mean that the sciences are degenerating but only that they are finding their own identity.

Finally, it should be evident that no science is entitled to prescribe its own method and language to any other science if the latter is to be worthy of the name. There is not one world-in-itself which demands one method, in order to guarantee one "scientific objectivity." [346] Each science is a way in which a specific scientific question encounters a specific scientific world.[347] The method and the language which guarantee the scientific character of a particular science can produce just the opposite effect for a different science and make its scientific character impossible.[348]

---

[344] J. Kockelmans, *op. cit.*, pp. 176ff.

[345] F.J.J. Buytendijk, *art. cit.* (in footnote 330), pp. 237-247.

[346] "The liberation from seventeenth century thinking, which had been reduced to a dogmatic schema, means that for the modern mind there is not just one absolutely real world but many worlds, which are no less real—and no more real—than the world projected by the physicist." Buytendijk, *art. cit.*, p. 237.

[347] "Or, cette rencontre et cette coexistence sont elles-mêmes, en vérité, susceptibles d'innombrables modalités correpondant aux diverses manières possibles d'apparaître pour l'objet et aux diverses manières pour moi de m'ouvrir à lui et de me comporter à son égard." De Waelhens, *Existence et signification*, Louvain, 1958, p. 107

[348] "Die Strenge der mathematischen Naturwissenschaft ist die Exaktheit. . . . Dagegen müssen alle Geisteswissenschaften, sogar alle Wissenschaften vom Lebendigen, gerade um streng zu bleiben, notwendig unexakt sein. Man kann zwar auch das Lebendige als eine raum-zeitliche Bewegungsgrösse auffassen, aber man fasst dann nicht mehr das Lebendige." Heidegger, *Holzwege*, p. 73.

8. REASON, SCIENCE AND METAPHYSICS

The preceding section showed how and on what conditions reason can rise to the level of science. Any pursuer of a positive science, however, starts from presuppositions which he himself does not make the theme of his considerations. These presuppositions are of a philosophical nature. The simple fact that physical science formulates certain specific laws presupposes the conviction that the specific being spoken of by this science is such that it can be approached and expressed by means of those specific laws. The physicist presupposes this, but does not justify his presupposition; he does not formulate a philosophy of natural things as natural things, but this philosophy lives in the way he pursues physical science. Similarly, the psychologist and the psychiatrist do not formulate a philosophy of man when they speak of man with the aid of specific psychological and psychiatric laws. But by the simple fact that they consider a certain type of law suitable for being used in their speaking of man, they reveal that they have a philosophical view concerning the specific being which man is. By adhering as closely as possible to the method of physical science, the psychologists and psychiatrists of the past revealed their implicit metaphysical conviction that man could be conceived as "another thing of nature."

Today there is explicit recognition of the fact that within the pursuit of the sciences philosophical affirmations are executed. Positivism is losing ground to make room for authentic "metaphysical" thinking. When the term "metaphysical" is used in this context, it obviously is taken as synonymous with "philosophical."

For the great metaphysical thinkers of the past, however, metaphysical thinking always was much more than transcendence of the thinking of positive science, and the explicitation of those specific modes of being whose philosophical concept is presupposed by positive science. For them metaphysics was the apex, the ultimate possibility of human questioning and answering, the question about the ultimate meaning of being.[349] They

---

[349]"La question: 'que sommes-nous finalement?' est dès lors inséparable de la question de 'L'être des existants en général'. Dans cette expression le mot 'être' signifie précisément *ce qui fait et fonde en fin de compte la diversité des êtres ainsi que l'unité qui les relie entre eux.* La métaphysique n'est rien d'autre que l'effort de la pensée en vue de répondre à cette suprême question. C'est pourquoi de tout temps la métaphysique a été définie comme la recherche de l'être." A. Dondeyne, "Dieu et le matérialisme contemporain," *Essai sur Dieu, l'homme et l'univers,* publié sous la direction et avec une introduction de Jacques de Bivort de la Saudée, Paris, 1957, p. 17.

viewed metaphysics as the question of what *ultimately* it means
that everything which is—no matter what—is said to *be*.[350]
Man uses the little word "is" most of the time in a thoughtless
fashion. He takes it for granted that being *is*. Within the unquestioned obviousness of life in a mythical sphere or within
the everydayness of life in a technocratic order [351] it seems that
man knows what he says when he says of anything, no matter
what, that it *is*. This unquestioned obviousness, however, is
very deceptive and merely a form of thoughtlessness. As soon
as man ceases to take being for obviously granted; as soon as
he wonders about being; as soon as he is able to ask himself
what he is saying when he affirms of anything that it *is,* metaphysical thinking, in the strict sense, is born.[352] Why is there
something rather than nothing?

Affirmation in Negation

The fact that in the history of thought human reason has
constituted itself as metaphysical reason implies that it is no
longer possible to reject metaphysical thinking without metaphysics. One who rejects metaphysics must begin by indicating
what, in his view, is defended by the metaphysician. Then he
will say, for instance, with Ayer that the results of such a way of
thinking cannot be verified,[353] and concludes that metaphysical
thinking is not concerned with anything. This is the way in
which Hume in his time rejected metaphysics, and today it is
still done in exactly the same way.[354]

It is obvious, however, that such a way of thinking implies a
metaphysics. For the motivation of the rejection implicitly contains the condition on which one is willing to affirm something
as something, and as not-nothing. The rejection says that
what cannot be verified (in the way the rejector understands
this term) is simply nothing. "Something," then, is verifiable in
a certain way; "nothing" is that which cannot be verified in that
way. There is here, therefore, an implicit doctrine about some-

---

350"So wird die Frage nach dem 'Sinn des Seins', danach, was damit
eigentlich gemeint ist, wenn wir sagen 'es ist etwas', und 'es ist so und so', zur
Grundfage der Metaphysik." L. Landgrebe, *Der Weg der Phänomenologie,*
Gütersloh, 1963, p. 78.
351Heidegger, *Einführung in die Metaphysik,* pp. 28-29.
352Landgrebe, *op. cit.,* pp. 77-78.
353A.J. Ayer, "Demonstration of the impossibility of metaphysics," *Mind,*
XLIII(1934), p. 339.
354G. Nuchelmans, "De kritiek op de Metaphysica," *Wijsgerig perspectief
op maatschappij en wetenschap,* III(1963), pp. 134-147.

thing *as* something, about being *as* being, i.e., as opposed to nothing.   One meets here the trend of thought which claims to seize "everything" is a rational grasp, for the rejector indicates the condition on which something can be called "something": one meets here the "radical" thinking which is traditionally called "metaphysical."   The rejection of metaphysics, therefore, itself also is a metaphysics.   For this reason even the most fervent opponents of metaphysics *tour court* have a place in the ranks of the metaphysicians: they figure in surveys of metaphysics with just as much right as the defenders of metaphysics.[355]

Metaphysics as Speaking About "Everything"

Metaphysics in the strict sense is the attempt to express the meaning of being *as* being.   Regarding particular and individual beings man can only say that they *are* because he understands being *as* being.   This point is the theme of metaphysics in the strict sense.   In other words, metaphysics is not concerned with "this" or "that" individual or particular being, but with that on the ground of which it can be said of the individual beings that they *are*.[356]   In the understanding of being *as* being, the opposite of being is nothing and *only* nothing.[357]

It should be clear now in what sense metaphysics may and must be said to speak about "everything."   Metaphysical thinking, in the strict sense, is the attempt to com-prehend "everything" and seize it in a single rational grasp.   In metaphysical thinking, in the broader sense—i.e., in the philosophizing that is implied in the pursuit of the positive sciences—there is also an attempt to arrive at a kind of com-prehending.   It consists in the orderly arrangement of specific objects into a specific region of being, in which the objects considered agree with one another. A metaphysics of the things of nature inquires into the meaning of the thing of nature *as* a thing of nature.   This question makes a specific meaning be the figure within an inner horizon but, at the same time, an entire region of being is, as it were,

---

355F. Sassen, "Wat betekent 'Metaphysica'?," *Wijsgerig perspectief op maatschappij en wetenschap,* III(1963), pp. 106-119.
356"Bei der Frage halten wir uns jedes besondere und einzelne Seiende als gerade dieses und jenes völlig fern."   Heidegger, *Einführung in die Metaphysik,* p. 3.
357"Der Bereich dieser Frage hat seine Grenze nur am schlechthin nicht und nie Seiende, am Nichts.   Alles was nicht Nichts ist, fällt in die Frage." Heidegger, *op. cit.,* p. 2.

cut out in reference to an external horizon and put into the foreground of the field of presence of the *existent* subject-as-*cogito*. The question about the meaning of the thing of nature as a thing of nature abstracts from the fact that *this* thing of nature is a grass seed or a geological layer; at the same time, by man's com-prehending rational grasp all things of nature are, as agreeing with one another, constituted into a single region of being, distinct from other regions.

Husserl gave expression to these ideas in his plan for so-called "regional ontologies." [358] He starts from the idea that the intentional subject contains many attitudes which cannot be reduced to one another. The scientific, artistic, technical, ethical, and religious intentionalities are always original and irreducible relationships. A consequence of this is that the "world" also, as the correlate of intentionality, is not a monistic edifice. A work of art is not an agglomerate of physico-chemical elements, and a state is not a series of psychological impulses.[359] The "worlds" connected with the scientific, artistic, political, technical, ethical, and religious attitudes of the intentional subject are specific regions of being—regions in which the objects agree with one another by their specific being such or such.[360] These specific regions of being are only accessible to the subject by means of an appropriate attitude.[361] If I assume the attitude of physical science, I do not see a work of art, and in a religious attitude I do not see a state. There is a unity of mutual implication of noetic activities and noematic correlates.[362]

All positive sciences are specific modes of being-present to a specific region of being. The specific character of these regions —in which the objects agree with one another through "regional" characteristics and are distinct from objects belonging to other regions—is not an explicit theme of the positive sciences themselves; nevertheless, they presuppose a certain understanding of that character. The historian does not make "the" historical his theme, the biologist does not thematize "the" biological, and the jurist does not make "the" rightness of rights his

---

[358]Husserl, *Ideen* I (*Husserliana, III*), *passim*.

[359]Max Müller, *Sein und Geist*, Tübingen, 1940, pp. 32-33.

[360]"Alle Gegenstände kommen darin überein, zu sein. Den Gegenständen eines bestimmten, unzurückführbaren Seinsbereiches, einer Region also, ist ein bestimmtes Sosein gemeinsam." Max Müller, *op. cit.*, p. 33.

[361]Müller, *ibid*.

[362]"Phänomenologie führt die erfahrene Welt . . . zurück auf das Zueinander von Grundarten des Seins und Grundarten des Bewusstseins." Müller, *op. cit.*, pp. 36-38.

topic.[363]   Nevertheless, they imply a certain understanding of these themes. The thematization of this understanding and of the corresponding regions is undertaken by the philosopher and results in "regional ontologies." In these ontologies "everything" called "historical" is understood as belonging to "the" historical; "everything" called "artistic" as belonging to "the" artistic; "everything" called "juridical" as belonging to "the" juridical; etc. In a regional ontology a specific being is understood as such, so that "all" objects of the region in question reveal themselves as agreeing with one another.

When in a regional ontology something is said of a specific object, i.e., when a predicate is added to a universal judgmental subject as referring to a specific region of being, the copula "is" is used. The judgment expresses that a specific object "truly" and "really" is what it is said to *be*; and, at the same time, the judgment also "says" that this object is *not* something else.[364] This intention is present in every way of saying "is," both in ordinary speech and in the speaking of the positive sciences and philosophy. In every judgment, the copula "is" is used, and in every judgment the subject who says "is" intends to express that the affirmed *is* "truly" and "really" such and such, regardless of the level on which, or the attitude in which the affirmation is made. This point is very important. Because the affirmation "is" can be made on many levels, it is obvious that the question how man can say "is" transcends *all* levels of saying "is." This question is not concerned with the possibility of any particular positive science or of any regional ontology. Similarly, the question of *the* "true" and *the* "real" is not the question of the "truth" and "reality" of what in a particular positive science or regional ontology is affirmed as "true" or "real." This means that in any positive science and in any regional ontology the answer to the question about the possibility and meaning of saying "is" and of *the* "true" and *the* "real" is presupposed, without being thematized in the positive sciences and regional ontologies.[365]

---

363 Müller, *op. cit.*, pp. 36-38.

364 "In einem jeden Satz gebrauchen wir das Wörtchen 'ist' als Verbindung zwischen Subjekt und Prädikat, zwischen Aussagegegenstand und Ausgesagtem, und wollen damit jeweils sagen: Es ist wahrhaft und in Wirklichkeit so und nicht anders." Müller, *op. cit.*, p. 40.

365 "Ueber allen speziellen Regionen und Bereichen, allen Einzelwissenschaften und Einzelfragen und ihren 'regionalen' Seinsvoraussetzungen gibt es eine allgemeine Voraussetzung eines jeden Denkens und Sprechens überhaupt." Müller, *ibid.*

The thematization of these most fundamental presuppositions is the task of metaphysics in the strict sense of the term. Transcending all specific regions of being, metaphysics asks what exactly is affirmed when man *on any level whatsoever* says of *anything whatsoever* that it "is," that it "truly" and "really" *is* and not *not-is.* Transcending all specific attitudes of saying "is," metaphysics asks what exactly is meant by *the* saying of "is" which is contained in all specific saying of "is." The answer to these "two" connected questions, then, is presupposed when any judgment whatsoever is pronounced. In any judgmental sentence a view of man "and" a view of being are implied.[366] This point is thematized in metaphysics in the strict sense. This metaphysics, then, is concerned with the saying of "is" *as such* "and" with being *as such.* This is what many authors wish to say when they affirm that metaphysics raises "the question of being."

Just as the positive sciences call for regional ontologies, so these regional ontologies call for transcendental ontology or metaphysics in the strict sense. At the same time, this "upward movement" indicates in what sense one may and should say that metaphysics in the strict sense speaks of "everything." At first sight, this claim seems fantastic. Yet from the preceding considerations it should be clear that the question about the meaning of the thing of nature *as* thing of nature inquires about "all" things of nature in such a way that this "all" may not be conceived as the sum total of the individual concrete things of nature. In a similar way it should be clear that metaphysics' speaking about "everything" in the strict sense does not mean that the metaphysician lets his gaze wander over plants, planets, rocks, machines, rivers, mountains, animals, and men in order to say something about each of them.[367] Speaking about "everything" is only then an intelligent speaking when the speaking subject occupies a standpoint from which a certain com-prehending becomes possible, and this com-prehending must be such that

---

[366]"Aber indem das 'ist' der Copula über alles formale Verbinden hinaus eben 'ist wirklich so', 'ist wahrhaft so' sagt, enthält es die Grundauffassung des Menschen über Sein als Wirklichkeit und Wahrheit." Müller, *op. cit.,* p. 41.

[367]"Wir befragen nicht dieses und nicht jenes, auch nicht es der Reihe nach durchgehend, alles Seiende, sondern im vorhinein das ganze Seiende, oder wie wir aus später zu erörternden Gründen sagen: das Seiende im Ganzen als ein solches." Heidegger, *Einführung in die Metaphysik,* p. 2.

whatever is, is grasped by it as agreeing with all that is and as excluding only nothing.[368]

"The Metaphysical in Man"

The metaphysical question in the strict sense is not an invention of metaphysics as a "science." [369] The question is implied in the *existent* subject-as-*cogito*, or rather, the question is an aspect of this subject and, therefore, a mode of being-man.[370] The subject-as-*cogito* himself is "metaphysical consciousness," "metaphysical reason." The metaphysical reason is a kind of "knowing" of what it means to say that everything of which it has been, will be, or is being said that it *is* belongs to reality, the order of being. In metaphysics, this consciousness is taken up in a critical and systematic fashion, made explicit, and developed. Metaphysics, then, is based on metaphysical reason, on a "determined" dimension of the subject's immediate presence to present reality, viz., the dimension in which the subject dwells in the universe, the universality of all beings as beings. Metaphysics presupposes "the metaphysical" in man.[371] For this reason, metaphysics presupposes a philosophical anthropology and a criteriology.

The phenomenological conception of reason leaves no room for an objectivistic metaphysics. Those for whom objectivism is a necessary condition for authentic metaphysics will claim that phenomenology can never develop into metaphysics. We, however, consider an objectivistic metaphysics a contradiction. Metaphysics can exist only within the sphere of intentionality. For one who recognizes this, a "first" answer can be given to the question, "Why is there something rather than nothing?" There

---

[368]Heidegger, *op. cit.*, pp. 2-3.

[369]"Metaphysik ist nichts, was von Menschen nur 'geschaffen' wird in Systemen und Lehren, sondern das Seinsverständnis, sein Entwurf und seine Verwerfung geschieht im Dasein als solchem. Die 'Metaphysik' ist das Grundgeschehen beim Einbruch in das Seiende, der mit der faktischen Existenz von so- etwas wie Mensch überhaupt geschieht." Heidegger, *Kant und das Problem der Metaphysik*, p. 218.

[370]"Hinsehen auf, Verstehen und Begreifen von, Zugang zu sind konstitutive Verhaltungen des Fragens und so selbst Seinsmodi eines bestimmten Seienden, des Seienden, das wir, die Fragenden, je selbst sind." Heidegger, *SZ*, p. 7.

[371]"Wenn die Interpretation des Sinnes von Sein Aufgabe wird, ist das Dasein nicht nur das primär zu befragende Seiende, es ist überdies das Seiende, das sich je schon in seinem Sein zu dem verhält, wonach in dieser Frage gefragt wird. Die Seinsfrage ist dann aber nichts anderes als die Radikalisierung einer zum Dasein selbst gehörigen wesenhaften Seinstendenz, des vorontologischen Seinsverständnisses." *SZ*, p. 15.

is something because man is—the man who, as "metaphysical reason," lets "come to pass" the being of all that is and who "brings about" the truth of being as being. This, however, is merely a "first" answer, beyond which we cannot yet go in this chapter.[372]

---

[372]W. Luijpen, *Phenomenology and Metaphysics*, Pittsburgh, 1965.

CHAPTER THREE

PHENOMENOLOGY OF FREEDOM

In the preceding chapters so much emphasis has been placed on being-in-the-world that it may have given rise to the impression that human *existence* is wholly static and lacks any dynamic dimension. This conclusion, however, is entirely wrong. To *exist* does not merely mean being-in-the-world but also being-"at"-the-world.[1] The particle "at" has here a meaning similar to the one it has in the expression "being at work": [2] it indicates that something is being done. Man is not *wholly fixed* in his world, but is dynamically in it. This dynamism is not a process, however, but the dynamism of human *existence* is the dynamism of subjectivity as freedom.

Anyone who meaningfully uses the term "freedom" expresses negatively a certain absence of determination and positively a certain autonomy. Both actually are aspects of one and the same reality—man.[3]

It is in this twofold sense also that the phenomenology of *existence* speaks of freedom. An opportunity for doing this was offered by the way various human sciences spoke of man; they considered man to be "the result of. . . ." The dots can be replaced by many things, for there was a time when practically all human sciences absolutized their specific method of inquiry as *the* method and were blind for anything that could not be caught in the net of their scientific apparatus.[4] In consequence of this attitude, man occurred in economics and sociology as nothing but the "result" of economic and social forces; in biology, as the "result" of all kinds of biological processes; and in orthodox psychoanalysis man was held to be the "result" of all kinds of drives dwelling in the substructure of the *id*. Man was considered as "all kinds of things," but always as the "result" of processes and forces, which, in deference to the prestige of physical science, were conceived to act unilaterally and deterministically. Thus man was actually conceived as another

---

[1]Merleau-Ponty, *PP*, pp. 496-520.
[2]Dondeyne, "Beschouwingen bij het atheïstisch existentialisme," *Tijdschrift voor Philosophie*, XIII(1951), p. 17, note 14.
[3]A. Dondeyne, "Truth and Freedom," *Truth and Freedom*, Pittsburgh, 1954, p. 30.
[4]S. Strasser, *Phenomenology and the Human Sciences*, Pittsburgh, 1963, p. 180-186.

thing; for, of a thing one can say, in the strict sense of the term, that it is the result of processes and forces.

1. Subjectivity as Freedom

All existentialists and phenomenologists have always objected to the view that man is nothing but the result of processes and forces. If man is *nothing but* a "result," then he *himself* is nothing, and this is not tenable.

To Be a Subject Is to Be Free

What a thing is can be fully explained in terms of its antecedents. The thing is nothing but the result of processes and forces; the being of a thing is a being-result. One who knows everything about the processes and forces causally acting on a thing, knows everything about the thing. It is merely a provisional point of rest in the endless evolution of the cosmos; it is nothing new with respect to the forces and processes which cause it.[5] The thing is nothing but a *part* of the material cosmos: it is not *itself* something transcending its antecedents.[6] The being of a thing is nothing but its belonging to the material cosmos.

Saying that the being of a thing is nothing but being-result, is the same as saying that the being of a thing is nothing but a being-necessitated, for determinism governs the world of things. The cosmic forces operate with necessity and give to the processes the constancy which the scientists assume in the formulation of their physical laws. If in individual cases they observe that their laws do not hold, then they know that other forces, operating with the same necessity, are at work and interfere with the forces whose action is formulated in the laws.

The forces operating with necessity in the cosmos work "blindly." This means that they do not have any knowledge of themselves as forces and of their results as results. The world of things is struck with "blindness." Things lie, as it were, crushed upon themselves, they are not for themselves or for other things. In short, the being of a thing is being a blindly determined result.

How, however, can such a thing be said? The statement

---

[5]De Waelhens, "Linéaments d'une interprétation phénoménologique de la Liberté," *Liberté, Actes du IVe Congrès des Sociétés de Philosophie de langue française*, Neuchatel, 1949, p. 82.

[6]D.M. De Petter, "Personne et Personnalisation," *Divus Thomas* (Piac.), 1949, p. 164.

that things are not for themselves and for other things—that they have no meaning for themselves and for other things—can be made only if the totality of reality is not identical with the totality of *things*. If there were nothing but things, processes and forces, there would be no meaning. But there is meaning. Paradoxically expressed, if there were nothing but things, processes, and forces, nothing would *be*, in the only sense which the verb "to be" can have, viz., being-for-man. But something is, there are things, processes, and forces.

Once this point is understood, it becomes wholly impossible to say that the totality of man—*all that man is*—is the blindly determined result of processes and forces.[7] Otherwise man would be a thing and, therefore (to use again the above-mentioned paradoxical expression), strictly speaking, nothing would *be*. But something is, thanks to the appearance of man. Man's being, then, cannot be called totally being-a-result. Being-man *itself* also is something. Being-man, likewise, cannot be totally being a part of the material cosmos. True, man's being is *also* a result, *also* necessitated, *also* a part of the cosmos; but it cannot *totally* be result, necessitated, and a part, for otherwise nothing would be.

What is the aspect of man's reality by virtue of which man rises above being the blindly determined result of processes and forces? The answer is his *subjectivity*. With the appearance of subjectivity in the endless evolution of the cosmos, a breach occurred in the "darkness" of matter. Man as subject is the "natural light," the light through which something is, in the only possible sense of this term.[8] It is by the being of man as subject that the being-a-result, being-a-part, being-necessitated (which also must be affirmed of man) are transcended.

Anyone who really wishes to say something by using the term "freedom" negatively expresses a certain absence of determination. It should be evident, then, that being-subject must be called being-free, for through his subjectivity man rises above his being-a-thing, his being-a-blindly-determined-result. No matter how many aspects there are in man with respect to which he must be called the necessitated result of processes and forces, nevertheless, these aspects cannot constitute the totality of man's being, for it is only through man's subjectivity that there are

---

[7] "La parole est l'excès de notre existence sur l'être naturel," *PP*, p. 229.
[8] Heidegger, *Vom Wesen der Wahrheit*, pp. 14-17.

necessity, results, processes, and forces.[9] If everything man is, is the determined result of processes and forces, man would be a thing, struck by the same "blindness" as all other things. Nothing would then be-for-man. But there is something, there are things, processes, and forces. Man's being as a subject is being-free as the "letting be" of the cosmos.[10]

It goes without saying that we are not concerned here with freedom as a quality affecting an action or a power. Freedom here refers to the *being* of man on the proper level of his being-man. The being of man as a subject is a being-free. Only on the basis of this idea is it possible to understand freedom with respect to human actions, and only on this basis one can understand the many senses which the term "freedom" has in contemporary philosophical writings.[11]

Positively considered, man's freedom as a subject implies a certain autonomy.[12] Not everything that man is is the result of processes and forces; the being of man as a subject is a certain being-a-*self*. Man cannot be fully explained in terms of his antecedents: the being of man as a subject is a being "from himself" (*aus sich*). Man's being is not being a mere part of the cosmos, not a mere belonging to the cosmos: as a subject man exists as a substance and belongs to himself.[13]

But, what is man *himself*? The answer admits no hesitation:

---

[9]"En effet, si la condition de l'homme est de découvrir et d'établir des significations, l'idée que le déterminisme pourrait s'appliquer à l'homme devient simplement absurde." De Waelhens, *art. cit.*, p. 83.

[10]"Die Freiheit zum Offenbaren eines Offenen lässt das jeweilige Seiende das Seiende sein, das es ist. Freiheit enthüllt sich jetzt als das Seinlassen von Seiendem." Heidegger, *Vom Wesen der Wahrheit*, p. 14.

[11]"Affirmer qu'ontologiquement l'homme est libre par définition et, encore, que la liberté est pour lui la condition de la vérité puisqu'un être non-libre ne pourrait dire ce que les choses sont, n'équivaut naturellement pas à résoudre tous les problèmes que l'existence de la liberté peut poser, ni même à nier que la liberté, relativement à l'homme, peut s'entendre en bien des manières. On pense pourtant que cette affirmation de principe permet seule de comprendre la portée exacte de ces difficultés ultérieures et le sens que l'idée de liberté devra revêtir lorsqu'on l'envisage dans les divers domaines de la philosophie et, notamment, sur le plan psychologique, moral, social, religieux." De Waelhens, *art. cit.*, p. 83.

[12]Generally man's ontological autonomy as a subject is approached by way of the autonomy of human action. By virtue of the principle that "acting follows being" the *self*-being of man is derived from his self-acting. Cf. De Petter, "Personne et Personnalisation," *Divus Thomas* (Piac.), 1949, p. 170.

[13]H.D. Robert, "Phénoménologie existentielle et Morale thomiste," *Morale chrétienne et requêtes contemporaines*, Tournai-Paris, 1954, pp. 208-209.

man *himself* is an "I," a person.[14] Thus man's freedom as a subject must be positively understood as a certain autonomy of being, a certain independence of being, a belonging to himself as a "being of his own" and therefore, also "not generated" (*ingeneratum*),[15] because he is not the result of processes and forces. Scholastic philosophy reserved the term "subsistence" to indicate man's autonomy of being.[16] As a subject, a person, as "I," man "subsists." [17]

To Be Free Is to Be Rational

The ontological superiority of man as a subject is equiprimordially his rationality. This point receives special emphasis in Boethius' classical definition: "an individual substance of a rational nature." [18] The being of man as an "I" means a certain ontological superiority with respect to the things of the cosmos. But this "I," as ontological superiority, i.e., as freedom, is the "natural light" through which man exists for himself and through which the world exists for man. It is the light through which there is objective meaning.[19] The traditional term indicating this light is "the light of reason." All rationalistic and scientistic prejudices must be removed, of course, to let man's reason appear in its original form. Man's reason is the "locus" where objective meaning appears and is the power to let it appear; and this "locus" and power evidently are the *existent* subject himself. Thus man is also traditionally defined as a "rational animal." To be a subject means to be free and, equiprimordially, to be rational.[20]

At the same time, however, the bond of freedom reveals

---

[14]De Petter, *art. cit.*, pp. 170-171.
[15]De Petter, *art. cit.*, p. 171.
[16]L. De Raeymaeker, *Philosophy of Being*, St. Louis, 1954, p. 240.
[17]De Petter, "Het Persoon-zijn onder thomistisch-metaphysische belichting," *De Persoon, Verslag van de dertiende algemene vergadering der Vereniging voor Thomistische Wijsbegeerte en van de vierde studiedagen van het Wijsgerig Gezelschap te Leuven*, Nijmegen, 1948, pp. 45-46.
[18]*De duabus naturis*, c. III.
[19]"On ne peut dire ni que l'homme libre veut la liberté pour dévoiler l'être, ni le dévoilement de l'être pour la liberté; ce sont là deux aspects d'une seule réalité." S. de Beauvoir, *Pour une morale de l'ambiguïté*, Paris, 1947, p. 99.
[20]"It is important explicitly to mention that in the case of the person the concept 'rational nature' does not relate to the concept 'subsistence' or 'supposit' as an extrinsic difference, but that rationality means a higher perfection of subsisting itself. More important even, in the strict and proper sense, it is only in a rational nature that there can be question of subsisting." De Petter, *art. cit.*, pp. 45-46.

itself inescapably. The subject reveals himself as freedom and freedom discloses itself as reason, that is, as the power to let meaning appear. But meaning is *objective*, and the light of subjectivity is an "objective" light. This implies that meaning is not left to the subject's arbitrariness. As a "natural light," the subject is the "letting be" of reality,[21] and as such he is bound to objectivity.[22] *Existent* freedom, then, is equiprimordially an *existent* being-bound.

All this remains unintelligible to anyone who is not willing to conceive freedom and objectivity in their most fundamental sense. There is no question here of freedom as the power to do this or that as one prefers.[23] Similarly, we are not concerned with objectivity as a quality of the judgment.[24] What we are referring to is precisely that which makes it possible to choose either this or that and which is the foundation on which the objectivity of the judgment can be based. It is man as subject who is this foundation.

2. Freedom as "Distance," as "Having to Be," and as "Project"

If being a subject means to be free, then the way one conceives the subject is crucial for the more precise description of the freedom ascribed to *man*. Obviously, if the subject who man is, is described as an isolated subjectivity, then freedom must be called absolute. As a mattter of fact, some contemporary phenomenologists do this,[25] but their views imply a departure from the phenomenological way of thinking.

Absolute freedom does not occur among men because the subject who man is, is not an isolated subjectivity.[26] The "I" occurs only as involved in the density of reality, the facticity of body and world, with which the "I" is not identical. The "I"

---

[21]"Die Freiheit zum Offenbaren eines Offenen lässt das jeweilige Seiende das Seiende sein, das es ist. Freiheit enthüllt sich jetzt als das Seinlassen von Seiendem." Heidegger, *Vom Wesen der Wahrheit*, p. 14.

[22]"Das Sicheinlassen auf die Entborgenheit des Seienden verliert sich nicht in dieser, sondern entfaltet sich zu einem Zurücktreten vor dem Seienden, damit dieses in dem, was es ist und wie es ist, sich offenbare und die vorstellende Angleichung aus ihm das Richtmass nehme." Heidegger, *op. cit.*, p. 15.

[23]Heidegger, *ibid.*

[24]Heidegger, *op. cit.*, p. 16.

[25]Robert, "Phénoménologie existentielle et Morale thomiste," *Morale Chrétienne et requêtes contemporaines,* Tournai-Paris, 1954, pp. 208-209.

[26]"Im Ich-sagen spricht sich das Dasein als In-der-Welt-sein aus." Heidegger, *SZ,* p. 321.

posits itself only in relationship, it *exists*, is intentional, situated.[27]
The ontological autonomy of the subject who man is, then, is
very relative, for it simply is not what it is without the body and
the world.   The freedom pertaining to man on the basis of his
being-a-subject, is equiprimordially a bond, and this bond must
be understood as a kind of "powerlessness."   Freedom is not an
"acosmic freedom": it is not the fully autonomous origin of
reality's meaning, for without this reality subjectivity is not what
it is.

"Zero Distance"

Reflecting upon the meaning of being-man—understood as
involved subjectivity, as situated freedom—one sees that the subject's involvement in reality implies a "distance which is, at the
same time, zero and infinite." [28]   Reality should be understood
here as the facticity of the world and bodily being, in the broad
sense of the term.   The statement that between the "I" and
reality there is a "zero distance," means that the "I"—as conscious "I," as self-affirmation—simply does not occur in any
other way than that of fusion with consciousness of reality, the
affirmation of bodily being and the world.   The "zero distance,"
then, is nothing other than what previously we have called "intentionality."

The "I" 's self-affirmation, however, lies on a twofold level,
and the same holds for the affirmation of the reality in which
the "I," by virtue of its intentionality, is involved.   It lies on the
cognitive level, that is, on the level of *recognition* of the "I" as
"I" and of reality as reality.[29]   At the same time, the "I" 's self-
affirmation and the affirmation of the reality, with which the
self-affirmation is fused through intentionality, lie on the affective level.[30]   The subject is not only a *cogito* but also a *volo* (I
will).   The affective "moment" of subjectivity is distinct from
the cognitive level.   The "I" 's self-affirmation contains not only

---

27"Si le sujet est en situation . . . c'est qu'il ne réalise son ipséité qu'en
étant effectivement corps et en entrant par ce corps dans le monde." Merleau
Ponty, *PP*, p. 467.

28De Waelhens, "Linéaments d'une interprétation phénoménologique de la
liberté," *Actes du IVe Congrès des Sociétés de Philosophie de langue
française*, Neuchatel, 1949, p. 81.

29"C'est en communiquant avec le monde que nous communiquons in-
dubitablement avec nous-mêmes." *PP*, p. 485.

30*SZ*, p. 54.

the *recognition* of the "I" as "I" and of reality as reality, but also a consent of the "I" to the "I" and, fused with it, to reality.

The terms "affirmation," "recognition," and "consent" obviously do not refer to explicit judgments and decisions of will on the part of the subject: they refer to the implicit "affirmation" which the *existent* subject himself, as "functioning intentionality," is and which underlies the judgment and decision of the will.[31] Savoring the first cigarette after breakfast or a good glass of wine; the joy caused by the birth of a beautiful child; the ecstacy of the bride; the happiness of finding a long-sought elusive truth; the roar of laughter following an hilarious joke; the emotion resulting from seeing a sunrise in the mountains—all these are examples of affective involvement in, and affirmation of reality. Fused with this consent of the "I" to reality, there is the "I" 's consent to itself. The self-affirmation of the "I" on the affective level means a certain fullness of being, a certain fulfillment and satisfaction, a certain rest and peace, which may be called "happiness."

"Infinite Distance"

The "I" 's involvement in reality, however, cannot be exclusively called "zero distance": it is equiprimordially "infinite distance" on both the cognitive and the affective levels. This means that the positivity of the self-affirmation which the "I" is, simply is not what it is without negativity, i.e., without self-negation; at the same time, the affirmation of reality which is fused with this self-affirmation is also affected by negativity.

As self-affirmation, the "I" is positivity of being. On the cognitive level, however, the *recognition* of the "I" as "I" implies negativity—namely, the denial of the "I" 's identity with any reality whatsoever, understood as the facticity of the body and the world. The "I" 's positivity of being, then, is not what it is without negativity of being: the "I" is not the All, but a finite positivity of being. Similarly, the cognitive affirmation of reality, with which the "I" 's self-affirmation is fused, implies negativity—namely, the denial of the claim that the reality of bodily being and the world is identical with the "I," and the denial of the identity of any reality, no matter which, with any

---

[31]Sartre, *EN*, p. 404.

other reality, no matter which.   No reality is the All; reality is a finite positivity of being.

The expert will easily recognize here a Sartrian inspiration. Unlike Sartre, however, we primarily conceive the "I" and intentionality as positivity.   For Sartre himself the "for itself" is pure "nihilation," which is wrong.[32] The "for itself'" is *also*, and essentially, "nihilation," but not exclusively.   For this reason, the "I"-subject is not pure "nothingness," but a positivity of being which is affected by negativity and is therefore finite.

In his work BEING AND NOTHINGNESS, Sartre mainly considers the negativity of intentionality insofar as it lies on the cognitive level, but in his literary works, especially NAUSEA, it is primarily the affective level that is discussed.   On this level also he absolutizes the negativity: the subject's affective involvement in reality is sheer nausea for him.   The whole introduction to BEING AND NOTHINGNESS drives the reader to a first climax, reached in the last two pages of the Introduction, where Sartre summarizes his vision of the "in itself."   Precisely these two pages provokes the same feeling of disgust as Sartre's principal novel NAUSEA.   It is no mere coincidence that in BEING AND NOTHINGNESS several terms recur which are the warp and woof of NAUSEA.   When Antoine Roquentin, the principal personality of the novel, in the city park of Bouville, comes to realize the meaning of uncamouflaged being, he describes his experience as follows:

> If anyone had asked me what existence was, I would have answered in good faith that it was nothing, simply an empty form which was added to things from without but did not change in their nature.   And then suddenly, there it was, clear as day: existence had suddenly unveiled itself.   It had lost its harmless look of an abstract category: it was the very paste of things, this root was kneaded into existence.   Or rather the root, the park gates, the bench, the sparse grass, all that had vanished: the diversity of things, their individuality, were only an appearance, a veneer.   This veneer had melted, leaving soft, monstrous masses, all disorder—naked, in a frightful, obscene nakedness. . . .
> All things, gently, tenderly, were letting themselves drift into existence like those relaxed women who burst out laugh-

---

[32]De Waelhens, "Zijn en niet-zijn," *Tijdschrift voor Philosophie*, VII (1945), p. 113.

ing and say: "It is good to laugh," in a wet voice; they were parading, one in front of the other, exchanging abject secrets about their existence. I realized that there was no half-way house between non-existence and this flaunting abundance. If you existed, you had to exist *all the way*, as far as mouldiness, bloatedness, obscenity were concerned. . . . We were a heap of living creatures, irritated, embarrassed at ourselves, we hadn't the slightest reason to be there, none of us, each one confused, vaguely alarmed, felt *In the way* in relation to the others. *In the way:* it was the only relationship I could establish between these trees, these gates, these stones. . . . *In the way,* the chestnut tree there, opposite me, a little to the left. *In the way,* the Velleda. . . .

And I—soft, weak, obscene, digesting, juggling, with dismal thoughts—I, too, was *In the way.* Fortunately, I didn't feel it, although I realized it, but I was uncomfortable because I was afraid of feeling it (even now I am afraid—that it might catch me behind my head and lift me up like a wave). I dreamed vaguely of killing myself to wipe out at least one of these superfluous lives. But even my death would have been *In the way.* *In the way,* my corpse, my blood on these stones, between these plants, at the back of this smiling garden. And the decomposed flesh would have been *In the way* in the earth which would receive my bones, at last, cleaned, stripped, peeled, proper and clean as teeth, it would have been *In the way:* I was *In the way* for eternity.[33]

And a litttle later he continues:

I hated this ignoble mess. Mounting up, mounting up as high as the sky, spilling over, filling everything with its gelatinous slither. . . . I was not surprised, I knew that it was the World, the naked World suddenly revealing itself, and choked with rage at this gross, absurd being. . . . That was what worried me: of course there was no reason for this flowing larva to exist. But it was impossible for it not to exist. . . . I shouted "filth! what rotten filth!" and shook myself to get rid of this sticky filth, but it held fast and there was so much, tons and tons of existence, endless; I stifled at the depth of this immense weariness.[34]

From these quotations it should be evident that Sartre simply

---

[33]Sartre, *Nausea*, New York, 1949, pp. 171-173.
[34]Sartre, *op. cit.*, pp. 180-181.

eliminates all positive moments from *existence*.[35] But *existence*, even on the level of *Volo*, undeniably also has a positive aspect. Sartre would be entirely right if he merely wished to say that all positivity is always also affected by negativity. *Existence* on the level of affectivity—which Heidegger calls "mood" or "tonality" (*Befindlichkeit*) [36]—is both a "finding oneself to be well" and a "finding oneself not to be well": the world is both a "home" and "alien to home." The consent to reality is never a consent without reserve. The subject who man is can never fully "say" yes to reality.[37] Neither money nor sexuality, science nor power, health nor the Revolution—in a word, nothing fully satisfies man.[38] The subject's affective "saying" of yes to the world includes also an affective no. All fullness of being-man is equiprimordially emptiness; all satisfaction is infected with dissatisfaction; all peace, rest and happiness with conflict, unrest, and unhappiness. The "yes" within *existence* excludes absolute "nausea"; the "no" makes absolute "affective adaptation" impossible. The world is my home, in which I long for a better fatherland.

"The Being for Whom, in His Being, This Being Is at Issue"

It is not impossible that the details put forward in our reflection on the subject's involvement in reality may have obscured the outlook on the totality of man's being. These details, however, were necessary to prevent overemphasis on some aspects at the expense of others, as occurs in Sartre's work. We must now try to comprehend man's being again in its totality and will do so with the help of a certain expression used by Heidegger.

When Heidegger wishes to point out that man is not just a thing among things but a subject, a person, he calls man the "being for whom, in his being, this being itself is at issue." [39]

35R. Verneaux, *Leçons sur l'existentialisme*, Paris, n.d., p. 118.

36*SZ*, pp. 134-140; "Das Gestimmtsein bezieht sich nicht zunächst auf Seelisches, ist selbst kein Zustand drinnen, der dann auf rätselhafte Weise hinausgelangt und auf die Dinge und Personen abfährt. Darin zeigt sich der zweite Wesenscharakter der Befindlichkeit. Sie ist eine existenziale Grundart der gleichursprünglichen Erschlossenheit von Welt, Mitdasein und Existenz, weil diese selbst wesenhaft In-der-Welt-sein ist." *SZ*, p. 137.

37". . . il manque à son assentiment quelque chose de massif et de charnel." Merleau-Ponty, *EP*, p. 81.

38S. De Beauvoir, *Pour une morale de l'ambiguïté*, Paris, 1947, pp. 65-75.

39"Das Dasein ist ein Seiendes, das nicht nur unter anderem Seienden vorkommt. Es ist vielmehr dadurch ontisch ausgezeichnet, dass es diesem Seienden in seinem Sein um dieses Sein selbst geht. Zu dieser Seinsverfassung

For a thing is not concerned with its being: it lies, as it were, crushed upon itself.[40]   A man is not bald just as a billiard ball is smooth; he is not ill just as a cauliflower is rotten; he is not a hunchback just as a willow tree is gnarled; for man is concerned with his bald pate, the malfunctioning of his organism, his mis-shapenness.   He has a relationship with what he is—bald, sick, hunchbacked, etc.—and he has this relationship as a subject. Heidegger expresses this by saying that *Dasein* has a "relation-ship to being" which is an "understanding of being." [41]   It is this that constitutes what man essentially is, what makes man's being differ from the being of a thing.   For this reason Heidegger says that for man *in his being* this being itself is at issue, thereby excluding that there would merely be question here of some-thing accidental to being man.

It is in man's relationship as a subject to what he is, then, that there are the above-mentioned positive and negative mo-ments on both the cognitive and the affective levels.   Nothing of all this is found in a thing.   A thing does not have a relation-ship to its own being; it is compact density and lies "crushed upon itself": [42] there is no possibility for the thing to ask ques-tions, to wonder or to be bored, to be sad or anxious, to hope or despair.

Freedom as "Having to Be"

The fact that being a subject is being free induced several phenomenologists to use the term "freedom" for the "distance" itself which, on the basis of man's being-a-subject, characterizes man as situated subjectivity.   They use this term in this way, even without first putting forward the subject's superiority of being, his subsistence.[43]   The same must be said with respect to

---

des Daseins gehört aber dann, dass es in seinem Sein zu diesem Sein ein Seinsverhältnis hat." *SZ*, p. 12.

[40]Sartre takes over Heidegger's thought when he says of consciousness: "L'être de la conscience est un être, pour lequel il est dans son être question de son être." *EN*, p. 116.

[41]*SZ*, pp. 12-15.

[42]"Mais si nous supposons une affirmation dans laquelle l'affirmé vient remplir l'affirmant et se confond avec lui, cette affirmation ne peut pas s'affirmer, par trop de plénitude. . . . Tout se passe comme si pour libérer l'affirmation *de* soi du sein de l'être il fallait une décompression d'être." *EN*, p. 32.

[43]"La liberté est échappement à un engagement dans l'être, elle est néan-tisation d'un être qu'elle est. . . . Simplement le surgissement de la liberté se fait par la double néantisation de l'être qu'elle est et de l'être au milieu duquel elle est." *EN*, p. 566.

an even more profound meaning of the term "freedom," viz., its "having to be" (*zu sein, avoir à être*). This meaning in its turn can only be understood after a more profound reflection upon freedom as distance.

The affective distance of the subject with respect to reality is an "infinite distance" and is therefore invincible. True, the subject consents to reality in an unmistakable way, but the reserve, the negativity affecting this consent cannot be annulled. No experience of value is such that the subject's *yes* is definitive and not also permeated with a *no*. This applies to every level of intentionality—for example, the technical, economic, political, social, medical, pedagogical, artistic, and intellectual levels. To the extent that an economic, social, or political system have a certain value, man can consent to them and also to himself as an economist, a sociologist or a politician. But this consent is never such that it escapes being infected by negativity. For this reason man çannot stand still: he is continually urged on by the negativity contained in his *existence*. Man is never finished, whether as an economist, an artist, a philosopher, or a physician, etc. The same applies to his world. Because man "gets bored" by the constituted [44]—because his *yes* can never be definitive—he must continually stretch himself forward to a new future. Man as a subject is not only a "natural light" but also a "natural desire."

To see this it is necessary that in reflecting upon freedom as infinite distance the greatest emphasis be placed upon affective "nihilation." Some of Sartre's expressions have to be understood in the sense of this affective nihilation in order to be fully intelligible. For example, one can say that "nothingness follows close on the heels of being" and pursues it,[45] because all affirmation is infected by an invincible "nihilation." Likewise, "nothingness lies in the very bosom of being, in its heart, as a worm": [46] this expresses that the affective "saying" of *yes* is never massive and definitive. The affective nihilation always means that the subjectivity retains a certain distance from reality, it does not

---

[44]Merleau-Ponty, *EP*, p. 79.
[45]"La condition nécessaire pour qu'il soit possible de dire non, c'est que le non-être soit une présence perpétuelle, en nous et en dehors de nous, c'est que le néant hante l'être." *EN*, p. 47.
[46]"Le néant ne peut se néantiser que sur le fond d'être; si du néant peut-être donné, ce n'est ni avant ni après l'être, ni d'une manière générale, en dehors de l'être, mais c'est au sein même de l'être, en son coeur, comme un ver." *EN*, p. 57.

fully hold fast to it, but maintains a certain reserve and reticence, an affective not-being-absorbed by facticity.

Such terms as "nihilating rupture," [47] "nothingness of being," [48] "hole in being," [49] and "decompression of being" [50] are all synonymous expressions, which can be used to convey that the subject's affective involvement in reality can never mean a definitive consent.

All this explicitates what phenomenology means when it calls the being of man a "having to be." Man is a task, a task-in-the-world. As long as man is man, his being is, and is essentially, a task. Man is never "finished," then, for a "finished" task is no longer a task. True, man can disregard the tasklike character of his being-in-the-world, but he then disregards himself as man. He then gives himself the mode of being of a thing: for a thing, being is not a task because it is not a subject, not free.

Freedom as "Project"

I would be meaningless to claim that man's being is a "having to be" if this "having to be" were not, so to speak, "preceded" by a "being able to be." Man's being cannot be a task if his being did not include any potential being. It should be evident, however, that this potential exists.

Reflecting upon his *existence*, man, it is true, "finds" himself as "already" merged with a particular body and as "already" involved in a particular world. He finds himself as an American, a Jew, intelligent, cripple, a worker, emotional, ill, rich, fat, etc. All this constitutes what he "already" is, his past. This "already" may be called man's "determinations," for there is question here of all kinds of "determinants." The most current terms today, however, are "situation" [51] and "facticity." [52]

The facticity of *existence* means that man, in a sense, is "fixed." Certain possibilities are excluded by it. An American for example, can never realize himself as a Frenchman, but at

---

[47]*EN*, p. 514.
[48]*EN*, p. 516.
[49]*EN*, p. 121.
[50]*EN*, p. 116.
[51]"Or, précisément, je suit *de fait* en tant que j'ai un passé et ce passé immédiat me renvoie. . . . Ainsi le corps comme facticité est le passé. . . ." *EN*, p. 392.
[52]"En tant que tel, le corps ne se distingue pas de la *situation* du pour-soi, puisque, pour le pour-soi, exister ou se situer ne font qu'un." *EN*, p. 372.

most as a frenchified American; a cripple cannot realize himself as an alpinist; one who is characterologically "inactive" can at most realize himself as an "activated inactive" man; one who is emotionally "explosive" cannot realize himself as "serenity personified" but at most as a "contained explosive" man; one whose I.Q. is 80 cannot realize himself as Secretary of Health, Education, and Welfare.

There is, however, no facticity which does not include any possibilities. If the determinations which make one factically a lawyer, dumb, ill, fat, a worker or an American did not include any possibilities, then he would not *really* be a lawyer, not *really* dumb, not *really* ill, fat, a worker, or an American. Potentiality co-constitutes the reality of facticity; the "not yet" co-constitutes the reality of the "already"; the future co-constitutes the reality of the past.

This statement applies to any facticity whatsoever. For example, I am never merely factically ill: my actual illness includes possibilities. I can use my illness as a means to raise myself over those who never experienced illness; I can seize it as an opportunity to revolt against God; accept the illness as a suitable expiation for my sins; or I can tyrannize my surroundings. An illness which does not include any possibilities is not a real illness.[53]

We should keep in mind, however, that the possibilities of which there is question here are not idle. There can be a *real* potential for being only on the basis of a specific actual being. Actual being makes potential being possible, and definite possibilities are only real on the basis of certain specific actualities.

Potential being, then, is not a matter of a purely logical possibility; it is not a mere absence of contradiction between two terms. Similarly, potential being is not like the being-possible of things, to which something "can happen."[54] Likewise, it should not be conceived as a little plan which one can drop if he likes.[55] The ability-to-be of which there is question here is an *existentiale*, an essential characteristic of man. Strictly speak-

---

[53]*EN*, p. 393.
[54]"Das Möglichsein, das je das Dasein existenzial ist, unterscheidet sich ebensosehr von der leeren, logischen Möglichkeit, wie von der Kontingenz eines Vorhandenen, sofern mit diesem das und jenes 'passieren' kann." Heidegger, *SZ*, p. 143.
[55]*SZ*, p. 145.

ing, this idea is implied in the very statement that man's facticity is no *real* facticity if it does not include any potential.

How must we conceive this potential being as an *existentiale*? The subject's superiority of being was described as a "light" for both the subject himself and the other than the subject. Insofar as the subject is a light for reality, we ascribed to him the "letting be" of reality. This is no creative "letting be" of reality, but only the dis-closure, the "rendering free" of a reality which reveals itself as "already" there. To be a subject is to stand consciously in reality as facticity. The subject's "letting be," however, is equiprimordially *Verstehen* [56]—a term which is well nigh untranslatable but sometimes rendered as "comprehending." Heidegger uses it to indicate that subjectivity is not merely the "rendering free" of the "already," of reality's facticity, but equiprimordially the "rendering free" of the "not yet," of reality's possibilities. *Verstehen* is "letting be" itself, insofar as it is the consciousness not only of factical being but also of potential being.[57]

Human *existence*, then, is the oppositional unity, the unity-in-opposition of factical being "and" potential being, of "already" "and" "not yet," of past "and" present. The term "project" is reserved to indicate this unity in opposition which man is.[58] Man does not lie "crushed" in his facticity, but *Verstehen* allows him a certain elbow room, the leeway of his potential being.[59] Man is an unfinished, "imperfect form in an imperfect tense" (Buytendijk).

Man's being, however, is a being-in-the-world. It stands to reason, therefore, that his potential being is a being-able-to-be-in-the-world.[60] To every possible way of *existing* there corresponds a possible meaning of the world. The project which man is is equiprimordially the project of his world.[61]

---

[56]*SZ*, pp. 143-146.

[57]"Dasein versteht sich immer schon und immer noch, solange es ist, aus Möglichkeiten." *SZ*, p. 145.

[58]"Warum dringt das Verstehen nach allen wesenhaften Dimensionen des in ihm Erschliessbaren immer in die Möglichkeiten? Weil das Verstehen an ihm selbst die existenziale Struktur hat, die wir den Entwurf nennen." *Ibid.*

[59]"Der Entwurf ist die existenziale Seinsverfassung des Spielraums des faktischen Seinkönnens." *Ibid.*

[60]"Als Seinkönnen ist das In-sein je Sein-können-in-der-Welt." *SZ*, p. 144.

[61]The French philosophers of existence also describe man as a "projet du monde."

Meaning as "Direction"

On the basis of the potential being contained in any factical meaning, it is possible to give a more profound sense to the term "meaning" than that of "appearing reality." Meaning reveals itself as "direction." The appearing profile of an ashtray is the meaning which clings to perception from a particular standpoint. But the factically appearing profile of the ashtray indicates the "direction" which my gaze must follow if it wishes to let appear that which factically does not appear. The subject, then, as "letting be" is the origin of meaning, but as *Verstehen* it is the origin of "direction." This is true for every level of *existence*. For example, the factical meaning of the world for a college graduate contains many references to possible modes of *existing* which are, as it were, sketches of the "direction" his *existence* can take in the world. Similarly, the factical value of a legal order indicates the "direction" in which *existence*, as projecting laws, can further realize itself.

The statement that for "man, in his being, this being itself is at issue," also assumes a new and more profound sense if one keeps in mind that subjectivity as the "letting be" of facticity is at the same time the *Verstehen* of possibilities.[62] The assertion that for man, in his being, this being itself is at issue now means that for man his possibilities and those of his world are also at issue.[63] Man is always "ahead" of himself and of his world [64] because his facticity is not what it is without the leeway of his potential being. This leeway, however, indicates the "direction" in which his *existence* can go.[65] All this applies again to every possible level of *existence*. If, for example, I ask about the meaning of a mode of *existing* of man as an economical being or a political being, I do not merely put factical value into question,

---

[62]"Das Seiende, dem es in seinem Sein um dieses selbst geht, verhält sich zu seinem Sein als seiner eigensten Möglichkeit. Dasein ist je seine Möglichkeit und es 'hat' sie nicht nur noch eigenschaftlich als ein Vorhandenes." *SZ*, p. 42.

[63]"Das Dasein ist Seiendes, dem es in seinem Sein um dieses selbst geht. Das 'es geht um . . .' hat sich verdeutlicht in der Seinsverfassung des Verstehens als des sichentwerfenden Seins. . . ." *SZ*, p. 191.

[64]"Dasein ist immer schon 'über sich hinaus', nicht als Verhalten zu anderem Seienden, das es nicht ist, sondern als Sein zum Seinkönnen, das es selbst ist. Diese Seinsstruktur des wesenhaften 'es geht um . . .' fassen wir als das Sich-vorweg-sein des Daseins." *SZ*, p. 192.

[65]"(Le temps) est à la lettre le sens de notre vie. . . ." Merleau-Ponty, *PP*, p. 492.

for these values are not purely factical. What is also at issue here is the direction which the mode of *existing* in question can take.

Above we said that it would make no sense to claim that man's being is a "having to be" if this "having to be" is not "preceded" by a "being able to be." Man's being could not be a task if man lay "crushed" in his facticity, i.e., if facticity did not reveal the leeway of potential being. It should be evident now that the term "preceded" is not correct: man's being is not "first" a being-able-to-be and "next" a "having to be," but these two are equiprimordial. The term "having to be," however, expresses more than "being able to be." "Having to be" reveals itself only when one sees that affective involvement in facticity does not imply a definitive consent but is permeated with "nihilation." For this reason man always wants to go forward and to reach ahead of every factical situation. His being-able-to-be offers him the necessary leeway in this matter.

We are still concerned here with the various moments of being-man on the strictly human level, in other words, with man as an involved subject. The being of man as subject revealed itself as a being-free. Next, we saw that the subject's involvement in reality implies distance. This distance itself also is called "freedom." A more profound reflection on distance disclosed "having to be" and the project. And here we must again note that in phenomenological writings the term "freedom" is also used for man's "having to be" and for his "being able to be." [66] In this usage the freedom of man as a subject is not always explicitly mentioned, but it is at least tacitly presupposed. For the being-able-to-be ascribed to man reveals itself as something very special in comparison with that of things, precisely because of the being-a-subject which characterizes man. For the potential being of human *existence* is a potential *of the subject*. Man's possibilities are *his own*. To a thing something can "happen," [67] but its various possibilities cannot be called possibilities of the thing *itself* because the thing is not a selfhood. Man, on the proper level of his manhood, is "master of his

---

[66] "Dire que le pour-soi a à être ce qu'il est, dire qu'il est ce qu'il n'est pas en n'étant pas ce qu'il est, dire qu'en lui l'existence précède et conditionne l'essence ou inversement, selon la formule de Hegel, que pour lui 'Wesen ist was gewesen ist', c'est dire une seule et même chose, à savoir que l'homme est libre." Sartre, *EN*, p. 515.
[67] *SZ*, p. 143.

situation" and holds his possibilities "in his own hands." The project he is is a *self*-project.

Just as "having to be" is not something accidental to being-man, but rather constitutes what man essentially is as situated subjectivity, so also his being-a-project is not like a "little plan" which he could discard if he so wishes but is an essential characteristic of man.[68] In his own way Sartre expresses this idea very conveniently when he points out that man "is not what he is but is what he is not." [69] Man is not what he is: he is not mere facticity, for facticity leaves him the leeway of his being-able-to-be. At the same time, man is what he is not: man is a being-able-to-be, but his is not factically this ability. This being-able-to-be, however, is not something superadded to man, and for this reason we must say that man *is* what he is not (factically).

If man as project is called "freedom," there is no compelling objection to Sartre's statement that man "is doomed to be free." [70] This expression means that man's *being* is a project, that there is question here of an essential characteristic which man cannot discard. One who speaks of the essence of a reality always wishes to indicate that through which something is what it is. "Essence" always implies a certain hypothetical necessity. "If," then a certain reality must be called "human reality," this reality must *of necessity* be *freedom*, because man's essence is freedom.

Just as the freedom of man as subject includes a being-bound —insofar as the subject who man is does not occur without the facticity of bodily being and the world—so also must freedom as project be called relative. Being-able-to-be is a potential being in terms of a particular facticity, a particular situation. A particular factical situation implies certain possibilities and excludes others. I am free to realize myself as a classical philologist, but this mode of potential being is implied only in the facticity of a college major in classics and not in that of a physical education major. I am free to realize myself as an alpinist, but not on the basis of a facticity which makes me a cripple. The situation, then, binds and limits me in many ways, and it is only in terms

---

[68]"Das Verstehen ist, als Entwerfen, die Seinsart des Daseins, in der es seine Möglichkeiten als Möglichkeiten ist." *SZ*, p. 145.

[69]"Pourtant, le pour-soi est. Il est, dira-t-on, fût-ce à titre d'être qui n'est pas ce qu'il est, et qui est ce qu'il n'est pas." *EN*, p. 121.

[70]*EN*, p. 515; "Etre libre c'est être condamné à être libre." *EN*, p. 174.

of these bonds to my situation that I am free. The project which I am is a "thrown project." [71]

3. To Be Free Is to Be Ethical

It happens rather frequently that freedom and being-ethical are seen as opposites. This view is based on a particular conception of freedom and being-ethical. Freedom is conceived as being without bonds, and being-ethical as being bound by laws that are "there." In such a view the opposition is, of course, inevitable. But the view is primitive, for the assumption that freedom can be conceived as being without bonds cannot be justified; moreover, this view leaves the origin of the moral law in darkness.

Even if freedom is not conceived as being without bonds but as "selfhood," there remains a certain opposition between being-free and being-ethical as long as the law is conceived as a norm which is "there," imposed upon freedom from without. There is opposition between a personalistic concept of man and a legalistic concept of ethical obligation.

Legalism—the view that morality is nothing but willingness to obey the externally imposed law—favored an impoverished and even pharisaic pursuit of the moral ideal.[72] If the good or evil of a human action depends solely on the agreement or disagreement with the law, then the attitude or mentality of the acting subject does not matter, so that a purely external compliance with the law suffices to speak of a good action. Such a view fosters self-complacency and pride: one need not make oneself any reproaches; one has acted *en règle*, according to the rule.[73] Moreover, one has here a ready-made criterion to judge others, viz., the external agreement or disagreement of their actions with the law. Observing that the other's action deviates from what the law prescribes, one has every reason to "wash one's hands in innocence" and to "thank God that one is not like him." This is pharisaism.

---

[71]"Und als geworfenes ist das Dasein in die Seinsart des Entwerfens geworfen." *SZ*, p. 145.

[72]J. Lacroix, *Personne et Amour*, Paris, 1955, pp. 36-41.

[73]"D'une part vis-à-vis de soi-même on sera porté à une sorte de satisfaction interne, de contentement intérieur d'autant plus grand qu'on se soumettra davantage jusque dans le détail aux plus petites prescriptions - et, comme disait saint Augustin, il y a quelque chose de pire que le vice, à savoir l'orgueil de la vertu." J. Lacroix, *op. cit.*, pp. 37-38.

When moral life is conceived in a legalistic fashion, moral education has no other possibilities than appeal to fear for the consequences of failure to observe the law. For there can be no question of a moral *ideal*, from which one could derive the strength to overcome obstacles: the law is conceived as imposed from without and, consequently, the law itself has to provide the motive for its observation. This motive is found in the threat of penalties, the fear of which must induce the person to observe the law. Educational value is thus attributed to the law itself and even to "regulations." [74]

Legalism was not merely a prevailing mentality in a certain period of moral history but is, more especially, a permanent temptation against which the authentically moral man must always struggle. Later we will see that this struggle implies the refusal to be satisfied with a minimum. It is the refusal to substitute for the creative aspect of moral life a process-like acting in agreement with the law; it is the refusal to sacrifice the progressive character of moral life to the "settling of old debts." [75]

Sartre's Deathblow to Legalism

Sartre found a very simple way to do away with legalism: he denies the existence of general norms and values. According to him, there are no universal norms because there is no God who has written such norms in heaven. [76] Sartre finds it very "annoying" that there is no God, but if he does not exist, someone has to invent values. Life does not have any *a priori* meaning: [77] man as a subject has to give meaning to it by inventing values.

Values, he holds, do not exist in themselves and have no meaning in themselves by virtue of which they can impose

---

[74]N. Perquin, "Het 'welopgevoede' Kind," *Dux,* XVIII(1951), pp. 432-434.

[75]J. Lacroix, *op. cit.,* pp. 41-45.

[76]"L'existentialiste pense, qu'il est très gênant que Dieu n'existe pas, car avec lui disparaît toute possibilité de trouver des valeurs dans un ciel intelligible; il ne peut plus y avoir de bien *a priori,* puisqu'il n'y a pas de conscience infinie et parfaite pour le penser; il n'est écrit nulle part que le bien existe, qu'il faut être honnête, qu'il ne faut pas mentir, puisque précisément nous sommes sur un plan où il y a seulement des hommes." Sartre, *EH,* pp. 35-36.

[77]"Si j'ai supprimé Dieu le Père, il faut bien quelqu'un pour inventer les valeurs. Il faut prendre les choses comme elles sont. Et par ailleurs, dire que nous inventons les valeurs ne signifie pas autre chose que ceci: la vie n'a pas de sens, a priori." *EH,* p. 89.

themselves on the will.[78] They do not lie like rocks in a land that has never been discovered, but always presuppose the subject. Sartre vigorously objects to the view that man encounters pre-given and ready-made goals or values as soon as he enters the world. Pre-given goals cannot determine the meaning of human activities, regardless of whether these goals come from God, nature, "my" nature or society.[79]

For Sartre, it follows from this that freedom is the *only* foundation of values and that nothing, absolutely nothing, justifies the acceptance of this or that particular value or scale of values.[80] My freedom is the groundless ground of all values.[81]

The firm anchorage, then, which traditional Christian morality has always offered does not exist according to Sartre.[82] There are no signs through which man knows what he ought to do. Sartre illustrates this point by means of an example. While a prisoner of war, he became acquainted with a Jesuit, whose father had died young and had left him behind in great poverty. He was able to attend a boarding school, but its directors continually reminded him that he had only been accepted as a charity case and denied him the scholastic distinctions which he deserved. Later he experienced disappointment in love, and in his military service, likewise, everything went wrong. Finally he began to see in all this a sign of God: it became clear to him that he was called to work for the triumph of religion, for holiness and faith. For this reason he had become a priest.[83] Sartre, however, concludes that the man *himself* and himself *alone* evidently gave to the "sign" the meaning he wished to ascribe to it. Why didn't he interpret "God's sign" as an indication that he should become a carpenter? Obviously because he did not wish to become a carpenter. Thus he himself was fully responsible for his decision.

---

[78]*EN*, pp. 75-76.

[79]"On posera les fins comme des transcendances . . . elles viennent de Dieu, de la nature, de 'ma' nature, de la société. Ces fins toutes faites et préhumaines définerons donc le sens de mon acte avant même que je le conçoive, de même que les motifs. . . . Ces tentatives avortées pour étouffer la liberté sous le poids de l'être . . . montrent assez que la liberté coïncide en son fond avec le néant qui est au coeur de l'homme." *EN*, p. 516.

[80]"Il s'ensuit que ma liberté est l'unique fondement des valeurs et que *rien*, absolument rien ne me justifie d'adopter telle ou telle valeur, telle ou telle échelle de valeurs." *EN*, p. 76.

[81]*EN*, p. 76.

[82]Sartre, *EH*, p. 47.

[83]*EH*, pp. 47-49.

Even if there were general norms, Sartre continues, they would be wholly useless for man. He illustrates the point with another example. During the war one of his students came to see him for advice. He did not know what he should do: go to England to join the Free French Forces or remain with his mother to support her.[84]   Triumphantly Sartre remarks that there is no system of universal moral norms which can answer this question. Christian morality preaches love and recommends the hardest way—but what is love? Serving France or supporting a mother—which is the hardest? Kantian morality teaches that man may never treat his fellowman as a means but must always consider him a purpose. But he who remains with his mother treats his fellow-combatants as means, and he who joins them treats his mother as a means.[85]   Therefore, universal norms of morality are useless. Even if there were a God, that would not make any difference in this respect.[86] "You are free; choose—that is, invent." [87]

The careful reader can hardly fail to notice that all kinds of questions are mixed here. For Sartre there are no values "in themselves"; *therefore*, man is the absolute source and the only foundation of values. God did not write any general laws in heaven; *therefore*, there are no general laws. No moral system can indicate what ought to be done here and now; *therefore*, all systems are superfluous. No sign from heaven guarantees man that his actions are good; *therefore*, man must invent his own norms in absolute autonomy. This is confusion confounded, and it gives Sartre all desirable elbow room for his own view of morality.

A Universal Norm in Spite of Everything

Nevertheless, according to Sartre, there exists a universally valid morality having a universally valid norm. This norm is freedom. Dostoevski said that if God does not exists, everything is permitted to man. "Indeed," adds Sartre, "this is the starting point of existentialism." [88] In absolute autonomy, man must create values, invent norms, and choose his morality.[89] He can

---

[84]*EH*, pp. 40-41.
[85]*EH*, pp. 42-43.
[86]"Même si Dieu existait, ça ne changerait rien." *EH*, p. 95.
[87]*EH*, p. 47.
[88]*EH*, p. 36.
[89]*EH*, pp. 78, 82.

choose what he wishes as long as he chooses freely.[90]   Freedom is the universal norm.

Sartre anticipates the possible objection that there exists no universal norm.   Of course, he admits, there is such a norm, but it is not writtten in heaven.   This norm is written in man himself as the truth, the reality, and the objective meaning of his human nature,[91] which is absolute freedom.   One could insist that Sartre literally rejects human nature: "there is no human nature whatsoever." [92]   In his terminology, however, this simply means that man is not a *thing* of nature.   For Sartre there is a "human universality of condition" [93]—a "human condition" [94]—and these terms indicate exactly the same as what other philosophers refer to when they speak of the nature or essence of man,[95] without attaching any materialistic sense to these terms.

The universal ethical law of absolute freedom is not written in heaven for Sartre, but is the expression of man's essence, his absolute freedom.   Thus it is possible also to judge the actions of others.   Those who depreciate their absolute freedom by trying to find in heavenly signs a guarantee for their actions or who point to their passions as an excuse for their deeds are in bad faith: they live inauthentically, immorally.   They disregard what they are—absolutely free.   They are cowards and rascals!! [96]

But, may man not freely choose to live in bad faith?   Sartre's answer is very definitely in the negative: "Here one cannot escape a judgment of truth." [97]   He who wishes to live in bad faith, disregards the *truth* of his essence, which consists in freedom as absolute autonomy.   The being of man is a "having to be" in the bond of his essence's objectivity.   For Sartre this essence is absolute autonomy.   Certain ways of choosing are based on the truth of his essence, others disregard this truth.[98] Man, therefore, can do good and evil.   The truth of his essence

---

[90]"On peut tout choisir, si c'est sur le plan de l'engagement libre." *EH,* pp. 88-89.
[91]"Ici, on ne peut échapper à un jugement de vérité." *EH,* p. 81.
[92]*EH,* p. 52.
[93]*EH,* p. 67.
[94]*EH,* p. 68.
[95]"Nous sommes donc dans la situation inverse de celle des psychologues puisque nous *partons* de cette totalité synthétique qu'est l'homme et que nous établissons l'essence d'homme *avant* de débuter en psychologie."   Sartre, *Esquisse d'une théorie des émotions,* Paris, 1948, p. 9.
[96]*EH,* pp. 84-85.
[97]*EH,* p. 81.
[98]"Certains choix sont fondés sur l'erreur, et d'autres sur la vérité." *EH,* p. 80.

imposes itself upon him as an obligation. For this reason the objectively universal moral law is at the same time also subjectively universal.[99] It imposes an obligation on every man, according to Sartre.

The Ethical Law

Is being-ethical a "standing under the law"? Must the ethical law be said to be a law that "is already there"? Is there opposition between freedom as "selfhood" and the law? Are there laws which hold for everyone, always and everywhere? Let us see to what extent it is possible to answer these questions on the basis of the insights we have acquired into freedom.

Man's being-a-subject is the basis of his "having to be" because the subject-as-*volo* includes an invincible negativity. This same subject as *cogito* is a light for himself and the world. This light is an objective light and, as such, is bound to the objectivity of *existence*. Man is a being for whom, in his being, this being itself is at issue, the *objectivity* of his being is at issue for him;[100] he is a being who is characterized by "understanding of being."[101] There is question here of a pre-predicative awareness of the reality of *existence*.

This pre-predicative awareness clearly contains moments of genuine "understanding," moments of insight into the *essence* of *existence*. The very fact that man understands himself as *existence* is evidence of such an insight: it belongs to the *essence* of man to *exist*. That by which man is precisely man—and not a thing or a God—is his *existence*, his being a subject-in-the-world. On the basis of this understanding it is possible to make objectively universal statements about man. On a more profound level of reflection *existence* reveals itself also as *essentially* destined for other *existences*, a destiny which man executes in love. There are many other essential characteristics of being-man which can be explicated in this way, but anything philosophical anthropology makes explicit is already implicitly "known" in the original light of the "understanding of being."

99"Ainsi, bien que le contenu de la morale soit variable, une certaine forme de cette morale est universelle." *EH*, p. 85.

100"Das Sicheinlassen auf die Entborgenheit des Seienden verliert sich nicht in dieser, sondern entfaltet sich zu einem Zurücktreten vor dem Seienden, damit dieses in dem, was es ist und wie es ist, sich offenbare und die vorstellende Angleichung aus ihm das Richtmass nehme." Heidegger, *Vom Wesen der Wahrheit*, p. 15.

101*SZ*, pp. 12-15.

If, then, we say here that the acting subject realizes himself in the world, it goes without saying that awareness of the bond with the objectivity of his own essence accompanies man in his action. For man himself is this awareness because he *exists* as *cogito*. The realization that he is bound to the objectivity of his essence forbids man to say about his *existence* anything which arbitrarily strikes his fancy or anything which a particular government or a particular tradition wishes to see recognized as "truth." We meet here the *ethos* of truth which has motivated so many authentic thinkers. Neither threats nor attempts to break their career, nor even violence could induce them to give up that *ethos*. The same consciousness also plays a role when man acts—that is, when he realizes the still unfulfilled possibilities of his *existence* as project. It is not only in speaking but also, and perhaps even primarily, in *acting* that man can recognize or disregard his own essence. In his actions man is accompanied by his awareness of the fact that he is bound to the objectivity of his own essence, and this awareness, this "companion," is man himself.

Once again, the subject-as-*volo* is the basis of man's "having to be" and the subject-as-*cogito* implies that man is bound to the objectivity of his essence. Realizing that there is question here of one and the same subject, we are now obliged to say that the being of the *existent* subject *is* a "having to be" in bond to the objectivity of his essence. If it is true, then, that the subject-as-*existence* essentially implies "destiny for other subjects-as existences," then the objectivity of man's own manhood obliges him to prevent that he ever destroy the others' subjectivity.[102] People who lived authentically preferred to sacrifice their lives rather than disregard in their actions the objectivity of their own essence.

We are speaking here of what is traditionally called "the ethical man." The "understanding of being," previously mentioned in a broader context, reveals itself here, in a more narrow framework, as what is traditionally called "conscience." And because of the fact that man himself is this "understanding of being," man's *being* must be called a "being-conscientious."

Since the beginning of authentic philosophical thinking, philosophers have tried to explicitate and conceptualize man's

---

102Obviously, to be ethical implies much more than this.

being as also being-ethical. Obviously, their intention was not to determine what the individual has to do or to omit in individual cases: they were concerned with explicitating the *essential* moments of man's being as a "having to be" in bond to the objectivity of his essence. Their endeavors resulted, precisely as explicitations of *essential* moments, in objectively universal norms—norms, therefore, which are not written in heaven, but are "impressed in the hearts of men." [103] The fact that these laws and norms, once they have been formulated, can begin to live a kind of isolated existence, divorced from their source, can become an occasion for the worst possible forms of objectivism and legalism.

Objectivism in Ethics

As we emphasized before, in legalism the law is conceived as "already there" and "imposed from without." This means that norms are conceived as norms-in-themselves. It is precisely this view that is denied, and rightly so, by Sartre and Merleau-Ponty. But they expresss themselves very badly when they formulate their rejection of that view as a rejection of "general norms." What they intend to deny is an implicit idea, underlying that view, about the ontological status of general norms—namely, the idea that such norms are in-themselves. For this reason they are subsequently able to admit again a general norm. For Sartre this norm is absolute freedom, for Merleau-Ponty the recognition of man by man.[104] Thus Merleau-Ponty is not a relativist; [105] and the same, in this respect, must be said of Sar-

---

[103]"Il y a au sein et à la racine du choix moral une visée de valeur constante et immuable que nous n'avons pas à inventer, ni à créer de toute pièce, mais à accepter et à faire nôtre: à savoir la reconnaissance de l'éminente dignité de la personne humaine et des valeurs constitutives de la personnalité." Dondeyne, "Les problèmes soulevés par l'athéisme existentialiste," *Sapientia Aquinatis, Communicationes IV Congressus Thomistici Internationalis,* Roma, 1955, p. 468.

[104]"Le marxisme avait vu qu'inévitablement notre connaissance de l'histoire est partiale, chaque conscience étant elle-même historiquement située, mais, au lieu d'en conclure que nous sommes enfermés dans la subjectivité et voués à la magie dès que nous voulons agir au dehors, il trouvait, par delà la connaissance scientifique et son rêve de vérité impersonnelle, un nouveau fondement pour la vérité historique dans la logique spontanée de notre existence, dans la reconnaissance du prolétaire par le prolétaire, et dans la croissance effective de la révolution." Merleau-Ponty, *Humanisme et Terreur,* Paris, 1947, pp. 19-20.

[105]"Dans une période donnée de l'histoire et de la politique du parti, les valeurs sont déterminées et l'adhésion est sans réserves, puisqu'elle est motivée par la logique de l'histoire. C'est cet absolu dans le relatif qui fait la différence entre la dialectique marxiste et le relativisme vulgaire." Merleau-Ponty, *op. cit.,* p. 129.

tre,[106] even though the content of his general ethical norm is not acceptable. Sartre and Merleau-Ponty rightly oppose themselves to the objectivism which legalism surreptitiously introduced as an implicit ontology in its affirmation of the objectivity of general norms. In this ontology values are merely "words" and these words are merely "empty shells." [107]

One who accepts ethical norms and affirms their objectivity, their truth or unconcealedness, is obliged explicitly to state that truth-as-unconcealedness must be "brought about," must "come to pass," and that this must be done by the subject-as-*cogito*. Now, we called the subject "freedom" because he *cannot* be the deterministic result of "blind" cosmic processes and forces. Thus we must say that truth-as-unconcealedness finds its origin in freedom.[108] This does not mean that the subject arbitrarily decides about truth,[109] but it does mean that the truth can never be the deterministic result of a causal process.[110] General ethical norms are born in history, and their truth "comes to pass" in the freedom which the subject-as-*cogito* is. When, at a given *place* or in a given *time*, the truth of a general ethical norm does not "come to pass" and is not "brought about," then we must say that this norm does not exist *there* and *then*. Only one who recognizes the "coming to pass" of ethical truth is able to overcome objectivism. Ethical norms are objective-for-a-subject.

In his opposition to objectivism Sartre goes so far as to claim that, even if general norms "were written in heaven," they could not help man. For he would still have the task of "deciphering" those norms in order to make them meaningful.[111] Sartre clarifies his assertion with the above-mentioned example of the situation facing one of his students during the war, and observes that no system of general norms can give any answer. Universal

---

[106]Sartre, *EH*, p. 85.

[107]"La décision . . . n'est pas affaire privée, elle n'est pas l'affirmation immédiate des valeurs que nous préférons, elle consiste pour nous à faire le point de notre situation dans le monde, à nous replacer dans le cours des choses, à bien comprendre et à bien exprimer le mouvement de l'histoire hors duquel les valeurs restent verbales et par lequel seulement elles ont chance de se réaliser." Merleau-Ponty, *op. cit.*, p. 23.

[108]"Die Existenzphilosophie . . . legt die Entscheidung ganz in die Freiheit des Menschen, dessen Dasein aus ihm selbst gestaltet werden muss, weil es keine verpflichtende Leitbilder über und ausser ihm gibt." F. Fechner, *Rechtsphilosophie, Soziologie und Metaphysik des Rechts*, Tübingen, 1956, p. 253.

[109]Fechner, *op. cit.*, pp. 209-210, 256, 261.

[110]Fechner, *op. cit.*, pp. 250-251.

[111]"L'existentialiste ne pensera pas non plus que l'homme peut trouver un secours dans un signe donné, sur terre, qui l'orientera; car il pense que l'homme déchiffre lui-même le signe comme il lui plaît." Sartre, *EH*, p. 38.

norms, therefore, even if they existed, would be entirely useless. "You are free, choose!"

Sartre is right here on one point, but tries to take advantage of this with respect to another point which does not have anything to do with the first. Obviously, "norms written in heaven," i.e., norms-in-themselves, cannot help man. They have to be "deciphered"—that is, their truth must be "brought about." But when Sartre advises his student to choose in freedom either to support his mother or to join the Free French forces, he actually has already made use of a general norm by simply disregarding a third possibility: his student could have decided to become a collaborator or a traitor. For Sartre this possibility does not even deserve mention because, by virtue of the general law that one may not destroy the subjectivity of one's countrymen, it was already excluded for him.[112] Thus the universal law is not entirely useless.

Next, it is a mistake to think that a universal norm *ought to be able* to indicate how man must act in *concrete* situations. Such an idea assumes that a general norm proves its validity by offering an insight into what here and now must be done; hence, the fact that general norms cannot do this would lead to the conclusion that they are useless. Now, it is obvious that no general norm can prescribe a concrete action, but this does not mean that Sartre's conclusion follows.

The insight into what must be done in concrete situations is born from the encounter of "having to be," the ethical ideal which man essentially is, with the concrete situation. The conviction that he is destined for the other is not enough to let man know what he must do here and now.[113] He has to investigate whether *this* deed is such that it fosters the other's subjectivity or destroys it. He cannot determine this by looking at the general norm, but has to consider the deed itself and the situation in which it is done. What has to be done here and now cannot be deduced from general norms, for these norms say nothing about the character of *this* deed and *this* situation. For instance,

---

[112]Dondeyne, *Contemporary European Thought and Christian Faith*, p. 197.

[113]"S'il est vrai que la foi chrétienne développe le sens de la personne humaine et nous oblige à promouvoir la justice et la paix dans le monde, par l'instauration d'un ordre temporel plus digne de l'homme, elle ne nous donne pas pour autant une image concrete de cet ordre." Dondeyne, "Les problèmes soulevés par l'athéisme existentialiste," *Sapientia Aquinatis, Communicationes IV Congressus Thomistici Internationalis*, p. 467.

whether a Rorschach test is a violation of someone's subjectivity or not cannot be deduced from the universal law which prescribes respect for other people: it can become evident only by investigating exactly what happens in a Rorschach test. The claim that such an insight can be derived from the general law is tantamount to the assertion that general esthetics enable an artist to conclude what he must paint on *this* wall and how he should do it.[114] The artist obviously cannot draw such a conclusion, and the same applies to the moral realm. The acceptance of general norms does not in itself guarantee and justify any moral choice. It is excluded that man does good of necessity, because general norms dictate a particular moral choice to him.[115]

Accordingly, universal laws are not useless but, on the other hand, they do not suffice for an authentically moral life. There are other reasons, however, in addition to those mentioned above for the fact that general laws are neither useless nor sufficient. Universal laws are especially insufficient because they do not explicitate moral life as an ideal of being-man, especially, when they are negative and express moral demands in a minimal way. An authentic moral life implies on the part of the subject an ever-renewed application to a task that is never finished. For the being of man is a "having to be" and is therefore never finished. Man can therefore never say that he *is* virtuous, without disregarding the proper character of being-virtuous. As a mode of being-man, being-virtuous is a mode of "having to be." In an authentically moral life, then, there is always progress. This progress does not consist in an ever more accurate observance of an increasingly more sharply defined law, but in a conscience which sees forever more clearly, and forever executes more faithfully, an ideal that has never been reached. Moral life also knows geniuses and inventors. They do not need minimalisti-

---

[114]"On ne déduit pas plus la morale de la loi qu'on ne déduit la science des axiomes de la raison ou l'art des principes de l'esthétique." J. Lacroix, *op. cit.,* p. 44.

[115]"La foi ne justifie aucun des choix qu'on peut être amené à faire dans une situation donnée; il faut se risquer, s'aventurer, et l'on ignore toujours ce qui en résultera et l'on ne doit pas pour autant cesser de s'en préoccuper, d'y veiller, de s'efforcer au besoin d'y porter remède. Peut-être a-t-on 'tort', peut-être va-t-on . . . déclencher des catastrophes; du moins doit-on savoir qu'elles risquent de se produire et ne pas se rassurer par avance en se disant: ce que je fais est nécessairement bon, puisque c'est la foi, qui me le dicte." Fr. Jeanson, "Les caractères existentialistes de la conduite humaine selon Jean-Paul Sartre," *Morale chrétienne et requêtes contemporaines,* p. 181.

cally defined laws any longer because, in their personal endeavor to attain the ideal, they always accomplish more than those laws prescribe.[116]

With respect to an authentically moral life, the "prevailing" laws are even a danger. For any moral life begains with the almost processlike observance of the laws which "prevail" in a society. Any violation of these laws is met or punished by the moral facticity of the society in a likewise almost processlike fashion. This implies the danger that moral life will never go beyond a certain automatic functioning under the law, thus giving rise to the worst possible kind of legalism and fixism,[117] which depreciates any authentically moral life. It would be wrong, nevertheless, to deny, because of this danger, the value of the law, understood as a kind of moral facticity of society. Yet, this is often done on the basis of a moral idealism. One *begins* by placing oneself above the law, in the conviction that the moral ideal can be reached without "passing through the law." [118] This attitude can be compared to another, similar mistake—the mistake of people who one day experience the attraction of authentic, personal philosophizing, join forces in a "circle," place themselves above every "ready-made truth" or "dogmatism," as they say, and then seriously think that in this way they can produce a valuable philosophical achievement. Such an expectation is an illusion: one can always notice that such people remain below the level of the so-called "ready-made truth." The same idea applies to those who, with an appeal to the personal character of the moral ideal, place themselves above the law: they end up below the law, below the minimum.[119] Man needs the law, at least in hours of waning enthusiasm, discouragement, and weakness, to remain steadfast and produce at least the minimum.[120] The "necessity" to deny the "prevailing" law governing a society as its moral facticity is an anthropological error. The

---

[116]"Plus un homme progresse en moralité et devient une personne, moins la loi a pour lui d'importance; plus la charité règne dans une âme . . . moins ses devoirs lui apparaissent comme des obligations." Lacroix, *Personne et Amour,* p. 52.

[117]Dondeyne, *art. cit.,* p. 467.

[118]Lacroix, *op. cit.,* p. 48.

[119]"De même que . . . celui qui s'élève au-dessus de l'intelligence sans passer par elle risque de tomber au-dessous, ainsi celui qui veut s'élever au-dessus de la loi sans passer par elle risque de tomber au-dessous." Lacroix, *ibid.*

[120]Lacroix, *op. cit.,* p. 53.

subject is not without a body; and, likewise, the moral subject is not without a "moral body." This is a point that pedagogists who champion freedom should never lose sight of.

The "Body" of Conscience

It stands to reason that we are concerned here only with the mature conscience, the personal conscience of man on the proper level of his being-man. This conscience, however, has certain infrastructures, a foundation having a biological, psychological, and sociological character, the reality of which has been disclosed principally in the past few decades by the corresponding sciences.[121] The specialists in these sciences managed to show that so-called "lack of conscience" is not infrequently the result of serious disturbances on an infrahuman level, for instance, through affective neglect in early infancy. The integrity of an adult conscience presupposes that these infrastructures underwent a favorable development. Strictly speaking, this goes without saying because man's subjectivity is not an isolated subjectivity but an embodied-subjectivity-in-the-world. It would be wrong to identify rudimentary and primitive forms of conscience with the adult conscience.[122] It is intentionally that we speak here of an "adult conscience" rather than the "conscience of an adult": in many so-called adults the development of their conscience did not go beyond one or the other of its rudimentary or primitive forms.

The adult conscience, however, cannot be identified with its infrastructures: the "knowing" anchored in these infrastructures is not the personal and objective knowing which belongs to the subject as "natural light"; moreover, the "having to be" and the "unrest" contained in these infrastructures cannot be understood as the striving for objective values and as ethical idealism. The personal conscience rises above its infrastructures and its primitive and rudimentary forms. Without being identical with them, however, the personal conscience continues to presuppose these infrastructures, as is evident also from the many "diseases of conscience." [123] Freud caused great confusion by simply

---

121H.M.M. Fortmann, "Het goede, het geweten en de moraal. Een paedagogische studie over de crisis in de opvattingen over moraal en geweten," *Dux*, XX(1953), pp. 436-442.
122G. Madinier, *La conscience morale*, Paris, 1954, pp. 13-20, 110-120.
123Gusdorf, *Traite de l'existence morale*, Paris, 1949, pp. 165-166.

identifying the personal conscience with those infrastructures.[124] This, however, does not give anyone the right to reject what Freud "saw." The personal conscience is not a "first datum," for it presupposes the infrastructures.[125] Freud must not be refuted but needs to be complemented.

The same applies to the sociologistic conception of conscience. It cannot be denied that one can find "in" the personal conscience the result of innumerable forms of social pressure as a kind of "social body." Without this "body," which is the result of a certain "way of doing things," of "accepted mores," the personal conscience is not what it is. This point is so evident that it could hardly escape becoming the basis of a kind of absolutism. For Lévy-Brühl and Durkheim, personal conscience is nothing but the product of actually prevalent moral views; nothing but a moment of "collective conscience." [126] A consequence of such a position is that man's personal "having to be" is reduced to a purely social *fact*, and that there can no longer be question of a *normative* morality but only of a "science of mores." [127] In this way the idea of "obligation" is wholly eliminated, and if, inconsistently, there is nonetheless question of obligations, then these are nothing but the "obligation" to respect the established norms.[128]

But, why would respect for such norms be an *obligation?* If a "way of doing things," guided by "established norms" inscribes itself, as it were, on my existence, this simply means that a certain facticity becomes inscribed in me. The statement that I am obliged to conform with this facticity has an entirely different meaning, which cannot be rendered acceptable by pointing to a particular facticity. On the proper level of my manhood *I* am the one who endeavors to evaluate the suggestions contained in my "social body," [129] and as long as I have not done

---

[124]"Sans doute, Freud prête-t-il à confusion, quand il appelle conscience morale cette structuration psychique qui la précède et rend possible la vraie moralité." W. Huber, H. Piron and A. Vergote, *La psychanalyse, science de l'homme*, Bruxelles, 1964, p. 213.

[125]"La vraie conscience morale assigne une tâche jamais achevée, puisqu'elle s'appuie sur sa préformation dans l'inconscient." W. Huber, H. Piron and A. Vergote, *op. cit.*, p. 214.

[126]Gusdorf, *op. cit.*, p. 31.

[127]"Il semble que la morale comme discipline normative perde toute signification." Gusdorf, *ibid.*

[128]"Le seul devoir est de respecter les normes établies." Gusdorf, *ibid.*

[129]"Il ne faut jamais se lasser de refaire le chemin de Descartes du doute au Cogito. Je pense signifie d'abord: je m'oppose pour évaluer. Je suis celui qui évolue les impératifs sociaux." P. Ricoeur, *Philosophie de la Volonté*, Paris, 1949, p. 119.

this, my conscience is not yet, in the full sense of the term, *my* conscience. Sociologism completely disregards the "personal initiative" of "placing oneself at a distance" because this distancing of oneself cannot be "produced" by that from which one places oneself at a distance. In its stead, sociologism puts the "collective conscience," in which man considers himself predestined by a kind of higher order, deriving from this order guarantees that it does not have.[130] Actually, however, this "higher" order is only a "lower" order, the order of the infrastructures of personal conscience. While it can never be denied that the personal conscience is based on social infrastructures, it cannot be reduced to its infrastructures.[131]

Evil

If the ethical moment *par excellence* of man's "having to be" *is* his destiny for his fellowman, then man's refusal to execute this destiny is the evil *par excellence*. Conscientious people are always aware of the possibility of evil in their lives, and for this reason they "examine their conscience." But what does this mean and how should it be done?

When man examines his conscience, he tries, as it were, to "catch" himself. He tries to catch himself where he thinks that he can be found. It is, of course, extremely important in this matter that man tries to find himself where he *really* can be found—that is, in the world—and not in an interiority isolated from the world *à la* Descartes. If man tries to find himself in the interiority of a Cartesian conscience, he will find nothing but "good intentions" and "evil thoughts." None of his fellowmen, however, derives even the slightest profit from his good intentions as long as these "dwell" in the interiority of his conscience; similarly, his evil thoughts harm no one. Intentions in the interiority are not *real* intentions: intentions are real when they enter the world. Because man's conscience *exists*, man must examine his conscience in and "at" the world.

The ethical level of a person or a society is not determined by ethical "principles." A society's worth is not identical with the value of the principles embodied in its constitution. Similarly, no one can measure how far a society has gone on the road to

---

[130]Gusdorf, *op. cit.*, p. 37.

[131]"Disons, si l'on veut, que la conscience morale est produite par les pressions sociales, mais non pas qu'elle *n'*est produite *que* par les pressions sociales. La doctrine doit être absorbée ou dépassée, beaucoup plus que rejetée; c'est le *ne que* qui est faux." Madinier, *op. cit.*, p. 19.

humanity by reading the texts written in gold on its monuments or by listening to the slogans of its orators.[132] The loftiest "principles" will not absolve a person or a society if they do not become embodied in the world. Such "principles" are not even *real* principles if they do not enter the world.

Because of his personal infidelity to the moral ideal, the authentically moral man is always inclined almost to apologize for the sublimity of his principles, especially when he defends them against others. He realizes that his principles are clean, but not his hands. Nevertheless, he will have to defend his principles, for truth, including moral truth, is, in principle, intersubjective. Unfortunately, however, truth is not *de facto* always intersubjective. Since a society of persons can only exist on the basis of a common truth, life becomes increasingly more difficult according as moral demands are more frequently denied —not theoretically but practically—by those who see and recognize the objectivity of these demands. For, when this happens, how will those who do not see learn to see?

No one, however, may reject his fellowmen's "doctrine" on the basis of their "practice." Otherwise he faces the choice between absolute scepticism and an absolute illusion about himself.

Objective Sinfulness

Not all sins are personal. Even those who try to realize the moral ideal as faithfully as possible are unable to do the "absolute" good.[133] If man were an isolated subjectivity, wholly locked up in itself and separated from the world, life as a "beautiful soul" would be a possibility. But such a subjectivity does not exist: man lives in the world, in history, among his fellowmen, and this has consequences.

First of all, man causes evil in the world because he does not know what he is doing. Human activity is characterized by this that man knows what he is doing. This knowing, however, is never an absolute possession of reality in a perfectly transparent

---

132"Quelle que soit la philosophie qu'on professe, et même théologique, une société n'est pas le temple des valeurs-idoles qui figurent au fronton de ses monuments ou dans ses textes constitutionnels, elle vaut ce que valent et elles les relations de l'homme avec l'homme. . . . La pureté de ses principes ne l'absout pas, elle le condamne, s'il apparaît qu'elle ne passe pas dans la pratique." Merleau-Ponty, *Humanisme et terreur,* Paris, 1947, Préface, p. X.

133Fr. Jeanson, "Les caractères existentialistes de la conduite humaine selon Jean-Paul Sartre," *Morale chrétienne et requêtes contemporaines,* Tournai-Paris, 1954, pp. 182-189.

idea. Hence human activity is also characterized by this, that man does *not* know what he is doing. For this reason man, while *intending* to give meaning and harmony to history, will *de facto* also cause meaninglessness and disharmony.[134] Man knows what he does but, at the same time, he also does not know it. Oedipus did not wish to murder his father and marry his mother, but he did.[135] The city of Athens did not wish to kill such a noble man as Socrates, but it did. The Reformers did not wish to destroy Christian unity, but a split did develop. There are innumerable other examples from various other realms of life. Well-meaning parents do not wish to make life impossible for their children by exaggerated discipline, but many do. Those parents who abstain from exaggerated discipline do not want to leave their children without any orientation by also abstaining from giving them any authoritative guidance, but some of them do. The bearers of public authority in a society do not wish to prevent the development of the community toward a new future by silencing advocates of "progressive" ideas, but some of them do. Others who do not silence the "progressives" in order to leave room for the development of the new future life of the community, do not wish to offer opportunities to corrupt the younger generation, but it can happen that they do. Curial and episcopal leaders of the Catholic Church do not wish to irritate its members or to make the Church ridiculous in the eyes of outsiders, but some of them do.

The fact that man *also* does not know what he is doing has terrible consequences in the realm of politics. Even if two "parties" intend to bring about the liberation of man, the universal recognition of man by man—justice—nothing whatsoever is guaranteed to them. For what the one considers to be the right way to justice and for which he is willing to sacrifice some of his fellowmen is for the other a flagrant violation of justice, against which he considers himself bound to defend his fellowman lest he himself become guilty of injustice.[136] The fact that man *also* does not know what he is doing makes it

---

[134]"Nous ignorons pour une très large part les conséquences de nos actes. Nous posons des actes et nous ne savons pas au juste quels en seront les retentissements, proches ou lointains. Tout ce que nous faisons est déformé, et nos intentions les plus généreuses subissent, en se propageant dans le monde, une sorte de réfraction souvent imprévisible." Jeanson, *art. cit.*, p. 186.

[135]Merleau-Ponty, *op. cit.*, Préface, p. XXXV.

[136]"La condition humaine ne serait-elle pas de telle sorte qu'il n'y ait pas de bonne solution?" Merleau-Ponty, *op. cit.*, Préface, p. XXXIV.

impossible for him to do the absolute good. Ethics implies war, but it is not possible to eliminate ethics without bringing war into the world.

In the second place, man brings evil into the world because his action in the world *also* produces side-effects which he rejects and of which he does not approve. The meaning which he creates is a good within a certain context. But there is no meaning which stands in only one context. One who creates meaning within a particular system of meanings must be resigned to the fact that he creates meaninglessness and evil within another system. For example, one who extinguishes a fire on the upper floor of an apartment building cannot prevent the lower floors from being flooded. Parents who bring a child into the world when a "regime of scarcity" prevails, must accept the fact that he increases the scarcity of available goods. One who strips a backward people of its pseudo-religiousness will make it impossible for many of them to give any structure to their lives. One who does not destoy an enemy having fifty I.C.B.M.'s when he still has the power to do so, must accept the possibility that ten years later he will be confronted with an enemy having five hundreds of those missiles. If the Russians turn their backs on China, they cannot prevent turning their faces to America. But if in the future the Russians would decide to join forces with China after all, then the Western protagonists of dialogue with Moscow have already struck future resistance a blow below the belt.

The question at issue here receives its full importance in the realm of politics. One who objects to the "evil" of flooded lower floors when fire is extinguished on the upper floors, makes himself ridiculous because this "evil" simply cannot be avoided. But in matters political the situation is entirely different. The politican who is not a barbarian will act with an appeal to the ethical ideal. He will have to exercise authority, use power, and apply force. He intends to defend his fellowmen against "evil" *tout court* and is ready to sacrifice victims in his defense. But this means that it is always possible for others to oppose him on the basis of the ethical ideal: he is making victims. What, however, is the meaning of their resistance? Those who resist the making of victims wish to establish meaning and harmony in history. But when *they* let their intention enter the world to defend fellowmen against "evil" *tout court*, they must exercise authority, use power and apply force. They, too, will make victims, other victims. It cannot be denied, of course, that they create meaning in history. But the absolute good is impossible. In reality, they do not oppose "evil" *tout court*, for they *also* create evil. Man cannot liberate himself from this evil by absolutely abstaining from any violence. For he who renounces all violence in a world in which violence "reigns" makes himself an accomplice of those who profit from the existing violence.[137]

In the realm of politics it is true, *par excellence,* that a meaning which is good in a certain context does not *exclusively* lie in that one context because in the political domain, more than anywhere else, others can seize that meaning, place it in another context than the one intended and orientate it to a future which was precisely not intended by the giver of that meaning. To give an example, the reproach is addressed to Pope Pius XII that he did not protest against the persecution of the Jews in the Third *Reich.* Things are presented as if his hands would have been clean if he had fearlessly preached the "principle of justice" in which he believed and had ordered all those who recognized his authority to put this principle into practice. But, may man preach justice and disregard the fact that his sermon will produce victims? Would Pius XII not have been reproached for sacrificing Christians—or for having caused the "Iron Curtain" to be drawn hundreds of miles more to the West—by inducing many soldiers to drop their arms? Such reproaches would then be made by precisely the same people who now complain about his action. The Dutch Cardinal De Jong *did* protest the persecution of the Jews and thereby caused new victims. Man sometimes cannot escape a situation in which he has no other choice than to "select" his victims. Would to God this were not true!

From all this it should be evident how reprehensible critics are, when their description of the objective evil in history situates this evil in the personal intentions of those who have to act, and who, even by not acting, act.[138] Politics is not *per se* absolutely

---

[137]"Choisir la non-violence, dans un univers où la violence est institutionnelle, revient à se rendre complice de ceux en faveur desquels la violence s'exerce." Jeanson, *art. cit.,* p. 182.

[138]"La véritable tragique commence lorsque *le même homme* a compris à la fois qu'il ne saurait désavouer la figure objective de ses actions, qu'il est ce qu'il est pour les autres dans le contexte de l'histoire, et que cependant le motif de son action reste la valeur de l'homme telle qu'il l'éprouve immédiatement." Merleau-Ponty, *op. cit.,* p. 67.

diabolical and politicians are not *per se* barbarians. But the absolute good is impossible.[139]

In the third place, man's involvement in the objective structures of the economic, social, and political world makes a pure conscience impossible as long as these structures *also* embody murder and slavery. Murder and slavery are consolidated in the facticity of history, institutionalized in tyrannical colonial systems, in inhuman economic orders, as well as in the intolerant fanaticism of both pseudo-religiousness and certain forms of atheism. I did not create the economic system in which seventeen per cent of mankind owns more than eighty per cent of the world's wealth. I am against that system because it offends my "principles." But this does not mean that my hands are clean, for in a certain sense I "agree" with the system by living off it.

It stands to reason that the evil here described is not a personal evil. Thus one cannot personally cleanse himself of it by withdrawing his hands in order to live with "clean" principles and "good" intentions in the "interiority" of his conscience.[140] One who withdraws his hands leaves everything as it is: he becomes guilty of the "sin of omission."[141] His "interior" life is no alibi for the catastrophes of history: there is no pure conscience in a rotten world. The ethical man is a task-in-the-world, a task which always is *also* a failure. But man will merely increase the evil if, on the basis of this failure, he eliminates his fellowman. In this sense it is true that "no revolution can *fully* count on the Catholic"[142] or any other Christian.

4. Freedom as Transcendence

When psychologists, pedagogues, and moralists speak of

---

[139]"Toute action ne nous engage-t-elle pas dans un jeu que nous ne pouvons entièrement contrôler? N'y a-t-il pas comme une maléfice de la vie à plusieurs?" Merleau-Ponty, *op. cit.*, Préface, p. XXXIV.

[140]"Dans la mesure même où un homme est moins sûr de soi, ou li manque de gravité et, qu'on nous passe le mot, de moralité vraie, il réserve au fond de lui-même un sanctuaire de principes qui lui donnent, pour reprendre le mot de Marx, un 'point d'honneur spiritualiste', une 'raison générale de consolation et de justification." Merleau-Ponty, *op. cit.*, Préface, p. XI.

[141]"Du seul fait que je continue d'exister dans ce monde, je me retire le droit de prétendre refuser le meurtre *absolument:* car le meurtre est déjà là car je vis de ce meurtre indéfiniment perpétré - sur d'autres hommes - par une organisation sociale dont je reste, à divers titres, obligatoirement solidaire. Je n'ai même pas besoin de lever le petit doigt pour être complice, il me suffit de m'abstenir." Jeanson, *art. cit.*, p. 182.

[142]Merleau-Ponty, *SNS*, p. 352.

freedom, they usually intend to refer to the freedom of human activity.[143] In the preceding sections we have explicitated more fundamental senses of the term "freedom." The sciences in question do not deny these senses, but are less immediately interested in them.

Human Action Is Not a Process

The characteristics of the freedom proper to human action should be readily accessible after the preceding considerations. Those who say that man's actions are free wish to convey that man's action is not a deterministic process, not a discharge of forces, and not a reaction. Man's action, on the proper level of his being-man, is the execution of the *self*-project which man is.

The being of a thing is being-the-result of processes and forces, but in human *existence* there is a moment which transcends being-the-result of processes and forces. As a subject, man is an "I," an *ego,* which *itself* possesses a certain autonomy of being with respect to the processes and forces acting upon man.

This autonomy of being reveals itself most clearly in the human action. For insofar as an action is human, man *himself* is the origin of this action. The "I" from which the action originates means a rupture in the chain of deterministic processes; the result of the action is a meaning which is "new" in reference to the forces acting upon man. The local motion of billiard ball *B* is nothing new with respect to the force with which billiard ball *A* strikes ball *B*. But when John bumps into Peter and makes him fall, the meaning of Peter's fall cannot be disclosed through mechanics, by calculating the force with which John bumped into him. Peter's position in space is "new" with respect to that force because of the attitude which Peter *himself* assumes toward his fall. Because man *himself* acts, his action is not a process. To the extent that man's activity is not a process, it is free.

Perhaps it is better to state explicitly that the human action always *co*-originates from man *himself*. For there is a danger that otherwise the *I*—the *selfhood* of man—is again isolated from his facticity. Subjectivity is not what it is, is no human

---

[143]De Waelhens, "Linéaments d'une interprétation phénoménologique de la Liberté," *Actes du IVe Congrès des Sociétés de Philosophie de langue française,* Neuchatel, 1949, p. 84.

subjectivity, without being involved in facticity.[144] If, then, I say that I *myself* execute a certain action, this excludes that the action is solely the result of a deterministic influence of facticity, but includes that this action is not what it is without facticity.[145]

The consequences of this insight are far-reaching. There is no personal philosophizing without the sedimented philosophies; no personal justice without a legal order; no personal religiousness without institutions; no personal love without sensuality; [146] no personal conscience without the biological and sociological conscience; etc. The meaning of asceticism in man's life can, therefore, never consist in "killing" his facticity, for without facticity man cannot do anything. On the other hand, because facticity is not what it is without subjectivity, the "I," i.e., the origin of the human action, can never be "produced" by the "pressure" of facticity. All "pressure" of facticity *presupposes* the subject, and therefore can never *explain* the subject's facticity.[147] Facticity, therefore, likewise, does not *explain* the action, for the latter originates in the subjectivity.[148] The specifically human character of the action, then, consists in this that the action is always to some extent done by man *himself*. If I wish to express the meaning of a certain action, I have to point to more than the influence of facticity: there is also the subject's spontaneity, and through this spontaneity a meaning is always a new meaning if only because the subject ratifies or does not ratify the facticity. The action, then, always comes *also* from the subject himself.

"Existence Precedes Essence"

Sartre expresses the priority of the acting subject, his freedom, in his notorious characterization of existentialism: *"Existence precedes essence."* [149] We call his characterization "notorious"

---

[144]Merleau-Ponty, *PP*, p. 467.

[145]"Il n'y a donc jamais déterminisme et jamais choix absolu, jamais je ne suis chose et jamais conscience nue." *PP*, p. 517.

[146]Humanus, "Zinnelijkheid en liefde," *Kultuurleven*, XXIV(1957), pp. 485-497.

[147]"Il *n'y a* d'état de fait - satisfaisant ou non - que par la puissance néantisante du pour-soi." Sartre, *EN*, p. 511.

[148]"En effet, dès lors qu'on attribue à la conscience ce pouvoir négatif vis-à-vis du monde et d'elle-même, dès lors que la néantisation fait partie intégrante de la *position* d'une fin, il faut reconnaître que la condition indispensable et fondamentale de toute action c'est la liberté de l'être agissant." *EN*, p. 511.

[149]Sartre, *EH*, p. 17.

because, for Sartre, his statement is inseparable from atheism. From the fact that man is not a paper-knife—that is, his being is not the being of a thing, and consequently, is not conceived and created by a "superior craftsman" [150]—Sartre concludes that man is what he makes of himself.[151] If one abstracts from his atheism, Sartre's statement that *existence* precedes essence can be put to good use; he intends it in particular to indicate that we must assign a certain priority to man's subjectivity,[152] even with respect to human activity: man's action is not the result of a causalistic influence exercised by facticity, in the way a process runs its course under the influence of a unilateral, deterministic cause.[153] Sartre's statement, then, means that man is not a thing like a paper-knife, a stone, a table, a kind of moss, or a cauliflower, and his life is not a process of corruption (*sic*).[154]

There is a second reservation that must be made with respect to Sartre's statement. A "certain" priority, we said, should be assigned to the subjectivity; for Sartre, this priority is absolute. It is not difficult to quote texts in which Sartre expresses the situated character of freedom. Every free selection of a purpose is accomplished, according to Sartre, in a particular empirical situation; [155] every choice of a purpose occurs in function of a particular past.[156] Thus we must say that the subject as freedom occurs only as involved in a particular facticity, and this facticity means a certain restriction with respect to the leeway of the subject as project.[157]

In this way the real world of freedom is distinct from the

---

[150]*EH*, p. 19.

[151]*EH*, p. 22.

[152]*EH*, pp. 60-62.

[153]"On voit ainsi dans quel sens et dans quelle mesure il nous est possible d'accueillir la thèse fondamentale de l'existentialisme, qui dans l'homme veut accorder à l'existence, c'est-à-dire à l'exercice de son activité autonome, une priorité sur l'essence; qui caractérise l'homme comme l'être qui doit par son existence, c'est-à-dire par la mise en oeuvre de sa liberté, se donner sa propre détermination." De Petter, "Personne et personnalisation," *Divus Thomas* (Piac.), 1949, p. 174.

[154]"Mais que voulons-nous dire par là, sinon que l'homme a une plus grande dignité que la pierre ou que la table? . . . . L'homme est d'abord un projet qui se vit subjectivement, au lieu d'être une mousse, une pourriture ou un chou-fleur." *EH*, pp. 22-23.

[155]"Ces fins, en effet, sont poursuivies à partir d'une situation empirique particulière, et c'est même cette poursuite qui constitue les entours en situations." Sartre, *EN*, p. 654.

[156]"Mais si la liberté est choix d'une fin en fonction du passé. . . ." *EN*, p. 578.

[157]*EN*, p. 655.

dream world. The possibility of realizing a project is required for freedom. Thus more is needed than the project itself. If the realization of a project required merely the conception of that project, there would no longer be any difference between the real world and a dream world.[158] But there is a difference. The real world is indispensable for freedom. The resistance of the world's facticity permits the subject to emerge as freedom. There is only a free subject when the subject is involved in a resistant world.[159]

To be free, however, is not the same as to attain what one wishes to attain, but rather to determine oneself to will and choose; in other words, it means autonomy of choice. This autonomy only reveals itself as real, as distinct from a dream or a mere wish, in man's action. Free choice and action are even identical; the distinction between free choice and a dream or mere wish always presupposes a beginning of realization.[160] A prisoner is not free to leave his cell, but he is free to try to escape. This freedom, however, is real, and not a dream or a mere wish, only through a "beginning of action." Thus there is no distinction between free choice, the free project, and the action. Intentions and choices cannot be separated from the action, no more than thought can be divorced from language. The action tells us what we *really* intend and choose.[161]

All this very clearly shows that Sartre conceives the subject, his free project and its execution, and his free action, as intentionality. Sartre attaches to this the consequence that no factical situation has any meaning "in itself" and that, therefore, it can never exercise a unilateral, deterministic influence on the subject.[162] Anyone who considers the matter without prejudice is willing to grant Sartre this, for it is obvious that the meaning of a factical situation is *co*-determined by the subject's project.[163] A huge rock only has the meaning "scalable" or "unscalable" in function of a climber's project; the rock has an entirely different

---

[158]*EN*, p. 562.
[159]"En sorte que les résistances que la liberté dévoile dans l'existant loin d'être un danger pour la liberté ne font que lui permettre de surgir comme liberté. Il ne peut y avoir de pour-soi libre que comme engagé dans un monde résistant." *EN*, p. 563.
[160]*Ibid.*
[161]*EN*, p. 564.
[162]*EN*, p. 568.
[163]"Dès l'origine, le milieu conçu comme situation renvoie au pour-soi choisissant, tout juste comme le pour-soi renvoie au milieu de par son être dans le monde." *EN*, p. 660.

meaning within the project of an estheticist; [164] and the rock is only a heavy obstacle within the project of one who wishes to remove it.[165] Similarly, the conditions of life of a laborer have no meaning "in themselves." The real meaning of this facticity depends on the subject who the worker is. The proletarian can lead a humiliated or a proud existence, according as he chooses resignation or the revolution. His facticity does not determine him to anything. Likewise, an illness is never *per se* unbearable: it can also be desirable, interesting, or useful.

Similar ideas apply also to the past. The past never has any meaning "in itself." Whether a crisis of puberty is a mere accident or a first sign of a future conversion depends on the subject. Whether a prison term is fruitful or miserable depends on the decision of the subject to give up stealing or to become a hardened criminal.[166] In the same perspective, one can say that the storming of the Bastille does not have any finished or definitive meaning.[167] No situation has any meaning "in itself," and no situation can exercise a unilateral, deterministic influence on the subject.[168]

While correct and authentically phenomenological as such, this thought is developed by Sartre in an unbalanced way. When above we related Sartre's rejection of views which consider the situation as existing "in itself," we had occasionally to close our eyes to certain expressions in Sartre's own text which, to say the least, could easily be misunderstood. He says, for example, "It is, then, our freedom which constitutes the limits it will encounter," [169] and "The rock discourages me when I have freely laid down the limits of my desire to climb it." [170] Although such texts could still be properly understood, they also offer every opportunity for misunderstandings. Or do we perhaps have to do here with an overestimation of the subject's importance, a surreptitious absolutizing of freedom? We are convinced that this is the case and we will prove it by explaining here Sartre's theory of freedom in reference to passions and emotions.

---

[164]*EN*, p. 568.
[165]*EN*, p. 562.
[166]*EN*, p. 579.
[167]*EN*, p. 582.
[168]"Il n'y a de liberté qu'en *situation* et il n'y a de situation que par la liberté." *EN*, p. 569.
[169]*EN*, p. 562.
[170]*EN*, p. 569.

Freud and Sartre on Passions and Emotions

Freud and Sartre are perhaps the most authoritative representatives of opposite standpoints in this matter. For Freud it is
certain that the actions of man—even his higher psychical activities, which manifest themselves in the pursuit of science and
art and in living a religion—are determined by influences arising
from the depth of an unconscious *libido*.

At first, Freud thought that his view applied only to pathological behavior. But when his analysis of dreams showed that
the same mechanisms operated in dreams as in pathological behavior, he gave a broader range of applicability to his thesis and
declared that it was valid also for normal behavior. For dreams
are perfectly normal. In cases of pathological behavior there
is no freedom according to Freud. Now, the same mechanisms
which determine pathological behavior operate also in dreams;
therefore, normal behavior also must be conceived as determined
by an unconscious *libido* since dreams are forms of normal
behavior.[171] Consequently, the freedom of normal behavior is
an illusion.[172]

From this it would logically follow that there can no longer
be question of responsibility. We must add, however, that psychological determinism belongs to what Freud "officially" taught
and explicitly affirmed. But implicitly and "really" Freud
taught something entirely different: his entire psychoanalytic
practice aimed at *liberating* his patients. He was convinced that
psychoanalysis would "give the 'I' of the sufferer the freedom
to decide for himself to act this way or that way." [173] Such a
text does not at all sound deterministic: "Where *Id* was, there
'I' must come to be." [174] Orthodox Freudianism, however, has
always interpreted him in a deterministic way.

Sartre opposes himself radically to determinism. "The existentialist does not believe in the power of passion," he says.[175]

171J. Nuttin, *Psychanalyse et conception spiritualiste de l'homme*, Louvain, 1955, pp. 135-142.
172W. Huber, H. Piron and A. Vergote, *La psychanalyse, science de
l'homme*, Bruxelles, 1964, p. 176.
173S. Freud, *Das Ich und das Es, Gesammelte Werke*, London, 1940,
XIII, p. 280.
174Freud, *Neue Folge der Vorlesungen zur Einführung in die Psychoana-
lyse, Gesammelte Werke*, XV, p. 86.
175"L'existentialiste ne croit pas à la puissance de la passion. Il ne pensera
jamais qu'une belle passion est un torrent dévastateur qui conduit fatalement
l'homme à certains actes, et qui, par conséquent, est une excuse. Il pense
que l'homme est responsable de sa passion." Sartre, *EH*, pp. 37-38.

He does not believe that a passion can be like a destructive torrent by which man is fatally swept along toward the performance of certain actions and which, therefore, could be an excuse for such deeds. Man is fully responsible for his passion. In Sartre's view it is wrong to present matters as if the autonomy of freedom can be ascribed to the will and denied to passion.[176] One is inclined to ask: Why? Is there then no difference between an act of will and passion?

Sartre does not deny the difference but, in connection with freedom, he considers the difference unimportant, because freedom precedes the act of will and passion. For freedom lies in the subject as project. A situation has no meaning "in itself," but only within a free project. Thus, according to Sartre, one can no longer say that a threat determined me to a passionate flight, for the threat is a threat only in terms of my free project to save my life. I can execute this project either by a passionate flight or by a rational resistance. I myself choose between these two possibilities.[177] I choose the act of will or the passion: whether the world is a rational world (the object of the act of will) or a magical world (the object of passion) depends exclusively on my choice.[178]

The lack of balance which, as we said, was to be feared, manifests itself here very clearly. It stands to reason, of course, that motives do not have any meaning "in themselves." They appear as motives only in function of a project. But Sartre should at least have emphasized that freedom as project is situated, i.e., that all projects are only possible within certain limits —for instance, the limits which passions and emotions impose on freedom as project. When this restriction is made, the question occupying Sartre returns: is it unthinkable that passions and emotions can be so violent that at a given moment there can no longer be question of a project in the authentically human sense of the term?

Sartre excludes an affirmative answer. Fear of a threat can never determine me, for a thing or a person appear as a threat only in function of my project to save my life. For Sartre, this means that the threat derives its meaning *solely* from my sub-

---

176"Et si la néantisation est précisément l'être de la liberté, comment refuser l'autonomie aux passions pour l'accorder à la volonté?" *EN*, p. 519.
177"Serai-je volontaire ou passionné? Qui peut le décider sinon moi?" *EN*, p. 520.
178*EN*, p. 521.

jectivity.[179]   In this way the subjectivity is isolated from the factical situation and absolutized as a project. With respect to the freedom of an action, then, it makes no difference whether the subject responds with a passionate action or with a free deed: the passionate action also is free, for it is executed in function of a wholly free project.[180]   This wholly free project is executed either through passion or through an act of will.[181]

Phenomenology has only one answer to the views of both Freud and Sartre: "lived experience" knows better.[182]

"Obvious Decisions"

Because man subsists, is a selfhood, it is possible to say that man *himself* acts. To be a subject, however, means to be a "light." It is important to indicate the meaning of this point explicitly here in connection with the proper character of man's acting on the distinct level of his manhood. Because man as a subject is a "natural light," the action originating from the subject is not a blind action. Processes work "blindly," they do not know anything about their actions and their effects. The acting of man as a subject is not a process because man executes his actions with consciousness of what he does. As a subject, as a "natural light," man *exists* in the truth; he puts himself at a distance, he "stands" in objectivity. The subject as light "liberates" the objective meaning of facticity and the objective meaning of the possibilities anchored in this facticity. Thus man "knows what he is doing." [183]

Man's acting, then, is distinct from that of animals. Psychologists have observed that in its behavior the animal simply follows the impulse of the strongest need.[184]   A determined impulse *per se,* within certain conditions, gives rise to a determined behavior: the animal's behavior is determined, as is the develop-

---

[179]"En fait, motifs et mobiles n'ont que le poids que mon projet, c'est-à-dire la libre production de la fin et de l'acte connu à réaliser, leur confère." *EN,* p. 527.

[180]*EN,* pp. 523-528.

[181]*EN,* p. 607.

[182]"Like every human concept, our concept of freedom is drawn from experience and must remain in contact with experience; otherwise it will end up by standing for an abstract and empty freedom which no longer has anything to do with true human freedom." Dondeyne, "Truth and Freedom," *Truth and Freedom,* Pittsburgh, 1954, p. 30.

[183]"Everyone agrees that to act freely is to act with knowledge of what one is doing and why one is doing it." Dondeyne, *ibid.,* p. 31.

[184]Nuttin, *op. cit.,* pp. 195-201.

ment of that behavior. This development is fixed and can be expressed in laws valid for the animal's own biological species. Thus the animal is, and remains, an element of material nature, and its behavior is a moment in the evolution of that nature. The animal is a stagnant being.[185] It produces no technology, no art, it projects no language, no social, political, or economic order. In the animal kingdom there is no culture of the mind and no education.[186]

The fact that man's free action is an action in which "man knows what he is doing" implies that a decision precedes his acting—that the subject *chooses* among the possibilities left to him by his facticity. Every facticity leaves the subject the leeway of a certain ability-to-be: man is a project. These possibilities are the subject's own possibilities: man is a self-project. When man acts, he *decides* to realize this possibility rather than that one. With respect to man's action on the proper level of his manhood, such a decision or choice is free. For the possibilities which any facticity leaves to the subject are this subject's *own* possibilities, and it is the subject *himself* who decides to realize this possibility rather than that one.

This choice, however, is not absolute, it does not start from "zero." [187] The choice is a decision about possibilities, but possibilities are real possibilities only on the basis of a certain facticity. The project which man is is a "thrown project." A choice is a decision about possibilities within a particular situation. An appeal is made to the subject in a certain way in terms of his factical situation, but this facticity does not have the character of a causalistic influence giving rise to the subject's action as a mere reaction.[188] On the proper level of being-man there is no situation which determines a human action. There is merely question of being-appealed-to by a particular situa-

---

185Nuttin, *op. cit.,* p. 196.

186"Que l'on songe, pour préciser quelque peu les idées, par ex. aux productions de la technique et de l'art, à la formation du langage, à l'organisation sociale, politique et économique, à la culture de l'esprit et à l'éducation." De Petter, "Personne et personnalisation," *Divus Thomas* (Piac.), 1949, p. 166.

187"Au nom de la liberté, on refuse l'idée d'un acquis, mais c'est alors la liberté qui devient un acquis primordial et comme notre état de nature. Puisque nous n'avons pas à la faire, elle est le don qui nous a été fait de n'avoir aucun don, cette nature de la conscience qui consiste à n'avoir pas de nature, en aucun cas elle peut s'exprimer au dehors ni figurer dans notre vie." Merleau-Ponty, *PP*, p. 499.

188"Le choix semble être une conception scientiste de la causalité incompatible avec la conscience que nous avons de nous-mêmes, et l'affirmation d'une liberté absolue sans extérieur." Merleau-Ponty, *PP*, pp. 498-499.

tion, and it can happen that a certain decision then becomes "obvious." [189]   The way in which facticity appeals to me co-motivates my decision. But the motive does not have any meaning "in itself": its meaning is co-derived from my subjectivity as a project. The motive is *taken* as a motive. My wretchedness does not drive me into a revolutionary party just as a storm drives a ship on the coast. But my wretchedness appeals to me in a certain way, through which the decision to join a revolutionary party becomes "obvious." The motive, however, is taken by me as a motive; it functions within a particular project, viz., the project to live prosperously. In function of a different project, e.g., that of resignation, the situation has a different meaning.

Applied to the relationship between free action and passion, this means that man's subjectivity puts itself at a distance from every instinctive impulse and breaks its compelling and determining influence. Man's action as human action, then, is not a being completely fascinated and carried away, as an animal is fascinated by a prey. [190]   On the contrary, it is a modifying interference in facticity, by virtue of which the subject distances himself and judges objective reality from a standpoint transcending the here and now appeal. [191]

It is necessary to keep in mind that we are all the time speaking here about human action as *human*. We do not say that all action which, in one way or another, can be ascribed to man is *per se* an authentically human action. [192]   Accordingly, we do not claim that passions can never determine man, and that an "action" may never be considered as a kind of "discharge" provoked by an instinctive impulse. Whether this is actually the case, however, can be determined only on the basis of the data of experience. One must then try to determine whether

---

[189]"Notre liberté ne détruit pas notre situation, mais s'engrène sur elle: notre situation, tant que nous vivons, est ouverte, ce qui implique à la fois qu'elle appelle des modes de résolution privilégiés et qu'elle est par elle-même impuissante à en procurer aucun." *PP*, p. 505.

[190]"Que je puisse dire le sens des choses, suppose que je ne sois pas emporté ou ravi par elles comme l'animal par la proie qu'il poursuit, que je puisse toujours les considérer en me plaçant en retrait par rapport à elles: c'est qu'on exprime en disant que je saisis l'étant comme tel ou que je suis capable de laisser cet étant être ce qu'il est." De Waelhens, "Linéaments d'une interprétation phénoménologique de la liberté," *Actes du IVe Congrès de Philosophie de langue française*, Neuchatel, 1949, p. 81.

[191]Nuttin, *op. cit.*, pp. 148-151, 160-163.

[192]We are referring here to the classical distinction between "act of man" and "human act." Our assertion is concerned with the human act.

and to what extent an objective evaluation of the motives *concretely* preceded the action, or whether the subject, for whatever reason, was not able to make such an evaluation.[193] If he could not make it, then the action cannot be considered a *human* action, a free action. As *man,* man is a "sick animal." [194]

The data of experience show clearly that every action is guided by a very complex set of motives. The complexity of the subjectivity's involvement in facticity does not permit anyone to claim that a concrete action is either free or determined. According to Nuttin, there are very few ways of behaving which "do not contain at least a certain influence or after-effect of insights and considerations which rise above matter. There is at least that specifically human restraint or hesitation with which an irresistible impulse is followed, or through which the instinct is followed through with less abandon." [195] From this standpoint it does not make sense to claim that man is "condemned to freedom." On the contrary, one should say that man's *task* is to be man, to act humanly. Thus freedom of action also appears as a task, and in this sense one can say that freedom has to be conquered.[196]

We wish to return here briefly to freedom as *choice,* but only to observe explicitly that in his choice man, strictly speaking, always faces *several* possibilities, even in those cases where he allegedly has only one possibility. For on the proper level of his manhood man can always choose for or against that possibility. This choice for or against is the essential element of freedom of choice, for it would be utterly meaningless to say that man can choose between several possibilities if he could not accept or reject them one by one.[197]

In choosing for or against a particular possibility man explicitly takes up a moment of the fundamental structure of his

---

193Nuttin, *op. cit.,* 149-150.

194"L'homme est absolument distinct des espèces animales, mais justement en ceci qu'il n'a point d'équipement originel et qu'il est le lieu de la contingence." Merleau-Ponty, *Signes,* Paris, 1960, p. 304.

195Nuttin, *op. cit.,* p. 162.

196"Mais du fait de son incarnation, ce sujet est toujours menacé de se laisser submerger par le vital, de ne vivre que pour celui-ci. Il éprouvera donc le besoin de se défendre contre cet engluement dans la matière pour sauvegarder sa liberté et pour conserver intacte la faculté même de jouir des objets, faculté qui serait compromise par un affaiblissement de la subjectivité personnelle. Une lutte incessante s'impose ainsi à l'homme, rançon de la liberté dans une personne incarnée." A. Brunner, *La personne incarnée,* Paris, 1947, pp. 191-192.

197*S.Th.,* I-II, q. X, a. 2.

essence as involved subjectivity. For the subject's involvement in his situation includes a positive and a negative moment on both the cognitive and the affective levels. We are interested here in the affective level. The subject's involvement in his situation means for him an affirmation and a nihilation of his situation, an affective "saying"-of-*yes* and, equiprimordially, also a "saying"-of-*no*. There is no reality to which man cannot consent to some extent; at the same time, there is no reality to which man can fully and definitively consent. No reality is the "be all and end all" for man as "having to be." Affirmation and nihilation are essential moments of man's being as *existent* subjectivity.

In his choice for or against a particular possibility man explicitly takes up the positive or the negative moment of his involvement in reality. His subjectivity as *Verstehen* means the anticipation, the "running ahead" of the objective value of the new meaning which his action will establish. Man, however, anticipates also on the affective affirmation and nihilation of the new meaning. Even before the action is done, the subject's intentionality includes a positive and a negative moment. When he chooses for or against a particular possibility, man lets the positive or the negative moment of his *existence* prevail. The freedom of choice is the explicit taking-up of what man, as involved subjectivity, essentially is. An *explicit* choice for or against a particular, not yet actual, meaning is possible because the "functioning intentionality" which man himself *is* includes a positive and a negative moment of reference to the future meaning.[198]

Freedom as "Movement of Transcendence"

When man on the proper level of his manhood acts, the subject who he is reaches beyond the facticity of his *existence* toward the fulfillment of a possibility that is not yet filled. The newly established meaning then remains as a new facticity of his

---

[198]"Unde, si proponatur aliquod objectum voluntati quod sit universaliter bonum, et secundum omnem considerationem, ex necessitate voluntas in illud tendit, si aliquid velit; non enim poterit velle oppositum. Si autem proponatur ei aliquod objectum quod non secundum quamlibet considerationem sit bonum, non ex necessitate voluntas fertur in illud. Et quia defectus cujuscumque boni habet rationem non boni, ideo illud solum bonum quod est perfectum, et cui nihil deficit, est tale bonum quod voluntas non potest non velle, quod est beatitudo. Alia autem quaelibet particularia bona, in quantum deficiunt ab aliquo bono, possunt accipi ut non bona; et secundum hanc considerationem possunt repudiari vel approbari a voluntate, quae potest in idem ferri secundum diversas considerationes." *S. Th.*, I-II, q. 10, a. 2.

existence. There is, however, no facticity without potentiality: the newly established meaning opens the subject to another new possibility, for man is a project. This statement applies to any action because man is *essentially* a project, a *continually recreated* openness.[199] Because the acting man continually evokes new lacunae and new voids, one can never say that man is "finished." For this reason Merleau-Ponty calls the acting man a "movement of transcendence," [200] a self-transcending movement. Sartre simply speaks of "transcendence," [201] and Heidegger of *"existence."* [202] As a self-transcending movement, then, the action is the execution of the project which man is. This execution is the being-"at"-the-world, mentioned at the beginning of this chapter. Man *is* this execution; hence it is not possible for man not to execute his own being-a-project. The *being* of man is "action." Even if a man decides no longer to realize himself, he still realizes himself, albeit as a lazybone, a good for nothing, a blockhead, and an idler. When man decides no longer actively to involve himself in the world, he still builds a world: a world in which broken dams cause thousands of victims; a world in which contagious diseases run rampant; a world in which nine out of ten children will have to die prematurely; a world of ignorance. Man cannot do nothing, for doing nothing also is doing something. For this reason we said that man *is* the execution of his being-a-project.

5. FREEDOM AS HISTORY

Once it is realized that man on the proper level of his manhood is the execution of the project he is, the implications of this insight justify the use of the term "history" to indicate the specific character proper to the dynamics of human *existence.* To understand this, it is necessary and sufficient to keep two things in mind. First, the dynamics of being-man is entirely different from that of things.[203] Terms such as process, evolution,

---

199"Cette ouverture toujours recréée dans la plénitude de l'être est. . . ." Merleau-Ponty, *PP,* p. 229.
200*PP,* p. 492.
201"Mais, précisément, par la transcendance, j'échappe à tout ce que je suis." Sartre, *EN,* p. 96.
202"Das 'Wesen' des Daseins liegt in seiner Existenz." Heidegger, *SZ,* p. 42.
203"On n'explique rien par l'homme, puisqu'il n'est pas une force, mais une faiblesse au coeur de l'être; (il n'est pas) un facteur cosmologique, mais le lieu où tous les facteurs cosmologiques, par une mutation qui n'est jamais finie, changent de sens et deviennent histoire." Merleau-Ponty, *EP,* p. 61.

growth, and movement are no longer proper in this context.[204] Secondly, man as "transcendent movement" is, as must be shown, the synthesis of the three ecstacies of time: present, past and future.

The special character proper to the dynamics in human *existence* has already been sufficiently discussed. At present we are mainly concerned with showing that *existence* as transcendence is "history." Describing man as *existence*, we indicated that it is a being-conscious-in-the-world. We saw also that in *existence* two levels must be distinguished: the level of the ego-body and that of personal consciousness and personal freedom. It goes without saying, therefore, that when *existence* is described as history, this history also must be sought on several levels: we must distinguish at least an infrahuman and a human history.[205] The "history" of the infrahuman—also called "cyclical time" [206] or "prehistory" [207]—leaves room for quasi-processes, but as soon as we reach the level of the properly human, the level of consciousness and freedom, terms such as growth, movement, process, and evolution become meaningless.

Nevertheless, it would be wrong to detach human history from infrahuman history.[208] It would amount to isolating subjectivity and facticity from each other. Freedom would then no longer be situated, it would no longer be human freedom, but an abstraction. Human action, as conscious and free, is framed in a prehistory. Conscious and free *existence* uses the results of this prehistory: it is a taking-up of a prepersonal tradition.

The human history of which we intend to speak here is man himself insofar as in his activity, creative of culture, he calls any facticity to life—i.e., placing himself at a distance, he seizes its objective meaning and he realizes the possibilities this meaning contains. An example may be taken from economic

---

[204]Dondeyne, "L'historicité dans la philosophie contemporaine," *Revue Philosophique de Louvain*, 54(1956), pp. 6-9.

[205]Kwant, "De historie en het Absolute," *Tijdschrift voor Philosophie*, XVII(1955), pp. 264-273.

[206]"Ce temps est celui de nos fonctions corporelles, qui sont cycliques comme lui, c'est aussi celui de la nature avec laquelle nous existons." *PP*, p. 517.

[207]*PP*, p. 277.

[208]". . . il faut que mon histoire soit la suite d'une préhistoire dont elle utilise les résultats acquis, mon existence personnelle la reprise d'une tradition prépersonnelle. Il y a donc un autre sujet au-dessous de moi pour qui un monde existe avant que je sois là et qui y marquait ma place." *PP*, pp. 293-294.

life to illustrate the point. In order to provide for his physical needs, man has given rise to a very complex system of institu‑ tions. This system did not just drop out of the sky, but was laboriously built by man. In the past changes have been continually made in that system, and in the future other changes will be made. There is "movement," then, in economic life. But what is the meaning of this term "movement" here? It is not more or less like the movements occurring in the crust of the earth in volcanic regions; not like the growth of a plant nor like the evolution of giant reptiles in the Cretaceous and Jurassic periods. The reason is that human subjectivity always plays a role in the economic "movement." It is man who becomes aware of the objective meaning of an economic system's facticity, and who, on the basis of this facticity, projects a more satisfactory system and then *himself* realizes the new system. The "matter" with which an economist works is a "human matter," and the changes in an economic system do not occur under the pressure of an economic facticity "in itself," but always are also brought about by the interference of human subjectivity.[209]

The same could be said with respect to language, art, social and religious life, the sciences, and philosophy.[210] Philosophy does not "evolve" and philosophical views do not "come about" just as things are brought about by things. On the contrary, authentic philosophizing is a taking-up of eternally the same problems, a reconsideration of previously given answers. It ratifies the previously given answer, rejects it, or tries to penetrate beyond it.[211] Without the subjectivity of human *existence* nothing can be understood of the "changes" occurring in the cultural world, and because of this subjectivity these "changes" are no processes.[212]

Untenable Views

Superficially considered, as is commonly done, history is the succession of events "in" time. Time is thereby conceived as a kind of stream,[213] and events in time are viewed as the suc-

---

[209] Merleau-Ponty, *EP*, p. 73.
[210] In connection with this matter, see Heidegger's development of the notion of *Wiederholung* ("repetition") in *SZ*, pp. 385-386.
[211] Dondeyne, *art. cit.*, pp. 14-15.
[212] G. Marcel, *L'Homme problématique*, Paris, 1955, p. 45.
[213] "L'histoire n'a pas de sens si son sens est compris comme celui d'une rivière qui coule sous l'action de causes toutes-puissantes vers un océan où elle disparaît." *EP*, p. 71.

cessive passing of little pieces of wood floating in the stream.[214] Thus the various moments are looked upon as "now"-points, as elements or atoms of time, and time itself as the succession of such points.[215] It is needless to argue the point: people generally speak of time as an objectivistic process, a stream without any witness, a flowing substance, a process "in itself" (Heraclitus).

The very image used in the description, however, shows that there can be no question of time without reference to a subject.[216] For what does it mean that one little piece of wood in the stream passes *after* the other? *After* is meaningless unless a perceiving subject is thought to be present to the passage of the pieces of wood, a subject who, while perceiving the second piece is able, as it were, to hold fast to the perception of the first. This *holding fast* is essential. One may not say that the past perception is no longer anything at all, for in that case one cannot say that the second perception occurs *after* the first, that the second piece passes *after* the first. And as soon as one can no longer say this, time no longer has a past, so that time is no longer time. Without a subject who in a certain sense holds fast to the past, any kind of "succession" is nonsense. Similarly, it is evident that "events" cannot be conceived as occurring in time if all subjectivity is thought away. Strictly speaking, the term "event" loses all meaning if an event is not conceived as an event-for-someone, an event for a subject.[217] Objectivism is unable to give an account of time.[218]

With respect to time it is essential to hold fast to the past and to anticipate the future. This, as we saw, requires a subject. It would be wrong, however, to say therefore that present, past, and future lie in the subject—that is, to consider the

---

214*PP*, p. 470.

215"Und so zeigt sich denn für das vulgäre Zeitverständnis die Zeit als eine Folge von ständig 'vorhandenen', zugleich vergehenden und ankommenden Jetzt. Die Zeit wird als ein Nacheinander verstanden, als 'Fluss' der Jetzt, als 'Lauf der Zeit'." *SZ*, p. 422.

216"Le temps suppose une vue sur le temps." *PP*, p. 470.

217". . . il n'y a pas d'événements sans quelqu'un à qui ils adviennent et dont la perspective finie fonde leur individualité." *PP*, p. 470.

218Some of Merleau-Ponty's expressions are rather unfortunate. When he says: "Le monde objectif est trop plein pour qu'il y ait du temps" (*PP*, p. 471), his way of speaking reminds us of Sartre's ideas about the in-itself. According to Sartre, the in-itself is fullness of being because the in-itself-for-me implies negativity. But it is meaningless to turn a qualification of the in-itself-for-me simply around and then to think that we may affirm that the in-itself is the fullness of being. Nothing whatsoever can be said of the in-itself—not even that it is "too full to be temporal."

ecstacies of time as states of an isolated consciousness. In this way time would be conceived as the succession of "now"-points˜ in an isolated consciousness instead of an objectivistic world.[219] Another consciousnesss would then be needed to be conscious of the succession of "now"-points as states of consciousness. Such a position would give rise to the question how the temporality of this consciousness can be explained in its turn without having to place each time a new consciousness behind the preceding consciousness.[220]

For one who understands the dimension in which the phenomenology of *existence* thinks, the preceding considerations are not really necessary. A consideration of time can offer an opportunity to find that dimension; but once the dimension itself is accepted, one no longer looks for time in an objectivistic world or in an isolated subjectivity.[221] The "locus" of time is in *existence*, presence, the reciprocal implication of subject "and" the human world. The question is now: what is *existence* as temporality?

Temporality Exists

Man is essentially *existence*, presence to the world, but his being-present is equiprimordially the present in the temporal sense. I am "now" in a particular way orientated to something which I myself am not, but without which I am not what I am. My presence constitutes at the same time my present.

My presence, however, is not finished. Neither I nor present being are "finished." In every presence there lies a retention, "now" present, of a former presence and a "protention," "now" present, of a future presence.[222] This means that no "now" is a real "now," no present is a real present without a future. The presence of the terminus encountered by *existence* is never finished; and the same holds for the present as temporality.

Something similar must be said of the relationship of present and past. My *existence* at this moment is not *real* without a

---

219*PP*, p. 472.

220"Si la conscience du temps était faite d'états de conscience qui se succèdent, il faudrait une nouvelle conscience pour avoir conscience de cette succession et ainsi de suite." *PP*, p. 483.

221"Mais l'analyse du temps . . . éclaire les précédentes analyses parce qu'elle fait apparaître le sujet et l'objet comme deux moments abstraits d'une structure unique qui est la présence." *PP*, p. 492.

222"Husserl appelle protensions et rétensions les intentionnalités qui m'ancrent dans un entourage." *PP*, p. 476.

reference to a future but neither without holding fast to a past. I could not even say that an act is past if this act were totally cut loose from the present, i.e., if it had vanished into nothingness. The past, then, is always present in a certain sense, and the same must be said of the future. Present, past, and future cannot be understood without one another; they imply one another, they are not what they are without one another.[223]

Thus it seems that we have reached an impasse. In every presence, we said, there are a retention, "now" present, of a past presence and a "protention," "now" present, of a future presence. Full emphasis must fall here on the presence of retentions and "protentions" in order to prevent the present from being cut loose from the past and the future. An isolated "now" is not a real "now." But if the past and the future are conceived as "presences," is not the synthesis of time's three ecstacies represented as an addition of "now"-elements, albeit as elements of the *existence*? Do retention and "protention" mean the *addition* of the past and the future to the present?

Such a representation is contradicted by experience. There is no present without *intrinsic* reference to the past and the future. The past and the future, then, are *present* in the present. Nevertheless, temporality is not an addition of "now"-elements because present, past, and future *are* not in the same sense.[224] Temporality is the never-completed unfolding of my subjectivity-in-the-world, the stream of my present. There is no plurality here of phenomena added to one another, but the one phenomenon of the stream.[225] In this one streaming phenomenon, my actual presence lets itself be discovered as the present, and my past and future as *absent* presences. Temporality, then, is not a simple being no longer and a simple being not yet, but a coming within my reach of nearby meanings and escaping my grasp as far-away meanings.

It may be useful to clarify the matter with an example. I am at this moment writing a philosophical book. I write: "There is no present without intrinsic references to the past and the future." When I am writing the word "without," my presence constitutes my present-as-temporality. I continue to hold fast

---

[223]*PP*, p. 479.
[224]"Il ne peut y avoir de temps que s'il n'est pas complètement déployé, si passé, présent et avenir ne *sont* pas dans le même sens." *PP*, p. 474.
[225]*PP*, p. 479.

to the words already written, i.e., my present holds on to my past. At the same time, I anticipate the words which I am still going to write. If I did not anticipate them, the word "without" would be entirely meaningless. Past and future, then, are present in the present, but as absent presences, for they are there as past and future presences.

An even more detailed description can be given. When I am writing the letter *i* of "without," I still hold on to the letter *w*. The *w* is still present under a certain profile, as are the other letters. When, next, I write the letter *t*, I again hold on to what preceded, to the *i* under profile *B*, and to the *w* under another profile (A^1) than the one I had when I wrote the *i*. In the writing of the letter *h* there occurs another modification in the present of the past: I hold on to the *w* under profile A^{11}, to the *i* under profile B^1, and to the *t* under profile *C*. The same could be said with respect to the anticipations.[226]

In conclusion, then, we must say that time is not found in an objectivistically conceived world or in an isolated subject. The "locus" of time is *existence*; or, rather, the subject-in-the-world is temporality.[227] Time is not composed of "now"-points synthetized from without, but time itself is the synthesis of present, past, and future and thus excludes any mere juxtaposition of data.[228] Temporality is an essential characteristic of an involved, situated subject, or rather, it is this subject himself. In Husserl's terms, temporality is "the living stream of presence."

Subjectivity-in-the-world means a break through the determinism of the cosmos—freedom. The subject is not merely *in* the world but also "at" the world; he is the execution of the self-project he is—transcendence. Even as transcendence the subject is freedom, he breaks through the determinism of the cosmos insofar as no facticity whatsoever determines man's action as a human action. Freedom as transcendence, however, is the synthesis of present, past, and future: it is temporality.

History in the Strict Sense

The temporality of the subject-in-the-world is called history when there is question of man's cultural activity in the stricter

---

[226]*PP*, pp. 477-481.
[227]"Il faut comprendre le temps comme sujet et le sujet comme temps." *PP*, p. 483.
[228]"Chaque présent, par son essence même de présent, exclut la juxtaposition avec les autres présents." *PP*, p. 483.

sense of the term. Even perception itself is a way of humaniz-
ing the world and, as such, is a cultural activity; but this term
applies all the more to all activities in the political, social, economic, artistic, scientific and religious life. There is more justification for speaking of the history of art than of that of a
perception or of the writing of the word "without."

Moreover, the accepted usage of the term "history" connotes
the intersubjectivity of human action. Of course, we do not wish
to imply that a perception does not have any intersubjectivity at
all, but merely observe that its intersubjectivity is not as strongly
emphasized as that of cultural activity in the stricter sense. The
history of cultural man is always a collective history, and the
more the world becomes one, the more also history will become
the history of all mankind.

In his cultural activity man is rooted in the past. This past
was constituted by the people who preceded him. Our ancestors,
in particular, the great men of the past, tried to humanize the
world, and all cultural activity of our time is a taking up of their
intentions. In his cultural activity man always distances himself
from the constituted, from facticity: he tries to seize its real
meaning in order to ratify or reject it, or else to modify it.[229] In
this way he is continually in dialogue with his fellowmen: the past
continues to live in the present and is projected toward a future.
Man is never "finished" and his world is never "completed."

6. Freedom, "Liberation" and Work

Any term which expresses something of "human reality" can
have a whole spectrum of meanings. Being-a-subject, we said,
is being-free; but anyone sees at once that, although all men are
subjects, they are subjects in different ways. There are "great"
subjects—people who are *I*'s in the full sense of the term, "full"
personalities, authentic human beings. But there are also people
whose subjectivity merely consists in this, that they barely rise
above not-being-a-subject: their subjectivity is, as it were,
crushed under a heavy burden of whatever kind. Their *I* is
actually only a "small" *I*, with hardly any leeway of possibilities,
powerless and impotent. What is the meaning of the subjectivity
of a farmer in India, who has to spend fifteen hours a day in

---

[229]Dondeyne, "L'historicité dans la philosophie contemporaine," *Revue philosophique de Louvain*, 54(1956), pp. 14-15.

laborious toil on a rockstrewn piece of land? What is the meaning of the subjectivity of an industrial worker who has found "shelter" in one of Rio de Janeiro's infamous slums? Or of a Javanese wracked by malaria, for whom medicine is out of the question? Or that of the neurotic who is torn apart by anxieties and collapses under the weight of his pseudo-religiousness? What is the meaning of the subjectivity of a woman in Arabian countries?

To be a subject is to be free, but this can mean all kinds of things. Man is distinct from the animal through his subjectivity, but before this *really* means anything, man's "freedom" must first be *liberated*. Man realizes himself, but this only *really* means something when man manages to break away from the load of a facticity which enslaves his freedom. The history of freedom will never be finished because any form of liberation gives rise to new forms of enslavement. No one can foresee the "direction" which history will take, but we do know where this history began and where—if in a particular place it did not yet begin—it must start. The history of freedom's liberation begins with work.

Work as Man's Coming to Be Man

It was Marx who first saw the essential importance of work for man's humanization and for liberating man's "freedom." According to Marx man realizes himself by turning to nature. By his turning to nature man is able to stay alive because he lives off nature. Even in this sense nature can be called man's "body." But this expression assumes a much more profound meaning when man makes nature the object of his activity by placing himself at a distance from it. This happens in human work. In and through work nature becomes the "inorganic body" of man [230]—a term Marx uses to indicate that there is an interaction, a "metabolism" between man and nature. In his work man objectifies nature, dominates nature, sets himself apart from nature, liberates himself, and becomes authentically human. Man—who with respect to nature knows that he is needy—is, strictly speaking, rich. For the existence of need in man is at the

---

[230]K. Marx, *Zur Kritik der Nationalökonomie, Ökonomisch-philosophische Manuskripte,* in Marx-Engels, *Kleine ökonomische Schriften,* Berlin, 1955, p. 103.

same time the existence of a necessity for man to realize himself. Not only the richness of man but also his poverty have a human and a social meaning.[231]

The animal is also involved in nature, but in an entirely different way than man. Hence the animal is not man. The animal is fully at one with its activity and does not at all distinguish itself from it. The animal's activity stands fully in function of its immediate, bodily needs.[232] Man, on the other hand, can place himself at a distance, he makes his own activity the object of his knowing and willing; his activity is conscious and free. Thus man is able to continually correct his own activity and raise it to a higher level, but the animal is and remains a stagnant being.

Man begins to distinguish himself from the animal as soon as he begins to *produce*, and the first things he produces are, of course, the necessities of life, food.[233]

These principles are independent of any particular form of society. Work is a process between man and nature—a kind of "metabolism" established by man between himself and nature, which man regulates and controls.[234] This metabolism presupposes in the first place the forces of man's body. Through these forces man acts upon nature, but, by changing nature, he also changes himself: he develops the powers and abilities which lie dormant in his own being.[235]

All this, however, assumes its full meaning only when man begins to utilize the mechanical, physical, and chemical forces of nature as means by which he can act upon things. This

---

[231]"Der *reiche* Mensch ist zugleich der einer Totalität der menschlichen Lebensäusserung *bedürftige* Mensch. Der Mensch, in dem seine eigne Verwirklichung, als innere Notwendigkeit, als *Not* existiert. Nicht nur der *Reichtum*, auch die Armut des Menschen erhält gleichmässig eine *menschliche* und daher gesellschaftliche Bedeutung." Marx, op. cit., p. 137.

[232]Marx, *op. cit.*, pp. 103-104.

[233]"Man kann die Menschen durch das Bewusstsein, durch die Religion, durch was man sonst will, von den Tieren underscheiden. Sie selbst fangen an, sich von den Tieren zu unterscheiden, sobald sie anfangen, ihre Lebensmittel *zu produzieren*, ein Schritt, der durch ihre körperliche Organisation bedingt ist. Indem die Menschen ihre Lebensmittel produzieren, produzieren sie indirekt ihr materielles Leben selbst." Marx and Engels, *Die Deutsche Ideologie*, Berlin, 1953, p. 17.

[234]"Die Arbeit ist zunächst ein Process zwischen Mensch und Natur, ein Process, worin der Mensch seinen Stoffwechsel mit der Natur durch seine eigne Tat vermittelt, regelt und kontrolliert." Marx, *Das Kapital, Kritik der politischen Oekonomie*, Berlin, 1957, p. 185.

[235]"Indem er durch diese Bewegung auf die Natur ausser ihm wirkt und sie verändert, verändert er zugleich seine eigne Natur." Marx, *op. cit.*, p. 185.

happens when he makes instruments and tools—he does this in a revolutionary way when he produces machines—for in this way he adds an extension to his own body.[236] As soon as work begins to develop a little, the necessity of tools imposes itself.[237] This implies that one can evaluate the perfection of past forms of society by the perfection of their means of work, their tools and instruments. Not the things produced, but the way they were produced divides the economic eras.[238]

Man, then, is a self-realizing being or—and for Marx this is the same—man is essentially a worker. Work makes man man. This is not all, however. Work becomes really productive only when man begins to make tools; besides, really productive work implies a division of labor: it must be executed as a social task. The product, then, is always a product of common or social labor: work produces society.[239] The division of labor actually means that people work for one another. Thus work really is mutual help, a characteristic which manifests itself most evidently in modern industrial labor. Man would simply disappear if he did not work. Exactly the same, however, is said when one asserts that man would disappear if people did not work *for one another*. Work, therefore, not only makes a man man but also makes him a fellowman.[240]

Co-existence in work also constitutes the interconnection in mankind's history. The fact that every generation finds at its disposal the means of work produced by the preceding generations means that every man is permeated with, and dependent upon the past.[241] The generation now living in its turn will continue to live in the future because it, too, leaves behind means of production which will serve as a starting point for the work of future generations. Man, then, is the origin and the product,

---

[236]Marx, *op. cit.*, pp. 186-187.

[237]Marx, *op. cit.*, pp. 187-188.

[238]"Nicht *was* gemacht wird, sondern *wie*, mit welchen Arbeitsmitteln gemacht wird, unterscheidet die ökonomische Epochen." Marx, *op. cit.*, p. 188.

[239]"Der Gegenstand als *Sein für den Menschen*, als *gegenständliches Sein des Menschen*, (ist) zugleich das *Dasein des Menschen für den anderen Menschen*, seine *menschliche Beziehung zum andern Menschen*, das *gesellschaftliche Verhalten des Menschen zum Menschen*." Marx and Engels, *Die heilige Familie*, Berlin, 1953, p. 146.

[240]"Eben in der Bearbeitung der gegenständlichen Welt bewährt sich der Mensch daher erst wirklich als ein *Gattungswesen*. Diese Produktion ist sein werktätiges Gattungswesen." Marx, *Zur Kritik der Nationalökonomie*, p. 105.

[241]Kwant, *De wijsbegeerte van Karl Marx*, Utrecht, 1961, p. 25.

the creator and the creature of history, and in this history work occupies the central position. Because of work's central position, history is a common history. The bond between men is not secured by any "political or religious nonsense" (*sic*), but by the continuity of the means of production.[242]

The original and novel point in Marx's description of work is his emphasis on work as man's self-realization. For Marx work is not purely a means to a goal lying outside work itself, but work is a goal in itself. Man wants to live, to be man; therefore, he wants to work, for working is living, is being-man. For this reason Marx is against work for *wages*.[243] The idea that the laborer must sell his power to work is unbearable to Marx, for in this way work does indeed become a means for a goal lying outside work itself. According to Marx, work must be performed as *the* way for man to realize himself, and this is no longer the case when work is wage labor. For the wage laborer, life is nothing but a means to live.[244]

While recognizing that the character of a means can never be totally eliminated from work, we think that work really cannot be reduced to a *means* to live. Even with respect to eating and drinking one should not say that we do this solely in order to live. Man wants to live, and eating and drinking themselves are ways of living.[245] Man does not eat and drink in the same way as an engine is supplied with oil and gas: there is a big difference between dining and taking pills. Dining is to a certain extent a goal in itself, and the same must be said even more of working. To work *is* to become man.

Modern Work

Although Marx's definition of work is original, his descrip-

---

[242]"Es zeigt sich also schon von vornherein ein materialistischer Zusammenhang der Menschen untereinander, der durch die Bedürfnisse und die Weise der Produktion bedingt und so alt ist wie die Menschen selbst - ein Zusammenhang, der stets neue Formen annimmt und also eine 'Geschichte' darbietet, auch ohne dass irgendein politischer oder religiöser Nonsens existiert, der die Menschen noch extra zusammenhalte." Marx and Engels, *Die Deutsche Ideologie*, pp. 26-27.

[243]Marx, "Arbeitslohn," *Kleine ökonomische Schriften*, p. 248.

[244]"Das Leben selbst erscheint nur als Lebensmittel." Marx, *Zur Kritik der Nationalökonomie*, p. 104.

[245]"Nous respirons pour respirer, mangeons et buvons pour manger et pour boire, nous nous abritons pour nous abriter, nous étudions pour satisfaire à notre curiosité, nous nous promenons pour nous promener. Tout cela n'est pas *pour* vivre. Tout cela est vivre." E. Levinas, *De l'existence à l'existant*, Paris, n.d., p. 67.

tion is not sufficiently supple and broad to be applicable to work as we know it today. Marx had in mind the kind of labor which in his era drew most attention, viz., the production of material goods.[246] But this kind of production is merely a "beginning."

As soon as the production of material goods has reached a certain level, i.e., when production has become so efficient that man is able to wrest a surplus from nature, there is room for modes of self-realization which lie beyond the self-realization contained in work conceived as "production." [247] The pursuit of science and art, sports and games, and many ways of taking care of one's fellowmen become posssible only when work, in the narrow sense, has reached a certain level of productivity. "Production," however, is always a necessary condition for those ways of human self-realization which themselves do not consist in the production of material goods.

As was mentioned, rationality is one of the moments on the basis of which human activity can be called human. It was Descartes who had the foresight to envision what man would be able to do in his work if he let himself be guided by the rationality presiding over the physical sciences. Descartes foresaw that man could become "master and possessor of nature" if he replaced the prescientific light of reason, which hitherto had guided work, by the rationality of the physical sciences.[248] Descartes' dream of the future has become reality in technology: work has become technical work.

It is from this time that dates the glorification of work as *the* way of man's self-realization and self-humanization and as *the* condition for the establishment of human relations and genuine peace. A "labor civilization" [249] arose along with a philosophy in which work may be called the central reference point. The French socialists Saint-Simon and Proudhon laid the foundation for Marx's philosophy of work.[250]

There is no reason to be surprised at this development. As we saw, work can only be called meaningful for man's *integral*

---

[246]Kwant, *Filosofie van de arbeid*, Antwerpen, 1964, pp. 14-15.

[247]P. De Bruin, "De structuur van het economisch arbeidsbegrip," *Tijdschrift voor Philosophie*, IV(1942), p. 128.

[248]Kwant, "Arbeid en Leven," *Arbeid, Verslag van de tweeentwintigste algemene vergadering van de Vereniging voor Thomistische Wijsbegeerte*, Utrecht, 1958, pp. 39-44.

[249]J. Lacroix, *Personne et Amour*, Paris, 1955, pp. 111-112.

[250]Lacroix, *op. cit.*, pp. 98-104.

humanity from the moment when, through his labor, he wrests a surplus from nature. Obviously, it was only through the introduction of technology that this condition was fully satisfied. Through work, moreover, man enters into relation not only with nature but also with his fellowmen. When man really begins to work, he continually has more and more to do with his fellowmen.[251] Saint-Simon and Proudhon saw this when, despising politicians, soldiers, jurists, "contemplatives," and philosophers, they described work as formative of society.[252] Work means man's coming to be man in the intersubjective sense.

If, however, productive labor has made man's integral self-realization posssible, we must note that from that very "moment," *every* way of human self-realization can be, and actually is, called work. There remains a difference between work and "occupation," in the sense of busy-ness; and there remains a difference between work and leisure.[253] But under certain conditions, any occupation can be work and any type of work a leisure pursuit.[254] One man's work can be the other's occupation. The boundaries are very uncertain in this matter: there are many activities which are both work and occupation, others which have much the character of work and little that of occupation or vice versa, others again which are passing from one category to the other. The truck gardener certainly works; the laborer who in his spare time cultivates half an acre for homegrown vegetables works and plays at the same time; but the retired gentleman, whose enthusiastic hobby is king-sized watermelons, can hardly be said to work.[255]

What are the conditions under which any occupation can be called work? What is the *modern* form of labor of which Marx could not yet speak? We have the impression that Kwant's answer to this question is better than those of Lacroix and Ricoeur. Lacroix uses a description of work which can be applied to any kind of occupation.[256] The result is that it remains

---

[251]"Le travail n'est pas seulement rapport de l'homme à la nature, mais relation de l'homme à l'humanité . . . une société ne s'édifie qu'autour d'une *oeuvre* réelle et à quelque degré commune." Lacroix, *op. cit.*, p. 83.

[252]"La paix pour et par la production, c'est-à-dire pour et par le travail, telle est donc l'idée centrale du saint-simonisme." Lacroix, *op. cit.*, p. 100.

[253]F. Tellegen, *Zelfwording en zelfverlies in de arbeid*, Delft, 1958, p. 6.

[254]Kwant, *Filosofie van de arbeid*, pp. 16-23.

[255]P. De Bruin, *art. cit.*, p. 131.

[256]"Le travail . . . est *liberté en acte,* c'est-à-dire effort pour actualiser des valeurs dans et par des mouvements, information nerveuse selon une norme, *émission de l'esprit,* pour reprendre la belle formule de Proudhon, dans la nature et par la méditation de l'organisme." Lacroix, *op. cit.*, p. 91.

obscure how work is distinct from simply being occupied with something. Ricoeur seeks the "counter-part" of work in the "word." [257] If this were true, Ricoeur and others who devote their energies to speech in its various forms could not be said to work.

Kwant describes modern work as that human occupation which is performed within the framework of the socially regulated satisfaction of needs, and for this reason implies a social "having to." [258] The material character of an occupation does not make it work, for one and the same occupation is sometimes work and sometimes not work. Similarly, whether a particular occupation belongs to the official "labor order" or not, does not decide the issue, for work is also done outside this "labor order." Finally, the more or less laborious character of an occupation or its financial remuneration do not make it work, for there are many ways of working which are not laborious and there is much work which remains financially unpaid.[259]

Work is to be occupied within the framework of providing for needs. These needs are not exclusively bodily needs. Because needs vary in the different phases of history, certain occupations *become* work. Where no need whatsoever is provided for, there no work of any kind is done. At the same time, work implies a social "having to," which, at least in the last instance, is imposed by the needs. The working man undertakes that which, in view of the needs, *has to* be done. Thus he himself cannot determine when he will begin or cease to work. The "having to" is regulated socially, sometimes by the official "labor order," sometimes by forms of social collaboration which lie beyond the official labor order.

Accordingly, work is very one-sidedly defined when it is described as a wrestling with nature, as man's turning toward nature in order to humanize it. Such a description can apply to certain forms of agricultural and industrial labor, but is hardly appropriate to many other forms of authentic work. Delivering speeches, having conferences, controlling and administering an enterprise, are ways of working, but not of "wrestling with nature" [260]—at least if this expression of Marx continues to be taken in the sense he originally attached to it.

257P. Ricoeur, *Histoire et Vérité*, Paris, 1955, pp. 183-212.
258Kwant, *op. cit.*, pp. 19, 20, 22, 24, 25, 27, 29, 32, 81.
259Kwant, *op. cit.*, pp. 12-19.
260Kwant, *op. cit.*, pp. 24, 34, 84.

If one can rightly say that man's freedom must be liberated before this freedom *really* becomes meaningful, then it is evident, we think, that work must be called the first step on the road to freedom. We do not wish to claim with Marx and Engels that the economic basis of society *determines* what a spiritualistic tradition calls the "higher, spiritual aspects" of man, society, and history.[261] But even if this determinism is not accepted, it should be recognized that there can be no question of genuine subjectivity and freedom unless man "goes to work." The West was first to recognize this necessity: it replaced the prescientific rationality of work by the rationality of the sciences—i.e., it changed work into technology, "invented" administration and the legal order, and thus liberated freedom. The necessity of work for the humanization of man is so evident that at present the "underdeveloped" countries also realize the need to take over these Western inventions if they wish to lead a life worthy of man.

As everyone knows, however, nowadays it is precisely the West that criticizes its own inventions. What does this criticism mean, if work is the first and most necessary condition for setting man's freedom free? Did this liberation result again in slavery, albeit it of a different kind than the slavery it conquered?

The Slavery of a Technocratic Order

No one can indict technology without making himself ridiculous. It is abundantly evident that most monuments of genuinely human greatness, no matter of what kind, are unthinkable without technology. It would be absurd to expect any good results from the closing of factories and laboratories.[262] Man acquired real power over nature only when his work began to be performed under the guidance of the physical sciences, with the means made possible by these sciences—in other words,

---

261"Die neuen Tatsachen zwangen dazu, die ganze bisherige Geschichte einer neuen Untersuchung zu unterwerfen, und da zeigte sich, dass *alle* bisherige Geschichte . . . die Geschichte von Klassen-kämpfen war, dass diese einander bekämpfenden Klassen der Gesellschaft jedesmal Erzeugnisse sind der Produktions- und Verkehrsverhältnisse, mit einem Wort der ökonomischen Verhältnisse ihrer Epoche; dass also die jedesmalige ökonomische Struktur der Gesellschaft die reale Grundlage bildet, aus der der gesamte Überbau der rechtlichen und politischen Einrichtungen sowie der religiösen, philosophischen und sonstigen Vorstellungsweise eines jeden geschichtlichen Zeitabschnittes in letzter Instanz zu erklären sind." Fr. Engels, *Herrn Eugen Dührings Umwälzung der Wissenschaft,* Berlin, 1954, p. 30.

262Marcel, *HCH,* p. 63-64.

when he began to use technology.[263]   To abolish technology
would mean anarchy, barbarism, starvation, disease, and death
—in a word, the loss of everything human that man has managed
to achieve in a long and bitter struggle.[264]

The rationality man uses in his technical work is a genuinely
human good, one of the most eloquent possibilities and expressions of human genius.   The power man has acquired through
his technology is an affirmation of his superiority over the mere
thing.   Technology can never be sufficiently appreciated.[265]

On the other hand, man has the duty to realize what will
happen if the spirit of technology becomes so far-reaching that
it is made an absolute.   The fact that this spirit is far-reaching
need surprise no one, for there is no other form of rationality
whose pursuit has been as convincingly fruitful as the rationality
expressing itself in physical science.   This fruitfulness, moreover, is confirmed by the real power given to man.   What, then,
is more tempting to man than to entrust himself entirely to the
perspective opened by science and technology, and to overestimate the promises resulting from such an adventure?   Is it not
possible that the physical sciences will solve *all* questions and
that technology will alleviate *all* needs?

Man has thought so but he was mistaken.   The physical
sciences are good and technology is beneficial, but the attempt
to absolutize the *spirit* of technology has given rise to what today
is often called "technocracy."   As early as 1933, Marcel pronounced his terrible indictment of it,[266] and subsequently
practically all philosophers who still retained any awareness of
man's integral destiny have sided with him.

In a technocratic society the spirit of technology is absolutized.   What does this spirit consist of, and what is this
absolutism?   Insofar as the spirit of technology belongs to the
realm of the *cogito*, it is determined by the rationality of the
sciences.   Absolutizing this rationality is called "scientism." [267]
The sciences of nature became very fruitful from the moment

[263]"Enfin, et c'est peut-être le point capital, nous nous rendons de mieux
en mieux compte que toute puissance au sens humain du terme implique la
mise en oeuvre d'une technique." Marcel, *EA*, p. 272.
[264]*HCH*, p. 50.
[265]*HCH*, p. 64.
[266]Marcel, "Position et approches concrètes du mystère ontologique,"
Le monde cassé, Paris, 1933, pp. 255-301.   Separately re-issued with an introduction by Marcel de Corte, Louvain, 1949.   The original pagination has
been retained in the re-issue.
[267]Marcel, *Homo Viator*, Paris, 1944, p. 195.

when man decided to question nature in a very special way, viz., by means of mathematical categories. Questioning nature in this way means approaching the world in a special way: in reply to the question addressed to it by physical science, the world shows a special objective face, viz., a quantitative face. The world reveals itself insofar as it is calculable and measurable.

It is easy to see to what absolutizing the attitude of physical science must lead, no matter how legitimate this attitude is within this science itself. The reality of everything in the world which cannot be measured or calculated, which cannot become a problem of physical science is simply meaningless for the adherent of scientism.[268] The non-measurable and non-calculable simply does not exist for him. To use again the example given before, water is solely and entirely H_2O for one who makes science the absolute: all other meanings of water are relegated to the realm of romanticism and mystification. For the technocrat the Rhine is simply "energy." But why do ordinary people love to take their vacation on the Rhine? One who goes for a swim in the Pacific from California's beaches most assuredly is not interested in H_2O. And what would remain of the lovely island of Capri if its reality is to be expressed only in terms of quantity?

The spirit of technology, however, belongs not only to the order of the *cogito* but infects also the level of man's *volo*, his affectivity. On this level it manifests itself in the desire to have and to control. We do not intend to deny the positive value of this desire, but what happens when this desire is absolutized? The progressive possibility to dominate the world asphyxiates man's power to wonder about the world.[269] The more technology dominates, the more man continually comes face to face with himself and his creations: he increasingly forgets that the world was already there before he transformed it into energy. The more he "possesses" the world through technology, the less he is capable of gratitude. Gratitude presupposes the reception of a gift,[270] but the world is no longer a gift, for it is conquered. In this way, pride is fostered.

The technical man, however, does not merely deal with nature but also enters into relationship with his fellowmen. To

---

[268]Marcel, *Position et Approches.* . . . . . . , pp. 258-272.
[269]Marcel, *Homo Viator*, p. 157.
[270]"Rendre grâce, cela suppose un don reçu" (Troisfontaines).

the extent that he has capitulated to scientism, human beings are not subjects for him. For the adherent of scientism people are "bodies," bodily "forces," "functions" in systems of tools and machines.[271] As such, they are measurable and calculable. The affective relationship of the technocrat to his fellowmen is also destroyed. Technocracy is a denial of one's "neighbor"; [272] the technocrat exploits man, even if he pays a "just" wage.

Let us repeat it, we are not speaking here of technology, but of the technocratic mentality. Its reality was described above almost entirely in terms of the technocrat's own *existence*. We must now briefly describe that same reality in terms of the *existence* of those who have become victims of technocracy.

Let us begin by observing that most victims do not realize the condition in which they are, at least not through an intellectual and reflective return to their own *existence*. They would not be able to make such a return anyhow. Life in a technocratic order is, like any way of life, not fully transparent to itself but rather a kind of semidarkness. Man knows what he is and does but, at the same time, he also does not know it. Only the sharpest minds are able to describe their own time, but even they can do it only when their era has already assumed very striking features.

The reality of life, however, does not merely manifest itself in explicit intellectual reflection: what Heidegger calls the "mood" of *existence* (*Befindlichkeit*) can also disclose that reality.[273] It is only on the level of this "mood," the tonality of *existence*, that the victims of technocracy are aware of their condition. In our technocratic order, not finding oneself well—at ease—has gained the upperhand over finding oneself at ease. According to Marcel's expression, our order is characterized by a "choking sadness." Man does not feel at home in a technocratic order because in this order his integral being-human, his authentically being-a-person, is mutilated. The world of technocracy is exclusively a mathematically calculated world, but

---

[271]"Le monde du problématique est en même temps celui du désir et de la crainte, qui ne se laissent point séparer l'un de l'autre; c'est aussi sans doute le monde fonctionnalisé ou fonctionnalisable que j'ai défini au début de cette méditation, c'est enfin celui où règnent les techniques quelles qu'elles soient." Marcel, *Positions et Approches* . . . . . , p. 281.

[272]"Mais comment ne pas voir que la technocratie consiste justement avant tout à faire abstraction du prochain et, en fin de compte, à le nier?" *HCH*, p. 200.

[273]Heidegger, *SZ*, pp. 134-140.

this world is empty and sounds hollow. In this world there is no longer any difference between day and night, and there are no seasons. The rhythm of life becomes more and more the rhythm of a machine,[274] in which man is a "function" and his fellowman "another function"; being-together becomes a "co-ordinate functioning" calculated by the psychotechnician.[275] Technocracy has deprived man of his *selfhood*, he is reduced to an anonymous entity, the impersonal "one."

It is excluded, however, that man can behave as an anonymous entity on one level of *existence* and as a person on a different level. The fact that the depersonalized people of a technocracy do not know what to do with their free time shows this. The impersonal "one" has lost his integral selfhood to such an extent that he slavishly follows any form of advertizing or propaganda. Goebbels, the Propaganda Minister of the Third *Reich*, realized this very well, and there are others who know it just as well.[276] Insofar as man profits from technocracy he has also lost his selfhood, for he has put the center of his existence and the basis of his equilibrium in television sets and motorcars.[277] He loses his selfhood in the products of his technology. From the religious standpoint, the victims of technocracy are among those people who "noiselessly apostatize." The loss of personality has become widespread.[278]

"Choking sadness!" The victim of technocracy is tempted to despair as soon as his blindness disappears: [279] nihilism prevails. Not technology, however, is nihilistic, but technocracy.[280] Marcel's expression clearly indicates the situation in which modern man finds himself. Technocracy means the *nihil*, the nothing of man's integral personality. Heidegger speaks of "forgetfulness of being" in his dialog with Ernst Jünger about the nihilism of our time.[281] Technology is a good, and it would

---

[274]Marcel, *Homo Viator*, pp. 112-113.

[275]"Dans notre monde de plus en plus collectivisé, le mot *avec* perd son sens et une communauté réelle apparaît de moins en moins concevable." R. Troisfontaines, *De l'existence à l'être, La Philosophie de Gabriel Marcel*, I, Louvain, 1953, p. 66.

[276]*HCH*, p. 43.

[277]*HCH*, pp. 46-47.

[278]G. Gusdorf, *Traité de l'existence morale*, pp. 9-20.

[279] *HCH*, p. 72.

[280]"C'est un fait à la fois mystérieux et profondément significatif que, dans le monde qui est aujourd'hui le nôtre, le nihilisme tend à prendre un caractère technocratique et que la technocratie est inévitablement nihiliste." *HCH*, p. 197.

[281]Heidegger, *Zur Seinsfrage*, Frankfurt a.M., 1956, p. 41.

be senseless if man were to try to rid himself of it,[282] to give up his "mastership." But, because man has let himself become fascinated by his own technology,[283] he has not succeeded in mastering his own mastership.[284]

If the immanent "intention" of the technocratic mentality would be fully realized, integral human life would be doomed to disappear. But, as shown by the above-mentioned "mood" of *existence*, technocracy has become unbearable to itself. The protest usually is still only of an affective nature, but this suffices to prevent the system from becoming self-enclosed. The affective breach with the system offers enough room for a suitable way of asking questions which can be the beginning of a "reversal." [285]

Camus bears witness to this possibility when he says: "It may happen that all of a sudden the whole scenery crumbles. To get up, take the streetcar, work for four hours in the office or factory, take the streetcar, eat, take the street car, work for four hours, eat, sleep—all the time in the same rhythm on Monday, Tuesday, Wednesday, Thursday, Friday, and Saturday—usually man has not trouble in following this routine. But one day the question 'why' arises. Everything 'begins' in this boredom, once it is colored by wonder. We say 'begins," for this word is important. Boredom lies at the end of the activities of a mechanized life, but at the same time, it puts consciousness into motion. It arouses consciousness and leads to the consequences. The result is either an unconscious return to the chain or a definitive awakening." [286]

A similar thought is voiced by Heidegger: "This Europe, in its ruinous blindness forever on the point of cutting its own throat, lies today in a great pincers, squeezed between Russia on one side and America on the other. From a metaphysical

---

[282]"Es wäre töricht, blindlings gegen die technische Welt anzurennen. Es wäre kurzsichtig, die technische Welt als Teufelswerk verdammen zu wollen. Wir sind auf die technischen Gegenstände angewiesen; sie fordern uns sogar zu einer immerzu steigenden Verbesserung heraus." Heidegger, *Gelassenheit*, Pfullingen, 1959, p. 24.

[283]"Unversehens sind wir jedoch so fest an die technischen Gegenstände geschmiedet, dass wir in die Knechtschaft zu ihnen geraten." Heidegger, *op. cit.*, p. 24.

[284]"*Livré à la technique,* ai-je dit: il faut entendre par là, de plus en plus incapable de la maîtriser, ou encore *de maîtriser sa propre maîtrise.*" Marcel, *Positions et Approches . . . . . ,* p. 282.

[285]Heidegger, *Die Technik und die Kehre,* Pfullingen, 1962.

[286]Camus, *Le mythe de Sisyphe,* Paris, 1942, p. 27.

point of view, Russia and America are the same; the same dreary technological frenzy, the same unrestricted organization of the average man. At a time when the farthermost corner of the globe has been conquered by technology and opened to economic exploitation; when any incident whatsoever, regardless of where or when it occurs, can be communicated to the rest of the world at any desired speed; when the assassination of a king in France and a symphony concert in Tokyo can be 'experienced' simultaneously; when time has ceased to be anything other than velocity, instantaneousness, and simultaneity, and time as history has vanished from the lives of all peoples; when a boxer is regarded as a nation's great man; when mass meetings attended by millions are looked on as a triumph—then, yes then, through all this turmoil a question still haunts us like a specter: What for?—Whither?—And what then?" [287]

As long as man is still somewhat human, capable of being bored, it remains possible for him explicitly to realize that work —the first step on the road to the liberation of freedom—can thereafter establish new forms of slavery. When he realizes this, then he can no longer escape the question of the meaning of his liberated freedom.

"Bourgeois" Philosophy's Alleged Sense of Doom

For any Marxist the above remarks about the nihilism of technocracy are an abomination. The Marxist is a technocrat "by definition." In his eyes, the pessimism with which certain thinkers of the West speak about technocracy is nothing but the last convulsion—the last for the umptieth time—of the bourgeoisie's sense of doom. [288] Such Marxists as Ermolenko, Calin, Gajdenko, and Narski claim that in its "existentialism" the West realizes its own decadence, the destruction of the social bonds within its society and the spiritual death struggle of its civic individualism. [289] The West's lamentations over the "mass man" of technocracy betrays, in the eyes of the Marxist, solely that the West is powerless to give a *real* answer to the question of what

---

[287]Heidegger, *Einführung in die Metaphysik*, pp. 28-29.

[288]"L'homme existentialiste et l'homme communiste semblent ainsi figurer deux représentations tout à fait opposées de l'homme moderne. L'un triste et déchiré, l'autre confiant et résolu." G. Gusdorf, *op. cit.*, p. 23.

[289]R. De George, "Heidegger and the Marxists," *Studies in Soviet Thought*, V(1965), pp. 289-298.

man is.[290] Heidegger is the prophet of doom. *par excellence.* But the Marxist will not shed any tears over the impending doom, for in his eyes bourgeois philosophy itself now expresses something which is *of necessity* implied in history, viz., the end of bourgeois society.

The Marxist himself has a very simple answer to the question about the meaning of liberated freedom. According to Marxism, work is the first step on the road to liberation, but at first this liberation is only to the advantage of a privileged few— those, namely, who have managed to seize control of the modern production apparatus.[291] These means are, however, by their very nature social: they can only be operated by many and produce for many, who depend on their products to stay alive. The simple "fact" that means of production which by their very nature are social are the personal property of individuals is for Marx the conflict *par excellence.*[292] People do not live in conflict with one another because of their subjective "intentions," but the conflict lies in the "objective" structures of society. The personal ownership of social means of production *is* absolute power of man over his fellowmen, *is* class struggle, *is* slavery for many, independently of "subjective" intentions. History, however—that is, of course, the history of work, of the economy— is on the road to liberating the enslaved freedom of the many. Not by virtue of the proletariat's "subjective" intentions, plans or initiatives, but through the "objective" reality of the proletariat history moves toward the historical moment when *the* conflict will be solved. Through an "objective" process, independently of the intentions of either the exploiters or the exploited, a moment will come when the proletariat will take over the means of production.[293] Then the possessors will be destroyed, and man will become authentically human: freedom will be liberated.[294] The negative solidarity, the solidarity in

[290]De George, *art cit.,* pp. 294-297.
[291]Marx, "Zur Kritik der politischen Ökonomie," K. Marx and Fr. Engels, *Ausgewählte Schriften in zwei Bänden,* Berlin, 1952, I, p. 338.
[292]Fr. Engels, "Die Entwicklung des Sozialismus von der Utopie zur Wissenschaft" in K. Marx and Fr. Engels, *Ausgewählte Schriften in zwei Bänden,* II, p. 127.
[293]K. Marx and Fr. Engels, *Die heilige Familie,* Berlin, 1953, p. 137.
[294]"Der Mensch eignet sich sein allseitiges Wesen auf eine allseitige Art an, also als ein totaler Mensch." Marx, "Zur Kritik der Nationalökonomie," in K. Marx and Fr. Engels, *Kleine ökonomische Schriften,* Berlin, 1955, p. 131.

suffering which the proletariat *is* will change into positivity.[295] *The* conflict will no longer exist, because the means of production will be socially owned. Brotherhood and peace will arise, of necessity! Man will become man in both the subjective and the intersubjective sense. The labor order will *be* humanity, love, brotherhood, and peace.

Summarizing, we may say that for Marxism the history of freedom's liberation through work is on the road toward a supreme form of freedom, viz., the universal recognition of man by man, brotherhood, and peace. This situation will be a reality when the proletariat has taken over the means of production, for then the conflict *par excellence* will be eliminated. Then *co-existence* in work will be intersubjectivity.

It is here that lies the great illusion of Marxism. It stands to reason that in and through modern work all men will have bonds with all other men. But every society which assumes social ownership of the modern means of production will have to appoint certain individual subjects to manage these means and divide their products. There is nothing, however, which can *guarantee* that no new class struggle will then arise. All workers will have bonds with all other workers in their labor, but nothing *guarantees* that this bond will be intersubjectivity. A world-wide labor order can be unmitigated hell if the subjects hate one another. For authentic intersubjectivity of free subjects more is needed than Marx believed.

---

[295]Marx, "Zur Kritik der Hegelschen Rechtsphilosophie," *Die heilige Familie*, p. 26.

CHAPTER FOUR

PHENOMENOLOGY OF INTERSUBJECTIVITY

Is the man I am unique? Is my existence an isolated existence? Am I "first" a man and do I "next" decide to have, or not to have, relations with others? These and other similar questions have not yet been raised, even though the topics that did come up offered a sufficient reason to investigate such matters. The man I am disclosed himself as a conscious-being-in-the-world, a being that cannot be isolated or separated from the world without losing his manhood. But in the world in which I dwell I encounter human beings, I meet them when I walk around, they look at me, make gestures at me, address me. Their looks, words, and gestures, however, give me reason to pause. I am the project of my world, and in my project I make the world a cultural world, but as soon as I encounter the other human being in my world, I realize that the other may not be submerged in my project: the other is not a worldly thing which receives meaning from my history as creative of culture.[1] What is my relationship with the others?

Opportunities to discuss this matter presented themselves several times, but in order not to interrupt a minimum of systematic presentation, we did not discuss the relationship of *existence* to other *existences*. In the present chapter we must now make this relationship the explicit topic of our discussions. In contemporary philosophy this relationship is expressed by saying that *existence* is *co-existence*.

1. To Exist Is to Co-Exist

The statement that *existence* is *co-existence* can have several meanings. Generally speaking, the term *"co-existence"* is used to indicate that on no level of his *existence* man is absolutely "alone." No aspect of man's being-man is what it is without

---

[1]"Regard de l'étranger, de la veuve et de l'orphelin et que je ne peux reconnaître qu'en donnant ou qu'en refusant, libre de donner ou de refuser, mais passant nécessairement par l'entremise des choses. Les choses ne sont pas, comme chez Heidegger, le fondement du lieu, la quinte-essence de toutes les relations qui constituent notre présence sur terre (et 'sous le Ciel, en compagnie des hommes et dans l'attente des dieux'). C'est le rapport du Même avec l'Autre, c'est mon accueil de l'Autre, qui est le fait ultime et où surviennent les choses non pas comme ce qu'on édifie, mais comme ce qu'on donne." E. Levinas, *Totalité et Infini, Essai sur l'extériorité*, La Haye, 1961, p. 49.

the "presence" of other men in it. The presence of others in my *existence* implies that my being-man *is* a being through others. If in a kind of thought experiment I would remove from my own being-man the being through others, I would come to the "conclusion" that I am removing the reality of my manhood itself. Being through others, then, is an essential characteristic of man.[2]

Two Objections

Before delving deeper into this matter, we may devote a few moments to objections raised sometimes against the radically social character of human *existence*.

No aspect of being-man, we said, is what it is without the presence of other human beings in it. One could argue, for example, that white blood corpuscles evidently constitute "aspects of being-man"; nonetheless, it could not be argued that they are a social reality. A bad answer can be given to this difficulty. One could be tempted to appeal to biology to show that, on the basis of heredity, it is meaningful to say that man is not entirely "alone" even with respect to his white blood corpuscles. The reason why we do not wish to refer to biology to argue in favor of the others' presence in my blood corpuscles is that we would not be speaking then about man on the level on which man is spoken of as *man*. The same would happen if one were to speak of the human heart as a muscle or as a pump. When existential phenomenology speaks of man, it does not refer to him as one of the many "ingredients" of the sciences, but it speaks of man as one who can pursue the sciences. We are not concerned here with man as an object of biology, but with man as a subject—the subject who also pursues biology; we speak of the being-man which is presupposed by the pursuit of the sciences. This is a man as *existent* subject, as project, as "having to be," and its execution, as history. Man is essentially history and, as such, he is radically social.

The answer to the second objection made against the thesis that *existence* is essentially *co-existence* is connected with the first

---

[2]"Das Mitsein ist ein existenziales Konstituens des In-der-Welt-seins. Das Mitdasein erweist sich als eigene Seinsart von innerweltlich begegnendem Seienden. Sofern Dasein überhaupt *ist,* hat es die Seinsart des Miteinanderseins. Dieses kann nicht als summatives Resultat des Vorkommens mehrerer 'Subjekte' begriffen werden." Heidegger, *SZ,* p. 125.

answer. This objection is the following. If *existence* is essentially *co-existence* and the term "essentially" is properly understood—i.e., taken to refer to that through which man is man and not something else—then it follows that in the hypothesis of a "first" man, this "man" may not be called a "man." We would be willing to accept this consequence to a certain extent, but not without indicating to what extent. According to estimates and calculations to which experts attach scientific value, mankind is at least five hundred thousand years old. What kind of man was that man who lived so long ago? Contemporary anthropologists sometimes find tribes who, according to their calculations, are fifty thousand years behind civilized man. One who studies what the being-man of these primitive tribes means can even ask himself whether these people can really be called men. The question can and must be answered in the affirmative: they are human beings. There is, however, also a standpoint from which the question can be answered in the negative: their being-man has not yet reached authenticity on any level. Nevertheless, they are human beings because and to the extent that what they are contains the possibility of rising to the level of authentic manhood—a possibility which a totem pole does not have. The level of authentic manhood, however, will never be reached if their *existence* does not begin to realize itself as *co-existence* in a much more comprehensive fashion.

Applying these ideas to the above-mentioned objection, we must say that the "first man" was not man on an authentically human level because his *existing* was not *co-existing*. The statement, however, that *existence* is *essentially co-existence* applies to man on the authentic level of his being-man. Besides, this is the only level on which there can be question of man. For, if, on the one hand, the "first man" is called man because and insofar as what he actually is contains the possibility of reaching the level of authenticity, it is then evident, that it is only on the basis of a certain understanding of being-man on the actual level of authenticity that there can be question of such a possibility.

Development of the Idea of Co-existence

The general remarks made above about *co-existence* need to be explored now in greater detail. We will do this while keeping in mind the distinctions made in the preceding chapters and consider here successively the *existent* subject as *cogito* (I think), *volo* (I will), and *ago* (I act).

The subject who *exists* as *cogito* evidently is *co-existence*. This statement applies to the prescientific, the scientific, and the philosophical levels of the *cogito*. Let us see each of these three levels.

On the pre-scientific level we find, for instance, the perception of a poker. Perceiving a poker is not a question of stimuli acting on my retina. If I hold a poker before a Papuan, there would be just as many stimuli on his retina as on mine, but he would not perceive a poker. I am able to perceive a poker because of several reasons. First, I have seen others *behave* in a particular way with respect to a poker.[3] This behavior made a certain meaning appear to me, for the meaning of a poker is connected with a certain way of acting. Secondly, this object received a clear "face" for me, distinct from other meanings, because other people gave this object a name: they used the *term* "poker", which is different from other terms. Not only the others' behavior but also their speech made it possible for me to perceive a poker.[4] It is *I* who perceive, but the perceiving *I* only is what it is because the behavior and speech of others are present in my *existence* as *cogito*. If their behaving and speaking were removed from my *existence,* I would not even be able to perceive a poker.

The same applies to the *cogito* on the level of the positive sciences. In the positive sciences there is a "seeing" which is a *personal* "seeing" of the man of science. But his personal seeing presupposes a tradition whose past can no longer be "discovered." This tradition was made by other people, and he who today pursues science lives on that tradition, no matter how great a genius he is. If a genius had to start from a zero level of "seeing," his "seeing" would not reach any scientific level. Other people are always present in one's personal *existence* on the scientific level, and it is they who make this *existence* possible.

Finally, the same applies to philosophizing. We considered this point extensively in Chapter One, where we called philoso-

---
[3]Dondeyne, "De mens en de geschiedenis," *De mens*, Utrecht-Antwerpen, 1958, pp. 32-33.
[4] Kwant, *Phenomenology of Social Existence,* Pittsburgh, 1965, pp. 79-81.

phizing a social enterprise *par excellence* and discussed the value of "classical" thinkers in philosophy. The "classics" of the philosophical tradition *make* us "see." One who today wishes to give *personal* expression to reality cannot avoid discussing a reality that has already been spoken of.[5] Reality "already" is an infinitely varied system of meanings, in which the philosopher "already" lives but of which he himself cannot be called the direct source.[6] One who with his hands tries to grasp things in the world or who walks the world on his feet, does not explicitly account to himself for the meaning his hands and feet have as "I who grasp" and "I who walk." In an analogous fashion, the personal thinker does not explicitly account to himself for the fact that the tradition of thinking has left in him—the "I who think"—a "body," which enables him to make his way in the world.[7] Because man is an "animal of words," he is able to speak *personally*.

Similar ideas impose themselves with respect to the subject as *volo*. The subject who on the affective level of his *existence* is involved in the world is characterized by a certain "mood": the "mood" proper to our time is totally different from that of the man who lived in a primitive world of culture. Between our phase and the primitive phase lies a long history made by other people. By making this history, they also "made" me in my "mood" of *existence*. In my affective life also I am a "child of the twentieth century." But it was the "children of the nineteenth century" who made me this.

The *co-existing* of *existence* manifests itself undeniably also on the level of subjectivity-as-*ago*. Marx was the first philosopher to put full emphasis on this point. For Marx the interconnection of history is constituted by *co-existence* in work. The fact that every generation begins with the tools of work produced by the preceding generations means that every man is tied to the past and dependent upon it.[8] The present genera-

---

5"Ainsi les choses se *trouvent dites* et se *trouvent pensées* comme par une Parole et par un Penser que nous n'avons pas, qui nous ont." Merleau-Ponty, *Signes*, p. 27.

6"Partout il y a sens, dimensions, figures par-delà ce que chaque 'conscience' aurait pu produire, et ce sont pourtant des hommes qui parlent, pensent, voient." Merleau-Ponty, *op. cit.,* p. 28.

7"Nous avons cet acquis comme nous avons des bras, des jambes, nous en usons sans y penser, comme nous 'trouvons' sans y penser nos jambes, nos bras, et Valéry a bien fait d'appeler 'animal de mots' cette puissance parlante où l'expression se prémédite." Merleau-Ponty, *op. cit.,* p. 26.

8 Kwant, *De wijsbegeerte van Karl Marx,* Utrecht, 1961, p. 25.

tion, in its turn, will live on in the future because it will leave behind means of production which serve as the starting point for the work of future generations. Man thus is both the origin and the product, the creator and the creature of history, and in this history work occupies the central position. Because of this central position of work, history is a common history. The bond between men, therefore, is not secured by all kinds of "political or religious nonsense" (*sic*), but by the continuity of the means of production.[9]

As we have shown, Marx takes the concept "work" in too narrow a sense and assigns too large a place to this narrow concept in his philosophy. It remains true, nevertheless, that Marx's emphasis on *co-existenc*e in what he calls work has made it possible for us to understand the radically social character of what we call the subject-as-*ago*. No man is "alone" when he acts: he always bases himself on meanings established by others.

At first sight it seems easy to show that the authenticity of *existence* presupposes other *existences* because we continually referred to the subject's involvement in the cultural world. The cultural world in which I participate, however, is by definition a system of meanings established by *others*. These meanings function as objective correlates of my *existence* as *cogito, volo,* and *ago*. Thus it would be absurd not to name other *existences* in the explicitation of my *existence*.

One could ask whether the same is true for *existence* insofar as it involves me in the "natural" world (assuming that this distinction makes any sense). That the "natural" world is a system of meanings pre-established by others is at least not as evidently true as a similar statement about the cultural world. And even if it were true, would such a statement about the "natural" world not have a different sense?

This difficulty offers us an opportunity to put the proper emphasis where it belongs. It is evident that the cultural world in which I am involved is a system of meanings established by others. But the proper reason why I call my *existence co-*

---

[9]"Es zeigt sich also schon von vornherein ein materialistischer Zusammenhang der Menschen untereinander, der durch die Bedürfnisse und die Weise der Produktion bedingt und so alt ist wie die Menschen selbst - ein Zusammenhang, der stets neue Formen annimmt und also eine 'Geschichte' darbietet, auch ohne dass irgendein politischer oder religiöser Nonsens existiert, der die Menschen noch extra zusammenhalte." K. Marx and Fr. Engels, *Die Deutsche Ideologie,* Berlin, 1953, pp. 26-27.

existence, why I must say that the others are "present" in my *existence,* so that my *existence* must be described as a being-through-others, lies in the fact that the others *make* me participate in the cultural world through their *behavior* and their *speech.* The proper meaning of the thesis that *existence* is *co-existence* lies in the fact that others *make* me be, so that my being is a being-through-others.

One who sees this realizes also that it does not make much difference whether one refers to the cultural world or the "natural" world if one wishes to show that *existence* is *co-existence.* For even when there is question of the "natural" world, the behavior and speech of the others make me be as *cogito, volo,* and *ago.* This is why the other is "present" in my *existence* and why *existence* is *co-existence.* This is also the reason why the distinction between the cultural world and the "natural" world cannot ultimately be maintained.[10] The "first" seeing of "first nature" does not occur anywhere, because for hundreds of thousands of years man has already been busy "opening the eyes" of fellowmen—or "throwing dust" into them.

The Social Body of Man

While paying attention to the details of *co-existence,* it could easily happen that we would lose sight of the totality. Man is, of course, "one": he is the unity of a *Gestalt,* and as such man *makes* man *be.* The fact that we distinguish *cogito, volo,* and *ago* in *existence* does not mean that we simply juxtapose isolated "elements." *Man* makes *man* be. For this reason we must say that "this" man is a New Yorker through New Yorkers, a smoker through smokers, a philosopher through philosophers, a Christian through Christians. Similarly, a mother is a mother through her children; a sick person is really sick only when he is visited or forgotten; a Negro is really a Negro only when Whitey refuses to admit him to his bowling alley or closes the doors of the university to him; an asocial family is really asocial only when other families want to have nothing to do with them, or when the social worker comes for a visit; a cute little button nose is really a cute little button nose only when others notice it;[11] a baldhead is a real baldhead only when he is called that by others. These examples clearly

---

[10] Merleau-Ponty, *PP,* p. 339.
[11] F.J.J. Buytendijk, *Ontmoeting der sexen,* Utrecht, 1962, p. 7.

show the complex *Gestalt* character which our making-one-an-other-be has. The *cogito, volo* and *ago* may and must be distinguished, but they cannot be separated from one another or from the totality.

The fact that it is the totality of man which makes man *be* manifests itself even more clearly if we direct our attention to those domains of being-man in which man either deliberately or unwittingly resorts to the formation of groups. This is the realm in which positive sociology is interested. The realization that individual *existence* cannot reach a level of authenticity unless *existence* embodies itself in forms of *co-existence* is the same as the observation of positive sociologists that the individual man is always found as already incorporated in certain groups, which are strongly determinant in his respect. The positive sociologists investigate the type of interaction and communication existing within a particular group.[12] When they discover a characteristic stability for a specific group,[13] they are able to predict, with a certain probability, that certain interactions will occur among the people in question.[14] The positive social sciences then, empirically detail the philosophical insight that *existence* is *co-existence*. They are pre-eminently "debunking" sciences:[15] they show how much the others, the group, are present in my *existence* when I think that it is *I* who thinks or acts. In every group there "predominate" more or less accepted views and more or less fixed patterns of acting. Every group lives a more or less stereotyped "way of doing things." That there is a "way of doing things" is a significant expression: it is as if the individual subjects do not count in the acting of the group.

Young people are often said to "enter" life. But this is not what happens. Rather, they are "pushed" into it. "Life" is governed by the "way of doing things." It refers to the way of moving, eating and drinking, taking recreation and being bored, thinking, being virtuous and sinful, engaging in politics and participating in worship, cultivating an art and appreciating it,

---

12J.A.A. van Doorn and C.J. Lammers, *Moderne sociologie,* 3rd ed., Utrecht, 1962, pp. 34-37.
13"Neither soccer club nor trade union, family nor circle of friends, society nor state could be topics of scientific inquiry if it were impossible to discover in them routine ways of acting and standardized attitudes." van Doorn and Lammers, *op. cit.,* p. 44.
14van Doorn and Lammers, *op. cit.,* p. 45.
15Erich Fechner, *Rechtsphilosophie, Soziologie und Metaphysik des Rechts,* Tübingen, 1956, p. 268.

advertising, working, having a sexual life, being ill, etc. Entering life is in the first instance not much more than being incorporated into the "way of doing things" which has become a fixed pattern within a group. This incorporation implies that the group makes the individual *existence* think, act, and be, in accordance with the group's patterns.[16]

The emphasis placed here on the quasi-process of making one another *be* clearly shows that making one another be is the indispensable condition for the authenticity of *personal existence.* This may seem to be in contradiction with the preceding paragraphs. Did we not say there that whatever an *existence* thinks that it is, thinks or does is in reality nothing but the result and repercussion of the group's "pressure"? How, then, can we now assert that making one another *be* is the indispensable condition for the authentic character of *personal existence?* Is it still possible to speak of the "person" and the "subject" if one takes seriously the unmistakable reality that we *make* one another be?

Sociologism

Sociologism answers this question in the negative:[17] man is nothing but the product of "social processes." It is necessary for the philosopher to have experienced at least once the serious temptation of adhering to sociologism if he does not wish to minimize the unmistakable importance of *co-existence,* of *making* one another be. Speaking of materialism, we pointed out that the materialist is *almost* right: the materialist takes seriously the insight that man is man on the basis of materiality. There are aspects of being-man which can be discussed by the sciences, and they treat these aspects as the results of cosmic forces and processes. Thus there is a temptation to present man as if he were nothing but the result of cosmic forces and processes. Similarly, the insight that man makes man think, act, and be includes a temptation to say that man is *nothing but* the result of social processes and forces.

---

[16]"In dieser Unauffälligkeit und Nichtfeststellbarkeit entfaltet das Man seine eigentliche Diktatur. Wir geniessen und vergnügen uns, wie man geniesst; wir lesen, sehen und urteilen über Literatur und Kunst, wie man sieht und urteilt; wir ziehen uns aber auch vom 'grossen Haufen' zurück, wie man sich zurückzieht; wir finden 'empörend' was man empörend findet. Das Man, das kein bestimmtes ist und das Alle, obzwar nicht als Summe, sind, schreibt die Seinsart der Alltäglichkeit vor." Heidegger, *SZ*, pp. 126-127.

[17]Kwant, *Phenomenology of Social Existence,* pp. 105 f.

In the history of my encounters with others, my life in many groups, these many encounters leave something behind in my own *existence*. In my dealing with others on all levels of my *existence* there occurs a quasi-process of sedimentation, and the quasi-effect of it is called "social facticity" [18] or my "social body." [19] Man has not only a "natural body" [20] but also a "cultural body" and a "social body." My "cultural body" [21] is the facticity which remains behind in my *existence* as a result of my personal actions.[22] My "social body" is the facticity which deposits itself in my *existence* in and through my togetherness with others. In *co-existence* the other "influences" me, but his "influence" is not a process in the strict sense of the term, as the influence of a thing upon a thing is a process. The reason is that my social body remains *my* body: it is the social body of the *existent* subject who I am.[23] As *existent,* the subject is immersed in the social body, gives meaning to it and "can still do all kinds of things with it," as, e.g., a baldhead gives a meaning to his bare pate and he "can still do all kinds of things" with this aspect of his "natural body." No more than the "natural body," then, the social body is an effect: it is not merely the result of unilateral and deterministic causes.[24] The "influence" of the other is a quasi-process, and the social body is a quasi-effect.

It is precisely the importance of the subject which is dis-

---

[18]Kwant, *op. cit.,* pp. 122-138.

[19]"Le corps en général est un ensemble de chemins déjà tracés, de pouvoirs déjà constitués, le sol dialectique acquis sur lequel s'opère une mise en forme supérieure." Merleau-Ponty, *StC,* p. 227.

[20]This *corps nature* obviously is not the reality of the human body studied by the biologist, but the "lived body."

[21]*StC,* p. 227, note 1.

[22]This does not mean that my "natural body" is not a social reality. It is such a reality because the others are "present" in my personal actions. Indirectly, then, the "cultural body" is also a "social body."

[23]"Wird mir daher mein soziales Ich auch aufgedrängt, ich kann mich doch *innerlich* gegen es wehren. Obschon ich unerbittlich an mein soziales Dasein gekettet bin und in ihm mein Selbstbewusstsein im Spiegel meiner Tätigkeit erhalte, kann ich mich ihm doch noch wieder als mich selbst gegenüberstellen. Trotz sozialen Gewinnes und Verlustes kann ich in allem Wandel ich selbst bleiben. Ich falle nicht mehr zusammen mit meinem sozialen Ich, wenn ich auch in jedem Moment zugleich in ihm bin. . . . Mein soziales Ich, das ich nicht aufhöre zu sein, so wenig ich aufhöre, als Körper da zu sein, wird mir selbst zum Gegenstand, aus dem ich mich zugleich zurückhalte." Jaspers, *Philosophie,* p. 320.

[24]"Ich bin nicht Ergebnis der soziologischen Konstellationen, denn ich bleibe, wenn ich auch in allem, was von mir objektiv in die Erscheinung tritt, durch mein soziologisches Dasein bestimmt bin, aus meinem Ursprung die Möglichkeit meiner selbst." Jaspers, *ibid.*

regarded and ultimately simply eliminated by sociologism. What man *personally* thinks and does presupposes the social body which "deposits" itself in man's *existence* through the others' *making*-be. This making-be and its quasi-effect—my social body—make it possible for me *myself* to think and act.[25] If man does not receive his social body from others, his thinking and acting cannot realize themselves on any level of authenticity. The fact that man receives his social body from others, however, does not mean that his personal thinking and acting are nothing but repercussions of the group's "pressure," for his social body itself—albeit a prerequisite for personal action—is not simply the effect of a social process. There is no contradiction between the subject and the social body,[26] but there is a unity of reciprocal implication.[27]

The proper importance of the subject in reference to the "weight" of the social body can perhaps also be detailed somewhat in the following way. If personal thinking and acting were nothing but the repercussion of the pressure exercised by the social body, then the undeniable fact that *new* meaning is sometimes established in history would be wholly unintelligible: for instance, the "Greek miracle" would have been impossible.[28] A meaning is new when at first it was not present in the way it is now present. This newness presupposes the spontaneity, the creativity of the subject, and these cannot be reduced to the "pressure" of what was already present. If the philosophy of Heidegger is called new, this does not mean that the past is not present in it. Heidegger, too, has a social body, and without this body his philosophy would not have reached any level. The newness of his philosophy means that Heidegger cannot be re-

---

[25] "Ich will nicht nur, um materiell da zu sein, meine Rolle ergreifen, sondern auch um ich selbst zu werden; ich kenne mich nur in ihr und bin doch mit ihr nicht identisch." Jaspers, *ibid.*

[26] "Ainsi nous savons, à présent, que la dialectique concrète c'est celle qui se dévoile à travers la *praxis* commune d'un groupe; mais nous savons aussi que l'indépassabilité (par l'union des individus) de l'action organique comme modèle strictement individuel est la condition fondamentale de la rationalité historique, c'est-à-dire qu'il faut rapporter la Raison dialectique constituée (comme intelligibilité vivante de toute *praxis* commune) à son fondement toujours présent et toujours masqué, la rationalité constituante. Sans cette limitation rigoureuse et permanente qui renvoie du groupe à ce fondement, la communauté *n'est pas moins abstraite* que l'individu isolé: il y a des bergeries révolutionnaires sur le groupe qui sont l'exact pendant des robinsonnades." Sartre, *Critique de la raison dialectique,* Paris, 1960, p. 643.

[27] Kwant, *op. cit.,* p. 163-177.

[28] Merleau-Ponty, *Signes,* p. 304.

duced to the "pressure" exercised on him by other previously constituted philosophies.

Accordingly, it is not the social body "alone" which builds meaning in the thinking and acting of personal *existence*. The unity of reciprocal implication of subject and social body thinks and acts.[29] Insofar as the subject through his spontaneity and creativity transcends the facticity of the social body, it is possible for new meaning to appear or to be created in history. Moreover, it is beyond dispute that the subject keeps his social body alive, neglects it, or even in some respects lets it die. The social body of man does not "live" solely and entirely through the group's pressure. The subject's non-identity with his social body makes it possible for him to distance himself from, or to consent to, his social body. This consent keeps the social body alive. If the subject no longer is able or willing to give his consent because the spontaneity of his subjectivity no longer finds support in his social body, then this body begins to degenerate. The patterns of group life do not have the stability of a rock.

Analogous ideas impose themselves with respect to the social facticity which lies on the side of the world. Canals and roads, cars and planes, books and libraries, works of art and museums, schools and hospitals, educational systems and medical institutions, industrial plants, methods of production and institutes for the poor—all these belong to the social facticity lying on the side of the world. They form part of man's "inorganic social body." They are the result of a long and common history. The subject has established the world's social facticity; it is the subject who keeps it alive and who also projects it toward a new future.[30]

Marx failed to realize this. He achieved the undeniable insight that the meaning founded by history transcends the initiative of the individualistically conceived subject in every direction. But this insight misled him because he was unable to conceive

---

[29]"Il est vrai que l'individu est conditionné par le milieu social et se retourne sur lui pour le conditionner; c'est même cela - et rien d'autre - qui fait sa réalité." J-P. Sartre, *op. cit.*, p. 52.

[30]"Il faut donc voir au niveau de la *praxis* individuelle (peu nous importe, pour l'instant, quelles sont les contraintes collectives qui la suscitent, la limitent ou lui ôtent son efficacité) quelle est la rationalité proprement dite de l'action." Sartre, *op. cit.*, p. 166.

any other subject.[31]   Marx knew only the Cartesian concept of subjectivity.   Conceived in this way, "the" subject could not possibly be called the subject of history.   This induced Marx to withdraw history entirely from the subject's initiative.   But history thus becomes a process and no longer is *really* history. Real history presupposes a subject, but a real subject implies the "flesh of history" [32] or social facticity.

Summarizing, we must say that *existence* is *co-existence*.[33] This does not mean that there is an agglomerate of superadded *existences*,[34] or, as Sartre holds, that man has to be with fellowmen for no other reason than that there happen to be fellowmen. Heidegger explicitly affirms that *co-existing* is an "existentiale," an essential characteristic of man.[35]   What for Heidegger is an insight into man's essence is for Sartre nothing but an "empirical observation." [36]   This need not surprise us, for Sartre's concept of the subject is Cartesian.   Such a view, however, is untenable.

Binswanger has more impressive objections to Heidegger and, by implication, to everything we have said above.   Binswanger does not deny that man's being must be called a being-"we"; [37] but in his eyes this admission fails to express what is most important, viz., that being-"we" is "the loving being-together of 'me' and 'you.' " [38]   When *existence* is called *co-existence* with a reference to the "social body" and the "flesh of history," nothing whatsoever has yet been said about this loving togetherness of me and you.

---

[31]Kwant, *The Phenomenological Philosophy of Merleau-Ponty*, Pittsburgh, p. 87.

[32]Merleau-Ponty, *op. cit.*, p. 28.

[33]Heidegger, *SZ*, p. 118.

[34]"Le monde communicatif n'est un faisceau de consciences parallèles. Les traces se broisillent et passent l'une dans l'autre, elles font un seul sillage de 'durée publique'." Merleau-Ponty, *op. cit.*, p. 28.

[35]"Das Mitsein ist ein existenziales Konstituens des In-der-Welt-seins. Das Mitdasein erweist sich als eigene Seinsart von innerweltlich begegnendem Seienden.   Sofern das Dasein überhaupt ist, hat es die Seinsart des Miteinanderseins.   Dieses kann nicht als summatives Resultat des Vorkommens mehrerer 'Subjekte' begriffen werden." *SZ*, p. 125.

[36]"Pourquoi devient-elle le fondement unique de notre être, pourquoi est-elle le type fondamental de notre rapport avec les autres, pourquoi Heidegger s'est-il cru autorisé à passer de cette constatation empirique et ontique de l'être-avec à la position de la coexistence comme structure ontologique de mon être-dans-le-monde?" Sartre, *EN*, p. 304.

[37]L. Binswanger, *Grundformen und Erkenntnis menschlichen Daseins*, Zürich, 1953, p. 267.

[38]"Das Wersein des Daseins im Sinne des 'Ich und Du' oder der dualen Wirheit finden wir jedoch nirgends." *op. cit.*, p. 65.

Heidegger's explanations, however, contain a passage in which he goes—at least in passing—beyond the framework of his own thoughts. He mentions the experience of being-alone, and describes it as a deficient mode of being-together *(Mitsein)*.[39] I can only be alone—I can only miss the other—if I am called to a being-together which is not identical with *co-existence* in the sense used in the preceding paragraphs. Even if I know myself to be alone, I still have a social body and my world is still a "common world" *(Mitwelt)*. Nevertheless, I feel alone. This means that *co-existence* has more than one dimension. We will return to this point later.

2. THE BODY AS INTERMEDIARY

It cannot be denied that the meaning of the world for the other is accessible to me. The letter I write is for me a matter of pen, paper, and an announcement; but for the recipient this same letter is perhaps something which he awaits in fear and trembling. *His* fear and trembling, however, are also meanings for me, they are accessible to me. I probably took these meanings into account when I wrote the letter. This means that I took the other subject into account: the other is not concealed from me but is accessible.

In everyday life such things are accepted as a matter of course. Anyone admits that the patient is accessible to the physician, the customer to the salesman, the student to the teacher. The thief is unconcealed from the policeman who catches him, the naughty child is not concealed from his mother. This does not mean, of course, that the other's subjectivity and his subjective intentions are ever fully transparent: they are and remain a mystery both for me and for the other subject himself. But this mysteriousness does not imply that I cannot *see* the other as a subject. If psychologists and philosophers have experienced the greatest difficulty in admitting, without qualifications, that it is possible for me to see the other subject, the reason must be sought in the fact that Cartesian philosophy had, strictly speaking, made this "impossible."

---

[39] "Auch das Alleinsein des Daseins ist Mitsein in der Welt. Fehlen kann der Andere nur in einem und für ein Mitsein. Das Alleinsein ist ein defizienter Modus des Mitseins, seine Möglichkeit ist der Beweis für dieses." *SZ*, p. 120.

The Impossibility of "Seeing One Another"

The Cartesian explicitations of the relationship between subject and body are the reason why it became impossible to conceive any direct contact between one conscious "I" and another conscious "I." For the subject was conceived as hidden and concealed in the machine to which the body was reduced. The subjectivity of the other person was, likewise, hidden and concealed in his body. In that case a direct contact of my subjectivity with that of another man is, of course, no longer conceivable: [40] my subjectivity is isolated from my body, my body is separated from the other's body and, finally, the other's subjectivity also is isolated from his body.[41] If "we" look at each other, this would mean that I "look at a machine" and that you "look at a machine." Thus I cannot really *see* that the other person is sad or happy, I cannot hear that he is furious or frightened to death.

Actually, however, no one admits that he cannot really do this. Anyone can do it. The philosophers knew this, of course, and for this reason they tried to restore this possibility *in spite of* Descartes' explicitations.

The usual argument was as follows. "Despite the fact that I am an interiority, my interiority manifests itself outwardly in bodily movements of expression. There exists a certain constancy in the relationship between my interior states and my bodily expressions: particular inner states are exteriorized in and by particular bodily movements. Now, I perceive in the other person the expressive movements through which I myself exteriorize particular inner states. This analogy gives me the right to conclude that an interiority is present in the other and that in him also there are those inner states to which I myself give expression by means of the bodily movements I perceive now in the other." [42]

Many psychologists went to great pains in order to formulate empirical laws governing the relationship between interiority

---

[40]"Si les âmes sont séparées par leurs corps, elle sont distinctes comme cet encrier est distinct de ce livre, c'est-à-dire qu'on ne peut concevoir aucune présence immédiate de l'une à l'autre." Sartre, *EN*, p. 277.

[41]"L'âme d'autrui est donc séparée de la mienne par toute la distance qui sépare tout d'abord mon âme de mon corps, puis mon corps du corps d'autrui, enfin le corps d'autrui de son âme." *EN*, p. 277.

[42]*EN*, p. 278.

and expression. They made distinctions between gross movements of expression, such as mimics and pantomimics, and more refined symptoms of expression, such as the pressure and frequency of pulse, depth of breathing, glandular secretions, and the electric conductivity of brain tissue. Inspired as they were by physical science, these psychologists felt at home here, for the symptoms of expression lent themselves to accurate measurements.[43] By means of appropriate instruments, they hoped to attain the exactness of physical science.[44]

It is not necessary to enter into details in this matter. Today, after many years of acceptance, it has become evident that the so-called argument from analogy does not "explain" the presence of, and the contact with the other subject *as* a subject. This means that the *de facto* existence of this contact with the other "in person" is not justified by the argument from analogy, i.e., it is not presented as a *possibility*. Within a Cartesian context, I simply *cannot see* the other. One could point out that such an argument from analogy is something which actually does not occur. If I hear someone groaning with pain, he is directly and "in person" present to me, without the slightest trace of any reasoning on my part by analogy. Thus, to say the least, one needs a large dose of optimism to base his certainty of the other's presence as another subject on reasoning by analogy.

Even if we disregard this point, there remains a much more serious difficulty: the above-described argument from analogy *presupposes* the presence "in person" of the other, the direct contact of my subjectivity with that of the other; yet its very purpose is to make this contact theoretically possible. "I perceive in the other person the expressive movements through which I myself exteriorize particular inner states," says the argument from analogy. But why do I speak here of *expressive* movements? Why not of mechanical movements? The reason is that I *presuppose* that the other is a subject and not a machine. Only in this presupposition is it possible for me to call certain bodily movements and symptoms *expressive* movements: without this presupposition, they are, in the Cartesian train of thought, purely mechanical movements. But the very purpose of the argument from analogy precisely was to justify the assumption

---

[43]F. Roels, *Handboek der Psychologie*, Utrecht, 1934, I, pp. 66-67.
[44]G. Dumas, *La vie affective*, Paris, 1948.

that the other is a subject. *Expression* was adduced in support
of this justification, but one can only speak of expression when
the other's subjectivity has already been recognized. Granted
that I give expression in a particular way to a particular inner
state, if I cannot *directly see* the other's subjectivity, then the
beings I see laughingly strolling around in the street can still be
conceived as machines. At most, one could say that probably
they are not machines.[45]

Accordingly, the argument from analogy presupposes the
very thing it intended to justify, viz., the presence of the other
as the other. Nevertheless, I am certain that the other is present
to me "in person." Thus it is not surprising that other theories
were invented to justify this certainty. Among these we may
name the empathy theories (Dilthey, Simmel, Scheler), but they
also have to presuppose what they intend to justify. For why
do I use the empathy method only to understand my fellowman,
and not to discover a malfunctioning in my alarm clock? While
the empathy theories make it possible to give a better description
of the means by which we can place ourselves in the other's
presence, they do not explain the fact that the other appears to
us as the other.[46] The other's unconcealedness is continually
presupposed.[47]

It could hardly be otherwise. The unconcealedness of the
other as the other is like an open door through which the phenomenologist finally enters again. It is not at all necessary to appeal to an argument from analogy or to an empathy theory to
"explain" the presence of the other as the other: the encounter
with the other is directly and immediately distinguished from
that with a mere *thing*. The other's body, "at which I look,"
is not "a" body belonging to the large family of "bodies," [48] but
human, a body *subject*. For this reason it directly reveals itself
as the other, as not-a-thing.[49] It is the other "in person"
whom I see shaking with fear, whom I hear sighing with cares.

45"On reconnaîtra volontiers que ces procédés peuvent seulement nous
donner d'autrui une connaissance *probable*: il reste toujours possible qu'autrui
ne soit qu'un corps. Si les animaux sont des machines, pourquoi l'homme que
je vois passer dans la rue n'en serait-il pas une?" *EN*, p. 278.

46*EN*, p. 279.

47*SZ*, pp. 124-125.

48"Ce n'est pas le *corps d'autrui* qui est présent à l'intuition réaliste:
c'est *un* corps. Un corps qui . . . appartient à la grande famille des corps."
EN, p. 278.

49Merleau-Ponty, *SNS*, p. 187.

I feel his cordiality in his handshake, the mildness of his voice and the benevolence of his look. Similarly, one who hates me, who is indifferent with respect to me, bored by me, afraid of me, who despises or distrusts me, who wishes to console me, seduce or rebuke me, convince or amuse me—he, too, is in person present to me. His look, his gesture, his word and his attitude are always *his* look, gesture, word, and attitude: he is immediately and directly present to me in person.

The fact that in Cartesian philosophy the human body was not conceived as *human* made it impossible to admit that I can see the other as the other. In Descartes' philosophy the "human" body was viewed as an object of the sciences. When the other subject looks at me, his eye is "he-who-looks-at-me," but for the sciences the eye is something entirely different: it is a lens; it has a cornea and a retina. Because it is a lens, the eye belongs to the objects of optic geometry. The dissection of cadavers showed that a bundle of nerves leads from the retina to the brain. When scalpels and microscopes became more perfect, it became possible to follow the course of those nerves from their starting point to their terminus. One who speaks in this way about the eye, does indeed speak of the eye, but in his analysis, he· *presupposes* an entirely different eye, viz., "my eye," understood as "I-who-see," the *human* eye.[50] When human eyes look at each other, human beings encounter each other. Their presence to each other is not the "presence" of lenses, or of things.

The presence of things reveals itself as an entirely different kind of presence. The way a rolling rock comes toward me in a narrow mountain pass is entirely different from the way an angry police officer comes toward me. My desk does not groan under my elbows; my pen does not give me a hurt look when I abuse it; I do not blame the apple which falls from the tree and strikes my head; and I do not expect that my dog will congratulate me on my birthday.

The other's unconcealedness, his direct presence to me as the other, I simply have to accept as something primordially given. Any "proof" for it is superfluous because it is immediately evident, and any attempt to make it acceptable to me that the other

---

[50]"(Ces connaissances) impliquaient, en outre, que nous pouvons *voir* cet oeil, le toucher, c'est-à-dire que nous soyons nous-mêmes pourvus d'un point de vue sensible sur les choses." *EN*, p. 373.

as the other can be present to me, appears to presuppose his presence to me.[51]

Is the Body "Intermediary" or Not "Intermediary"?

From the preceding considerations it should be clear that there is at least a danger of misunderstanding in the assertion that the body "mediates" in human encounters. Encounters between men are possible because man in a certain sense "is" his body. Insofar as man "is" his body, the encounter of man with his fellowman occurs without any intermediary whatsoever. With respect to the bodily movements of expression spoken of by the argument from analogy, one could say that they must be conceived as intermediaries, or rather as attempts to be intermediaries, because the reasoning from analogy starts with the *separation* between the subject and the world. But precisely this separation must be rejected. Man does not "have" "a" body.

As Marcel has convincingly shown, the categories of "having" do not without qualifications apply to "my body." The object of "having" exists "to a certain extent" independently of me; it reveals a distance from me, I can dispose of it and do away with it.[52] I "have" a car, a pen, and a book. "My body," however, does not exist independently of me, as does my pen; it does not reveal the same distance from me as the pen; I cannot dispose of "my body" and do away with it, as I dispose or do away with my collection of stamps.[53] For "my body" is not "a" body: "my body" is that which embodies *me*.

For the same reason "my body" is not an instrument, as a hammer or a microscope are instruments. Instruments are extensions of "my body": if, then, I consider "my body" as an instrument, of which body is "my body" an extension? "My body" is not an instrument because it is mine, because it is merged with the conscious "I" which I am.[54]

---

[51]Heidegger uses different terms to indicate the variety of man's relationships with the worldly thing and the other. To the worldly things I am related in an attitude of "concern" (*Besorgen*), but my relationship with the other is called "solicitude" (Fürsorge). "Das Seiende zu dem sich das Dasein als Mitsein verhält, hat aber nicht die Seinsart des zuhandenen Zeugs, es ist selbst Dasein. Dieses Seiende wird nicht besorgt, sondern steht in der Fürsorge." *SZ*, p. 121.

[52]Marcel, *EA*, p. 225.

[53]Marcel, *JM*, p. 301.

[54]"Si je pense mon corps comme instrument, j'attribue par là, disons à l'âme dont il serait l'outil, les virtualités même dont il assurerait l'actualisation; cette âme, je la convertis en corps, et par conséquent le problème se pense à nouveau pour elle." Marcel, *RI*, p. 29.

If the separation between subject and body is undone, one can understand that in the look, gesture, attitude, and word of the other I really encounter the other as subject. The other's body is "his body." The other lives "in person" in his look, his gesture, his attitude, and his word.[55] Thus I encounter the other as the other, as a subject, when he looks at me with love, hatred or indifference; when he makes a gesture toward me, assumes a threatening attitude, or addresses words to me, for his bodily form is the embodiment of his subjectivity.

Only to the extent that there exists "a certain" non-identity between subject "and" body may one say that in the encounter of human beings the body offers "a certain" mediation. To exclude Cartesianism, we must say that man "is" his body. The dividing line between subject "and" body must be blotted out.[56] But even when this line is blotted out, there remains "a certain" non-identity between the subject "and" the body. The subject who I am is not without qualification my feet or my nose.[57] In a certain sense, then, I "have" "my body," for if I were to say without any qualifications that I am "my body," I would be fully encompassed by the world of mere things. (Let us add that the statement, "I am my body," without any qualifications, is a contradiction, because the term "my" does not retain any meaning.) The subject who I am would be "annulled," and therefore also my body as mine and the world as my world. Insofar as there exists "a certain" non-identity between subject "and" world, I must say that I "have" "my body." My body is the transition from what I *am* without qualification to what I *have* without qualification. I am a subject and I have a car. But with respect to "my body" neither "being" nor

---

[55] *JM,* pp. 325-329.

[56] "Notre siècle a effacé la ligne de partage du 'corps' et de l' 'esprit' et voit la vie humaine comme spirituelle et corporelle de part en part, toujours appuyée au corps, toujours intéressée, jusque dans ses modes les plus charnels, aux rapports des personnes. Pour beaucoup de penseurs, à la fin du XIXe siècle, le corps, c'était un morceau de matière, un faisceau de mécanismes. Le XXe siècle a restauré et approfondi la notion de la chair, c'est-à-dire du corps animé." Merleau-Ponty, *Signes,* p. 287.

[57] "Cette identité supposée est un non-sens; elle ne peut être affirmée qu'à la faveur d'un acte implicite d'annulation du *je* et se change alors en une affirmation matérialiste: mon corps, c'est moi, mon corps existe seul. Mais cette affirmation est absurde; le propre de mon corps est de ne pas exister seul, de ne pouvoir exister seul. Nous réfugerions-nous alors dans l'idee d'un monde des corps? Mais qu'est-ce qui confère l'unité? qu'est-ce qui le pense comme monde? et d'autre part, que devient dans ce monde purement objectif le principe d'intimité (*mon* corps) autour duquel se constituait l'orbite existentielle?" *RI,* p. 30.

"having" can be affirmed *without qualification*.[58] "My body" lies precisely "midway" between these two,[59] and to this extent one can say that the body acts as an "intermediary" in the encounter between human beings.

The body does not merely "mediate" in the other's disclosure of himself, but is also a possibility for him to conceal himself. I, too, can conceal myself. Man can simulate, pretend, dissimulate, mask, and lie in his relation with his fellowmen. And again, it is the body that acts as an "intermediary." But precisely in understanding the many modes of concealing oneself, man's unconcealedness for his fellowman is affirmed. Self-concealment is possible only on the basis of unconcealedness.

There is still another reason why the body must be said to be an "intermediary" in my encounter with the other. There exists "a certain" non-identity of subject "and" body, there is "a certain" distance between them, but there is even a "greater" distance between the subject who the other is and the world of the other. Since, however, the human body is the transition from subject to world, in the encounter with the other, I participate also, through the "mediating" function of his body, in the meaning which the world has for him. The body of the other not only makes it possible for me to encounter *him* but also to enter into his world, that complex of meanings existing *for him*. Through the intermediary of his body, the complex of meanings for him also becomes a complex of meanings for me.

When, for instance, I am seated alongside the driver, I enter by "way" of the behavior of the other's body and its extension— the car—into the meaning which the road, hills, curves, narrow bridge and oncoming traffic have for him. If I am nervous because of his excessive speed, he enters by "way" of my body into the meaning the narrow bridge we are entering has for me. When I watch a carpenter at work, I am by "way" of his body involved in his world, and the meanings which saw, hammer and nails have for him disclose themselves to me. I place myself in the meaning which my garden and trees have for the neigh-

---

[58]"Etre incarné, c'est s'apparaître comme corps, comme ce corps-ci, sans pouvoir s'identifier à lui, sans pouvoir non plus s'en distinguer - identification et distinction étant des opérations corrélatives l'une de l'autre, mais qui ne peuvent s'exercer que dans la sphère des objets." *RI*, p. 31.

[59]"L'expérience du corps propre au contraire nous revèle un mode d'existence ambigue." *PP*, p. 231.

borhood boys when I see them sneaking in under the hedge.
The words my friend uses in describing distant lands I have
never visited place me in his world. Through his words I enter
into his world and his world becomes meaningful to me: his
world becomes my world, our world.

To Co-exist as to "Accompany"

All this indicates the very special way of the other's presence
to me. The encounter with the other reveals him to me as "not
a thing," but as *existence,* as an origin of meaning. Because the
other is not a thing, he "accompanies" me: [60] he is my "companion," and for this reason I can speak of "we." A thing
is not really my companion.

Is it right, however, to say so explicitly that the other accompanies *me*? Why should he be *my* companion? Am I not
his companion? Who are the others? Are they, perchance,
the rest of mankind, from whom I distinguish myself? By
what right, however, would I "first" affirm myself and "next" the
others as the mass above which I elevate myself? No, rather,
the others are those from whom I do not distinguish myself: they
are those among whom I *also* am.[61] *We* accompany one another.

In the following pages we will use the term "to accompany"
to refer to *co-existing* in the above-described sense, viz., *co-
existence* in "encounter" with, and "presence" to the other as a
subject. When in the preceding section we described *existence*
as *co-existence,* "encounter" with, and "presence" to the other
as the other did not receive the emphasis and relief we have
in mind now. We called *existence "co-existence"* and intended
to describe *existence* as the unity of the reciprocal implication
of subjectivity "and" the social body. We saw there that my
"social body" is the quasi-effect of a "way of doing things"—
initiated and carried by others, but a "way" in which I as a
subject was not at first involved. The reception and carrying of
a "social body" as the quasi-effect of a "way of doing things" lies
far less on the level of the personal "encounter" with, and the

---

[60]"Dieses Seiende ist weder vorhanden noch zuhanden, sondern ist so, wie
das freigebende Dasein selbst - es ist auch und mit da." *SZ,* p. 118.

[61]" 'Die Anderen' besagt nicht soviel wie der ganze Rest der Übrigen ausser
mir, aus dem sich das Ich heraushebt, die Anderen sind vielmehr die, von
denen man selbst sich zumeist nicht unterscheidet, unter denen man auch ist."
SZ, p. 118.

"presence" to the other as other than does the mutual "accompanying" with which we are now concerned. Before discussing the various forms of accompanying each other, however, we must first clarify here a terminological question.

To indicate the mutual implication of subject "and" world, we have used the terms "encounter" and "presence." Here, where there is question of the other as the other, these terms are used again; but they have now an entirely different sense, for the other reveals himself as a meaning which is distinct from that of a thing. It is to emphasize this difference in meaning that we use the term "accompany." The encounter with the other—his presence—reveals the other to me as one "like-me-in-the-world," a meaning which I never notice when I encounter things. Because the other is like-me-in-the-world, he is my "companion-in-the-world."

The same applies to the term "dialog." I am a dialog with the world because what I am is not conceivable without the world, and my world is not without me. A dialog is not conceivable without the two "partners" who "speak" with each other. But the way in which the other participates in the dialog with me when I encounter him differs radically from the way the worldly thing answers my questions. The other subject answers me as another "I," he answers me as I answer him when he asks me a question, and this is something which no thing is able to do.

Modes of "Accompanying One Another"

It is the task of positive sociology to describe the manifold forms of accompanying one another and to attempt to formulate the empirical laws governing the interaction and communication existing within those forms of being a "we." It goes without saying that this task will never be finished. One has only to recall how variegated the ways are of man's behavior toward his fellowmen. The "we" means a relation of the "I" to another "I," a "You." Obviously, this relationship varies all the time, e.g., when there is question of working together, drinking together, travelling together in the same plane, having an accident together, etc. The "we" of a labor union differs from that of a military barracks and that of a convent, the "we" experienced by patients in a hospital ward differs from that of a youth hostel, a hockey club, a lecture hall, or a cinema. Examples could be multiplied *ad infinitum,* and it is very difficult to bring order to this enormous variety of forms.[62]

The situation of these "we"-forms is similar to that of the world's meanings. My world is an enormously complex system of nearby and remote meanings corresponding to my actual or no longer actual attitudes. Any attempt to absolutize a particular attitude makes a genuine understanding of my world impossible. The tendency, however, to absolutize a particular attitude and the corresponding system of meanings, appears difficult to overcome. Yet, giving in to it means an impoverishment of man and an ever-increasing danger of becoming totally blind to whatever cannot be pressed into certain categories.

The insight that absolutizing a particular standpoint implies impoverishment and blindness, imposes the greatest prudence on us in connection with the recognition of the many forms in which "accompanying one another" occurs. It is essential to realize that this pluriformity lies on different levels. People speak of "human relations" in the family, the school, the factory and office, the armed forces, medical help, spiritual care, etc.[63] One can describe these relationships and try to formulate the "rules of the game" governing the fundamental forms of man's dealing with his fellowmen. This is done, for instance, by Josef Pieper.[64] Obviously, such an attempt is the work of the sociologist. One can, however, also observe that in the many changes which have occurred in human relationships, we have "lost genuine humanity," [65] and that "intimate values, enriching man in a definite humane sense" [66] have disappeared. This is done, for example, by F. Rutten. Such an observation no longer asks about actual sociological forms of accompanying one another, but is interested in the conditions which permit us to call human relationships "human" in the full sense of the term. For our relations can also be inhuman.

All this indicates that the pluriformity of accompanying one another lies on different levels. We realize that, in no matter

---

[62]M. Nédoncelle, *Vers une philosophie de l'amour,* Paris, 1946, pp. 125-138.
[63]F.J.Th. Rutten, *Menselijke verhoudingen,* Bussum, 1955.
[64]J. Pieper, *Grundformen sozialer Spielregeln,* Frankfurt a.M., 1955.
[65]Rutten, *op. cit.,* p. 11.
[66]Rutten, *op. cit.,* p. 46.

which sociological form [67] of *co-existence,* we always either approach or draw away from an *ideal* of mutual companionship which is, at the same time, an ideal of authentic humanity. If in a labor organization all functionaries are perfectly attuned to one another, so that the goal of the organization is realized, one could—perhaps—say that, sociologically speaking, there is here a perfect form of accompanying one another. But at the same time, it is possible and even probable that these sociologically perfect human relations are inhuman.[68]

Thus there is every reason for making a distinction between *sociological* forms of companionship and others, which we will from now on call *ethical.* In any sociological form man can be authentically human, less human, or even inhuman. This idea obviously presupposes that man *is* not in the same way as an ashtray or a cauliflower *is,* but the being of man is a "having to be," it has a certain destiny.

The sociologists investigate the character of the many forms which human companionship can have with a special intention or attitude. The ethicists do the same, but with a different intention. We will limit ourselves here to those fundamental ethical forms. At present, we can merely enumerate them, without attempting to justify the division: they are hatred, indifference, love, and justice.

To speak true to life about love and justice, however, is possible only if one sees that these terms do not refer to *commandments*—at least not if commandments are understood as laws that "hang in the air" and are imposed upon man from without. If they are conceived in this way, one can never show that man *ought* to love and be just, in the sense in which one always wishes to understand this "ought," viz., as a demand flowing from man's being as something which his very manhood demands—an inner "ought," and not an externally imposed requirement. Love and justice are modes of being-man as characterized by his "having to be." Hatred and indifference

---

[67] We do not wish to dispute here whether or not the term *"sociological* form" is correct. Our intention should be evident.

[68] We abstract here from the fact that when the relations are not *human* it is usually also impossible to speak of a *perfect* labor organization and the *perfect* realization of its aims. This is the reason why even those who wish to foster purely economic interests are also interested in the humanity of their labor organizations.

also are modes of being-man, now being understood as modes in which man *ought not* to realize himself.

The fourfold division is not a division into four "pieces." Hatred, indifference, love, and justice are not juxtaposed as things, as marbles, wigs, courts of justice, and clouds. They are modes in which the one, concrete man can and does realize himself. One can even say that "all four" are always realities in the concrete man, but the accent falls on one of them.

3. PHENOMENOLOGY OF HATRED

For the phenomenology of hatred we base ourselves fully on Sartre's explicitation of the "look." At first, such a procedure may not seem warranted, for a look is not *per se* a look, or stare, of hatred. We agree, but think that what Sartre says of "the" look applies solely to the stare of hatred. This causes complications, however, when one tries to understand Sartre's own personal attitude with respect to important *human* questions of our time. Through his participation in the resistance against the Nazis, his standpoint in the Algerian question, and his attitude toward the great social questions of our time Sartre seems to deny everything he says in his philosophy of the look, if this look has to be exclusively understood as a stare of hatred. We will return to these difficulties later.

As all other phenomenologists, Sartre considers it entirely superfluous to prove the existence of the other as the other; this existence is immediately evident and any attempt to prove it presupposes what it wishes to prove.[69] This general position, however, receives a wholly unexpected turn when Sartre investigates in which situation the existence of the other as the other—as another "I," as subjectivity—becomes accessible to me. This existence is not disclosed to me when I look at the other but only when the other looks at me.[70] The subject who the other is always reveals himself as "he who looks at me" [71] and never as anything else.

What the Look Is Not

Catching the other's look is not the perception of a quality—

---

[69]Sartre, *EN*, pp. 278-279.

[70]"Et dans l'épreuve du regard, en m'éprouvant comme objectivité non révélée, j'éprouve directement et avec mon être l'insaisissable subjectivité d'autrui." *EN*, p. 329.

[71]*EN*, p. 315.

"looking"—among other qualities—such as "blue," "beautiful," or "cross-eyed"—of an eye or of an object functioning as an eye. Sartre speaks of an object "functioning" as an eye because the look does not merely disclose itself in the convergence of the pupils in my direction but also in the snapping of twigs— e.g., during an assault in the dark—in the sound of footsteps, followed by silence, in the half-open position of shutters or the slight motion of a heavy curtain.[72] All these objects "function" as an eye. To catch the look of someone who looks at me, Sartre says, *is* not the perception of his eyes or of certain qualities of his eyes. The eyes are there, but I cease to perceive them thematically, they are neutralized, do not play a role, and no statement is made in their regard. Eyes which look at me are not eyes which I can explicitly find beautiful or ugly. The other's look masks his eyes. I cannot catch the look of someone unless the perception of his eyes falls into the background.[73] To catch someone's look, then, is not to perceive an object-in-the-world; rather, it is becoming conscious that I am being *looked at*. The look of the other who looks at me proceeds from his eyes and throws me back upon myself.[74] If during an assault I suddenly hear twigs snapping behind me, I am thrown back upon my own vulnerability and I understand at once that I am being *looked at*.[75]

To Be Looked at

What does it mean that I am being looked at? Sartre's example clearly illustrates the exclusive meaning which the look has for him, a meaning from which subsequently he does not deviate. Imagine, he says, that, driven by jealousy, I press my ear against the door of someone's room or that I look through the key hole to catch the occupant in a compromising situation.

---

[72]*EN*, p. 315.
[73]Accordingly, I am able to perceive and express the qualities of the other's eye, but only when the experience of the "look" withdraws to the background. In other words, to the extent that I perceive that someone's eyes are beautiful or blue, I am not influenced by his "look." We will see that this means that I do not experience my own "being looked at." "Je dirais volontiers ici: nous ne pouvons percevoir le monde et saisir en même temps un regard fixé sur nous; il faut que ce soit l'un ou l'autre." *EN*, p. 316.
[74]"Saisir un regard n'est pas appréhender un objet-regard dans le monde (à moins que ce regard ne soit pas dirigé sur nous), c'est prendre conscience d'être regardé. Le regard que manifestent les yeux, de quelque nature qu'ils soient, est pur renvoi à moi-même." *EN*, p. 316.
[75]*EN*, pp. 315-316.

In doing this, I am fully with the "object" of my listening or looking and with the door or the key hole, which for me have the meaning of being obstacle or instrument of my actions. My own *existence,* the acts through which I am with those objects, escape me.[76] Suddenly I hear footsteps in the corridor, followed by silence. Someone else is looking at me! At the very moment I realize that I am being looked at, I also experience my being an object for the other.

My experience of being looked at by the other discloses to me the look, the stare, i.e., the meaning of the other's subjectivity. This experience costs me my own subjectivity, my own freedom, for under the other's stare I am as a thing in his world. I experience the death of my own subjectivity. What this means becomes clear to me if I call to mind what it is to be a "living" subject. As a "living" subject, I am the co-source of the system of meanings which the world is for me. When unsuspectingly I look through the key hole, the walls, the door, the lock, the key hole and the semidarkness of the corridor derive their meanings as obstacle or instrument from my subjectivity. In a certain sense they are organized by me and function at the service of my intentions. As a "living" subject, I am a self-project, I am not what I am, but am what I am not. I am master of the situation and hold my possibilities in my own hands. As a "living" subject, I am also the execution of my self-project: I am the spontaneous transcendence and co-source of ever-new meaning.

All this, however, changes when the other's subjectivity appears on the scene. The other deprives me of my subjectivity as co-source of meaning. My world shows a face whose meaning no longer stands in function of my intentions.[77] The meanings of the door, the walls, and the darkness of the corridor, organize themselves in such a way that I no longer control them:

---

[76]"Je suis pure conscience des choses et les choses . . . m'offrent leur potentialité comme réplique de ma conscience non-thétique (de) mes possibilités propres." *EN,* p. 317. More simply expressed, there is a thematic consciousness of objects which permeates the non-thematic consciousness of my own acts: "conscience *de* quelque chose" and "conscience (de) soi." *EN,* pp. 19-20. My own acts, then, are not reflected upon: "Ils ne sont nullement connus, mais je les suis." The claim that these acts are not "known" can be understood if one takes Sartre's concept of knowledge into account. For Sartre, knowledge is always the thematic affirmation of an object: "connaître, c'est-à-dire poser comme objet." *EN,* p. 329.

[77]"Mais, du coup, l'aliénation de moi qu'est l'être-regardé implique l'aliénation du monde que j'organise." *EN,* pp. 321-322.

they relate now to the other's subjectivity.[78]   The key hole now shows me its most fearful aspect.

Next, the other's stare means the death of my subjectivity as "being able to be." I could try to hide from his look in a dark corner of the corridor, but the other transcends, dominates, and controls that possibility by his own power to dispel that darkness with his flashlight. I am present to my own ability to be, my own possibilities; I seize them, but as absent.[79] I seize them insofar as the other has foreseen them and already prevented them.[80] My possibility to hide becomes for the other his possibility to unmask me and identify me. Every action I execute against the other can become, under his stare, an instrument serving him against me. Under the other's stare I am no longer the master of the situation and I no longer hold my possibilities in my own hands.[81]

Finally, under the other's stare my freedom as transcendence becomes immobile. All spontaneity and "mobility" of my subjectivity as transcendence is paralyzed and frozen under his stare.[82] I have to consider myself as a slave, for I depend on a freedom which is not mine.[83]

The feeling of shame I experience summarizes what I am in the eyes of the other. Looked at by him, I am ashamed. Shame is always shame of myself. I am ashamed of my freedom insofar as it escapes me and becomes a mere object under the other's eyes. Shame is the recognition that I am the object the other stares at and judges.[84] He merely has to look at me and, at once, I am what I am.[85] When the other sees me seated, I *am* for him *seated* just as this inkwell *stands* on the table. For the other, I *am bent* over the key hole just as a tree *is bent* by the wind; I *am* for him *indiscreet* just as a table *is round* or a cauliflower *is rotten*: for him I *am* a thing in the midst of

---

[78]"Mais avec le regard d'autrui une organisation neuve des complexes vient se surimprimer sur la première." *EN,* p. 321.

[79]"Elle est là, cette possibilité, je la saisis, mais comme absente." *EN,* p. 322.

[80]"Cette tendance à m'enfuir, qui me domine et m'entraîne et que je suis, je la lis dans ce regard guetteur et dans cet autre regard: l'arme braquée sur moi. L'autre me l'apprend, en tant qu'il l'a prévu et qu'il y a déjà paré." *EN,* p. 322.

[81]*EN,* pp. 321-323.

[82]"Aussi ai-je dépouillé, pour l'autre, ma transcendance." *EN,* p. 321.

[83]*EN,* p. 326.

[84]"Or, la honte est honte de soi, elle est reconnaissance de ce que je suis bien cet objet qu'autrui regarde et juge." *EN,* p. 319.

[85]"Il suffit qu'autrui me regarde pour que je sois ce que je suis." *EN,* p. 320.

things.[86] His stare strikes me, so that I am for him what I am; but, at the same time, his stare also extends to my world,[87] making me *be* "bent over the key hole." [88] It is this *being* of which I am ashamed.

In a single sentence Sartre fully generalizes his above-mentioned view of the meaning which the other's subjectivity has: if there exists even a single person, no matter who or where and regardless of the relations he has to my being, then the very fact that his subjectivity arises before me, makes me have an "outside," a "nature," and makes me be an object.[89] "My original fall is the existence of the other." [90] Thus I am always in danger. But the danger in which I am is not an unfortunate circumstance: it is the permanent structure of my being-for-the-other.[91]

It may be useful to state explicitly that Sartre does not wish to see his expressions interpreted in the most literal sense. The emergence of the other's subjectivity destroys my subjectivity as freedom and "makes me a thing." This should not be taken literally,[92] for I am fully *conscious* of the fact that in the other's eyes I am a "thing." Thus I obviously am not a thing as the things of the world are things. Nevertheless, the expression is meaningful, for Sartre wishes to indicate that the terms "subjectivity" and "freedom" can have a long scale of senses. They can refer to a kind of "fullness" of human authenticity, the spontaneity of an authentically human life. For this reason we spoke above of the "living subject." But they can also refer to a subjectivity and freedom which lie crushed under a weight. The fact that I am conscious of being crushed implies that I am a subject. But what does this mean? Simply that I cannot

---

[86]"Et ce que je suis . . . je le suis au milieu du monde." *EN*, p. 322.

[87]". . . car le regard d'autrui embrasse mon être et corrélativement les murs, la porte, la serrure; toutes ces choses ustensiles, au milieu desquelles je suis, tournent vers l'autre une face qui m'échappe par principe." *EN*, p. 319.

[88]"Si je suis vu comme assis, je dois être vu comme 'assis-sur-une-chaise', si je suis saisi comme courbé, c'est comme 'courbé-sur-le-trou-de-la-serrure', etc." *EN*, p. 321.

[89]"S'il y a un Autre, quel qu'il soit, où qu'il soit, quels que soient ses rapports avec moi, sans même qu'il agisse autrement sur moi que par le pur surgissement de son être, j'ai un dehors, j'ai une nature. . . ." *Ibid.*

[90]*Ibid.*

[91]". . . je suis en danger. Et ce danger n'est pas un accident, mais la structure permanente de mon être-pour-autrui." *EN*, p. 326.

[92]"Ce n'est pas, à proprement parler, que je me sente perdre ma liberté pour devenir une chose." *EN*, p. 321.

say that I am not a subject. There is no longer question of the "fullness" and spontaneity of authentic subjectivity. Under the other's stare my freedom degenerates into an "attribute" of the "thing" I am for the other.[93] I am "for myself" what I am for the other, but I have no control over what I am for the other. My freedom has no longer any *real* content.

Hatred

We now have enough data to observe that "the" look of which Sartre speaks is a very special kind of look, and that its meaning is absolutized and generalized by him without the slightest sign of reserve. Sartre's look is the hateful stare, the look which does not accept me as a subject, which does not tolerate that I as a subject project my own world, but which throws me down as a thing among the things of the world by murdering my possibilities. This, however, does not mean that what Sartre says about the look does not express any reality. On the contrary, his explicitations are an ingenious description of the hateful look, and that look is a reality. We do not have the slightest intention of denying this reality.

At the same time, we have no intention of admitting that Sartre's explicitations describe "the" look—i.e., that man can only look at his fellowman with hatred.[94] The example chosen by Sartre in starting his descriptions forced him to pursue his chosen path to the end, especially because he did not add any other examples which could have broadened the field of his inquiry. Sartre, then, does not speak of "the" look, but only of a very special way of looking at a fellowman. In addition to that look, however, there is also a benevolent look, a look of favor, a merciful and forgiving look, an understanding, exhorting, encouraging look—in a word, a loving look. Sartre does not mislead us by what he says but by that about which he keeps silent and by surreptitiously suggesting that there cannot be anything else than what he expresses in his analysis.

An Objection

This is not the end of the trouble, however. On the occasion of a self-made objection, Sartre tries to penetrate deeper

---

[93]"(Ma liberté) est là-bas, hors de ma liberté vécue, comme un attribut donné de cet être que suis pour l'autre." *Ibid.*
[94]E. Mounier, *Introduction aux existentialismes*, Paris, 1947, p. 99.

into the meaning of the look. What value has the certainty I have that I am being looked at? I experience this certainty on the occasion of the appearance of certain objects in the world, such as the other's eyes or the snapping of twigs. But I can be mistaken: the snapping of twigs during an assault in darkness can be caused by the wind. In such a case, of what value is the certainty I have that I am being looked at? For there is no one looking at me. My shame—the experience of being an object for the other—would be merely a pseudo-shame, it would be shame for no one.[95]

Sartre uses this difficulty to re-emphasize the purely incidental relationship between the eye and the look. Being looked at does not depend on the object manifested by the look. Catching the other's eye *is* not the perception of his eye or of an object functioning as an eye. One must even say that the perception of an object makes it impossible to have at the same time the experience of the look—of being looked at; I experience the other's look only when his eyes no longer play any role and are "destroyed." [96] Being looked at by the other, then, is not connected with his body,[97] but it is only on the occasion of the appearance of certain objects that I experience that I am being looked at. The fact that I am being looked at is certain; the fact that the other's look is connected with this or that object is never more than probable; at any rate, this connection is not more than occasional.[98]

The example taken by Sartre as his starting point again serves to illustrate his view. When I stand bent over the key hole, I can be mistaken if I think that I am hearing *footsteps,* but I do not err in my certainty of *being looked at.* The other's look is so real that I abandon my plan or, if I persevere in it, I can hear my heart beat and I sharpen my ears to the slightest sound, the least creaking of the stairs. I am not mistaken about the other's presence. The other is everywhere, under me, above me, in the neighboring rooms, in a dark corner of the corridor. Only the empirically verifiable "being there"—the concrete, his-

---

95*EN*, p. 335.

96"Le regard, nous l'avons montré, apparaît sur fond de destruction de l'objet qui le manifeste." *EN*, p. 335.

97"Si donc l'être-regardé, dégagé dans toute sa pureté, n'est pas lié au corps d'autrui plus que ma conscience d'être conscience, dans la pure réalisation du cogito, n'est liée à mon propre corps. . . ." *EN*, p. 336.

98*EN*, p. 336.

torical event which we express by saying: "There is some-
body in the room"—remains doubtful, but not his presence.[99]

Moreover, someone's absence, properly understood, reveals
precisely his more original presence. Let us say that I arrive
at Peter's room and notice that he is absent. I would not dream
of saying then that the Sultan of Morocco is absent. Peter's
absence, therefore, is not the non-existence of Peter's relations
with a particular place, as is the case with the Sultan of Morocco;
on the contrary, I speak of Peter precisely in relation to a particular place when I say that he is absent. This place, however,
is not determined by its location or by Peter's relations to a particular place, but by the presence of other human beings. I
can say, e.g., that Peter is absent from a picnic, but he is absent
for Theresa: his absence is a concrete way of being situated
with respect to Theresa. To be absent is a way of being present.[100]

The distance between Peter and Theresa is irrelevant. In
London, India or America, or on a lonely island—everywhere
Peter is present to Theresa who stayed in Paris, for being present is a question of man being situated with respect to others,
independently of the latitude and longitude of a place. It is
evident, however, that man is situated in many ways with respect
to others. As a European, I am situated in reference to Afri-
cans; as a white man, with respect to Negroes; as an adult, in
relation to adolescents; as bourgeois, in reference to the out-
casts of society; as a taxpayer, with respect to the Internal Reve-
nue Service; as an author, in regard to my readers; etc.[101]
Man, then, is present with respect to everyone, and this presence
is more fundamental than the empirically verifiable "being
there" or "not being there." [102]

It should also be clear now why my certainty of the other's
presence is justified. I can be mistaken in the object revealed
by the other's look—by my being looked at—but not in the

[99]*EN*, pp. 336-337.

[100]"Etre absent, pour Pierre par rapport à Thérèse, c'est une façon particulière de lui être présent." *EN*, p. 338.

[101]All examples added by Sartre to his starting point stand directly in
function of this starting point, viz., the being looked-at of someone who
peeps through a key hole. Even the picnic does not reveal any new dimension of presence: "Et cette présence originelle ne peut avoir de sens que
comme être-regardé ou comme être-regardant, c'est-à-dire selon qu'autrui est
pour moi objet ou moi-même objet-pour-autrui." *EN*, p. 339.

[102]"Ainsi les concepts empiriques d'absence et de présence sont-ils deux
spécifications d'une présence fondamentale." *EN*, p. 338.

presence of this look. The emergence of certain objects in my
world is merely the occasion on which I experience myself as
thrown into the arena.[103] It would be wrong to speak of a
plurality of looks in this context, for plurality belongs only to the
objects which presuppose my world-projecting look. Similarly,
it is wrong to synthesize the human presence and to conceive
it as the presence of a single infinite subject, the omnipresent
God.[104] I experienced only the pre-numerical presence of the
others. When under the look of a class or an audience I give
a lecture or deliver a conference, the others' presence remains
undifferentiated. I never experience either one synthetized look
or many distinct looks. But when I wish to check whether
my audience has understood me, I look at them and then I
suddenly see "heads" and "eyes" appear. The others' pre-
numerical presence is then dissolved and reduced to a plurality
of objects. At the same time, however, the other's look—the
experience of being looked at—disappears.[105]

"And in This Way I Recover Myself"

From these descriptions it is evident that there is only one
way for me to regain my subjectivity, which is frozen by the
other's stare. I am an object for the subject who the other is,
but I am never an object for an object. To liberate myself
from my state of being-an-object, I will rise and try to reduce
the other to an object by my stare.[106] For as soon as the other
appears to me as an object, his subjectivity degenerates into a
"quality" of the object whose appearance made me become its
victim. His subjectivity thus becomes a "quality" of, for example, his eyes, just as being blue or ugly are qualities of them.
The other "has" his subjectivity, then, just as a box "has" an inside. "And in this way I recover myself." [107]

In this way all concrete human relations are, in principle,
settled for Sartre: either the other rejects me and reduces me

---

103"L'épreuve de ma condition d'homme, objet pour tous les autres
hommes vivants, jeté dans l'arène sous des millions de regards et m'échappant
à moi-même des millions de fois, je la réalise concrètement à l'occasion du
surgissement d'un objet dans mon univers." *EN*, p. 340.
104*EN*, p. 341.
105*EN*, pp. 340-342.
106"L'objectivation d'autrui . . . est une défense de mon être qui me
libère précisément de mon être pour autrui, en conférant à autrui un être
pour moi." *EN*, p. 327.
107*EN*, p. 349.

to a thing in his world, or I keep his subjectivity under my control by making it an object for me. There are no other possibilities. Subjectivity, in the sense of a subject to subject relationship, is not conceivable. Nevertheless, man will not cease to strive for such a relationship: love, masochism, desire, hatred, sadism are just so many different attempts to realize the intersubjectivity of which man dreams.[108] But these attempts are in vain.[109] Human relationships are fully exhausted by the twofold possibility of either transcending the other or letting myself be transcended by him. The essence of interhuman relationships, therefore, is not "being with" but conflict.[110] Love is "essentially a fraud," [111] a sly maneuver by which I seize control of the other's subjectivity without depriving him of his liberty.[112]

For this purpose I will "first" identify myself with my being-an-object in the other's eye. To love the other means "first" to accept that I am an object for the other and that the other is a subject. But I cannot accept that I am "simply" an object for him: that would be masochism.[113] I wish to be a *privileged* object. But I can only be a privileged object if the other loves me. I will that the other makes me his goal and freely binds himself to me.[114] But I do not wish to be the "chosen one," in the sense that I would have been chosen by my beloved above others who could *also* have been chosen.[115] I will the other to accept that he can no longer be freedom without my being-an-object-for-him.[116] I will the world to organize itself for the other in terms of the center which I am for him.[117] I will to be the "unsurpassable" for the other, the one without whom

---

[108]*EN*, pp. 428-503.

[109]"Vainement souhaiterait-on un nous humain dans lequel la totalité intersubjective prendrait conscience d'elle-même comme subjectivité unifiée." *EN*, p. 501.

[110]"L'essence des rapports entre consciences n'est pas le Mitsein, c'est le conflit." *EN*, p. 502.

[111]*EN*, p. 445.

[112]"En tant qu'autrui comme liberté est fondement de mon être-en-soi je puis chercher à récupérer cette liberté et à m'en emparer, sans lui ôter son caractère de liberté." *EN*, p. 430.

[113]*EN*, p. 446.

[114]"(L'amant) veut être aimé par une liberté et réclame que cette liberté comme liberté ne soit plus libre." *EN*, p. 434.

[115]*Ibid.*

[116]"(L'amant) ne veut pas *agir* sur la liberté de l'Autre mais . . . être donné d'un coup avec elle et dans son surgissement même comme la limite qu'elle doit accepter pour être libre." *EN*, p. 435.

[117]*EN*, p. 437.

there exists no freedom for him.[118]   I will this and have to
will it in order not to be an "ordinary object" under his look.
It is only when through his love I have become a privileged object that I am liberated from my shame and secure.[119]   Only in
this way I can escape from his look; or rather, only in this way
I am the "object" of an entirely different look.[120]   I am no longer
a utensil, a means, an obstacle, but the absolute goal of the
other.   "How good I am to have eyes, hairs, eyebrows. . . ." [121]

It is not possible, however, that through the other's love I
really become a privileged object for him.   For "to love me"
means for the other "first" to accept that he be an object in my
eyes and that I am a free subject.   But the other cannot accept
"simply" to be an object in my eyes.   He wishes to be a *privileged* object.   But he can only be a privileged object if I love
him, if I make him my goal, if I accept no longer to be able to
be freedom without his being-an-object-for-me, if I accept that
he is the "unsurpassable" for my freedom, so that he is liberated
from his shame and secure because he is the "object" of an entirely different kind of look.   But it is impossible that through
my love the other *really* becomes a *privileged* object.   For "to
love the other" means "first" to accept that in the other eyes I
am an object, etc., etc.   The possibility of love keeps being
shifted away *ad infinitum*.[122]   Both I and the other would have
to be at the same time unfreedom and freedom, which is impossible.   For this reason, the attempt to realize the "ideal" of
love must of necessity fail.   Consequently, this "ideal" may not
be called a *real* ideal.[123]   For to love is "willing to be loved."
But how, then, could the other love me?   His love also is a will
to be loved,[124] and any will to be loved means a will to *possess*

118"Mais si l'Autre m'aime, je deviens *l'indépassable,* ce qui signifie que
je dois être la fin absolue." *EN,* p. 436.

119"Si ce résultat pouvait être atteint il en résulterait en premier lieu que
je serais *en sécurité* dans la conscience de l'Autre." *EN,* p. 436.

120"De ce point de vue, mon être doit échapper au *regard* de l'aimé;
ou plutôt, il doit être l'objet d'un regard d'une autre structure." *EN,* p. 437.

121*EN,* p. 438.

122"Si l'autre m'aime, il me déçoit radicalement par son amour même:
j'exigais de lui qu'il fonde mon être comme objet privilégié en se maintenant
comme pure subjectivité en face de moi; et dès qu'il m'aime, il m'éprouve
comme sujet et s'abîme dans son objectivité en face de ma subjectivité.   Le
problème de mon être-pour-autrui demeure donc sans solution.   Les amants
demeurent chacun pour soi dans une subjectivité totale." *EN,* p. 444.

123*EN,* pp. 443-444.

124"Chacun veut que l'autre l'aime, sans se rendre compte qu'aimer
c'est vouloir être aimé et qu'ainsi en voulant que l'autre l'aime il veut seulement que l'autre veuille qu'il l'aime." *EN,* p. 444.

the other's *freedom*.   There is an internal contradiction here.[125]
"Respect for the other's freedom is an idle word." [126]

The "Us"-Object and the "We"-Subject

According to Sartre, the great complexity of human relations
does not modify the fact that the essence of these relations is
conflict.   Sartre recognizes the reality of the "us"-experience,
but he describes this experience also in terms of being looked
at.   In the "us"-experience there is a third who looks at
"us." [127]   My relation with the other is nothing but "conflict,"
but when a third looks at "us," I experience not only my own
self-estrangement but also that of the other.   His being-an-
object, however, is not simply parallel with my being-an-object;
I experience that we, as equivalent and solidary meanings, occur
in the world of the third—he has "us" in his power.[128]   In the
absence of a third, I fight with the other, but under the stare
of a third I experience that "we" are fighting.   Under his stare
we *are fighters*.   We are ashamed because a third looks at "us."
Certain situations very clearly reveal the "us"-object to us.
The class consciousness and solidarity of the laborers, for example, with respect to their oppressors, is nothing but the experience of being stared at by a third, viz., the ruling class.[129]
Through the look of the ruling class, "we" live in estrangement.
Class consciousness arises because we take up our common estrangement.[130]   The Jews also are solidary, and the same is true
for citizens of the same country, but only under the eye of the
anti-Semite [131] and the foreign occupiers.[132]   If the term "love"
has any meaning, it could be used for these modes of solidarity.   To love is to hate the same enemy.
The "us"-experience, then, does not imply more than was
explained above: it is merely a more complex form of being
looked at.   At the same time, it follows that there is only one

---

125J. Wahl, *Les philosophies de l'existence*, Paris, 1954, p. 120.
126*EN*, p. 480.
127*EN*, pp. 486-495.
128*EN*, pp. 489-490.
129*EN*, pp. 491-494.
130"Le Nous-objet ne se découvre que par l'assomption que je fais de
cette situation, c'est-à-dire par la nécessité où je suis, au sein de ma liberté
assumante, d'assumer *aussi* l'Autre, à cause de la réciprocité interne de la
situation." *EN*, p. 490.
131Sartre, *Réflexions sur la question juive*, Paris, 1946.
132J-P. Sartre, *"Morts sans sépulture," Théâtre*, Paris, 1947, pp. 185-268.

possibility of liberation: the oppressed class will rise and with its stare reduce the oppressing class to "them"-objects.[133]

It did not escape Sartre that there exists also a "we"-subject. This subject is revealed to us through our common goals and instruments. "We" use a highway and a gas pump; "we" oppress the workers and "we" destroy our oppressors. There is question here of a certain solidarity between subjects. But for Sartre this "we" does not have any ontological importance. It is a purely psychological, purely subjective experience of an individual consciousness; in other words, it is only the way in which "I" experience myself among others [134]—only an ethereal symbol of an absolute solidarity between subjects which cannot be realized.[135]

Death

The hope that "we human beings" could ever attain an authentically human "we," in which we would affirm one another's subjectivity, is, according to Sartre, idle because every subject seeks the death of the other's subjectivity.[136] Sartre lugubriously develops this idea when he tries to understand the meaning of death.

From the standpoint of the "for itself"—i.e., from that of my transcendence, my self-realizing subjectivity—death is absurd. For death "simply" puts an end to my transcending: we die "into the bargain." [137] My ability to be solidifies into the compact density of the "in itself." This can give no meaning to my life; on the contrary, death deprives my life of all meaning.[138]

In terms of the "being for itself" dying does not have any discernible meaning; but it does have meaning in terms of my "being for the other." The experience of my "being for the other" reveals me to myself as looked at, as an object, a thing in the world. The other transcends my transcendence by his

---

133*EN*, p. 490.
134"Il s'agit seulement d'une manière de me sentir au milieu des autres."
EN, p. 497.
135"Les subjectivités demeurent hors d'atteinte et radicalement séparées."
EN, p. 498.
136"Vainement souhaiterait-on un nous humain dans lequel la totalité intersubjective prendrait conscience d'elle-même comme subjectivité unifiée."
EN, p. 501.
137". . . nous mourrons toujours par-dessus le marché." *EN*, p. 633.
138"Ainsi la mort n'est jamais ce qui donne son sens à la vie: c'est au contraire ce qui ôte par principe toute signification." *EN*, p. 624.

look; his look means the death of my ability to be. Now, death is the other's definitive triumph over me.[139] As long as I am alive, I am able to transcend his transcendence by my look, but death deprives me of this possibility of self-defense. I become definitively a prey of the other's stare. I am what I *am*, a thing—just as the other has always considered me. One who wishes to understand the meaning of his future death must conceive himself as the future prey of the other.[140] As long as I live, the other will try to murder my subjectivity, but it is only when I am dead that he definitively triumphs over me.

Retrospect

When the reader of BEING AND NOTHINGNESS finally manages to escape from Sartre's fascinating genius, he will pronounce only one verdict: a splendid analysis of a degenerate society. But he will refuse to accept that even in the degeneration of the twentieth century there exists nothing but hatred which cannot bear that the other is a subject, which simply cannot stand the thought that he realizes himself in the world, and which, therefore, cannot rest until the other is definitively reduced to the compact density of an "in itself." Above we mentioned that the "we" assumes very many forms. In Sartre, however, all of them are reduced to a single fundamental pattern: the conflict between the hateful look and the hated being looked at. He leaves no room for any genuine *co-existing,* for intersubjectivity in the sense of being-subjects-together. We have only one reply to such a position: "There are more things in heaven and earth than are dreamt of in your philosophy."

Is the above-described interpretation of the look correct, or does it perhaps fail to do justice to what Sartre really wished to say? There are authors who vote for the second alternative. According to Jeanson and Simone de Beauvoir, it is wholly to be excluded that Sartre really wished to say that man is essentially and of necessity nothing but a barbarian and a murderer. For otherwise, how could Sartre devote himself to the liberation of man as a subject, as he actually did and continues to do? If respect for one another's subjectivity is an empty word, what would be the sense of fighting for freedom's liberation?

---

[139]*EN*, pp. 624-625, 629.

[140]"Etre mort, c'est être en proie aux vivants. Cela signifie donc que celui qui tente de saisir le sens sa mort future doit se découvrir comme proie future des autres." *EN*, p. 628.

Undeniably, Sartre did engage in the fight for freedom. He defended and undertook an "authorship of involvement" and the aim of this involvement was the liberation of man.[141] A professional writer who takes his work seriously, says Sartre, will have to be a revolutionary.[142] He wishes to change the world and history. While he does not act in the same way as the practically involved revolutionary, his action is not less effective. He acts by "naming," and "naming" things is to change them.[143] One who calls the injustices of the world injustices contributes to liberating man from them. When Sartre writes, he aims at liberating man's freedom.[144] For man "is" not free just as a rock is sharp. Man's freedom must be liberated from the economic, social, and political pressures which crush freedom.

Concern for man's concrete freedom also kept Sartre from definitively joining the Communist Party. Personally, he always felt sympathy for Marx's doctrine, but he saw the Party as a violation of Marx's ideal. According to Sartre, the Communist Party is most certainly not a revolutionary party. Its aim is not the liberation of man but the protection of Russia.[145] Its revolutionary ideal became an "ordinary" ideology, one which cannot stand being criticized and does not tolerate freedom. In the eyes of the Party, writers and intellectuals are suspect because they freely joined the Party. By freely joining, they demonstrated a suspicious sense of independence, for they could leave the Party with the same freedom with which they joined it. They are subjected to a long Kafkaesque trial. The judges are unknown and the records secret. The final verdict is a condemnation. The invisible accusers need not prove the guilt of the accused, but the latter has to demonstrate to them that he is not guilty.[146] Such procedures violate freedom, but Communism indulges in them.

---

[141]"Ainsi qu'il soit essayiste, pamphlétaire, satiriste ou romancier, qu'il parle seulement des passions individuelles ou qu'il s'attaque au régime de la société, l'écrivain, homme libre s'adressant à des hommes libres, n'a qu'un seul sujet: la liberté." Sartre, *Situations,* 34th ed., Paris 1948, II, p. 112.

[142]Sartre, *op. cit.,* pp. 276-277.

[143]"Ainsi le prosateur est un homme qui a choisi un certain mode d'action secondaire qu'on pourrait nommer l'action par dévoilement." Sartre, *op cit.,* p. 73.

[144]"C'est pourtant cette homme libre qu'il faut *délivrer,* en élargissant ses possibilités de choix." Sartre, *"Présentation," Les temps modernes,* I(1945), p. 19.

[145]Sartre, *Situations,* p. 280.

[146]Sartre, *op. cit.,* pp. 281-282.

Sartre is also opposed to the claim of Communism that it represents the absolute good. Joseph de Maistre used to say: "The married woman is of necessity chaste because she married before God." That's nonsense, of course. But a correspondent of ACTION writes: "The Communist is the *permanent* hero of our time, for the Communist Party is the party of heroes." What a "grace of state"! [147] For Sartre, there exists no such "grace of state." The claim to have such a grace disregards the reality of man, for if there were such a grace, how could one still be critical?

Evidently, one who speaks in such a way, and knows what he is saying, cannot at the same time assert that respect for freedom is nothing but an empty word. For this reason Jeanson proposed to interpret BEING AND NOTHINGNESS as Sartre's description of being *inauthentically* human [148] and as a plea to transcend inauthenticity because the latter must necessarily fail.[149] What Sartre *describes* would thus be precisely what Sartre criticizes, and the failure of being-man *described* by him would be the proof for the impossibility of inauthenticity. As Jeanson presents the matter, those who agree with Sartre's claim that life is absurd—and there are many—really disagree with him, and those who oppose him for his claim assert nothing but what Sartre himself really wishes to say. While Jeanson defends the position that BEING AND NOTHINGNESS in its entirety must be understood as a rejection of "bad faith" and inauthenticity,[150] De Beauvoir is of the opinion that such a statement can only be made with respect to a large part of the book.[151]

In a splendid book about love according to Sartre, Joseph Arntz has tried to offer proofs for Jeanson's view insofar as it

---

147Sartre, *op. cit.,* p. 281.

148"Toutes les descriptions de *L'Etre et le Néant* se refèrent à cette attitude d'échec et de mauvaise foi. Mais, tout comme dans le cas des relations avec autrui, Sartre prend soin de signaler qu'il serait possible d'adopter une attitude différente." Jeanson, *Sartre par lui-même,* Paris, 1955, p. 58, note.

149"De cette *'attitude d'échec' L'Etre et le Néant* constitue à la fois la description et la dénonciation." Fr. Jeanson, *op. cit.,* p. 31.

150"*L'Etre et le Néant* est tout entier consacré à la description de cette attitude d'échec, qui est une attitude de *mauvaise foi*. Loin de représenter la morale de Sartre, *L'Etre et le Néant* dévoile au contraire, dans ce souci d'être, l'attitude spontanée que la morale aura à convertir pour engager le mouvement d'authentification." Jeanson, "La conduite humaine selon J-P. Sartre," *Morale chrétienne et requêtes contemporaines,* Tournai-Paris, 1954, p. 176.

151S. De Beauvoir, *Pour une morale de l'ambiguïté,* 8th ed., Paris, 1947, p. 66.

is concerned with the possibility of love.[152]   After a very detailed examination Arntz comes to the conclusion that, as a matter of fact, Sartre really only wished to describe inauthentic love and called only *this* form of "love" a failure.[153]   For Arntz, then, there is no contradiction between Sartre's denial of the possibility of "love" and Sartre's personal efforts (including those in the realm of reflection) for the liberation of freedom.   In a certain sense Jeanson and Arntz, who defend Sartre, agree with those who oppose him.   Both parties agree about what it is that Sartre actually wrote, viz., that the inauthenticity of human relations must of necessity terminate in failure.   The disagreement is about what Sartre *himself* "really" wishes to say.   Does he mean that there exists nothing but inauthenticity and, therefore, also nothing but failure, or is he a moralist calling mankind to authenticity?

We will not attempt to settle this question, but pay some attention to a supposition which Arntz would rather not make, viz., that Sartre would have given up his original position.   Is this possibility really "extremely improbable"? [154]

In his Preface to Jeanson's book about his morality Sartre praises Jeanson for not looking at his ideas as "finished" and "dead" but as unfinished and in motion.[155]   He praises Jeanson because the latter had become so familiar with his thoughts that he was able to *transcend* Sartre's own standpoint, precisely at the moment when Sartre *himself* did the same.[156]   Such a remark makes the "extremely improbable" somewhat probable at least.   Arntz cannot accept that within two years Sartre would abandon a theory which took him years to develop.[157]   But in THE WORDS, his autobiography, Sartre himself speaks in a different tone.   My best book, he says there, is the one I am now writing; then comes the last one published, but I am already beginning to be disgusted with it.   If the critics should now condemn it, they may hurt me, but in six months I will be on the verge of agreeing with them.   But no matter how valueless they consider the book, they should place it above all my previous writings.   I

152J. Arntz, *De liefde in de ontologie van J-P. Sartre,* Nijmegen, 1960.
153Arntz, *op. cit.,* pp. 286-318.
154Arntz, *op. cit.,* p. 284.
155Jeanson, *Le problème moral et la pensée de Sartre,* pp. 13-14.
156"Vous avez si parfaitement épousé le développement de ma pensée que vous en êtes venu à dépasser la position que j'avais prise dans mes livres au moment que je la dépassais moi-même." Jeanson, *op. cit.,* Lettre-préface de J-P. Sartre, p. 14.
157Arntz, *op. cit.,* p. 284.

do not care if they belittle everything I write, as long as they "maintain the chronological order of value." [158]

This statement is entirely consonant with the sphere depicted by Sartre in his autobiography. He describes himself as a man who, with the greatest of ease, can disavow one book after the other, but who continues to believe in his "mandate" of being a writer and an elect. At the age of thirty, he says, I managed to describe in all sincerity the unjustified existence of my contemporaries and exonerate my own in NAUSEA. "*I was* Roquentin: in him I showed without complacency the texture of my life." At the same time, however, Sartre adds, I was I, the elect, the chronicler of hell, "bent over the juices of my own protoplasma." Later, he continues, I gaily proved that man is impossible. I, too, was impossible, different from the others only because I had a mandate to prove that impossibility. But this impossibility thereby became my inmost possibility, the springboard of my glory. A prisoner of that evident contradiction, I failed to see it. A fraud to my very bones and deceived, I happily wrote about our unhappy existence. I spoke "dogmatically," but I doubted everything except that I was the elect of doubt. With one hand I rebuilt what I destroyed with the other.[159] Now, however, the dream is finished. "I have changed," Sartre says. My past illusions have been smashed, I have lost them. For about ten years, I have been waking up, cured of a long madness. I cannot get over it and "I cannot think without laughing of my past mistakes." I mistook my pen for a sword, but now I realize that man is powerless. But it does not matter: "I write books and will keep writing." [160]

If Arntz considers it extremely improbable that Sartre would have denied his ideas, he starts from the otherwise legitimate assumption that he is dealing with a writer who does not hold himself entitled to launch ideas in the same way as an engine blows off steam.[161] But from THE WORDS it is evident that Sartre is not such an author. It stands to reason that an author

---

[158]Sartre, *Les Mots*, Paris, 1964, pp. 200-201.
[159]Sartre, *op. cit.*, pp. 209-210.
[160]Sartre, *op. cit.*, pp. 210-211.
[161]"On ne peut là-dessus donner à un auteur le droit de produire ses idées comme la locomotive sa fumée: il faut qu'il mette en place ce qu'il pensait hier dans ce qu'il pense aujourd'hui. Et autant il aurait tort de chercher dans ses écrits d'hier toutes ses idées d'aujourd'hui,—ce serait avouer qu'il n'a pas vécu, rien acquis entre-temps,—autant il doit expliquer le passage." Merleau-Ponty, *Les aventures de la dialectique*, 13th ed., Paris, 1955, p. 306.

can never claim that his ideas of today can already be found in his works of yesterday. Otherwise he would not have continued to live. But he falls short if he leaves his changes unexplained. As Merleau-Ponty points out, "No one is interested in the mere fact that yesterday he thought this while today he thinks that." [162] For this reason Arntz tries to find continuity in Sartre's thought. Sartre, however, pushes his principle of "nihilation" so far that he continually places himself, as it were, outside himself and splits with laughter at his own expense. For this reason he could hardly avoid refusing the Nobel prize. One who accepts a prize accepts also the "seriousness" with which the members of the jury take his work "seriously." But Sartre is unable to do this.

This lack of seriousness on Sartre's part explains why we do not wish to determine what he "really" wished to say when he wrote his philosophy of "the" look. As it stands in BEING AND NOTHINGNESS, it is for us a philosophy of hatred. An ingenious piece of philosophy, let us admit it—one that is surpassed only by Jerzy Kosinski.[163]

4. PHENOMENOLOGY OF INDIFFERENCE

Care must be taken not to misunderstand the statement that, by hatefully looking at the other, I "see" nothing in him but a thing, an object. I most certainly "see" the "other": I am certainly conscious of his subjectivity, I encounter the other "in person." Sartre was one of the first to affirm this point, in opposition to a Cartesian position only recently overcome. What Sartre says of the look contains exclusively the explicitation of the *answer* man gives to his consciousness of the other's subjectivity: being looked at must be understood as a way of being treated by the other. By my look, I reduce the other to an object; by his look, he murders my subjectivity. What Sartre says of the look, then, is not really concerned with my *consciousness* of the other's subjectivity or his consciousness of my subjectivity, but solely with my or his *answer* to this consciousness. According to Sartre, this answer can only be hatred.

Hatred means that I cannot accept that my fellowman is a subject, cannot bear that he realizes himself as a person, brings

---

162M. Merleau-Ponty, *op. cit.*, p. 306.
163Jerzy Kosinski, *The painted bird*, New York, 1965; cf. A. C. Zijderveld, "Het gedoodverfde individu," *Wending*, XXII(1967), pp. 285-305.

about his own personal history. Hatred means a refusal to dwell "together" in "our" world and to bring about "our" history. Hatred is an attempt to reduce the other's subjectivity to a factor in my project of the world, to integrate him into the system of meanings I project for myself. Doing that is slavery and murder. He who hates his brother is a murderer, for he destroys the subjectivity by which his brother is a human being.

We have repeatedly mentioned that "being companions," or fellows, has more variations than Sartre would have us believe. There is also love, which is exactly the opposite of hatred. But before we start the phenomenology of love, it may be useful to see that even the schema love—hatred is insufficient to do justice to the complexity of human relations. Love is the very counter pole of what Sartre says of the hateful look. In "between" these two, however, lies a way of relating to fellowmen which perhaps occurs most frequently, viz., the way of indifference. This attitude must now be discussed.

The "We" of Indifference

I am indifferent with respect to most people. I encounter them in my world and I immediately recognize their subjectivity. I address each of them as "you," for I realize that I am dealing with another "I," a being which is "like me" in the world, which "accompanies" me in the world, with which I am "together" in the world.

The terms "encounter," "accompany," "you," "together," and "we" can have many meanings.[164] Generally speaking, they imply the recognition that the human being I encounter in my world differs from the things in that world. I never turn to a thing "in the second person," never call it "you." I realize that I can never receive a personal answer from a thing and for this reason I do not address things as I address a person, a "you." [165] Similarly, it is nonsense to say that things "accompany" me or that I am "together" with things. But all such terms becomes

---

164"Il est clair au surplus qu'il existe dans le domaine de la rencontre toute une gamme qui va de l'insignifiant au plus hautement significatif; plus je m'approche de la limite inférieure, c'est-à-dire d'une insignifiance radicale, plus la rencontre peut être traitée comme entrecroisement objectif; humainement parlant elle n'est d'ailleurs là qu'un coudoiement." Marcel, *ME* I, p. 153.

165"Je ne m'adresse à la deuxième personne qu'à ce qui est regardé par moi comme susceptible de me répondre, de quelque façon que ce soit— même si cette réponse est un 'silence intelligent'." Marcel, *JM*, p. 138.

increasingly more meaningful as human relations become more meaningful, more profound, more genuinely human.[166]

We submit that the "we" most frequently encountered by the phenomenologist is the "we" of indifference—the empty, unfeeling, dull "we" of a society which is increasingly losing its humanity. It may be useful to start with an example. What meaning does the man behind the ticket counter have for most travellers? One has only to watch the way most people express themselves when they need a ticket. They snap: "Chicago, round trip, coach" and put some dollars on the revolving disk. A few seconds later, the ticket appears on the same disk, together with their change. What does the man behind the counter mean to them? His meaning is the function which he fulfills, and for him all the people whom he encounters in his function are identical with the label "traveller."

How many "human beings" does the ticket clerk "encounter" during his eight hour shift? One can say 756, but also only two—the two who addressed him in an "entirely different way." To "encounter" can have many meanings. The above-mentioned example demonstrates the "we" of indifference. There is a "we"-consciousness, which is not the case if I take a ticket from an automatic dispenser. But what is the meaning of the "you" contained in this "we"? Nothing but that of a quality, "ticket clerk", and for the man behind the counter "I" am nothing but a "traveller." In such a "we" the "encounter" means nothing but the confrontation of one quality or function of the "I" with a quality or function of the "you." It is the function which brings us in contact with each other, and this contact is limited to the meeting of those functions. In such a case, the other does not concern me and I do not care who stands behind the counter. He is for me simply a ticket clerk, I identify him with that quality. If someone else were to take his place, I would not care, just as the man behind the counter remains indifferent as to who snaps "Chicago, round trip, coach." The "we" of this contact is the "we" of indifference.

The "He"

For this kind of a "you" one can appropriately reserve the term "he." [167] For the explicitation of the "he" shows the same as

---

166*JM*, p. 169.
167*JM*, p. 171.

the analysis of the indifferent "you." The experience of the "he, there before the class," the "he, there on the operating table," the "he, there behind his desk" can be fully expressed in a series of predicates, the expression of an agglomerate of qualities ascribed to "him" in an objective judgment: "he" is ill, "he" is a bookkeeper, "he" is sensuous, authoritarian, learned, a publisher, handsome, prudent, spendthrift, Jewish, colored, etc. The experience of the "he" is like the experience of a "filled out questionnaire," [168] a "source of information," [169] a "file card" which is its own archivist.[170]

Exactly the same reveals itself when our relations in the above-mentioned sense are "mutual": "he" is a teacher and "I" am a student; "he" is a doctor and "I" am ill; "he" is authoritarian and "I" am his victim; "he" is a farmer and "I" am a technician; "he" is a Jew and "I" am a Christian. In other words, "he" is a file card and "I" am a file card. "We" are filled out questionnaires.

The principle of Christian ethics: "Judge not lest you be judged" appears to be open to a philosophical interpretation.[171] As soon as I judge the other—i.e., reduce him to the qualities I express in objective predicates, as soon as I classify him, or put him into a category—the judgment is also pronounced upon me. I need not wait till the end of time, for the judgment is executed at once: I experience myself as identified with my qualities, the bearer of predicates, classified and categorized. I experience myself as "alone" and therefore also as "condemned."

When we clearly realize this, we feel spontaneously inclined to protest: are "we" not more, much more than those qualities and predicates? But, what are "we," then? What can "we" be? What ought "we" to be?

It is not difficult to recognize in the above-described "we" the "we" of bureaucracy, administration, and a world ruled by technocracy. It is the "we" of indifference, in which no one is someone because no one cares for anyone. But "seeing" in the other nothing but a "he" is a way of treating the other, a way in which I encounter him. That way of treating the other is a reality, just as Sartre's hateful stare is a reality. But is it the only possible way I can meet my fellowman? Obviously not.

168Marcel, *RI*, p. 49.
169*JM*, p. 174.
170*RI*, p. 71.
171*JM*, p. 65.

This may be the appropriate place to refer again to one of Heidegger's arguments in favor of "being with." Heidegger points out that the experience of being alone refers to a more original being called to being-together: being alone is a deficient mode of "being with." [172] His point is well taken. One can experience this in the "we" of indifference, at least if one does not systematically close oneself to that experience. In the "he," I experience the other as "absent," as "far away" from me. No geometrical distance is involved here, for it could easily happen that the other is geometrically close to me and, nonetheless, "far away" from me.[173] What is at stake here is a certain "fullness" of being-man, and it is in reference to this "fullness" that I experience the other as "far" from me and myself as "alone." It can happen that I walk around with the other, talk with him, even work together with him day after day, and that, in spite of all this, he remains "far" from me.[174] My experience of "being alone" corresponds to such a situation. It is as if I am identified with the qualities which I have in the eyes of the other.[175]

An Objection

The objection could be raised that we are going too far here by speaking about indifference in connection with simple functional encounters, such as that between a ticket clerk and a traveller. The term "indifference" has a pejorative meaning, it refers to a relationship that is not what it ought to be. But can one seriously claim that the encounter between the ticket clerk and the traveller ought to be more than the meeting of functions? What ought a waiter to be more than a waiter? Or a teacher more than a teacher? Can one expect more of a quarterback than that he be a quarterback? In summary, can one reproach functional relations for being functional? Why, then, should the pejorative label "indifference" be attached to functionality within society?

It was not at all our intention to suggest that functionality in society is something which ought not to exist. One who wishes to eliminate the "bearing of functions" and, conse-

---

[172]Heidegger, *SZ*, p. 120.
[173]Marcel, *ME* I, p. 221.
[174]*RI*, p. 48.
[175]Dawiet van Sonsbeek, *Het zijn als mysterie in de ervaring en het denken van Gabriel Marcel*, Antwerpen, 1966, pp. 118-131.

quently, functional encounters would stupidly eliminate all humanity which has been established as facticity in our society in the course of history. We do not call functional relations "indifference" because they are functional but only because, and to the extent that, they are *purely* functional. In purely functional relations there is *not a trace* of affectivity. Obviously we do not claim that every functional encounter must be permeated with the highest degree of love, but we do assert that every functional encounter ought to participate in a *general* affective attitude toward man, so that it ceases at once to be *purely* functional. The point is not that an explicit act of love is needed, but that there ought to be a loving disposition. The latter practically cannot be defined, but its presence in interhuman relationships is experienced as something beneficial and its absence as something painful. This absence from an encounter is rightly called "indifference." Something is lacking that ought to be there. Man experiences himself as "alone" and the other as "far away."

Am I not more than the sum total of my qualities? [176] Am I not more than the object of an "objective" judgment? [177] What does it mean that I am "alone" when the other is "far" from me? The fact that I "miss" the other, that I can "miss" him points to a more original call, the call to togetherness.

Encounter

If nothing but the "we" of indifference were possible, the term "encounter" could not have the authentically human meaning which is ascribed to it.[178] In the authentically human sense the term is loaded with affectivity, an affectivity of which there is no trace in the "we" of indifference. Used in its authentically human sense, the term betrays a kind of participation in the personal life of the other for whom I "care." But this is precisely what is lacking in indifference. If there were nothing but the "we" of indifference, the encounter of human beings would

---

[176]"Je suis toujours à tout moment plus que l'ensemble de prédicats que serait susceptible de mettre en lumière une enquête faite par moi-même—ou par tout autre—sur moi-même." *JM*, p. 196.

[177]"Certes je puis me décrire—mais outre qu'il n'est point aisé de comprendre comment cette description est métaphysiquement possible, ne faut-il pas dire que ma réalité la plus profonde déborde infiniment cette description?" *JM*, p. 215.

[178]"Rencontrer quelqu'un, ce n'est pas seulement le croiser, c'est être au moins un instant auprès de lui, avec lui; c'est dirai-je d'un mot dont je devrai user plus d'une fois, une coprésence." *RI*, p. 20.

not be much more than a bumping into each other of certain qualities. But there are cases in which obviously more is experienced than just that.

Let us assume that I am standing in a car of the Métro, the Paris subway. The car is filled to overflowing, and whenever the train lurches, I bump into one of my fellow travellers. Nobody pays any attention to this: we are for one another "travellers in a full subway car." On the platform of the Saint-Michel station, from which another train has just departed, only one man is waiting. He opens the door of the car to enter and "bumps" into me, who happens to stand near the door. It is possible that he will just "bump" into me, but also that something entirely different will take place between this man and me.[179] A certain feeling may grow between us, if only because of the trouble I take to try and make room for him, the friendly smile on his face or the tone of his voice when he says: "I am sorry" while his foot lands on my toes. What is that between this man and me—that reality between us—which both of us feel when we get out and go our separate ways? "Nothing," a materialist would answer, but he is wrong. It is "almost nothing," but during the short trip it exercised a kind of hidden circular "causality" in such an effective way that, if the next day I happen to meet the same man again in the Louvre, I would at once be inclined to speak to him and say: "Hey, are you also here?"[180]

What happened between this man and me? Did I "bump" into him as I could bump into the door of the subway car when it suddenly closes? If matters are presented that way, my encounter with that man becomes unintelligible. We again use the term "encounter," but the term now expresses a reality, a "we" with a much more profound meaning, permeated with genuine humanity and affectivity. This "we" is not the "we" of a realized indifference, for that man was one for whom I "cared." I did not wish him to miss this train, in spite of the lack of

[179]"Mais il suffit parfois d'une rencontre de regards, ou d'une parole, ou d'un service échangé, pour que deux êtres sachent immédiatement qu'il y a entre eux une sorte de communauté métaphysique et qu'à travers la médiation des qualités ils découvrent déjà une solidarité de leurs essences personnelles." Nédoncelle, *La réciprocité des consciences*, Paris, 1942, p. 17.

[180]These thoughts paraphrase a suggestion made by Marcel in *ME*, I, p. 153.

room. He, too, "cared" for me, as was evident from the tone of his voice when he gingerly stepped on my toes.

The most striking aspect of our stiuation, however, is that the objective qualities, which could have been said of both of us, remained wholly in the background during our encounter. Only now I realize that this man was somewhat stout and that there was something wrong with his left eye. But I did not reduce him to the predicates "fat" and "cross-eyed." If I had done this, what happened between us would never have become a reality; and, on meeting him the next day in the Louvre, I would not have spoken to him, but simply would have said to myself: "There is that cross-eyed fatso again."

5. PHENOMENOLOGY OF LOVE

In what was said above about hatred and indifference these modes of being-man revealed themselves as modes of "accompanying one another." We reserved the term "accompanying one another" for *co-existing* in encounter with, and presence to the other as a subject. In this encounter and this presence there are several specific possibilities of *"treating"* one another as subjects." Love also is such a possibility.

The example given at the end of the preceding section could serve as a starting point on the road toward a correct concept of what love really means. For we are spontaneously convinced that in the stiuation suggested in that example there really is a first beginning of what may be called authentic love. We must now see what the proper character is of authentic love.

Subjectivity as Appeal

The loving encounter always implies the other's appeal to my subjectivity. A call goes out from him, embodied in a word, a gesture, a look, a request. His word, gesture, look or request signify an invitation addressed to me, the true meaning of which is very difficult to express in words. No matter, however, in what form the other's appeal embodies itself, it always contains an invitation to me to step, as it were, out of myself, to break with my pre-occupation with myself and my fascination with my own concerns.

Perhaps this is already saying too much. We said the other's appeal is an "invitation to me to step out of myself." But under what conditions is it possible to "see" that this is so? The compulsive way in which I am centered on myself and my own concerns makes it clear why I have such difficulty in understanding the other's appeal to me. To *see* a certain reality, I need more than eyes; to understand the meaning of the other's appeal to me, I need a special attitude, and this attitude itself implies that I have already broken away to some extent from pre-occupation with myself.[181] One who is wholly permeated with pride or cupidity "sees" nothing, for the other's appeal has nothing violent about it, it is not brutal, not bent on conquest, it does not jolt me and always leaves open the possibility of refusal.[182] It does not present itself as a demand, for it is too humble to demand anything. But this is also the reason why it is possible for me not to see the other's appeal. If I am fully pre-occupied with myself, absorbed in my pursuits, obsessed by my thoughts and my desires, I will not understand the other's appeal. Fully pre-occupied with myself, I am *a priori* convinced that I am excused, no matter what the other's request may be, even though I do not explicitly realize that I have that conviction.[183] "Excused beforehand from everything," I am insensitive to any appeal.

In daily life I am used to playing a role: I am a physician, a middle class citizen, a teacher, a judge, priest, intellectual, or laborer. As a judge I face the delinquent, as a teacher the student, as a physician the patient, as a priest the seeker or the sinner. But who are they, those delinquents, students, patients, seekers, and sinners? They are those who address an appeal to me, but I will not understand their appeal if I identify myself with the role I have to play. This identification means that I am pre-occupied with myself, so that I close myself to the *real* appeal of the other to me.

What the Appeal Is Not

Is it possible to render the appeal with which we are concerned here more explicit? To begin with the easier part, let us first say what the appeal is not. It may not be understood as the attractiveness proper to one or the other bodily or spiri-

---

[181]Marcel, *EA*, p. 152-155.
[182]"Dans transitivité non-violente se produit l'épiphanie même du visage." E. Levinas, *Totalité et Infini*, p. 22.
[183]*EA*, pp. 101-102, 105-106.

tual quality of the other subject.[184] The other's attractive qualities can perhaps invite me to a "being near the other," but is
this enough to speak of love? Would love be impossible if
the other's qualities are not attractive? Or would it have to cease
if those qualities cease to attract? Qualities can give rise to
an enamoredness in which the desire to "be near the other" is
inherent, but is love not much more? As long as only the
other's qualities speak to me, whether positively or negatively,
my answer will not be more than an answer to a "he" or "she."
One who really loves, however, realizes that the other's qualities or merits matter little or nothing: they fall into the background to make room for what the other is, over and above a
particular facticity, over and above a "file card." [185]

Similarly, the other's appeal to me may not be understood
as identical with any explicit request. A request could be explicitated as the expression of a factical situation for which
provisions have to be made. Such a request is not the other's appeal to me, as is evident from the fact that, even if I materially
satisfy that request, the other often goes away very much dissatisfied. He will be dissatisfied, for instance, if he realizes
that I do not wholeheartedly do or give him what he asks; that I
receive him or speak to him only in a passing way; that he
disturbs me, is too much for me; that I am distracted or ab-
sent-minded.[186] I satisfy his request, yet he is dissatisfied. The
reason is that his appeal to me is more than his explicitly formulated request: the other does not merely "make" a request,
he "is" an appeal.

"Be With Me"

Understanding the other's appeal to me does not relate to
his facticity but rather to what he is over and above his facticity, viz., a subject. His subjectivity *itself* is the appeal addressed to me, it is an appeal to me to share in his subjectivity.

184"La manière dont se présente l'Autre, dépassant *l'idée de l'Autre
en moi,* nous l'appelons, en effet, visage. Cette *façon* ne consiste pas à
figurer comme thème sous mon regard, à s'étaler comme un ensemble de
qualités formant une image. Le visage d'Autrui détruit à tout moment, et
déborde l'image plastique qu'il me laisse, l'idée à ma mesure et à la mesure
de son *ideatum*—l'idée adéquate." Levinas, *op. cit.,* p. 21.

185"C'est en vain que l'amant dénombre les caractères, les mérites de
l'être aimé; il est certain a priori que cet inventaire ne lui rendra pas son
amour transparent pour lui-même." *JM,* p. 226.

186G. Marcel, "Positions et Approches concrètes du Mystère ontologique," *Le monde cassé,* Paris, 1933, p. 293.

Marcel tries to express this appeal in the words "Be with me." [187]
It is the other's appeal to me to leave my self-centeredness, to
share in his subjectivity, to accept, support, and increase it.

A New Dimension of Existence

If I am to understand the appeal: "Be with me," I must already have overcome to some extent my fascination with myself.
But, on the other hand, it is precisely the other's appeal to me
that enables me to liberate myself from myself. His appeal reveals to me an entirely new, perhaps wholly unsuspected, dimension of my *existence*. Who am I? Am I not more than the
sum total of my objective qualities,[188] more than a filled-out file
card? Am I not more than the role I play, more than my facticity? I am, indeed, more than my facticity because I am its
bearer as a subject and, therefore, as freedom. As freedom, I
"nihilate" and transcend every form of facticity; as freedom, I
continually extend myself toward a never finished future in order
to establish myself always more securely in my world. But
in every new phase of the history of my "building my nest in
the world," I always find myself again as the "bearer of objective
qualities," as a "filled out file card," as the "player of a role," as
facticity. Who am I?

Understanding the other's appeal to me puts my freedom
and my security at stake,[189] because the appearance of his subjectivity as appeal to me reveals me to myself in an entirely new
dimension—the dimension of my destiny for the other. The
world with its space and time constitutes, in the first instance, the
ex of my *existence;* but the appearance of the other's subjectivity as appeal gives to my *existence* a dimension of "depth." [190] I
am called to realize myself in the world, but not as an egoist.
The other's appeal to me makes me "see," in "the second in-

---

[187]"Pour que cette unité soit, il faut d'abord, semble-t-il, qu'il y ait appel,
invocation, un 'sois avec moi' plus ou moins clairement énoncé. Il faut que
cet appel soit entendu, sans nécessairement que le sujet sache qu'il l'entend,
et c'est sur la base de ce co-esse mystérieux que la vision pourra s'édifier."
JM, p. 169.

[188]*JM*, pp. 215-216.

[189]"L'infini débordant l'idée de l'infini, met en cause la liberté spontanée
en nous. Il la commande et la juge et l'amène à sa vérité." Levinas,
op. cit., p. 22.

[190]"Le visage se refuse à la possession, à mes pouvoirs. Dans son
épiphanie, dans l'expression, le sensible, encore saisissable se mue en résistance
totale à la prise. Cette mutation ne se peut que par l'ouverture d'une
dimension nouvelle." Levinas, *op. cit.*, p. 172.

stance," the truth about my own being and calls me to bring about this truth—that is, to realize myself in the world *for the other*. The appearance of the other's subjectivity as appeal calls me to "conversion," to a change in my self-realization. The truth of my own essence prescribes to me that I conquer the world in order that *the other* can *exist*.

Love as "Yes" to the Other

The other's appeal and my consciousness of my destiny demand that I give an answer. But I realize that this answer must be adapted to the appeal: "Be with me." A piece of information, a crust of bread, a coin *are* not the answer sought of me. On the contrary, I realize that they can be means by which I could cheaply escape the answer which I really owe the other. The other's "Be with me" is an appeal to my *being,* to being-together. Giving him a piece of bread or some money can mean that I reply to his appeal by saying: "Be satisfied if I give you from what I *have*." Thus I would have again locked myself up in my own world—in myself—in the hope that the other will never again disturb me. I remain alone, and the other remains far away.

If the other's appeal does not go out from his facticity, the appropriate answer to that appeal, likewise, does not primarily refer to his particular facticity. This is the reason why my destiny for the other is so difficult to define. The appeal *is* not an explicit request, the answer is not the material granting of a desire. Sometimes the refusal to satisfy a particular request can be the only way I can *really* answer the other. The answer to the other's appeal is an answer to his subjectivity. As an embodied subject, the other is the source of meaning and of new meaning, he continually and freely gives meaning and new meaning to his facticity and his world. As a subject—as another "I," a selfhood—the other freely makes his way through the world, brings about his history, goes forward to his destiny. His appeal to me means that he invites me to affirm his subjectivity, to offer him a possibility to *exist,* to consent to his freedom, to accept, support and share in his freedom. My "yes" to his appeal is known as *love*.[191]

---

[191] ". . . l'amour est une volonté de promotion. Le moi qui aime veut avant tout l'existence du toi; il veut en outre le développement autonome de ce toi; . . ." Nédoncelle, *Vers une philosophie de l'amour*, Paris, 1946, p. 11.

As used in the above context, there is little danger that the term "love" will be misunderstood, but the same cannot be affirmed of its everyday use. There the term often means an insipid kind of sentimentality or a lax permissiveness.

Love, however, has nothing to do with sentimentality. This should be evident from the preceding considerations and from the meaning of sentimentality. Sentimentality does not *act,* does not accomplish anything in the world. One who joins others in singing the German song "All people become brothers," or the American "We shall overcome," and cries with emotion on the way home, has not made the world more human, has not loved anyone. Love is the "yes" to the other's subjectivity, but this subjectivity occurs only as immersed in the body and involved in the world. "Willing" the other as a subject is equiprimordially a "willing" of the other's body-for-him and of a piece of the world-for-him. The man who loves his fellowman takes care of the other's body, is concerned about the other's needs for his material life, builds hospitals, constructs roads, tames rivers, blocks the sea, establishes traffic laws, opens schools and prisons, humanizes the economic, social and political structures of society, etc. He does all this in order that it may be possible for the other to be a subject, a self, and free.

It was the purely spiritualistic conception of love that made Marx call all speaking of love "religious nonsense." Thus his own feeling for his felllowman finds no place in his philosophy. As long as the "yes" to the other is conceived as "dwelling" in a Cartesian interiority, Marx's protest makes sense: it is a protest against sentimentality. On the other hand, however, it is certain that the relations between men cannot be humanized if love does not enter the world as a subjective inspiration. Humanity does not come into existence "with the necessity of a natural process." [192]

Similarly, love is not permissiveness. Permissiveness could be described as openness or adaptability to the other's arbitrariness and caprice. Love is the "yes" to subjectivity as freedom. But to affirm, will, and support the other's freedom is not the same as giving in to the other's arbitrariness; for his *real* freedom is at the same time a being bound to the truth of his own essence

---

[192]Marx, "Geschichtliche Tendenz der kapitalischen Akkumulation," K. Marx and Fr. Engels, *Ausgewählte Schriften in zwei Bänden,* Berlin, 1952, I, p. 434.

and the true destiny of his being. Let us call this destiny, in the most general way, "happiness," without making here an attempt to answer the question in what this happiness consists. It could be material possessions, power, wisdom, virtue, sexuality, perhaps even the "possession" of God. No matter what I think about the answer to that question, obviously my conviction about what human happiness is will give an orientation to my love for the other. For in executing my "yes" to the other's subjectivity it is not possible for me to have no opinion, no intention with respect to freedom's destiny. (Not to have any opinion is also having an opinion.) Similarly, I cannot be indifferent to what the other—whose selfhood I affirm —himself thinks about this destiny. If, for example, the other thinks that his freedom has its destiny in the subjection of everyone to the absolute arbitrariness of one, then my love for him and for all obliges me to oppose him and to close to him—if necessary by force—the roads through the world which would lead him to his "destiny."

How simple it is to write this! But we are actually touching here again a mystery: the absolute good is impossible. There exist "absolute barbarians," people who are always ready to sacrifice others to their arbitrariness and lust. Our "yes" to their subjectivity and to that of their satellites may and must assume the form of resistance and opposition. Love must sometimes make victims, and he who does not wish to accept this simply makes "other victims." The principle of "man's recognition of man" excludes intolerance and tyranny.[193] But there can be no tolerance of intolerance.

Appeal to the Beloved

Is the other the only one with whom love is concerned? This would be going too far: in my love I am also concerned with myself. This statement can be misunderstood, however. We are still dealing here with love as an active turning to the other, not with the legitimate desire *to be loved* by him. Insofar

---

[193]"Aimer, c'est s'intéresser à ce que l'autre est à la première personne et dans son pour-soi, c'est s'efforcer de le constituer dans son intimité, c'est le vouloir comme liberté et principe d'initiative. C'est pourquoi l'objection d'intolérance et de tyrannie, si fréquemment faite à la charité, ne peut s'adresser qu'à une charité mal entendue et mal pratiquée. Qui aime vraiment veut l'autre en tant que sujet et s'efforce de le constituer comme tel." G. Madinier, *Conscience et Amour*, Paris, 1947, p. 127.

as my own subjectivity is an appeal to the other's *existence,* a call upon him to actively participate in my subjectivity, love is also concerned with myself. But this is not the point at issue here. Even in love as active turning to the other, love is in a certain sense also concerned with myself. Let us see in what sense.

Because love wills the other's freedom, it is in a certain sense defenseless. It displays infinite trust and by this very fact it surrenders itself to the other. This surrender contains an appeal of the lover to the beloved. The trust revealed by love and its defenselessness themselves are an appeal of the lover to the beloved. Love is not solely concerned with the other.

Again, however, it is easier to say what this appeal is not than to indicate its meaning at once in a positive way. The appeal of love to the beloved is not the will to draw somehow advantage from one's affective inclination to the other. One who loves cannot possibly try to promote his career or seek a promotion and, at the same time, keep his love pure. If, for instance, a sick person discovers that the nurse, who so "lovingly" takes care of him, does so only in order to become as quickly as possible head nurse or to gain an "eternal crown in heaven" for herself, the patient does not feel that he is really loved.

Secondly, the appeal of love to the beloved does not mean that the lover would wish to force, dominate, or possess the other. Love wills the other's freedom. Love is not satisfied if the other goes in a particular way through the world, not even if that way is good and secure, as required by the destiny of human freedom. Love desires that the other *himself* chooses this good way or avoid that dangerous way.[194]

Sincere availability, then, implies that I forego the temptation to seek my own advancement by loving the other and to dominate the other. Love, however, still contains another moment of self-denial, one which is more difficult to grasp. In love I destine myself for the other, but I vaguely realize that, in doing this, I also go forward to my own destiny. Even if I have never studied a theory about man's destiny, I experience in love that I am on the road toward my own destiny, the fulfillment of my own being as "having to be." Love is the availability of my subjectivity, my belonging to the subject who the

---

[194]"Aimer, c'est vouloir l'autre comme sujet." Madinier, *op. cit.,* p. 95.

other is. In giving and surrendering myself, however, my own proper "selfhood" is revealed to me. My proper self is the available self. In a certain sense I lose myself in love, but this "loss" is not really a loss. I "lose" my inauthenticity. As *existence* I am a certain "yes" to the world and equiprimordially a certain "yes" to myself. This "yes" to myself could easily harden into exclusivism and try to conquer the whole world for myself. But my understanding of the other's subjectivity as an appeal to me and my "yes" to his freedom, strip me of my hardened, egoistic "I." At the same time, the other discloses to me the possibility of consenting to myself—on the basis of my "yes" to his freedom—in a way which at first lay beyond my vision. Is love's appeal to the beloved, then, perhaps a request to offer me the possibility of fulfilling my own manhood? The question we are asking here is the very difficult question of whether love can be wholly disinterested. Is it possible for man to will something without willing it in "his own interest"? With respect to love this question is of special importance, for, in any case, love wills the other's "interest."

It is impossible for man, we think, to love his fellowman in such a way that his love would not *actually* be in the lover's own "interest." It is impossible for man to disregard the fact that love, as active turning to the other, is equiprimordially the fulfillment of his own being, understood as "having to be." [195] But this does not mean that love aims at this fulfillment, i.e., that one's own self-fulfillment is the motive of love. Just the opposite is true. In love, man goes forward to his destiny; he finds the fulfillment of his manhood, provided this fulfillment is not the motive of his love. If the other were to thank me for my affectivity, and I would brush away his thanks by saying that I was interested only in my own self-fulfillment, he would at once understand that I did not really love him. I would ultimately be interested only in my own "career."

Love's appeal to the beloved can only be properly understood when one sees that in willing the other's subjectivity, his freedom can be fruitful only if the other ratifies this will by his own "yes." Love does not wish to force, and for this reason

---

195"L'être qui s'exprime s'impose, mais précisément en en appelant à moi de sa misère et de sa nudité—de sa faim—sans que je puisse être sourd à son appel. De sorte que, dans l'expression, l'être qui s'impose ne limite pas mais promeut ma liberté, en suscitant ma bonté." Levinas, *op. cit.*, p. 175.

it is, in a certain sence, defenseless in reference to the other. Love wills the other's freedom and therefore becomes fruitful only by the other's free consent. The lover, however, *cannot will* that his love be not understood, not accepted, not fruitful. That's why love appeals to the beloved, an appeal which we would like to explicitate in the words: "Accept that I be at your disposal." Even if love is obliged to close certain roads through the world for the beloved, it cannot do otherwise than will that the other *himself* avoid those roads. Love is not satisfied with making it materially impossible for the other to go certain roads. This is what is meant by saying that love refuses to force the other. Love's appeal to the beloved thus means a prayer to the beloved *himself* to see that this road and not that one will lead his subjectivity to its destiny. The prayer: "Accept that I be at your disposal" thus means "See for yourself and realize in freedom your own happiness." The only fruit love may hope for is that the other will *exist*.[196]

The Creativity of Love

The lines which slowly become visible in the explicitation of love converge in one point, viz., the "you." It is always the "you" that is at issue in love, and wherever the "you" is not at stake love loses its authenticity or is even wholly destroyed. Love only becomes possible when I am sensitive for the other's subjectivity as not identical with his qualities, not even with his most noble or most perfect qualities. Secondly, it is the other's subjectivity which is an appeal to love, and not his facticity. The explicitation of his facticity yields an explicitly formulated request, but this request is not identical with the appeal to love. Again, love "wills" the other's subjectivity, and not my own promotion, career, or perfection, and even less my control over the other. All this can pithily be expressed by saying that the motive

---

[196]One may ask whether love implies *per se* reciprocity. Insofar as my love is fruitful only through the other's "yes," the question must be answered in the affirmative. If I love the other, I cannot will that he does not accept my ready availability. In this sense, then, it is true that in love "not everything turns around the other." "Liebe, in der sich 'alles nur um Dich dreht', ist ebensowenig sich-selbst mehrend und zehrt sich ebenso an ihrem eigenen Feuer auf, wie Liebe, in der sich 'alles nur um Mich dreht.'" L. Binswanger, *Grundformen und Erkenntnis menschlichen Daseins*, Zürich, 1953, p. 121. That "not everything turns around the other," however, really means for Binswanger that love is not love unless I am loved with the same intense love with which I myself love. It seems to us that this thesis, which Binswanger presupposes from the very first page of his book, is very debatable.

of my love is "you." I love you because of you, because you are who you are. I love you because you are lovable, but you are lovable because you are who you are.

This "you" does not have here the neutral sense of "another 'I,' " of "subjectivity like my subjectivity," or of the "he" revealed to me in any encounter whatsoever with the being called "man." This "you" most certainly is not the hateful subjectivity of the other who, as Sartre holds, wishes to murder my subjectivity.

The "you" of whom there is question here is the "you for whom I care." This expression, however, says almost nothing if the reality to which it refers is not alive in me.[197] What this "you" means I know by experience, in the broad sense; it is accessible to me as something present to me, on condition that I love the other.[198]

Scientific experience, with its own special attitude of asking questions, tells me nothing about the "you for whom I care." [199] The reality of this "you" is not disclosed to me by an objectivistic psychology limited to an enumeration of psychical qualities or the description of the other's character, temperament, aptitudes, inclinations, deviations, etc. An objectivistic psychology discloses the other's subjectivity as a "filled-out questionnaire," a "he." [200] This does not mean, of course, that love can only make a subjectivistic judgment of the other—that, e.g., it can no longer observe that the other is stupid, uncouth, or immature. The very opposite is true. Love, however, refuses to reduce the other to a series of predicates, and it is precisely love which makes the lover clearly see what the other is over and above his qualities.[201]

All this merely establishes a fact. But after the preceding reflections it is possible to give due weight to this fact and this may perhaps open a road for us by which we can more deeply

---

[197]"Diese Wahrheit kann nicht in Sätzen von objektiver Gültigkeit ausgesprochen, ausgesagt, mitgeteilt und 'gezeigt,' sondern nur 'gelebt' werden." Binswanger, *op. cit.*, p. 111.

[198]Marcel, *ME* II, pp. 11-13.

[199]"Das aber heisst, dass das Seinkönnen in der Wahrheit rein gegenständlicher Erkenntnis und das Seinkönnen in der Wahrheit der Liebe, mit andern Worten dass theoretisch-wissenschaftliche Wahrheit und Wahrheit des Herzens rein als solche 'inkommensurabel' sind." Binswanger, *op. cit.*, p. 110.

[200]"Le jugement porte essentiellement sur un 'lui,' sur quelque chose qui est censé être 'catégorisable' en dehors de toute réponse." *JM*, p. 162.

[201]"L'amour porte sur ce qui est au delà de l'essence, j'ai dit déjà que l'amour est l'acte par lequel une pensée se fait libre en pensant une liberté. L'amour en ce sens va au delà de tout jugement possible, car le jugement ne peut porter que sur l'essence." *JM*, p. 64.

penetrate into the true character of love, understood as active turning to the other.[202]   The emphasis will have to fall here on the *active* nature of this turning to the other.   We would like to conceive this activity as creativity.

In which sense can the subject be called "active" or "creative"?   As was pointed out, the truth of every judgment is founded upon a more profound truth, viz., the unconcealedness of reality for the knowing subject.   Reality's unconcealedness implies the unveiling "activity" of the subject, by which reality is, in the full sense of the term, "reality," i.e., appearing reality. Knowledge is always an encounter in which the subject "lets" reality "be," respecting and accepting it in its own real character.   This "letting be" of reality is not pure activity but also passivity, for it implies respect for, and acceptance of what reality is.   Only when reality is respected and accepted, can knowledge be objective.   Thus the knowing subject's activity is rather limited, precisely because of the passivity which it contains.   It is not a creative activity.

The moment of activity contained in *existence* as being-"at"-the-world—as acting—clearly differs from the activity moment proper to knowledge.   To do carpentry is more than being sensitive and open to reality, and the same must be said of the artistic act.   It makes sense to call the subject's activity in such matter a creative activity.   In doing carpentry work or engaging in artistic work, I do not merely "let" reality be, but I "make" it be.   I build a new meaning.

We would like to ascribe to love also a kind of "making be," the building of a *new* meaning.   But this *making*-be within intersubjectivity differs from the *making*-one-another-be previously emphasized when we stated that *existence* is *co-existence*. We then stated that man is a New Yorker through New Yorkers, a smoker through smokers, a philosopher through philosophers, a Christian through Christians, that a mother is a mother through her children; that a sick person is really only sick when he is visited or forgotten; [203] that a Negro is really only a Negro when he is refused admittance to a bowling alley by its white proprietor; that an asocial family is really asocial only when

---

[202]The reader will have noticed that we intentionally and systematically have excluded from our analysis the phenomenological data of reciprocal love.   This was done in order to avoid confusion and misunderstanding.

[203]J.H. van den Berg, *Psychology of the sickbed*, Pittsburgh, 1966, pp. 40f.

other families refuse to have anything to do with it or when the social worker comes for a visit; that a cute little button nose is really a cute little button nose only when a boyfriend notices it; [204] similarly, a baldhead is really a baldhead only when others ridicule him; a Jew is only a Jew because of the pressure of anti-Semitism; and a boy is really only a boy through a girl.[205]

We realize that these examples should be much more differentiated than they are in the preceding enumeration. Otherwise they are open to all kinds of objections. This risk cannot be avoided, however, without unduly extending this section. Those who wish to object to them should keep in mind that they can easily overshoot their mark. One could, for example, say that a Jew is a Jew also when there are no anti-Semites, that a sick person is sick even when he has no visitors and that a baldhead is bald even when he is not ridiculed because of his bald pate. But such an objection is a mistake: it presupposes that being a Jew is a purely biological matter, that a sick person is sick just as a cauliflower is rotten; and that the baldhead is bald just as a billiard ball is smooth. Such a view disregards the *human* aspect of being a Jew, sick, or bald. A baldhead is not bald as a billiard ball is smooth because a baldhead as a subject is related to his bald pate: he occupies a standpoint with respect to it and can still "do something with it." Man's being is a *human* being because man is the being for whom, in his being, this being itself is an issue. Applied to the baldhead, this means that the reality of a bald pate is distinct from the smoothness of a billiard ball, because the baldhead is a subjectivity which gives meaning to this particular facticity. The kind of meaning, however, which he gives to it depends to a large extent on the way others treat him. This is why we said that a baldhead is really a baldhead only when others ridicule him.

Disregarding, then, the inaccuracies contained in the formulation of the preceding examples, one can see at once their essential point. In my encounter with the other I am the bearer of a being-for-the-other which is, at the same time, a being-through-the-other. But does the other *make* me be? The examples clearly show this: the other *makes* me be "facticity." On the level with which we are concerned here the quasi-process of *making*-one-another-be results in certain "determina-

---

[204]F. Buytendijk, *Ontmoeting der sexen,* Utrecht, 1952, p. 7.
[205]E. De Greef, *Notre destinée et nos instincts,* Paris, 1945, pp. 157-159.

tions" which settle as a kind of sedimentation in *existence* and make it possible to affirm of the *existence* certain predicates expressing this "social facticity." Our *making*-one-another-be makes us bearers of a "social body."

The *loving* encounter, however, does not *make* the other be "facticity" but "subjectivity." [206] Love "creates" the subject. This obviously does not mean that without the other's love I am not a subject. But the statement that I am a subject can have many meanings. It can indicate that I am not a thing, even if my freedom is smothered or crushed in any way whatsoever. It can also indicate that I live in a fullness of manhood which changes every obstacle into a value and allows me to affirm myself as the "king of creation." In other words, the term "subject" has a full scale of meanings. This point should be kept in mind when one tries to understand the creativity of love.

By calling love creative, we ascribe a certain "influence" to it, but this influence must not at all be conceived in a causalistic fashion. The efficacy of love may under no conditions be reduced to the efficacy of a unilateral, deterministic cause, in the sense of physical science. The reason is that the use of such scientific concepts would make it impossible to understand what what love really is: the reality of love—as it is accessible to us in our "lived experience"—cannot be expressed in physical concepts. This should be evident at once when we call to mind the essential moments of love: appeal, destiny, availability, self-denial, and acceptance refer to a reality which implies reciprocity and freedom. These elements are precisely a denial of unilateral and deterministic causality and, therefore, cannot be "explained" through it.

Perhaps there is no better way to arrive at a measure of understanding of love's creativity than a phenomenological analysis of being-loved. What does it mean that the other loves me— that he turns actively to me in love? His loving turning to me *makes* my subjectivity *be* insofar as, through his affection for me, he mysteriously participates in my subjectivity, supporting and favoring it in such a way that I no longer "alone" project my manhood and "alone" go forward to my destiny, but now do so

---

[206]"Est-ce à dire que la volonté de promotion soit une volonté de création? Peut-être. En principe, l'amant aspire à engendrer intégralement l'être de l'aimé." Nédoncelle, *Vers une philosophie de l'amour*, p. 15.

"together" with the other. The other's love gives me to myself if this "being myself" is understood in the sense of a certain fullness of being.[207] Anyone who receives genuine love undeniably knows from his own experience the reality of love's creativity, but this creativity is particularly evident in the pedagogical situation, at least when the latter is what it ought to be.[208] Through the educator's love the child is, as it were, "raised above himself": through the educator's "power" of affection an obstacle loses its invincibility, the person who is being educated becomes "master of the situation" and able to realize himself on a level he would never have reached if he had been left "alone." [209]

The realization that one is no longer "alone" testifies perhaps most eloquently to love's creativity. Love creates a "we," a "being together" that is experienced as wholly different from every other kind of "we" experienced in other encounters. The "we" of love can only be expressed—if it can at all be expressed —in such terms as "fullness," "fulfillment," and "happiness."

My world also is "re-created" by the other's love.[210] This world is the correlate of my self-realizing subjectivity. But through his love the other makes the little "I" I am a big "I." Through his love the world shows its kindest face to me and becomes accessible for me in my self-realization.[211] Through the other's love the world becomes "my homeland"; I feel at home in it and like it.[212] Children whose parents are unfeeling psychopaths are destined to meet only the harshest meanings of the world. For them the world is only resistance, something which from their early youth inspires them to protest and revolt.[213] Without love, the world is hell for man.[214] Without love, the man for whom the time of death has come can only

---

[207]"Who cannot say to his friend or beloved: 'You have given myself to me, I have received my soul from your hands" (Gustave Thibon).

[208]"Le 'nous' devient fécond et créateur; de nouveaux 'toi' sont suscités, et l'enfantement se prolonge dans l'éducation qui est par excellence oeuvre d'amour, puisqu'elle consiste non pas à façonner une nature, comme en un dressage, mais à susciter un sujet existant par soi, sentant et pensant à la première personne." Madinier, *op. cit.*, p. 133.

[209]This idea is the starting point of Carl Rogers' client-centered therapy. Cf. J. Nuttin, *Psycho-analyse et conception spiritualiste de l'homme*, Louvain, 1955, pp. 109-124.

[210]Max Picard, *Die unerschütterliche Ehe*, Erlenbach-Zürich, 1942, pp. 13-25.

[211]"Nil homini amicum sine homine amico" (Augustinus).

[212]"Seit ich in Deiner Liebe ein Ruhen und Bleiben habe ist mir die Welt so klar und so lieb" (Goethe).

[213]See the film of Bunuel *Los Olvidados*.

[214]"Pas besoin de gril, l'enfer c'est les Autres." Sartre.

curse the world and history, but he who dies in love can die in peace.

No one, we expect, will any longer be surprised now that above we refused to conceive the "influence" of love in a causalistic way. For the lover's creative affection only bears fruit if the beloved accepts this affection. His "yes" ratifies the lover's affection and makes it fruitful. He who loves the other wills the other's subjectivity, his freedom and transcendence; he, therefore, can only will that the other *freely* consents to the love offered to him, for love is precisely the willing of the other's freedom. Here, again, the pedagogic situation is particularly illuminating. The educator knows that his love is not understood if the person to be educated simply does what he says because the educator is "boss." The educator's love is only fruitful when the person who is being educated "opts" for his education (Kriekemans). The "influence" of love, then, is not "causal," but a mysterious exchange between subject and subject.

There is only one word to express correctly what love is: it is grace.[215] I can only say "yes." Or is perhaps even this "yes" also, in part, given to me?

To finish this section, let us return briefly to a point mentioned at its beginning, viz., the clear-sightedness of love. The "you for whom I care" is accessible to me, on condition that I love the other. Neither the experience of physical science nor that of an objectivistic psychology can "verify" the reality of this "you." Only love "sees," and what I see is beyond dispute. The indisputable character of this "you"-reality can be understood to some extent now that we have seen that love is creative. For through love I "create" that which I see, I "make" the other "be" what I see. Thus it is impossible for one who does not love to see what the lover sees. In a certain sense the lover does not even care whether others deny what he affirms, for he knows that, if they do not love, they can only deny something else than what he affirms. For this reason he does not even try to "prove" that he is not mistaken: "It is impossible to come to an agreement with one who is unwilling or unable to see" (Husserl).

[215]"Je demeure convaincu que c'est seulement par rapport à la grâce que la liberté humaine peut être définie en profondeur." G. Marcel, *L'Homme problématique*, p. 71.

6. Phenomenology of Justice

Any study of love, conceived as "humanity" *par excellence,* is almost forced to devote attention also to justice.[216] Justice is usually conceived as the willingness to abide by the legal order and, if this is done, it is not difficult to show how much "humanity" there is in society, because its members simply do what is prescribed by positive law.

Today, however, one can observe the strange phenomenon that many of those who pursue the positive sciences of law refuse to identify "justice" with the "legal order," and to define justice as the willingness simply to do what positive law prescribes. This fact is all the more remarkable because not too long ago the general opinion existed that nothing remained to be added when the pursuers of the various positive sciences of law had spoken *as jurists.* In the nineteenth century, the jurists generally held the conviction that "justice" and "positive law" were identical. They lived in an era of legal positivism.[217]

The Strength of Legal Positivism

In a positivistic conception of justice there obviously is no room for a *philosophy* of right or law. For, no matter how one wishes to define such a philosophy, it will have to speak about justice and injustice. If, however, justice and injustice are identical with what positive law permits or prohibits, then there is no way in which a philosophy of right could add anything to what has already been said by the positive science of law.

When society passes through an era of internal peace, the legal order can reach such a high standing and respect that it becomes almost inviolable. Practically everyone's interest demands that the legal norms be held indisputable and definitive. Only for the disadvantaged does the legal order of such a peaceful area appear to be a problem. They have the impression that the legal order is simply the product of arbitrary decisions made by the ruling powers. The law forbids, for instance, to beg near the entrance of a church, to steal bread or to sleep under bridges. All this is forbidden to both the rich and the poor.[218]

---

[216]See, e.g., the controversy between Renouvier and Secrétan, related by Madinier, *op. cit.,* pp. 25-51.

[217]Hans Welzel, "Naturrecht und Rechtspositivismus," *Festschrift für Hans Niedermeyer,* Göttingen, 1953, p. 279.

[218]Fechner, *Rechtsphilosophie,* Tübingen, 1956, pp. 9-10.

After the chaos of World War II, however, there was no longer anyone for whom the legal order was simply inviolable. Everyone realized that this order had been corrupted by the arbitrary decisions of those in power.[219] This corruption had to be disposed of. Legal vacuums arose in every field, and new regulations appeared necessary. But on the basis of what principles could those regulations be made? Thus there arose again a call for "the natural law," which is the core of the philosophy of right and law.[220]

This restoration of the "natural law," however, does not mean that legal positivism is an unimportant phenomenon in the history of the philosophy of right and law. On the contrary, legal positivism rejects the philosophy of law, but presents itself as *the* philosophy of law and justice *tout court*. It simply identifies justice with the legal order, with the rules laid down by law, customs, jurisprudence and the institutions erected in the course of history. Although this view of justice is not tenable, it has arguments in its favor that are very strong. Anyone should be sensitive to the idea that a society's value is in direct ratio to the value this society attaches to man's relationship with his fellowman; anyone should be able to see also the important role which the *act* of establishing a legal order plays in the *actual* humanization of interhuman relationships. But one who sees these points also sees that there can be no question of justice, in the provisional and still vague sense of humanity, if the legal order itself is not explicitated as an essential aspect of justice *tout court*.[222]

---

[219]G. Radbruch, "Die Erneuerung des Rechts," *Die Wandlung,* II(1947), pp. 8-16.

[220]"Auf weiten Gebieten entstanden rechtsleere Räume, die einer Neuordnung von Grund aus bedurften. Es waren jedoch selbst die Richtmasse dazu zerstört, verzerrt oder in Vergessenheit geraten. Dies führte zum Ruf nach dem Naturrecht, das wie ein Phoenix aus der Asche des Positivismus emporstieg und eine vorher nicht geahnte 'Wiedergeburt' erlebte. Mit ihm gewann die Rechtsphilosophie (deren Kernstück die Naturrechtslehre ist) erneute Bedeutung." Fechner, *op. cit.,* p. 3.

[221]"Das edelste 'Bewusstsein' und die schönste 'Idee' als solche tragen auch nicht eine Linie zum Wachstum, zur Aenderung, überhaupt zur Entstehung des Rechts bei. Sie sind ohne *That* nichts. Der Gedanke muss erst noch einen besonderen Weg gehen; ohne diesen Gang ist noch keiner Recht geworden, wird keiner Recht und kann keiner Recht werden." K. Bergbohm, *Jurisprudenz und Rechtsphilosophie,* Leipzig, 1892, I, pp. 544-545.

[222]"Obwohl ein bedenkliches Zeichen des Verfalls rechtsethischer Substanz und Ausdruck eines hybriden Glaubens an die rechtschaffende Kraft des (National-)Staates, darf der 'Positivismus' nicht nur unter diesem Aspekt beurteilt werden. Denn: so sehr die 'Rechtssicherheit' als *einziger* Rechtswert den Naturrechtsgedanken zu verneinen scheint (weil sie die 'Gerechtigkeit'

The act of establishing a legal order, however, presupposes a certain *power*, the power to impose and enforce decisions and regulations. One who has a clear insight into the demands made by the ideal of humanity and does not have the power to impose and enforce certain decisions and regulations *does not really accomplish anything*. He can demand and preach humanity, but he cannot bring it about; he can hope for peace, but he cannot establish it. Because there is no humanity without a legal order, because there is no legal order unless it is established by power, and because, generally speaking, the state actually has this power, one can understand that the legal positivist simply identifies justice with what the state demands. Justice, in the provisionally vague sense of humanity, presupposes order. But there is no order, no actual and real humanity, unless it is *established*, and it can be established only by someone—or some authority—who has the power to do this. Barbarism, the war of all against all, is more effectively contained by a primitive emergency proclamation than by an ideal of justice.[223]

Nevertheless, this cannot be the last word. History has taught us this in a terrible lesson. As late as 1932, the German legal positivist Gustav Radbruch wrote in the third edition of his RECHTSPHILOSOPHIE that he who holds power to impose rules of laws proves by that very fact that he is called to make rules of law. For the judge it then becomes a professional obligation to change the law's will-to-validity into actual validity. The judge may merely ask himself what legally ought to be done, and not what is just. The judge must put aside his own sense of justice and follow the dictates of the law. Priests and ministers who preach against their own convictions are despicable, but not so judges: a judge who does not allow himself to be sidetracked by his own sense of justice is praiseworthy.[224]

---

ausser acht lässt, d.h. die 'differentia specifica' zwischen iustitia und utilitas verkennt)—so liegt eben doch auch in der 'Positivität' des Rechts selber etwas 'Natürliches', zur 'Natur der Sache' Gehörendes. Grund dafür ist, dass eben (doch) letzten Endes alles Recht *da* sein, 'gelten', sich 'realisieren', 'verzeiten' will; es liegt das in der (wesensnotwendigen) 'Wirklichkeit' des Rechts begründet, in seiner 'Praxis' als Friedensordnung." Erik Wolf, *Das Problem der Naturrechtslehre*, Karlsruhe, 1955, pp. 95-96.

[223]"Die gedanklich idealste Ordnung, die diese wirklichkeitsformende Kraft nicht besitzt, ist kein Recht, während die unvolkommenste Notordnung, welche jene wirklichkeitsgestaltende Macht aufweist die essentielle Funktion des Rechts erfüllt." Welzel, "Naturrecht und Rechtspositivismus," *Festschrift für Hans Niedermeyer*, pp. 286-287.

[224]Hans Welzel, *art. cit.* p. 279.

Thus instructed, says Hans Welzel, the German jurists entered the Third *Reich*. Theoretically it had already been established for them that they could not resist if they were ordered to condemn to death all blue-eyed children, on condition that the authorities giving the order had the power to impose their commands. This theoretical powerlessness then also appeared to be a practical impotence to resist. After the fall of the Third *Reich,* legal positivism revealed itself as an hypothesis wrecked by the gruesome reality of history. The same Radbruch who had made the German jurists powerless before Hitler's system wrote in 1947 that the legal sciences should again reflect upon the age-old wisdom that there exists a higher right than the law —a "natural right," a "divine right," a "right of reason"—and that injustice remains injustice as measured by this right, even if that injustice is given the form of a law.[225]

One who identifies right with the legal order is *almost* right, and the same is true for one who identifies right with power. He is *almost* right and, therefore, he is not right.

The Untenable Character of Legal Positivism

In spite of the power of legal positivism, its identification of right and the legal order makes it untenable. First of all, the legal rules used by the jurists have been *made.* The rules of law which existed formerly, those that exist now and those which will exist in the future are the work of man. They are made, not found somewhere as a traveller discovers a mountain. Why does man make those rules? Obviously, *in order that there be justice,* and not in order that there be legal rules. The fact that rules of law are made in order that there be justice means that the aim pursued by the making of those rules is the establishment of "rights," in the provisionally still vague sense

---

[225]"Die überkommene Auffassung des Rechts, der seit Jahrzehnten unter den deutschen Juristen unbestritten herrschende *Positivismus* und seine Lehre 'Gesetz ist Gesetz', war gegenüber einem solchen Unrecht in der Form des Gesetzes wehrlos und machtlos; die Anhänger dieser Lehre waren genötigt, jedes noch so ungerechte Gesetz als Recht anzuerkennen. Die Rechtswissenschaft muss sich wieder auf die jahrtausendalte gemeinsame Weisheit der Antike, des christlichen Mittelalters und des Zeitalters der Aufklärung besinnen, dass es ein höheres Recht gebe als das Gesetz, ein Naturrecht, ein Gottesrecht, ein Vernunftrecht, kurz ein übergesetzliches Recht, an dem gemessen das Unrecht Unrecht bleibt, auch wenn es in die Form des Gesetzes gegossen ist,—von dem auch das auf Grund eines solchen ungerechten Gesetzes gesprochene Urteil nicht Rechtsprechung ist, vielmehr Unrecht." Radbruch, "Die Erneuerung des Rechts," *Die Wandlung,* II(1947), pp. 9-10.

of humanity. If this is true, then right and legal rules can no longer be identified.

Secondly, man continually keeps revising the legal rules, the reason being his conviction that the complex of laws also contains injustices. Anyone who is somewhat familiar with the law knows that this is really true. But the fact that the complex of laws contains injustices does not mean that among those laws there are some laws which go counter to the laws: they are unjust because they go against justice, against humanity. Man must continually revise the legal rules in order that there be less and less injustice, i.e., in order to make the laws more in harmony with justice.[226] This, again, shows that justice and the rules of law must not be identified.

Finally, it is possible—as does happen—to manipulate the complex of laws in such a way that one can commit the greatest injustice efficiently and with impunity. If justice and law were identical, then such a possibility could not exist. The fact, however, that it does exist and does happen shows that the identity of justice and law cannot be maintained.

We realize, of course, that all this is an abomination in the eyes of a man like Hans Kelsen, who spent his entire life in trying to "purify" the philosophy of law from such questions. On the basis of the "purity" he demands for the theory of law, Kelsen refuses to call a legal order good or bad, just or unjust. Those who occupy themselves with such questions make value judgments, pursue politics or lapse into subjectivism. The theory of law can only be an "objective science" if it abstains from such questions.[227]

The American jurist Roscoe Pound counters this position by pointing out that if the philosophy of law must, for the sake of the "purity" of the theory of law, reject every value judgment, then it actually gives up everything that gives worth to a philosophy of law.[228] The same point keeps recurring all

---

[226]"On peut et, en un sens, on doit même en appeler de lois et d'institutions moins bonnes à des lois et à des institutions plus parfaites, et, contre la justice existante et définie par les moeurs, les coutumes, les institutions et les lois, travailler à l'établissement d'une justice meilleure." Madinier, *Conscience et Amour*, pp. 54-55.
[227]H. Kelsen, "Was ist die Reine Rechtslehre?," *Demokratie und Rechtsstaat, Festgabe zum 60. Geburtstag von Zaccaria Giacometti*, Zürich, 1953, pp. 152-153.
[228]Quoted by G.E. Langemeyer, *Inleiding tot de studie van de Wijsbegeerte des Rechts*, Zwolle, 1956, p. 134.

the time: the attitude of asking philosophical questions is not the same as that of positive science; *therefore,* says the legal positivist, in philosophy there can be no question of being "objective" and "scientific." The only legitimate conclusion, however, would be that the objectivity and scientific character of philosophy differs from that of positive science. But that which is different from what is accepted within a particular positive science cannot be rejected simply because it is different.

There would be few, if any, objections to Kelsen's view of the "purity" of the theory of law if he had merely wished to say that the jurist as a jurist does not have the task of asking philosophical questions.[229] Within the questioning attitude of the positive sciences of law the question whether a positive law and a legal order are just or unjust does not occur—just as the question of the ethical meaning of bacteriological warfare does not occur and cannot occur in bacteriology. The bacteriologist, *as* bacteriologist, does not ask any ethical questions. But Kelsen goes much further: he considers it a fatal form of presumption for a "pure theory of law" to ask any question about the justice or injustice of a legal order.

It is true, of course, that the positive sciences of law cannot ask this question. But one who reflects upon positive law and the positive sciences of law—*and this is what Kelsen is doing*—does not pursue a positive science but philosophizes about the law. He imposes upon the philosophy of law the same demands as on the positive sciences of law, and refuses to let it ask certain questions *because* the positive sciences of law are unable to ask these questions. Thus, in order that the theory of law be "pure," he demands that the *philosophy* of law be a positive *science* of law. But how can this demand be justified on the basis of a positive science of law? One who holds such a position must logically accept the consequence that *any arbitrary content* can be put into the law, for the positive sciences of law cannot show that this is not possible. Philosophy of law, therefore, according to Kelsen, may not deny it either; other-otherwise it is not "pure." All this, however, simply shows that the philosophy of law *cannot* and *may not* be "pure" in

---

[229]"Der Positivismus ist die *praktische* Beschäftigung mit dem Recht selbst; in dieser geht er ganz auf und hält sich dabei an das Dichterwort: 'Bilde, Künstler! Rede nicht'." Welzel, *art. cit.,* p. 282.

the sense Kelsen gives to this term. In other words, the philosophy of law cannot be a kind of positivism.

Thus it follows that even for those who dominate the positive sciences of law there remain fundamental questions which can never be answered by those sciences. The first of these questions has already been formulated above: what exactly is the principle or "right" that serves as an orientation point for the rules of law [230] and guides man to be just?

The Normative Character of the Legal Order

All jurists are convinced that the legal order *ought* to be observed. But this conviction inevitably gives rise to certain crucial questions. Why must the legal norms be obeyed? Is it because there is a legal rule prescribing obedience? Such an answer merely evades the question, for one can at once ask why such a legal rule must be obeyed. The positive sciences of law have the task and the duty to reflect upon all kinds of details and shades of meaning with respect to the obligatory character of various positive rules of law. The most fundamental question, however—viz., the ground on which the obligatory character of the entire legal order as such is based—cannot be answered by a reference to a positive rule of law. Legal positivism, which identifies right and legal order, leaves the entire legal order without a foundation. Although the positive sciences of law can be specific with respect to all kinds of particular obligations, they cannot account for the obligatory character of the entire legal order by referring to a particular obligation.

This same idea can also be expressed in a different way, one which has the advantage of clearly showing the relationship between the following two questions: what is right in contradistinction to the legal order? and, what is the foundation of the "ought" contained in the legal order? Within the framework of a constituted legal order the statement that man ought to be

---

[230]"Diese Begriffsbestimmung . . . ist also nicht juristischer, sondern vorjuristischer, d.h. im Verhältnis zur Rechtswissenschaft apriorischer Natur. Der Rechtsbegriff ist nicht ein gewöhnlicher, zufälliger, sondern ein notwendiger Allgemeinbegriff, das Recht ist nicht deshalb Recht, weil die einzelnen Rechtserscheinungen sich ihm einordnen lassen, vielmehr sind umgekehrt die Rechtserscheinungen nur deshalb 'Rechts'-erscheinungen, weil der Begriff des Rechts sie umfasst." Radbruch, *Rechtsphilosophie*, vierte Auflage, nach dem Tode des Verfassers besorgt und biographisch eingeleitet von Dr. Erik Wolf, Stuttgart, 1950, p. 129.

just means that he ought to obey the rules of law. In this context, then, justice must be described as the willingness to conform to the demands of the legal order. This willingness presupposes man as a *subject,* and the "ought" ascribed to justice implies that this willingness is not something left to the subject's own arbitrary decision, not something to which he can remain, without prejudice, sensitive or insensitive, but an attitude which is *obligatory.* If, then, the subject *himself* is not obliged, better even, if being-a-subject *itself* does not imply a certain obligation, then it remains fundamentally unexplained that the legal order has an obligatory character. If the subject *himself* cannot be explicitated as an "obligation," one can endlessly repeat that the legal order has an obligatory character, but this repeated assertion does not really mean anything. A certain "ought" must be inherent, not to the legal order, but to the subject: he *ought* to be just.[231]

We can now formulate the second fundamental question of the philosophy of law. The first asked about the essence of the principle or right by which the legal order is orientated. The second is concerned with the essence of the "ought" of justice, understood as a being-obliged to what is right. The legal order is not identical with justice or right; it sometimes even goes counter to it. In such a case justice makes it a duty for man to reform or overthrow the legal order. Man "ought" to be just. This "ought" remains unexplained in legal positivism, which cannot even justify the normative character of the legal order and remains helpless before arbitrary and inhuman laws. Radbruch, especially, has shown this very clearly since World War II.[232]

---

[231]"Schon wenn wir fragen, *wer* denn hier soll, und den Menschen als den 'Adressaten' des Sollens, sein Verhalten zur Welt als die Wirlichkeit erkennen, an die dieses Mass gelegt wird, drängt uns sogleich, hinter all den so sicher sich gebenden Vorschriften *was* er soll, nach dem Grunde der uns so selbstverständlich gewordenen Tatsache weiterzufragen, dass er überhaupt 'von Rechtswegen' soll. Was soll denn solches Sollen? Wozu die ganze Welt des Rechts? Was geht sie ihn an, diesen Menschen, dessen Da-sein in dieser Welt doch nicht erst 'von Rechtswegen' begonnen hat." Werner Maihofer, *Recht und Sein, Prolegomena zu einer Rechtsontologie,* Frankfurt am Main, 1954, p. 37.

[232]"Der Positivismus hat in der Tat mit seiner Überzeugung 'Gesetz ist Gesetz' den deutschen Juristenstand wehrlos gemacht gegen Gesetze willkürlichen und verbrecherischen Inhalts. Dabei ist der Positivismus gar nicht in der Lage, aus eigener Kraft die Geltung von Gesetzen zu begründen." Radbruch, "Gesetzliches Unrecht und übergesetzliches Recht," *Rechtsphilosophie,* 4th ed., Stuttgart, 1950, p. 352.

The "Inspiration" Underlying The Idea of the Natural Law

Speaking about legal positivism, we showed that "right," *tout court*, cannot be identified with the legal order and that, therefore, justice cannot be identified with the willingness to execute the prescriptions of the legal order. We indicated that the question concerning the essence of right and justice is *the* question of the philosophy of law. To anyone who is familiar with the history of the philosophy of law it is evident that the philosophical question about the essence of right and justice is identical with the historical question about the essence of natural right and the so-called "natural law." We will not hesitate to raise this question again. In doing it, we will not be guided by any artificially defined "traditional concept of the natural law"; similarly, we will not worry about the objections that can be raised against the naturalistic, rationalistic, and objectivistic conceptions of the natural law formulated in the history of man's thinking in terms of the natural law. We refuse, however, to permanently fasten the use of the terms "natural law" and "natural right" to untenable conceptions of the natural law; consequently, we also refuse to drop these terms themselves. It does not make sense to reject a particular term solely because in the past that term was used to express views which one cannot accept. One who rejects a term for this reason is exposed to the danger of no longer being able to "see" the ultimate "inspiration" which moved thinkers to introduce that term.

The historical use of the term "natural law" points to an "inspiration" guiding life and thought in which the *humanity* of the legal order was the point at issue. The "struggle about the natural law" must be viewed as the search for a foundation and a critical norm of the legal order.[233] One who refuses to stop this search teaches that there is a natural law; one who rejects this search is a legal positivist.

Even the most rigorous legal positivist defends the absolutism of positive law because he cares for establishing humanity. Ac-

---

[233]"In allen diesen Möglichkeiten so problematischer und fragwürdiger Art . . . äussert sich das gleiche Bedürfnis. Man möchte den zufällig geltenden, sich oft widersprechenden und sich verändernden Rechtsnormen, Rechtseinrichtungen und Rechtsanschauungen einen rechtfertigenden Grund und ein kritisches Richtmass geben, um das Wesentliche ('existentielles' Naturrecht) vom Beliebigen, das Bleibende ('institutionelles' Naturrecht) vom Vergänglichen allen Rechts zu unterscheiden." Wolf, *Das Problem der Naturrechtslehre*, Karlsruhe, 1955, p. 5.

cording to legal positivism, the absolute validity of positive law and the authority of the State is the only way to be "just." But according to those who claim that there is a natural law, precisely this absolutism makes it possible to do violence to humanity—a violence of which history offers many examples. What, then, is this *humanity* for which both legal positivism and the defenders of the natural law are fighting?

Struggle Against Inhumanity

That the humanity of justice has to be *conquered* from inhumanity is a point which Hobbes and Spinoza have more strongly emphasized than anyone else. According to Hobbes, man in his natural condition is fully guided by egoism. Life is wholly dominated by a paralyzing fear of death because in the natural condition there prevails a war of all against all. Man is a wolf for his fellowmen; there simply is no question of sympathy, disinterestedness, and love. The natural condition is identical with barbarism, in which nothing human can flourish.[234]

Similar ideas can be found in Spinoza. With respect to "what is in man," he does not wish to ridicule, deplore, or blame, but simply to observe and understand them, just as he also tries to observe and understand what happens in the atmosphere, such as heat, cold, or storms.[235] One who adopts this attitude, Spinoza thinks, must come to the conclusion that the religions teach people that they should love one another, but also that this teaching is not very effective in overcoming the egoism, the lust for power, vengeance and honor of men or their envy. In the church people accept the doctrine of love, but in the church they do not have to deal with one another. Where they have to deal with one another, however—that is, in the market place and in political life, where their interests are in conflict—they let themselves be guided by entirely different inclinations.[236] Then they try to destroy one another.

---

[234]Hobbes, *Leviathan* (Ed. Michael Oakeshott), Oxford, 1946, p. 82.

[235]"Et ut ea, quae ad hanc scientiam (Politicam) spectant, eadem animi libertate, qua res Mathematicas solemus, inquirerem, sedulo curavi, humanas actiones non ridere, non lugere, neque detestari, sed intelligere: atque adeo humanos affectus, ut sunt amor, odium, ira, invidia, gloria, misericordia, et reliquae animi commotiones, non ut humanae naturae vitia, sed ut proprietates contemplatus sum, quae ad ipsam ita pertinent, ut ad naturam aëris aestus, frigus, tempestas, tonitru, et alia hujusmodi." Spinoza, *Tractatus Politicus*, c. I, § 4.

[236]Spinoza, *op. cit.*, c. I, § 5.

This aspect of being-man has been unfolded in our time in an unsurpassed fashion by Sartre in his philosophy of the "look," the stare of hatred. Sartre tries to express there the essence of man's relationship to his fellowmen.

It is hardly necessary to mention that what Hobbes, Spinoza and Sartre say about our being-man-together-with-others is part and parcel of reality. It is the reality of inhumanity, of barbarism. The term "barbarism" should not be understood here as if it referred to a phase of history which is past in some parts of the world but still fully actual in other parts. Spinoza explicitly points out that his assertions can be "read" in man's *essence*,[237] and for Sartre conflict is the *essence* of interhuman relations. We need not consider here whether these thinkers are right in using such strong expressions although we are inclined to deny it. Yet it appears undeniable that barbarism is more than a phase of history which is past in some countries but still fully actual in others. What Hobbes, Spinoza, and Sartre "saw" in human *co-existence* is part of the truth. Our question here is whether barbarism is the whole "truth about man."

The Theory of the "Social Contract"

Before examining the question formulated above, we first wish to observe that, if man is *nothing but* willingness to destroy his fellowmen, it is entirely useless to "explain" the origin of positive law and public authority by means of a so-called "social contract." One who wishes to understand the essence of positive law and the rights it "gives" must try to account for the "rightness" of these rights and the normative character of the legal order. One who only points to man's fear of his fellowmen may perhaps be able to explain psychologically that enemies visit one another and come to terms because they realize that their mutual interest demands restraint on their enmity. The reason, however, why such a "contract" would have normative value remains wholly unexplained. As a matter of fact, he cannot adduce any reason at all for it.

A certain "ought" can only be ascribed to a "social contract" between men if man himself *is* a certain "ought" with respect to his fellowmen. If the contemporary social legal order is *nothing but* a contract between "master" and "slave," based

---

[237]Spinoza, *op. cit.*, c. III, § 18.

upon mutual dread of an all-out war between both parties, or if the Civil Rights Law of 1964 is *nothing but* an agreement between Whites and Negroes, based on the realization that both parties would destroy each other if they did not come to an agreement between Whites and Negroes, based on the realization that both parties would destroy each other if they did not come to an agreement—then neither party would have any reason not to repudiate their agreement as soon as it finds itself in a situation where it no longer needs to fear the other party. With respect to the *essence* of the legal order and its normative character, a "social contract" explains nothing because fear offers no explanatory ground for the "ought" proper to the legal order. "I fear" is entirely different from "I ought."

Undoubtedly it is true that in the course of history fear has often been the *occasion* leading to the conclusion of a "social contract," thus preventing a massacre. But this is not the essential point. What is essential here is the answer to the question why those who fear or who no longer have anything to fear "ought" to observe the "social contract" or, in more general terms, the legal order. The attempt to account for the normative value of the legal order can only succeed if the philosophy of law is able to show that man himself *is* a certain "ought" with respect to his fellowmen.

The "Origin" of "Natural" Rights

It seems undeniable to us that the inhumanity of barbarism is not the last word in human relations. At a particular moment in the history of certain societies there arose, through the intermediary of an "ethical genius," a "vision" of man's essence which, *as a matter of principle,* broke through the inhumanity of barbarism, understood as the execution of man's willingness to destroy his fellowman's subjectivity. No such principle is involved when man, involved in a war of all against all, "sees" that such a war can only terminate in the total destruction of "society," and, therefore, tries to stop barbarism by means of a "social contract."

No "ethical genius" is needed to "see" that a social contract sometimes *de facto* establishes humanity. But a transcendence of inhumanity, *as a matter of principle,* is only secured when an "ethical genius" at a given moment of history "sees" man as essentially destined for the other, a destiny which man brings to execution by his "yes" to the other's subjectivity. Man's being discloses itself to the "ethical genius" as a "having to be in the world for the other," and this disclosure imposes itself upon man with a binding force. For the subject-as-*cogito* is a "light" unto himself and this light is an objective light—i.e., it does not permit man to deny that which appears in this "light." [238] Bound by the objective "light" of his subjectivity-as-*cogito,* man "sees," thanks to an "ethical genius," that his essence implies a being destined for the other. Man himself *is* a certain "ought" with respect to his fellowman. An age-old tradition calls the execution of this "ought" "love," and it understands this love as the acceptance, the willing, supporting, and fostering of the other's subjectivity, selfhood, and freedom.

Thus man appears to himself as a very paradoxical reality. On the one hand, he is willingness to destroy the other's subjectivity. Acting according to this willingness is called "hatred" or "being a wolf for the other." On the other hand, he experiences himself as destiny for the other, and acting according to this destiny is called "love." Experiencing himself as both "wolf" and "destined" for his fellowman, man "sees," thanks to an "ethical genius," that the *minimum* demand contained in his being destined for the other consists in not permitting the "wolf" in him to devour the other.

The *minimum* demanded by the requirement of love—a requirement which human *existence* as *co-existence* itself *is*—is thus formulated as the most fundamental right of the other. The other's right is the minimum of my "yes" to his subjectivity, a "yes" called for by my *existence* as a "having to be for the other"—that is, as an "ought" on the level of *co-existence.* Thus the other's "right" is a "natural" right, better, an "essential" right, for it is contained in the "nature," the "essence" of *co-existence.* For the execution of his "having to be for the other" belongs to that through which man is *authentically* man and, therefore, to his "nature" or "essence." In a certain sense he is not a man if he does not execute that "having to be"—viz., he is not man on the *level of authenticity.*

238"Il y a au sein et à la racine du choix moral une visée de valeur constante et immuable que nous n'avons pas à inventer, ni à créer de toute pièce, mais à accepter et à faire nôtre: à savoir la reconnaissance de l'éminente dignité de la personne humaine et des valeurs constitutives de la personnalité." Dondeyne, "Les problèmes soulevés par l'athéisme existentialiste," *Sapientia Aquinatis, Communicationes IV Congressus Thomistici Internationalis,* Romae, 1955, p. 468.

Because the other is an embodied subject in the world, his "natural" right has two aspects. On the one hand, it is a "subjective" title to do something or have something, insofar as his subjectivity occurs as the correlate of my "yes"-to-his-subjectivity, called for by the essence of my *existence* as *co-existence*. On the other hand, my fellowman's "natural" right has an "objective" side because the subject who the other is as intentional subject occurs only as immersed in the body and involved in the world. As correlates of his right, as a subjective title, his body and (a part of) his world are "his," his "right." [239]

We realize that this brief summary is an abomination in the eyes of the legal positivist. His ire is caused by the seeming surrrender of everything he calls "right," in the sense of "law" and "order," to the "subjectivism and relativism" of man's personal inspiration—all of it in the name of love! This so-called subjectivism and relativism will be discussed later; for the present, we simply wish to emphasize that our view does indeed do away with the objectivism and absolutism of legal positivism. Positivism identifies justice with the willingness to do what is demanded by positive law. For this reason, it *cannot* accept that justice would ever oblige man to overthrow the legal order. At the same time, positivism is unable to justify the "ought" it ascribes to this legal order. Such an explanation is only possible if man *himself* can be called a certain "ought" with respect to his fellowman.

We have indicated this "ought" in the preceding paragraphs. The legal order is normative because it participates in, and is the embodiment of the minimum of man's "having to be for the other" which *existence* as *co-existence* is. If the legal order itself, however, does violence to the subject, then this order is unjust precisely for this reason. By virtue of the minimum demand of love—i.e., by virtue of justice—man is then obliged, if necessary, to overthrow the legal order. Justice, therefore, cannot be identified with the willingness to observe the legal order. Justice is the willingness to respect rights, conceived as

---

[239]We intentionally avoid the term "objective right" because jurists use this term in a different sense than the one intended here. Unfortunately, there is no way to avoid the term "subjective right." It should be clear, however, that our use of this term does not refer to the powers which the legal order assigns to those living under it. Cf. J. van Kan, *Inleiding tot de rechtswetenschap,* 8th ed., Haarlem, 1951, pp. 52, 172-182.

the subjective and objective correlates of the minimum contained in the "yes" of my *existence* to the other's *existence*.

The "we" of justice, understood as an ethical form of *co-existence* and as the fundamental transcendence of barbarism, as *humanity,* evidently cannot be identified with any sociological form of *co-existence,* not even with the "we" of the proletariat, as conceived by Marx. Humanity, as the fundamental transcendence of barbarism, is born from man's "yes" to his fellowmen. No sociological "we," however, carries a guarantee that it will be human.

The Ethical Genius

It goes without saying that, unlike Thomism, we do not conceive the objectivity of natural rights and natural duties in an objectivistic sense. To be objective is to be objective-for-a-subject. As soon as this is said, however, one can no longer avoid the question for whom rights and the demands of justice are objective. "The" subject brings about the truth of rights and the demands of justice; through "the" subject the truth of *existence* "comes about" and "originates." But, who is this subject?

In our time, things which formerly used to be done only through the love of the best members of a society are affirmed as rights. This fact makes it possible to give an answer to the above-formulated question. "The" subject for whom the rights and demands of justice are objective is, at first, the best of a society and, after them, all those who, thanks to them, are able to "see" what they "saw." [240] We grant that there are many difficulties in this view but, in spite of them, it seems to us that this standpoint is irrefutable. A right is not objective "in itself": it is objective for a subject, and this implies a certain "seeing," a certain "bringing about" or "letting come to pass" of the unconcealedness of the demands of justice and their correlate called "rights." This dis-closing of the demands of justice, in its turn, implies that within *co-existence,* my subjectivity "brings about" or "lets come to pass" truth as the unconcealedness of the-other-as-appeal-to-my-*existence,* so that in my own *existence* the truth of my "having to be for the other" is "brought about" or "comes to pass."

---

[240]H. Bergson, *Les deux sources de la Morale et de la Religion,* Paris, 1942, pp. 29-30.

It would be impossible, however, that this could happen in an *existence* encompassed by greed or pride, or in one which is involved in a war of all against all and is willing to do anything that will make it possible for him to realize himself as a monster. The "coming about" of the objectivity of right presupposes an "ethical genius," one in whose *existence* truth as the unconcealedness of the-other-as-appeal-to-his-*existence*, and of his own *existence* as destiny for the other, is "brought about" at a given moment in the history of a society. The "coming about" of this truth means *in principle* the emergence of humanity, and the minimum of this humanity is formulated as the most fundamental right of the other.

If we apply this view to the question of natural rights, it becomes evident that there is no natural right which, as an "in itself" of either an ideal or a real character, is immutable, eternal, and valid for all. The objectivity of natural rights must be "brought about" through an historical act in the *co-existence* of the "ethical genius." The latter, however, "brings about" the truth of *co-existence* in the name of all who call themselves human beings; he "brings about" a truth which is, in principle, intersubjective.

The fact that an "ethical genius" "brings about" a truth which is, in principle, intersubjective is not the important point here. He would do the same if, suffering from a toothache, he would "let come to pass" the reality, the truth, the objectivity of his toothache. He can never consent to anyone who denies his toothache without destroying his own affirmation. This is about all that can be said about this intersubjective truth. If anyone denies it, the "ethical genius" will not mind it very much, for in such a denial his very *essence* is not at issue.

The matter is entirely different, however, when there is question of "bringing about" the reality, truth, and objectivity of natural rights. The "ethical genius" "brings about" the truth of the *essence* of *existence* as *co-existence*; he "brings about" the truth of that by which man is man, even if provisionally only a very modest level of authenticity is involved. The "ethical genius" "brings about" truth about man, *tout court*; in other words, he brings about an objectively universal truth, a truth which applies to "all people, at all times, and in all places." [241]

---

[241]"Quand nous disons que l'homme est responsable de lui-même, nous ne voulons pas dire que l'homme est responsable de sa stricte individualité,

This objectively universal truth is, in principle, intersubjective.[242]

By "many people, at many times, and in many places," however, the objectively universal and fundamentally intersubjective truth—reality and objectivity of natural rights—is *de facto* not "brought about." This means that "there" and "at that time" there are no natural rights. It may happen that, if not in theory, at least in practice, the truth of natural rights is absolutely denied. None of this, however, makes the "ethical genius" doubt what he "sees" as a demand of humanity, he "brings about" the truth of the *essence* of *co-existence* "on behalf of all."

Natural right, conceived as the correlate of the minimum of love, continually changes its boundaries, as we will see later in more detail. Hence, the natural law is never "finished," but takes part in an endless history. If we keep this in mind, we realize that many societies at many times and in many places live in many different historical phases of the natural law. It stands to reason that this situation causes enormous difficulties in the mutual relationship of different peoples.

Nevertheless, there is a standpoint from which it can be said that the natural rights are immutable and eternal. They derive this immutability and eternity from the immutability and eternity of the initial demand of justice.[243] Even though the truth of the natural law is an endless history,[244] the "already" of

---

mais qu'il est responsable de tous les hommes." Sartre, *L'existentialisme est un humanisme*, p. 24.

[242]"En effet, il n'est pas un de nos actes qui, en créant l'homme que nous voulons être, ne crée en même temps une image de l'homme tel que nous estimons qu'il doit être. . . . ; et rien ne peut être bon pour nous sans l'être pour tous. . . . Ainsi, notre responsabilité est beaucoup plus grande que nous ne pourrions le supposer, car elle engage l'humanité entière." Sartre, *op. cit.*, pp. 25-26.

[243]"Mais, si une morale ne représente jamais qu'un acquis historique, comment justifier son contenu qui sera sujet à des révisions et à des élaborations incessantes? La seule réponse à cette question est de montrer que ce contenu est fidèle à l'exigence morale initiale, qu'il réalise dans le présent et pour l'avenir une reconnaissance de la dignité de l'homme." A. Wylleman, "L'élaboration des valeurs morales," *Revue philosophique de Louvain*, 48(1950), p. 245.

[244]"In der Rechtsphilosophie entstünde durch den 'geschichtlichen Wesensbegriff' eine ganz neue Lage. Das 'Entweder-Oder' von zeitlosem 'Naturrecht' und blossem 'Positivismus' ontischer Geschichte wäre überwunden zugunsten eines 'geschichtlichen Naturrechts', welche Bezeichnung zunächst ebenso paradox erscheint (vom üblichen Gegensatz Natur und Geschichte aus gedacht) wie die andere mögliche eines 'existenziellen Wesensrecht" (vom üblichen Gegensatz Wesen und Existenz aus gedacht). Was in beiden Termini zum Ausdruck käme, wäre die unbeliebige Notwendigkeit der Geschichtlichkeit des Seins selbst." Max Müller, *Existenzphilosophie im geistigen Leben der Gegenwart*, Heidelberg, 1949, p. 105.

the initial demand of justice can never be destroyed by the "now" of the same demand. The "already" of the natural law's un- concealedness is taken up and integrated in its "now." In this sense, the natural law and its rights are immutable.

Their eternity is connected with this. Anything which in any phase of history has ever become unconcealed as a demand of the *essence* of *co-existence,* and which—on the basis of its unconcealedness—has ever compelled man to a fundamentally intersubjective affirmation, will compel him to the same affirma- tion in every subsequent phase of history; thus, in no phase of history will the denial of the same unconcealednesss ever be justi- fied for any subject.

The Necessity of The Legal Order

The statement that the objectivity of natural rights is "brought about" in the *existence* of the "ethical genius" does not at all imply that by that very fact any kind of humanity is *established.* The "ethical genius," the "heroes and the saints," the best people in a society, are the personal representatives of what is best in mankind. At first, however, they stand alone. They are like a "voice in a wilderness" of inhumanity and bar- barism. They are convinced, however, that the demands of humanity which they discern are objective and, because they see that these demands are anchored in the *essence* of *existence* as *co-existence,* they know themselves to be "functionaries of man- kind" (Husserl). They know that, bearing witness to the truth about *co-existence,* they express things which must be recog- nized by everyone. The "heroes and the saints," the geniuses and inventors in the realm of ethics,[245] have a task of mediation to fulfill with respect to their fellowmen. They make it possible for others to see what they themselves see.[246] In spite of all this, however, they do not *establish* humanity; humanity does not yet "rule."

The demands of justice and right only become a reigning humanity when those who "see" put forward representatives— i.e., when they give authority and power to certain persons to bring about in reality the minimum of love by imposing rules endowed with a compelling force, and thus tame the "wolf"

---

[245]"Il y a de l'invention en morale." G. Madinier, *Conscience et Amour,* p. 58.
[246]H. Bergson, *op. cit.,* pp. 85-86.

who would otherwise make himself felt in human *co-existence*. To make justice "reign" demands a legal order.

To show the necessity of the legal order one could appeal to all the arguments which induce the legal positivist to be a legal positivist. The positivist wants *matter of fact* humanity, *matter of fact* order, *matter of fact* peace. He is so fascinated by the undeniable importance of the legal order for the actual *realization* of humanity that he simply loses sight of the justifying ground and the critical norm of this order.

The demands of justice become a *reigning* humanity, when a positive rule of law, imposed with compelling force, is formulated as that which imposes itself as a demand of humanity, in the encounter of man's "yes" to his fellowmen and to the actually existing relations and conditions. In this way, that rule then becomes embodied in those relations. This "process" of embodiment cannot be dispensed with.[247] For if the demands of humanity are not embodied in the existing relations by a compelling legal order, man would at best be "left to the mercy" of his fellowmen's spontaneous love—if his fellowmen belong to the "best of society," that is. If they don't, then he would be left to the "mercy" of "wolves." And even with respect to the best, he would still be left to the mercy of wolves, in case the spontaneous love of the best in a society would show "lapses" or moments of weakness.[248]

The legal order, therefore, is wholly indispensable for making the minimum of love "reign" and for guaranteeing it as much as possible. The establishment of a legal order is a first step on the road to the *effective* humanization of the many sociological forms of *co-existence*—the first success in taming the "wolf," the first victory over barbarism. The legal order takes the necessary steps to effectively establish and maintain humanity; it guarantees a certain stability to the humanity that has

---

[247]"To give concrete form to the minimum demands of love, we need a legal order whose rules of law clearly determine the required objective performances and which, through its legal institutions, makes it possible to force recalcitrants to comply with the demands of the law. Thus the existing laws mirror what, at a given moment, is established as the minimum demands of love or humanity in a particular society." L. Janssens, "De inhoud van de rechtvaardigheid wordt steeds rijker," *De gids op maatschappelijk gebied*, 1960, p. 127.

[248]"Recht zwingt. Aber gerade an dieser Grenze wird auch ihr Bezogensein deutlich, wird Recht zum Halt in Stunden der Schwäche. . ." Fechner, *Rechtsphilosophie*, p. 241.

already been attained.[249]   By looking at the legal order ruling a
society, one can see how far that society has progressed in taming the "wolf." The stability of the rules of law is the expression
of the firm will a society has not to sink below a certain level
of humanity.[250]   The legal order is the barrier which permanently prevents the "wolf" in man from getting his chances.[251]

When love and the "juridical attitude" are confronted with
one another, it is easy to show that the "humanity" of love cannot hold a candle to the "humanity" established by the royal
order.   People engaged in litigation before a court of law often
present a sorry spectacle.   No matter, however, how much one
is disgusted by that spectacle, one cannot remain insensitive to
the fact that engaging in a lawsuit is a great advance over settling matters through a brutal physical fight.[252]

Authority and Power

Rules of law cannot establish humanity in a *compelling* way
unless they are imposed by an authority having power.   When
the truth of a natural right is "brought about" in *co-existence*
through an "ethical genius," it depends largely on the response
of the society whether or not humanity will *de facto* be established.[253]   There will be many who do not "see" what the "ethical

---

[249]"Positive law reveals a static aspect because it is an expression of what,
at a given moment, has been reached by civilization: it preserves what has already been accomplished in the development of society lest society lose conquered ground and lapse again into man's exploitation by his fellowman. Love
keeps guard lest we abandon what its energy and inspiration have already
achieved in human relationships and laid down in positive laws.   To clarify
this static aspect of the law, justice has been described as love which maintains its conquests but does not go beyond them." Janssens, "Naastenliefde en
rechtvaardigheid," *Kultuurleven,* XIX(1952), p. 15.

[250]"Le moraliste constate cette pression de la justice dans le droit et
quand il la considère dans la conscience, où elle est un vertu, il peut la
définir comme une volonté de ne pas rétrograder dans le chemin parcouru
par l'oeuvre ancestrale de l'amour." Nédoncelle, *Vers une philosophie de
l'amour,* p. 87.

[251]"La justice est l'ensemble des règles que la charité a inventées pour
s'assurer et s'établir parmi les hommes d'une façon durable.   Ces règles sont
un cran d'arrêt et un parapet; elles représentent un certain état d'unité et
d'harmonie au-dessous duquel une société n'accepte pas de descendre."
Madinier, *Conscience et amour,* p. 128.

[252]Pieper, *Grundformen sozialer Spielregeln,* p. 86.

[253]"The question that arises here immediately is: How will society react
to their message?   This reaction is just as important as the intuition of the individuals.   In the experience of justice this reaction functions as the counter
pole of the individuals' intuition." Gits, *Recht, persoon en gemeenschap,* pp.
335-336.

genius" "sees" as a demand of justice. Thus, the best of the society have as their primary task to educate their fellowmen— to make them "see" so that they, too, will understand the demands of justice.[254] As soon as this has been sufficiently done, the society will put forward, or rather "elevate" one or more persons who, as bearers of authority, will see to it that justice and right become realities. These persons derive their authority from the "having to be" which *co-existence* itself is and, on the basis of this "having to be" the rules they establish are normative.[255] As bearers of authority, they represent the "having to be" of *co-existence*, and only to the extent that they represent this "having to be" are they bearers of authority.[256]

Historically speaking, this theory often means revolution against an oppressive situation and, philosophically speaking, the theory is a justification of such a revolution. In other cases, where it does not lead to a revolution, the person or persons "at the top" are forced to a "change of heart." By conforming to the demands of justice, a tyrant can become a legitimate bearer of authority. In this connection it is striking that the constitutions of the most modern states, basing themselves on the American Constitution and on the Declaration of the Rights of Man and of the Citizen made by the French National Assembly of 1789, primarily formulate the personal rights of freedom of the individual with respect to the State.[257] Similarly, the first part of the General Declaration of Human Rights of the United Nations is mainly negative: it formulates the limits of governmental authority.[258] Only to the extent that the bearers of authority represent the "having to be" of *co-existence* are they really bearers of authority.[259]

To exercise authority, however, they need power. This point also has been heavily emphasized by legal positivism, and justly so. As late as 1932, Radbruch wrote in the third edition

---

[254]"Aussi compte-t-il seulement sur un long effort de l'humanité et sur une lente éducation pour former les hommes et les rendre toujours plus raisonnables. En attendant il importe de se prémunir contre les retours offensifs de l'égoïsme vital." J. Lacroix, *Personne et amour*, p. 13.

[255]We abstract here from the ways and techniques by which legal rules are established.

[256]Gits, *op. cit.*, p. 332.

[257]J.J. Loeff, "De sociale grondrechten van de mens," *Handelingen der Nederlandse juristen-vereniging*, 83 (1953), p. 103.

[258]F. van der Ven, *Sociale grondrechten*, Utrecht, 1957, pp. 89-97.

[259]Gits, *op. cit.*, p. 332.

of his *Rechtsphilosophie*: "He who is able to enforce the law thereby proves that he is called to make the law." [260]   To make justice and right actually rule, power is essential [261]—to such an extent that those who identify right and might are *almost* right.   To defend this identification does not always mean a cynical disregard of justice.   "Power ideologies often go hand in hand with pessimistic anthropologies.   Such pessimism can be a matter of principle, but it can also be the result of certain political experiences, in which case it must be viewed as the expression of a disenchanted and disappointed idealism.   Power is then not exalted for its own sake but as the only and the last means to prevent chaos." [262]   Humanity must become an accomplished fact and this requires power.   Those who dearly wish to make humanity rule, but have never been tempted to identify might and right,[263] do not yet understand the human meaning of power. Humanity cannot be established as the actual rule by mere "expressions of love." [264]

Our own era makes us painfully aware of this truth.   There exists no significant body of international law because there exists no supra-national authority.   One who would like to consider the United Nations as such an authority cannot ignore the fact that the action of this organization will remain weak as long as it does not have its own supra-national armed forces.

Radical pacifists and anti-militarists also make a mistake when they deny the importance of power.[265]   They are for a just peace, but without any armies; they want right without might. This is a utopian view, based on an anthropological error.   As matters stand today, the anti-militarists can only afford to defend their error because there are others who fulfill their military duties in protecting the anti-militarists' homeland.

---

[260]Quoted by Hans Welzel, "Naturrecht und Rechtspositivismus," *Festschrift für Hans Niedermeyer,* p. 279.

[261]"Tout droit exprime un certain rapport de forces.   Un droit que ne soutient aucune force peut faire illusion un moment: il ne tarde pas à s'écrouler et la réalité remplace bientôt l'apparence.   Aussi ne suffit-il pas de dire que le droit sans la force est inefficace: il faut affirmer qu'il n'existe pas." Lacroix, *op. cit.,* p. 15.

[262]R.F. Beerling, *Kratos, Studies over macht,* Amsterdam, 1956, p. 177.

[263]"Those who are more or less inclined to attribute greater weight to the factual character of the law than to its normative character will tend to occupy this standpoint." Beerling, *op. cit.,* pp. 173-174.

[264]"Le grand danger de l'heure, surtout pour les chrétiens, est celui d'une sorte de *surnaturalisme désincarné* qui est prêt à sacrifier la force, qui méconnaît le rôle du droit et s'imagine résoudre tous les problèmes par des témoignages d'amour." Lacroix, *op. cit.,* pp. 29-30.

[265]Lacroix, *op. cit.,* p. 14.

The "Pressure" of the Legal Order as a Quasi-process

Speaking of *existence* as *co-existence*, we emphasized that others influence man in whatever he is. In every society there prevail more or less accepted views, and more or less fixed patterns of actions. Every society has a more or less stereotyped way of doing things. At first, man as a *person* has little to do with life, for things "run their course" in his life. When "life begins" for him, this means at first not much more than that he is introduced to the way "things are done," to the way that has become a more or less fixed pattern. The group makes the individual *existences* think, act, and be. This quasi-process of making one another *be* is the indispensable condition for the authenticity of *personal existence*. For the group's "pressure" establishes in the individual *existences* a "social body," so that the "soul" of authentic, personal *existing* can emerge. Without this "social body," no individual *existence* can reach any level of authenticity.[266]

This idea applies *par excellence* to the legal order as materialized humanity. Authentic, personal *existence* presupposes a social body, which is established by social facticity, and the legal order is an aspect of this social body. The "ruling" law "runs its course" and "functions." Those who live in a society experience its "pressure." They try not to deviate from the law because they know that if they violate the legal order, the latter will "automatically" act against them. The legal order "reacts" at once. As soon as a legal order is established, it begins, as it were, to lead a life of its own and "acts" normatively on those who are subject to it. If anyone tries to disregard the norm and escape from its "pressure, the law "proceeds" against him in a trial, in which legal justice is blindfolded.

It is of the greatest importance that the members of a society undergo the "pressure," the "action," "reaction," and "processes" of the legal order. For this "pressure" establishes in their individual *existences* a social body, and this body *is* ma-

---

266"Der Mensch, jeweils in einer geschichtlich geschaffenen Situation erwachend, hat in jeder Generation neue Möglichkeiten doch nur, weil er schon seinen Grund in einer überlieferten Lebenssubstanz hat. Er würde— was nur im Grenzfall zu denken ist—aus dem Nichts seines vitalen Verstandesdaseins existieren müssen, wenn die Situation ihn in die Weltlosigkeit atomisierter Vereinzelung würfe; er würde in schmerzvoller, aber blinder Verzweiflung leben, nicht wissend, was er eigentlich will; er würde zerstreute Dinge ohne Transparenz ergreifen und sich verkrampfen im leeren Aushaltenkönnen des Nichts." Jaspers, *Philosophie,* 1948, p. 263.

terialized humanity. It makes them share in the achievements
attained by past struggles against the inhumanity of the "wolf" in
man, even though they themselves had no share in those struggles. They can lead a life that is at least to some extent human,
but they owe this at first to the fact that they do not live themselves, but "are lived," just as simple technicians are what they
are because they *themselves* did not first have to invent the
wheel. Because living in and according to the legal order establishes in the individual *existences* a "just social body," many
human *existences* live on a relatively human level, a level which
they would not have reached if they *themselves* had to be just.
And even when they *themselves* are just, their being-just still
implies the social body because it is this social body that makes
possible man's "soul," his selfhood.

Is This View Anti-personalistic?

One may ask whether this emphasis on social facticity, and
the social body established by it, does not deny personalism with
its accent on the subject. It must be admitted that there are
philosophers of existence, phenomenologists and even jurists who
pay little or no attention to the importance of being "ruled" by
the legal order, and who, therefore, show hardly any apprecia-
tion for it.[267] Some of these greatly emphasize the wholly original and irrepeatable aspects, the radically personal and unique
facets of *existence*; these thinkers will have the greatest trouble
in finding in the description of the legal order as anonymous
and materialized humanity, those aspects emphasized by them.
Does not the anonymity of the impersonal "they" deny the subject's authenticity? Does not the accent which we place on the
importance of undergoing the pressure of the legal order, conceived as materialized humanity, imply the denial of the subject's
authenticity? Is our view anti-personalistic?

Those who think so fail to pay attention to the fact that
the philosophers of *existence*—and the phenomenologists whom
they quote to show that "subject" and "legal order" are mu-
tually exclusive—speak with more circumspection about the
subject than is insinuated in certain summaries of their views,
such as those presented by Hans Welzel and H. Hommes. Em-

---

[267]Georg Cohn, *Existenzialismus und Rechtswissenschaft*, Basel, 1955,
pp. 78-79.

phasis on the subject's authenticity and on the demands imposed by this authenticity does not *per se,* or even *de facto* always, mean a denial of the importance of the social body, of the social facticity of the world, or of the pressure exercised by the objective structures of society. On the contrary: for Heidegger, the subject's authenticity, man's proper *self*-being is not an exceptional state divorced from the "they," but an existential modification of this "they" which must be conceived as an *essential* moment of *existence.*[268] Thus, according to Heidegger, social facticity is not denied by the subject's authenticity, but is first supposed and then transcended by it.

Jaspers shows a similar conviction when he says that the existence of an order is necessary for the individual;[269] that society is indispensable for the existence of that order[270] that tradition and authority must be listened to;[271] that dutiful acting is a condition for the authenticity of action;[272] that established relations are needed in the contacts which even existentially united human beings cannot do without,[273] so that their being-together will always be a mixture of "fellowship and communication."[274] For Jaspers, social facticity underlies any form of the subject's authenticity. Authenticity always presupposes a "heritage," and this "heritage" is the history others have made.[275] If the subject does not "remember" this "heritage," he is uprooted and perishes.[276] It is out of the question, therefore, says Jaspers, that from time to time the whole of tradition must be destroyed, in order to give man an opportunity to begin afresh. Man must continue to live in the tension between the conservative preser-

---

[268]"Das eigentliche Selbstsein beruht nicht auf einem vom Man abgelösten Ausnahmezustand des Subjekts, sondern ist eine existenzielle Modifikation des Man als eines wesenhaften Existenzials." Heidegger, *SZ,* p. 130.

[269]Jaspers, *op. cit.,* p. 607.

[270]Jaspers, *op. cit.,* p. 349.

[271]"Um nicht ins Bodenlosen zu gleiten, *vertraut* sich daher der philosophisch erwachende Mensch als mögliche Existenz *der Tradition an,* solange nicht ein ihn selbst vernichtender Widerspruch auftritt; er *gehorcht* der Autorität. . . . Sein Selbstsein *drängt sogar zur Autorität,* wo das Selbst noch nicht aus Eigenem zur Klarheit kommt." Jaspers, *op. cit.,* p. 266.

[272]Jaspers, *op. cit.,* p. 157.

[273]Jaspers, *op. cit.,* p. 377.

[274]"Faktisch ist überall die Verflechtung von Geselligkeit und Kommunikation, des sozialen Ich und der Möglichkeit des Selbstseins so unlösbar, dass eine *Spannung* beider und ein Kampf des Einzelnen *um* wahrhafte Kommunikation zun Wesen gesellFigen Dasseius gehört." Jaspers, *op. cit.,* p. 379.

[275]Jaspers, *op. cit.,* p. 858. Other texts of Jaspers are quoted by Erich Fechner, *op. cit.,* pp. 231-237.

[276]Jaspers, *op. cit.,* p. 210.

vation of the previously established order and the unlimited risk of total destruction.[277]

From all this we can conclude that even those philosophers who occasionally put much—even too much—emphasis on the subject create no contradictory opposition between "subject" and "social body," and, therefore, none between "subject" and the "ruling legal order." [278] There is a unity of mutual implication between authentic subjectivity and social facticity. Social facticity is the "body" which makes it possible for the "soul" to be "soul."

To continue in the same language, one could ask, how many human beings are there who really "have" a "soul" of any importance? How many are authentic subjects? How many are there whose *selfhood* is ready for so much humanity that *of themselves* they do what is prescribed by the legal order? No one, of course, can answer this question. But anyone knows that in every society there are always many who do not reach the level of humanity attained by the "ethical geniuses" whose vision and actions gave rise to the legal order. For this reason it is a great good that *all* members of society undergo the "pressure," the "action," the "reaction," and the "processes" of the legal order. The "rule" of the legal order gives to all *existences* a social body whose "weight" "drives" them to a particular way of acting. This "weight" is the weight of materialized humanity. In its turn, this weight "produces" humanity. Such a view is not anti-personalistic, but simply recognizes the undeniable fact that, although all men are called to the authenticity of being subjects, many do not attain authenticity in this respect.

Accordingly, the term "justice" can have a whole spectrum of meanings. Of the "ethical genius" one can say that he is just, but also of the young criminal who has learned from his father to be wary of the police, and who therefore carefully abstains from murder.[279] That, too, is important. If only mankind had some kind of international "police," the fear of which would prevent nations and countries from taking each other by the throat!

---

[277]"Es ist eine unwahre Redensart: von Zeit zu Zeit müsse wieder einmal alles vernichtet und von vorn angefangen werden. Im geschichtlichen Dasein ist es Wahrhaftigkeit, in der Spannung zu bleiben zwischen dem tradierenden Bewahren eines Bestandes und dem grenzenlosen Risiko des Zerstörens." Jaspers, *op. cit.*, p. 759.

[278]Jaspers, *op. cit.*, pp. 608, 631.

[279]J. J. M. v.d. Ven, *Existentie en recht*, Antwerpen, 1966, pp. 62, 67-68.

Mutability of the Legal Order

If the encounter of love's subjective inspiration with the actually existing relationships among men and the actual conditions of the world calls for a legal order, then it should be obvious that every legal order must continually be revised. For neither love's inspiration nor the actually existing relations and conditions are fixed realities.

When above we spoke of the legal order as materialized humanity, and emphasized the importance of the "pressure" and "action" of this order, we did not refer to the highest but to the lowest form of living in a legal order. Those who are simply compelled to realize the lowest level of life in a legal order do not even see where living by the law originates and where it leads. Their life is a quasi-process.

The situation is entirely different for the "ethical genius," that is, for the best of a society. If the legal order embodies the minimum demands of love, then again the best of a society are unable to be satisfied with whatever results have already been achieved. Because love knows no limits, the legal order is never "finished." The love of the best makes them clearly see what humanity demands, but, at the same time, every forward step on the road to society's humanization means that the "ethical genius" begins to occupy a standpoint from which it is possible to discern those demands with even greater clarity. The very "seeing," then, of the "ethical genius" is an history without end.[280] What is implied in being destined for the other only becomes accessible and clear in the history of man's effective love for his fellowman.[281]

It should be obvious, therefore, that we do not wish to represent matters as if the "ethical genius" has *a priori* a perfect and transparently clear idea of humanity and can deduce particular applications from it.[282] In reality, at first there is only a very vague and poor "seeing" without much content, which leads to an equally vague and poor idea. This idea is subsequently enriched in the never-ending history of "seeing," but it can never be made fully transparent.[283] Every phase of "seeing"

---

[280]v.d. Ven, *Grundrechte und Geschichtlichkeit,* Marburg, 1960.

[281]A. Wylleman, "L'élaboration des valeurs morales," *Revue philosophique de Louvain,* 48(1950), pp. 243-246.

[282]v.d. Ven, *op. cit.,* p. 28.

[283]"Pour qu'une évidence absolue et sans aucun présupposé fût possible, pour que ma pensée pût se pénétrer, se rejoindre et parvenir à un pur 'con-

opens up a new future of "seeing," and a "seeing" that would not open up to such a future would not be a *real* "seeing." [284]

In many places and at many times, we said, men live in different historical phases of humanity. An "ethical genius" is needed to induce a society to abolish the burning of widows as inhuman. But the idea of humanity needed for this is not so transparent that one can also see the widow's right to a pension in it. The view that there is such a right requires a long history of humanity. It is within history—not outside or above it—that the idea of justice really lives. Because this history is never finished,[285] there is also room for "inventions" in the realm of justice.[286]

As soon as an "invention" is made in the realm of inter-subjectivity's demands, the legal order becomes antiquated, at least in a certain sense. That order, then, only embodies a phase in the history of humanity which has already been over-come in the lives of the best of society. If the legal order is not then changed, it would become an obstacle to the authentic life of *co-existing* men. The legal order has, of course, of necessity and inevitably, a static aspect also, precisely because this order must establish *security* of human rights. It can happen, however, that exclusive attention to this static aspect makes man lose sight of the origin and aim of the legal order.[287] It can happen that legal rules and institutions begin to lead, as it were, an autonomous existence and that jurists handles those laws and institutions as if they were autonomous entities. Such jurists de-serve to be called "dehydrated jurists" (W. Pompe),[288] and their

---

sentement de soi à soi', il faudrait, pour parler comme les kantiens, qu'elle cessât d'être un événement et qu'elle fût acte de part en part, - pour parler comme l'Ecole, que sa réalité formelle fût incluse dans sa réalité objective, - pour parler comme Malebranche, qu'elle cessât d'être 'perception,' 'sentiment', ou 'contact' avec la vérité pour devenir pure 'idée' et 'vision' de la vérité." Merleau-Ponty, *PP*, p. 453.

[284]*PP*, p. 453.

[285]"Les concepts juridiques sont des constructions humaines, toujours perfectibles, pour nous approcher toujours davantage de l'Idée éternelle de charité." Lacroix, *Personne et amour*, p. 29.

[286]"Il n'y a pas une dignité humaine objectivement concevable. Le progrès de la justice consiste précisément à inventer une dignité humaine toujours plus haute et plus riche. Le progrès ne consiste pas à s'approcher de plus en plus près d'un idéal de dignité humaine *conçu* avant que ce progrès ait eu lieu. Il y a de l'invention en morale." Madinier, *Conscience et amour*, pp. 57-58.

[287]"Trop souvent, l'aspect statique de la justice a fait oublier son origine et sa nature." Nédoncelle, *Vers une philosophie de l'amour*, p. 87.

[288]"I recognize that this is a danger for the jurist, but jurists who study only the law are, in my opinion and that of many other jurists, nothing but

"justice" is, in Nédoncelle's words, only capable of settling "old debts," without any sign of creativity.[289] A petrified legal order is not much more than a sediment of humanity and, at the same time, an obstacle to the attainment of greater humanity.[290]

The fact that the minimum of love continually shifts its boundaries makes it possible to understand that things which were formerly considered acts of charity or love are now viewed as demands of justice.[291] What the best formerly did out of love for their fellowmen is now demanded of everyone and enforced by the legal order.[292] Because justice prescribes only the minimum requirements of love, it stands to reason that traditional morality considers obligations of justice graver than obligations of charity, for man has a greater obligation to the minimum than to that which transcends the minimum.[293]

The importance of the actually existing social relations for the establishment of the legal order cannot be sufficiently emphasized. If man does not show himself "sensitive" to their *reality* when he establishes a legal order and solely relies on the "inspiration" of love, then the legal order which he establishes will be an ethereal system built in a vacuum. The legal

---

dehydrated jurists." W. Pompe, "Gedachtenwisseling over phaenomenologie van het recht," *Annalen v.h. Thijmgenootschap*, 58(1960), p. 101.

[289]"La justice est une charité aux yeux bandés, une mémoire opinâtrement active qui ne crée rien mais règle de vieux comptes avec une précision sévère." Nédoncelle, *op. cit.*, p. 87.

[290]"If the law is described in terms of the moral ideal, it amounts of necessity only to a poor 'sediment' of a moral life which is much broader and richer. If, on the other hand, the law is described in terms of the bottom layer of the group's life, it reveals itself to us as the first manifestation of a new life that makes itself felt in the group." Gits, *Recht, persoon en gemeenschap*, p. 357.

[291]L. Janssens, *"Naastenliefde en rechtvaardigheid,"* *Kultuurleven*, XIX (1952), p. 15.

[292]"It suffices to have a brief look at our modern basic rights: man's right to his life and the integrity of his body, his honor and his reputation; the various public freedoms: freedom of movement, thought and religion, freedom of education, freedom of organization and assembly, freedom of the press and correspondence; the rights of ownership: acquisition of property through occupancy or work; contracts: the obligations arising from freely made agreements, the possibility of disposing of one's property among the living and the dead; the rights of work: the right to work, the right to the product of one's work, the right to a minimum needed for existence; political rights: the equality of all citizens before the law, the right to a legally determined way of obtaining one's rights and of being judged, the abolition of privileges, the right to participate in the country's government and to be admitted to public office . . ." Gits, *op. cit.*, pp. 367-368.

[293]"At the same time it is evident that the duties of justice are most urgent and must be first fulfilled. This does not mean that justice ranks higher than love or can be separated from it. But justice deals with the strictly necessary minimum of love's obligations." Janssens, *art. cit.*, p. 12.

order intends to put order in the actual conditions, and therefore demands a realistic view of those conditions.

When these conditions—that is, the sociological forms of *co-existence*—change, this is a sign that the legal order also must be modified. If this is not done, real life outgrows the man-made structures, with all the consequences this implies, as history has repeatedly shown. The supporters of the *Ancien Régime* and of liberalistic capitalism tried in vain to contain the changed conditions within the structure of a static legal order. Some colonizing nations endeavored to do the same, and one or the other still keeps trying to do this. Such an effort is doomed to ultimate failure.

The same idea applies to a more modest realm which jurists deal with in their everyday work. The relative equilibrium reached by a society in a particular phase of its history can never last long. As soon as the rights and duties about a particular subject matter have been weighed and laid down in laws, things happen in the actually existing conditions and situations which make new measures necessary. For instance, rules may laboriously have been established to safeguard the health of workers in a particular process of production. These rules assume, let us say, that steam is used as a source of energy. By the time these rules are finally fixed, a number of factories have already given up the use of steam and switched to electricity. By this very fact a large part of the laboriously constructed legal order is then antiquated and new regulations are required. Every historical situation differs from all others and therefore requires appropriate provisions. For example, man's right to traffic safety calls for different regulations depending on whether a society uses donkeys, bicycles, motor cars, or jets for its transportation.

The Necessity of Love

From all this it should be evident that Marx's theory about the history of humanity is one-sided. For Marx, love has no importance, as is evident even in his youthful critique on Feuerbach. Marx reproaches Feuerbach for abolishing religion on the one hand, and introducing a new religion on the other, viz., men's love for one another. If Feuerbach had been sensitive to the importance of *praxis,* he would have noted that not love but work, with the socio-economic structures resulting from it, brings people together and unites them. For this unity Feuerbach substituted the unity of the human species, the inner and dumb universality which binds all men together in a natural way.[294] This is an "abstraction," says Marx. The *real* unity among men arise from social life,[295] and the continuity of history is secured by the continuity of the means of production, not by any "political and religious nonsense." [296]

According to Marx, the objective reality of the capitalistic system contains the fall of this system, regardless of the capitalists' intentions. Private property propels itself to its own destruction, but solely through a development that is independent of the capitalist, of which he is not conscious, and which he does not want, but which is conditioned by the "nature of the matter," that is, it destroys itself by producing the proletariat with its own objective laws.[297] The Communist future is contained in the objective reality of the proletariat, independently of the proletariat's intentions.[298]

It should be evident that in this theory both the subject and the subject's turning to another subject in love are unimportant. According to Marx, the legal order of the liberal capitalistic system mirrors the actually existing relations and conditions of capitalism.[299] After the Revolution, however, he holds, those actual relations and conditions will be different, and this difference will express itself in a different legal order, viz., that of communism. But on what grounds can Marx call the capitalistic order unjust and the communist order just? If a legal order is nothing but a mirror image of actual conditions and relations, one can no longer call any legal order whatsoever either just or unjust. *In reality* Marx can only call the legal order of liberal capitalism unjust because he saw it as a viola-

---

[294]Marx, "Thesen über Feuerbach," *Die Deutsche Ideologie,* Berlin, 1953, p. 595.
[295]"Alles gesellschaftliche Leben ist wesentlich praktisch." Marx, *op. cit.,* p. 595.
[296]K. Marx and Fr. Engels, *Die Deutsche Ideologie,* pp. 26-27.
[297]"Das Privateigentum treibt allerdings sich selbst in seiner national-ökonomischen Bewegung zu seiner eignen Auflösung fort, aber nur durch eine von ihm unabhängige, bewusstlose, wider seinen Willen stattfindende, durch die Natur der Sache bedingte Entwicklung, nur indem es das Proletariat *als* Proletariat erzeugt." K. Marx and Fr. Engels, *Die heilige Familie,* Berlin, 1953, p. 137.
[298]K. Marx and Fr. Engels, *op. cit.,* p. 138.
[299]Fr. Engels, "Ludwig Feuerbach und der Ausgang der klassischen Deutschen Philosophie." K. Marx and Fr. Engels, *Ausgewählte Schriften in zwei Bänden,* pp. 369-370.

tion of his fellowman's subjectivity and because Marx's entire personal life was encompassed by his attempt to embody in a new legal order *his* "yes" to his fellowman, his love. But this inspiration of Marx's entire personal life does not occur in his philosophy.[300]

Thus we arrive at the conclusion that the mutability of the legal order finds its explantion neither in love *alone* nor in the changed conditions and relations *alone*. But it is rather in the encounter of these two aspects of human *co-existence* that the necessity of new legal rules makes itself known.

---

[300]Nevertheless, Marx accuses the capitalists of greed: "Die einzigen Rader, die der Nationalökonom in Bewegung setzt, sind die Habsucht und der Krieg, der Habsüchtigen, die Konkurrenz." Marx, "Zur Kritik der Nationalökonomie," *Kleine ökonomische Schriften,* p. 97.

CHAPTER FIVE

THE METAPHYSICAL IN MAN

Hitherto we have spoken of "two" dimensions of man's *existence*: his being-consciously-"at"-the-world "and" his being-destined for his fellowman, which he executes in love. The words "two" and "and" are put between quotation marks in order to avoid the impression that the dimensions of *existence* can be added to each other as one adds numbers in arithmetic. Obviously, that is not the case. Philosophical reflection upon man explicitates man's "understanding" of himself and, in a spiral-like procedure, acquires in this explicitation an insight into levels of being-man which are neither identical with one another nor simply capable of being added to one another. The one essence of man reveals itself in different dimensions.

Speaking of the "primitive fact" of existential phenomenology, we said that, for us, this "primitive fact" is *existence* or intentionality, conceived as the subject's openness to all that is not this subject himself. That which is not the subject himself, we saw, refers to both the world and the other, albeit in different ways. At the same time, we emphasized that nothing gives us the right arbitrarily to close the openness which man is. Nothing justifies the assertion that the being of man is *nothing but* a being-consciously-"at"-the-world and thus, *a priori*, to eliminate even the possibility of an authentic "affirmation" of God. At the same time, however, we are not absolved from the duty critically to investigate what is tenable and what is untenable in an "affirmation" that is as generally made as is the "affirmation" of God.

Nevertheless, it is not our intention to make the "affirmation" of God explicitly the theme of this chapter. The present-day confusion of thought simply does not permit this. It is almost impossible to say anything about either the "affirmation" of God or the "denial" of God without having to fear that one will be misunderstood. Atheists cannot state their atheism without seeing certain theists and believers in God "prove" hermeneutically that those atheists "really" are theists and believers in God. Others claim those "exegetes" can deliver their "proofs" only because they have no idea of what an authentic "affirmation" of God means. Others, again, claim that God is dead—

not just that our *image* of God is no longer viable, but that God himself is dead. Yet, they do not wish to be called "ordinary" atheists, for, according to them, God did exist at one time, but he no longer exists now: God is really dead now.[1] Still others assert that "God exists," but they are unmasked as atheists.

In a certain sense this confusion is inevitable. It is indeed possible, for example, that one who affirms the existence of God really affirms a pseudo-God. We have the impression, however, that the confusion is greater than is absolutely inevitable because the presuppositions of both the "affirmation" of God and the "negation" of God often remain insufficiently clear. The consequence is that many people do not realize what they themselves or what others affirm or deny.

In this chapter we will limit ourselves to a contribution to the necessary spade work which must precede the "affirmation" as well as the "negation" of God. At the same time, we hope to show in what sense it is meaningless to exclaim in the midst of the confusion: "Does God exist or not?" Let us begin with a description of the "actual state of the question."

1. MYTHS

For Auguste Comte the "stories of myths" belong to the "imaginary state," the first stage of development of the human mind. In this first stage man connects the phenomena of nature with God, gods or spirits, making use only of his imagination.[2] For Comte, this does not mean, however, that this stage was unimportant. Primitive man and the child do not yet have any other possibilities of explanation. By inventing myths, they enter the road of trying to find explanations. Obviously, this is important, for the human mind otherwise would never reach the stage of maturity, the stage of scientific explanation.[3] Once this stage is reached, however, there will be no room for the "affirmation" of God. "Theology" will only have an "historical existence" for future investigators.[4]

---

[1]Thomas J. J. Altizer and William Hamilton, *Radical Theology and the Death of God*, New York, 1966, Preface, p. X.

[2]"Or, chacun de nous, en contemplant sa propre histoire, ne se souvient-il pas qu'il a été successivement *théologien* dans son enfance, *métaphysicien* dans sa jeunesse, et *physicien* dans sa *virilité*." A. Comte, *Cours de philosophie positive*, Paris, 1907, I, p. 4.

[3]*Cours*, I, p. 7.

[4]"Ayant acquis par là le caractère d'universalité qui lui manque encore, la philosophie positive deviendra capable de se substituer entièrement, avec

For Comte, then, myths are unscientific old wives' tales which are told for lack of scientific explanations. Those tales belong to the phase of mankind's unscientific backwardness. The "affirmation" of God will disappear without any campaign against God. Comte rejects myths in order to posit his "negation" of God. The same holds for all adherents of scientism.

Comte's expectations, however, have not been filled. Myths have not disappeared, and for the past half century they are no longer being interpreted solely as "fictions," "fables," "fabrications of the mind," and "illusions." Today we try to accept myths as they were understood in primitive societies and gradually we have begun to see that a standpoint is possible and necessary from which myths are "true." [5]

Rudolf Bultmann occupies a special place in this new outlook upon myths because of his program of "demythologizing." [6] The aim of this program is to let the "affirmation" of God have its own truth. For this "affirmation" has always made use of myths; hence, if the myths are not understood according to their own, specific "truth," they falsify the "affirmation" of God.

For Bultmann it is certain that the atheist is right when he refuses to take part in the "affirmation" of God, if such an "affirmation" would demand that he accept as an *historical* or a *scientific* truth something which cannot possibly be verified according to the normal course of affairs in the domains of the sciences of history or of physical science. [7] In particular with respect to what Christianity preaches, the atheist will say: "This is only a myth." [8] Bultmann agrees with this "atheism." However, he only rejects myths insofar as they are falsely interpreted —that is, considered to be true in the historical sense or the

---

toute sa supériorité naturelle, à la philosophie théologique et à la philosophie métaphysique, dont l'universalité est aujourd'hui la seule propriété réelle, et qui, privées d'un tel motif de préférence, n'auront plus pour nos successeurs qu'une existence historique." *Cours* I, p. 13.

[5]"Au lieu de traiter, comme leurs prédécesseurs, le mythe dans l'acceptation usuelle du terme, i.e. en tant que 'fable' 'invention', 'fiction', ils l'ont accepté tel qu'il était compris dans les sociétés archaïques, où le mythe désigne, au contraire, une 'histoire vraie' et, qui plus est, hautement précieuse parce que sacrée exemplaire et significative." Mircea Eliade, *Aspects du mythe,* Paris, 1963, p. 9.

[6]R. Bultmann, "Neues Testament und Mythologie," *Kerygma und Mythos,* I, 4th ed., 1960, pp. 15-48; "Zum Problem der Entmythologisierung," *Kerygma und Mythos,* II, pp. 179-190; "Zum Problem der Entmythologisierung," *Kerygma und Mythos,* VI-1, pp. 20-27.

[7]Bultmann, *art. cit., Kerygma und Mythos,* VI-1, pp. 23-24.

[8]S. Ogden, "The Christian Proclamation of God to Men of the So-called 'Atheistic Age,'" *Concilium,* 16(1966), p. 94.

sense of physical science, without being subject to the methods of verification accepted in the sciences of history or physical science. Unlike Comte, Bultmann does not in this way posit the "negation" of God, but only that the "affirmation" of God has a character all of its own.

The proper reason why Bultmann rejects the myths in the above-mentioned interpretation does not lie in the fact that their content is *de facto* not verifiable, but that this content is not conceivable by those sciences. It is simply inconceivable that in the domains of physical science and history one accepts the specific laws governing those domains and, at the same time, does not accept them by positing that God sometimes overrides these laws.[9]   Moreover, and this is more important, this is not conceivable because he who affirms the possibility that God overrides the historical and scientific laws thereby shows that he conceives God as the world and no longer as God.[10]

In connection with the above-mentioned aim of limiting ourselves here to a description of the "state of the question" with respect to the "affirmation" and "negation" of God, it may be useful to add that the view which represents God as a factor "puncturing" the laws of nature and history [11] is sometimes called the "supernaturalistic," [12] "metaphysical," [13] or "theistic" [14] view.   As we will see, however, these very terms, used in a different context, have an even broader sense than the one referred to here.

While some thinkers motivate their "negation" of God with their rejection of the mythical, Bultmann and his followers demand this rejection in order that the "affirmation" of God can be authentic.   Bultmann's rejection, however, starts from the

[9]"Wenn nun in unserer Auffassung Natur und Geschichte durch eine bestimmte Gesetzmässigkeit beherrscht sind, so können wir freilich nicht zu gleicher Zeit annehmen, dass sie es nicht seien, dass sie der Willkür überirdischer Mächte ausgeliefert sein können." Fr. Theunis, "Prolegomena zum Problem der Entmythologisierung," *Kerygma und Mythos*, VI-1, p. 146.

[10]"Der gedankliche Inhalt des Mythos ist schlechthin undenkbar, eben weil in ihm von Gott Weltliches gedacht und ausgesagt wird; weil er nur bejaht werden kann, insofern Gott als Welt gedacht wird und nicht als Gott." Theunis, *art. cit.*, p. 147.

[11]Bultmann, "Jesus Christus und die Mythologie," *Das Neue Testament im Licht der Bibelkritik*, Hamburg, 1964, pp. 11-13.

[12]John A. T. Robinson, *Honest to God*, London, 1963, pp. 29-35.

[13]Paul van Buren, *The Secular Meaning of the Gospel*, London, 1963, pp. 82, 167, 191, 198; C. A. Van Peursen, *Hij is het weer! Beschouwingen over de betekenis van het woordje "God"*, Kampen, 1967, pp. 8, 33.

[14]I. Sperna Weiland, *Oriëntatie, Nieuwe wegen in de theologie*, Baarn, 1966, pp. 107-110.

standpoint that myths can be interpreted falsely, i.e., as true in the historical sense or the scientific sense. Bultmann rejects this interpretation and for this reason he does not at all have to reject "the" myths. The proper intention of myths, however, must be brought to light. Myths do not at all intend to convey an historical or a scientific truth. Myths intend to speak about the essence of man as *existence*: [15] they must be existentially interpreted.[16]

Reflection upon man, Bultmann holds, is not exhausted by the "objectifying" thinking of the sciences of history and nature. True, man can be considered as an element of history and of nature, as an ingredient of the sciences. But in myths man does not occur as such an element and for this reason, the myths, taken according to their own intention, are *true*. Myths intend to "speak of man's authentic reality," to express his "understanding of his *existence*," [17] to give expression to the idea that it belongs to man's essence to recognize that the available world in which he lives does not have its ground and purpose in itself and that man is not his own master.[18] Myths "objectify" the Transcendent (*das Jenseitige*) as the "world here" (*das Diesseitige*): contrary to their real intention, they represent the Transcendent as the spatially distant, with His power rising above and exceding human power.[19] According to Bultmann, it is precisely to express the most profound dimension of man's "understanding of his *existence*" that the myths use the term "God."

Wholly in line with all this is the view of those who see mythical speech as *the only way* in which God and things divine

---

[15]"Der eigentliche Sinn des Mythos ist nicht der, ein objektives Weltbild zu geben; vielmehr spricht sich in ihm aus, wie sich der Mensch selbst in seiner Welt versteht; der Mythos will nicht kosmologisch, sondern anthropologisch - besser: existential interpretiert werden." Bultmann, *art. cit., Kerygma und Mythos,* I, p. 22; cf. also *Kerygma und Mythos,* II, p. 183 and VI-1, p. 24.

[16]We use our own terminology here. Bultmann himself says that myths demand an *existential* interpretation.

[17]Bultmann, *art. cit., Kerygma und Mythos,* VI-1, pp. 24-25.

[18]"Im Mythos findet der Glaube Ausdruck dass die bekannte und verfügbare Welt, in der der Mensch lebt, Grund und Ziel nicht in sich selber hat. . . . Und in eins damit gibt der Mythos dem Wissen Ausdruck, dass der Mensch nicht Herr seiner selbst ist, dass er nicht nur innerhalb der bekannten Welt abhängig ist, sondern dass er vor allem von jenen jenseits des Bekannten waltenden Mächten abhängig ist, und dass er in dieser Abhängigkeit gerade von den bekannten Mächten frei werden kann." Bultmann, *art. cit., Kerygma und Mythos,* I, pp. 22-23.

[19]Bultmann, *art. cit., Kerygma und Mythos,* VI-1 and I, p. 22, note 2.

can be spoken of, provided that this speaking correctly understands itself.[20] This is only then the case, some thinkers hold, when one sees in mythical speech the "coming about" of the essence of *existence* as orientation to the Transcendent. In mythical speech man does not speak "about" his *existence* or "about" God, but he "brings about" his *existence* and "confesses" God.[21] Mythical language is the language of proclamation. This is also the reason why there are false myths: there are proclamations which mislead, disorient, point to a way that leads nowhere.[22] But even then the name of the "theme" or the "hero" of which the myth speaks must be written with a capital.[23]

2. METAPHYSICS

Because the right understanding of myths requires interpretation, it is not surprising that some people ascribe this task to metaphysics, particularly if one keeps in mind that metaphysics has always laid claim to the ability to speak about God. If, however, we limit ourselves here to a description of the "state of the question," we must observe that, just as with respect to myths, so also in reference to metaphysics there are many different standpoints.

Some thinkers reject metaphysics and, consequently, the possibility of "affirming" God. This is the standpoint taken by many adherents of analytic philosophy. For Ayer this standpoint implies that one should reject not only theism but also atheism and agnosticism with respect to the "existence" of God. The statements of the atheist and the agnostic are also metaphysical statements and therefore meaningless.

Metaphysical statements claim to refer to a suprasensual world.[24] Such statements cannot be verified, that is, in the way Ayer understands this verification;[25] consequently, they are meaningless.[26] Therefore, the existence of God can never

---

[20]E. Cornélis, "Mythe en religie," *Annalen van het Thijmgenootschap,* 53(1965), p. 67.
[21]van Peursen, *op. cit.,* pp. 32-37, 52-57.
[22]van Peursen, *op. cit.,* p. 54.
[23]Jacques Ellul, "Mythes modernes," *Diogène,* 1958, pp. 29-49.
[24]A. J. Ayer, "Demonstration of the impossibility of metaphysics," *Mind,* 43(1934), p. 339.
[25]Ayer, *Language, truth and logic,* London, 9th ed., pp. 5-16.
[26]Ayer, *op. cit.,* pp. 35-45.

be proved. For, if such a proof were possible, the premises from which the "affirmation" of God would follow, would have to be certain. But in the supposition that those premises are verifiable, they would not be more than probable because subsequent verification could take away their truth. Only *a priori* statements are certain because they are tautologies. From tautologies, however, only other tautologies can follow, but not the existence of God.[27] The statement, "God exists," is not even probable. Such a statement could be probable only if it were empirically verifiable, derived, for example, from the regularity with which certain phenomena occur in nature. But if the statement, "God exists," were reduced to the affirmation of a regularity in nature, the religious man would object and say that what he wishes to "affirm" is a transcendent being. In that case, says Ayer, the term "God" is a metaphysical term. The statement, "God exists," is neither true nor false but meaningless,[28] and the same must be said of the statement, "God does not exist." [29]

For Ayer, this means that agnosticism is also condemned. The agnostic claims that he does not have the means to determine which of the two statements is true: the statement, "There is a transcendent God," and the statement, "There is no transcendent God." For the agnostic one of the two is true, but he does not know which one. The agnostic should see that both statements are nonsensical, i.e., that the question, "true or false?" cannot be asked. Only when divinities are identified with natural objects are statements about them meaningful. If, for instance, someone says that the occurrence of a thunderstorm is required and sufficient to observe that Yahweh is angry, his statement is meaningful, for all he really affirms is that there is a thunderstorm.[30] In sophisticated religions, however, a "Person" is supposed to control the empirical world, without being localized in it. He is considered to be "higher" than the empirical world and is placed beyond this world. He has superempiri-

---

[27]Ayer, *op. cit.*, pp. 114-115.
[28]"But in that case the term 'god' is a metaphysical term. And if 'god' is a metaphysical term, then it cannot be even probable that god exists. For to say that 'God exists' is to make a metaphysical utterance which cannot be either true or false." Ayer, *op. cit.*, p. 115.
[29]Ayer, *op. cit.*, pp. 115-116.
[30]Ayer, *op. cit.*, p. 116.

cal attributes. But in that case the term "God" is a metaphysical and therefore meaningless term.[31]

Other thinkers, however, reject metaphysics with the avowed intention of letting the "affirmation" of God have its own truth. They "confess" God but reject a "metaphysical affirmation of God." This expression can have various senses, which should not be confused.

First of all, there is the "metaphysical affirmation of God" in the sense of post-Kantian idealism, to which we referred in Chapter One in connection with spiritualism. The subject's relative priority is made so absolute there that the qualifications of the Subject finally agree with the "names" traditionally given to God. The Absolute Subject is then considered to act in and through the "little" subject. Actually, however, this amounts to saying that the "little" subject claims to think with "divine" authority and to act with a "divine" guarantee. Precisely for this reason, however, some people say, the "metaphysical affirmation of God" must be rejected, for it fails to do justice to the authentic character of the "affirmation" of God.[32]

Secondly, there is the "metaphysical affirmation of God which is sometimes called "supernaturalistic" or "theistic." Its rejection can perhaps best be understood as a rejection of the consequences flowing from the Cartesian idea of God. As we pointed out before, Descartes did not really lose anything through his methodic doubt, but simply attached to everything of which he doubted the label "thought of." In the first instance, Descartes reduced the *human* body, the *human* world, and God-for-*man* to the idea of the body, the idea of the world, and the idea of God. He realized of course that, by doing this, he had not given expression to the "whole" *reality* of the human body, the human world, and God-for-man. God-for-the-subject, the world-for-the-subject, and the body-for-the-subject are "more" than ideas. Descartes, however, had reduced the human aspect—the *being*-for-the-subject of everything which is not the subject himself—to an idea-in-the-subject; thus, this being-"more," to which he had to give expression, could no longer be conceived as a being-for-the-subject. This being-"more" had

---

[31]"It is only when we enquire what God's attributes are that we discover that 'God,' in this usage, is not a genuine name." Ayer, *ibid.*

[32]G. Gusdorf, *Traité de métaphysique*, Paris, 1956, pp. 102-132.

therefore to be conceived as "inhuman," as being a body in itself, a world in itself, a God in himself.

At the end of his third MEDITATION Descartes offers his *a posteriori* argument for the existence of God. He observes that he has an idea of God as an Infinite Substance, Eternal, Immutable, Independent, Omniscient, and Almighty. Now, this idea, argues Descartes, could not have come from me myself, for as a finite being I am unable to produce the idea of the Infinite. Only an Infinite Substance can have caused this idea in me; therefore, God exists.[33]

In the light of the preceding paragraphs, this "Infinite Substance" must be conceived as a God in himself, an "inhuman" God, one who is in principle and of necessity "separated" from man—a God with whom man in principle has no relationship, for in Cartesianism the God-for-man is an idea of and in the subject. What God is "over and above" an idea-in-the-subject, is God in Himself. The "affirmation" of such a God is the "metaphysical," "supernaturalistic," or "theistic" "affirmation" of God which is rejected by many in order to safeguard the authenticity of the "affirmation" of God.

All things considered, the idea of such a "metaphysical God" is older than Descartes' philosophy. It can also be found in the objectivistic philosophy of order proposed by Scholasticism.[34] As was pointed out, in this philosophy every essence, that of man included,·was given a place in "brute reality." Being—as the "totality of reality"—was represented as a collection of essences which in themselves are necessarily, universally, immutably, and eternally "true"—outside the encounter which human *existence* is. They are "true" in that way because and to the extent that they are created by God. But one who represents God as the creative Origin of the order of being, and conceives this order as reality "divorced" from man, implicitly conceives God also as a God in Himself with whom man, in principle, has no relation whatsoever.[35]   God is the Transcendent-in-

---

[33]René Descartes, *Meditationes de prima philosophia,* Introduction et notes par Geneviève Lewis, Paris, 1946, pp. 45-46.

[34]Fr. Gogarten, *Die Wirklichkeit des Glaubens, Zum Problem des Subjektivismus in der Theologie,* Stuttgart, 1957, pp. 7-24.

[35]"Wollte sich der mittelalterliche Mensch eine gedankliche und begriffliche Klarheit über das Ganze der Welt, in der er lebte, verschaffen, so war das einzige Mittel, das er dafür hatte, eben die griechische Philosophie, soweit sie ihm bekannt war. Mit deren metaphysischen Begriffen hat dann die

Himself, "metaphysically out there." [36] If, "after" this, one still wishes to speak of God's revelation of Himself or of His action with respect to man, then there is question of the self-revelation and action of a Being with whom man, *in principle, has no relations at all.* One who still "believes" is then forced to conceive his believing as to accept on authority the "truth" of judgments, statements, "articles" about God, understanding the "truth" of these judgments as their agreement with God-in-Himself. This is the position which some people reject when they reject the "metaphysical," [37] "theistic," [38] and "supernaturalistic" God. "Theodicy, that is atheism," exclaimed Marcel.[39] Those who deny an "inhuman" God do this only in order to be able to "affirm" God-for-man.

The "metaphysical affirmation of God" is even more vehemently opposed by others when they observe that the "affirmation" of God as Cause no longer differs from the affirmation of causes made by the sciences.[40] As soon as metaphysics wishes to be a "science" in order to maintain itself with respect to the sciences,[41] as soon as it calls the "Supreme Being" [42] the "First Cause" [43] in the way the sciences speak of "cause" with respect to the beings they discuss, God is represented as the first cause in a series of causes. In that case the denial of the "metaphysical God" comes closer to the "divine God" than does His "affirmation." [44]

Those who reject the "metaphysical affirmation" of God—understood as the "affirmation" of a God-in-Himself—also reject "metaphysical" agnosticism with respect to the "affirmation"

---

mittelalterliche Theologie die Wirklichkeit Gottes und die der Welt als ein metaphysisches Reich gedacht, das unter Gott, dem Schöpfer, als seinem ewigen Haupt von einer hierarchischen Rangordnung alles Seiende durchwaltet ist." Gogarten, *op. cit.,* p. 14.

[36]J. Robinson, *Honest to God,* London, 1963, p. 13.

[37]"Das Wort 'Gott ist tot' bedeutet: die übersinnliche Welt ist ohne wirkende Kraft. Sie spendet kein Leben. Die Metaphysik, d.h. für Nietzsche die abendländische Philosophie als Platonismus verstanden, ist zu Ende." Heidegger, *Holzwege,* p. 200.

[38]"For, to the ordinary way of thinking, to believe in God means to be convinced of the existence of such a supreme and separate Being. 'Theists' are those who believe that such a Being exists, 'atheists' those who deny that he does." Robinson, *op. cit.,* p. 17.

[39]Marcel, *JM,* p. 65.

[40]Heidegger, *Identität und Differenz,* p. 55.

[41]Heidegger, *Über den Humanismus,* p. 6.

[42]Heidegger, *Was ist Metaphysik?,* p. 19.

[43]Heidegger, *Nietzsche,* II, p. 415.

[44]Heidegger, *Identität und Differenz,* p. 71.

of God. Karl Jung's work can serve as an example of this agnosticism. Jung emphasizes that he wishes to speak about "God" solely from the standpoint of one who pursues the empirical psychology of religion. He says that when he speaks of "God," this expression only refers to certain specific, empirically verifiable contents of consciousness, psychical facts or processes. He points out that, as a pursuer of empirical science, he must impose this limitation on himself because psychology is psychology and not philosophy or theology. For the psychologist "God" is an empirical datum, not a "metaphysical entity." For this reason Jung objects when others interpret his psychology as if it were a metaphysics.[45]

Jung, however, goes beyond "imposing a methodic restriction on himself" when he explains what, in his opinion, "metaphysicians" do when they speak of God. "Metaphysicians," he holds, believe that they are able to know something about God as a non-psychical entity, as "objective reality." They claim, he thinks, that they know something about the unknowable things of "the world to come" and about God-in-Himself. Jung rejects the possibility of such "knowledge" as fantastic and pretentious,[46] and on the basis of this rejection he calls himself a "metaphysical agnostic."

This agnosticism, however, does not make any impression on people who reject the "metaphysical affirmation of God" in order to defend the authenticity of the "affirmation" of God. They point out that this agnosticism is nourished by the same ideal as the "metaphysics" which they cannot accept because of its objectivistic standpoint.

Finally, mention must be made of those thinkers who do not consider it necessary to reject the "metaphysical affirmation of God" in order to defend the "affirmation" of the "divine" God. They do not interpret metaphysics in an idealistic, objectivistic-realistic or scientistic sense and consider such interpretations simply as degenerations of an authentic metaphysical inspiration. They defend a "human" metaphysics and the possibility of a metaphysical "affirmation" of the Transcendent God-for-man. In their eyes, the recognition of man's deepest dimension as "functioning intentionality" is identical with the

---

[45]Han M. M. Fortmann, "Als ziende de Onzienlijke," III, a, *Geloof en ervaring,* Hilversum, 1965, pp. 51-54.
[46]Fortmann, *op. cit.,* p. 54-58.

"affirmation" of God-for-man. For them, the "proof" of God's existence explicitates the being of man as orientation to the Transcendent.

From this much too concise survey of the "actual state of the question" the conclusion can be drawn, we think, that there exists a certain "trend" or "direction" in man's "thinking about God." Negatively expressed, this direction can be indicated as the impossibility of asking as a meaningful question whether God exists or not, at least if one assumes that the answer can be "yes" or "no," without a previous inquiry into the possibilities and impossibilities of the "saying" of *is* which man himself is as "functioning intentionality." This means that contemporary thought rejects the Scholastic and the Cartesian "affirmation" of a God-in-Himself, regardless of whether one wishes to call such an "affirmation" "metaphysical," "theistic," or "supernaturalistic." Today the rejection of representational realism, which is characteristic of existential phenomenology, is carried over to our "speaking about God." There is hardly anybody left [47] who fears that the "affirmation" of God-for-man is a form of atheism.

Positively expressed, the "actual state of the question" in man's "speaking about God" indicates the necessity of what Kant calls a "transcendental doctrine of method," [48] and what Heidegger refers to as "fundamental ontology" [49] in connection with his inquiry into the meaning of Being. To express what the religious man means when he uses the term "God" implies giving expression to the depth of man's essence as "functioning intentionality."

As was pointed out, it is not our intention to make the "affirmation" of God the explicit theme of this chapter. We merely wish to investigate the pointers given by contemporary philosophy when it thinks that it gives expression to the deepest dimension of man's essence. Let us begin with the "atheism" of Sartre.

3. THE ATHEISM OF SARTRE

One who only pays attention to Sartre's definitions of the *subject* who man is always has the impression that Sartre, in

---

[47]H. Geurtsen, "Fenomenologie en atheïsme, Kritische studie," *Bijdragen,* XXIV(1963), p. 312.

[48]I. Kant, *Kritik der reinen Vernunft,* Berlin, 1913, Band III, p. 7.

[49]Heidegger, *SZ,* pp. 13, 183.

speaking of man, has in mind a subject who is really involved, intentional, and *existent*.[50] The same happens when one's attention is solely focused on Sartre's phenomenological analyses of the human body: it would be inconceivable for him to think that Sartre could still divorce the subject from the facticity of the body and the world.[51] A really intentional subject, then, should be understood as an intentional—and therefore relative —freedom, a freedom which is meaningless without involvement in the facticity of the body and the world. An absolute autonomy of the subject should therefore be out of the question, for an intentional subject implies the facticity of that which the subject is *not*, viz., body and world.

The way Sartre speaks of worldly *things*, however, makes one fear the worst. He calls the worldly thing an "in itself," he affirms that it is being in the proper sense, the only being deserving to be called "being." The question which evitably arises here deals a lethal blow to Sartre's phenomenology. If the "in itself" is a reality divorced from the subject, how can the subject still be a really intentional subject? If one detaches intentionality's correlate from the intentional subject, must one not also accept that the subject is then detached from its correlate? But in that case there exists no *real* correlation, and the subject's freedom becomes an absolute freedom.

For Sartre, as for all other phenomenologists, to be a subject is to be free.[52] It is excluded for him that the subject would be the determined result of thinglike processes and forces. This conviction may perhaps be considered to be one of the reasons why Sartre calls the subject "nothingness." For, if the term "being" is reserved for the being of a thing—and if one wishes to make it clear that the being of the subject is not, like that of a thing, the determined result of thinglike processes and forces— then, terminologically speaking, what else can one do but call the subject "non-being," "nothing"? [53] If, however, the subject as

---

50"Toute conscience, Husserl l'a montré, est conscience de quelque chose." Sartre, *EN,* p. 17.
51"On sait qu'il n'y a point, d'une part, un pour-soi et, d'autre part, un monde, comme deux touts fermés, dont il faudrait ensuite chercher comment ils communiquent." *EN,* p. 368.
52"Nous avons montré que la liberté ne faisait qu'un avec l'être du Pour-soi." *EN,* p. 529.
53"Ces tentatives avortées pour étouffer la liberté sous le poids de l'être . . . montrent assez que la liberté coïncide en son fond avec le néant qui est au coeur de l'homme." *EN,* p. 516.

freedom is separated from the facticity of the body and the world, the subject can hardly be conceived otherwise than as absolute freedom. But is the "affirmation" of God still possible for such a freedom? Can such a freedom still accept the consequences of the "affirmation" of God?

God is not absent from Sartre's work. On the contrary, He is everywhere present,[54] but only to be rejected over and over again.[55] Sartre denies that man is in any way dependent upon God. God is not the king of mankind, for man is free. If God had wished to rule over man, He should not have created man free. At the very moment God created man as a free being, this freedom turned against God: as freedom, man does not belong to God. Thus there is no one to give orders to man. Man has only one law, his own, and that law is his freedom.[56] The gods know this; it is their painful secret. Once freedom emerges in man's heart, the gods are powerless against this man.[57] They could annihilate him, but they cannot make man in his *freedom* belong to the gods.

The idea is clear: God does not exist, for man is free. A really existing God would crush man's freedom to death. But it is an indisputable fact that man is free; therefore, God does not exist.[58]

Although Sartre really has only one argument to deny God's existence, he develops this argument in a threefold way. Let us see how.

God as the "Superior Craftsman"

Traditional reflection, says Sartre, has always called God man's Creator. Man's creation was conceived by analogy with the production of an object by a craftsman. A craftsman who makes an object first has an idea of the object to be made and then makes the object in accordance with his idea. The essence of a paper knife precedes the knife's production and actual existence, for it exists *first* in the craftsman's mind and is *fixed* in his plan.[59]

---

[54]This was true until the publication of Sartre's *Critique de la raison dialectique,* Paris, 1960. In this work God no longer occurs.
[55]H. Paissac, *Le Dieu de Sartre,* Arthaud, 1950, pp. 9-11.
[56]Sartre, "Les Mouches," *Théâtre,* Paris, 1947, pp. 84, 86.
[57]Sartre, *op. cit.,* pp. 111-113.
[58]Paissac, *op. cit.,* pp. 16-17.
[59]Sartre, *EH,* p. 18.

Exactly in the same way, says Sartre, people speak about man's creation by God. God is represented as a "superior craftsman," one who, before He creates, knows exactly what He will create and then gives man being in accordance with His idea. Thus the idea "man" is in God's mind what the idea "paper knife" is in the craftsman's mind, and God produces man just as the craftsman produces the paper knife. Man's being is fixed beforehand and, because God's creation extends over the whole of man's life, man's entire life is fixed beforehand. In other words, man is a fixed sample of a fixed species, and his life is more or less like the growth and swelling of a pea.[60]

Sartre rejects this doctrine because man appears here only as "just another thing." It is true, of course, that there are thinglike aspects in man, he has an essence—that is, a certain facticity which makes him resemble a thing; but the proper character of *man* consists precisely in this that as *existence*—as a self-realizing subject—he has a certain priority over his essence and that as a subject—as freedom—he gives meaning to his essence and in this way "makes" himself.[61] Accordingly, there is no idea of man, man cannot be defined, for whatever can be said of man can only be said *a posteriori*, in function of the way the subject has realized himself. He who wishes to speak about man must "take his starting point in subjectivity," [62] for "*existence* precedes essence." [63] This expression, Sartre holds, means nothing but that man has a higher dignity than a thing.[64]

Accordingly, for Sartre the idea of a Creator God cannot be reconciled with the reality of man as freedom, project, and history. But man's reality is beyond dispute; therefore, no reality can correspond to the idea of a Creator God.

God as the Other par Excellence

Sartre's theory of intersubjectivity also makes it necessary for him to reject God. Those who accept the existence of God conceive Him as the Other *par excellence*.[65] But every other means the death of my subjectivity. If God is the Other *par excellence*, He is the one who "looks" or stares at all subjects;

---

[60]*EH*, pp. 19-20.
[61]". . . et il sera tel qu'il se sera fait." *EH*, p. 22.
[62]*EH*, p. 17.
[63]*EH*, p. 17.
[64]*EH*, pp. 22-23.
[65]"Dieu n'est ici que le concept d'autrui poussé à la limite." *EN*, p. 324.

the one for whom all subjects experience themselves as objects, the one whose presence is intolerable for every subject. God is the being who stares at every one and Himself cannot be stared at: [66] He is the "unstared stare." [67]   To accept God, then, would mean to accept being a thing. To accept God would imply an alienated *existence*, an estrangement from my being-man as freedom. [68]   Is the situation, then, such that I must accept God and that freedom is an illusion?   No, for man is free: therefore, he must rise up against God, reject Him, in order to continue to be free.   Man owes it to his manhood to deny God. [69]

These ideas remind us of Nietzsche's standpoint.   Nietzsche said that he could not bear the thought that there was a God and that he, Nietzsche, was not that God. [70]   A God whose look inquisitively and brutally penetrates into the dirtiest corner of the human soul must die.   Man must avenge himself on such a witness, for man cannot tolerate that kind of a witness to live. [71]

The Idea of God as a Contradiction

For Sartre God is not only the one who crushes man's freedom to death—not only an unbearable and intolerable stare—but the very idea of God, defended by the religions as the expression of a *reality*, cannot possibly correspond to any reality because it is an internal contradiction.   Let us see why.

Sartre uses his fundamental concepts of the in-itself and the for-itself in his attempt to speak about the Being which the religions call "God."   What he means by the in-itself has already been explained; hence, it is not necessary to repeat his description here in its entirety.   Moreover, Sartre himself does not use all the qualifications of the in-itself in his reflections on God.

---

[66]*EN*, p. 495.

[67]"Une seule fois, j'eus le sentiment qu'il existait.   J'avais joué avec des allumettes et brûlé un petit tapis; j'étais en train de maquiller mon forfait quand soudain Dieu me vit, je sentis Son regard à l'intérieur de ma tête et sur mes mains; je tournoyai dans la salle de bains, horriblement visible, une cible vivante."   Sartre, *Les Mots*, Paris, 1964, p. 83.

[68]"La position de Dieu s'accompagne d'un choisisme de mon objectivité; mieux, je pose mon-être-objet-pour-Dieu comme plus réel que mon Pour-soi, j'existe aliéné et je me fais apprendre par mon dehors ce que je dois être. C'est l'origine de la crainte devant Dieu."   *EN*, p. 350.

[69]"L'indignation me sauva: je me mis en fureur contre une indiscrétion si grossière, je blasphémai, je murmurai comme mon grand-père: 'Sacré nom de Dieu de nom de Dieu de nom de Dieu.'   Il ne me regarda plus jamais." Sartre, *Les Mots*, p. 83.

[70]Fr. Nietzsche, *Also sprach Zarathustra*, Stuttgart, 1960, p. 91.

[71]Nietzsche, *op. cit.*, pp. 294-295.

Unlike consciousness, the in-itself is not a being which refers to itself, not a being for which "its being is an issue." In Heideggerian terms, the in-itself is not characterized by "understanding of being." It lies "crushed upon itself," that is, it does not show the "nihilating" distance which characterizes consciousness, it does not include any negativity but is full positivity.[72] The in-itself *is* in the full sense of the term: it is the fullness of being and does not need anything else to be what it is.[73]

This suffices, according to Sartre, to make one see that the God of whom the religions speak must be an in-itself. For God is conceived as a Being having the fullness of being, a Being fully sufficient unto itself, which does not need anything else to be what it is.[74] At the same time, however, the religions conceive God as for-itself, as consciousness.[75] But, according to Sartre's general characterization of the for-itself, the for-itself is diametrically opposed to the in-itself: for the for-itself is nothing but negativity and, by definition, it needs the in-itself to be able to be for-itself; hence it is never self-sufficient.

The contradiction, then, is evident. God would have to be the identity of the in-itself and the for-itself, of pure positivity and pure negativity, of self-sufficiency and the lack of self-sufficiency, of independence and dependence. God would have to be an intentional being which is not intentional. Therefore, the idea of God is an internal contradiction, so that no reality can correspond to it.[76]

This alleged contradiction, however, fails to make much impression on anyone who realizes that the contradiction is the result of Sartre's clear-cut betrayal of the phenomenological dimension of thought, the reciprocal implication of subject and object. Sartre accepts this dimension in his phenomenological descriptions, but nothing remains of it in his ontology. What possible sense can be attached to the "fullness of being" ascribed to the in-itself when one accepts that one can meaningfully speak only of the in-itself-for-us? The in-itself-for-us certainly does not appear as fullness of being. What, then, justifies Sartre to withdraw the intentional movement of con-

---

[72]*EN*, p. 119.
[73]*EN*, pp. 33-34.
[74]"Et Dieu n'est-il pas . . . un être qui est ce qu'il est, en tant qu'il est tout positivité et le fondement du monde?" *EN*, p. 133.
[75]*EN*, p. 133.
[76]*EN*, pp. 133, 707-708.

sciousness and claim that the in-itself is the fullness of being? True, the religions call God the Supreme Being, the Fullness of Being, but Sartre's identification of God with the in-itself-as-fullness opens an abyss between him and religion which can no longer be bridged. In Sartre's opinion, the definition of God is a contradiction; actually, however, his own attempt to speak about the in-itself is a contradiction.

Similar remarks could be made with respect to the for-itself. The religions affirm that God is the Supreme Being and that, therefore, his being lies on the level of consciousness. But when Sartre denies all positivity to consciousness, denies to consciousness the dignity of being the highest mode of being,[77] and conceives consciousness as pure "nihilation," his assertion that the religions conceive God as a for-itself again open an unbridgeable abyss between his affirmation and that of religion.

This is not all, however, and not even the main point. We must add that religion does not call God a conscious Subject without any qualification. True, God is conceived as a conscious Subject, but *not without any qualification*; for the conscious subjects man encounters are intentional subjects, and this is precisely not the way the religions conceive God: God is not an intentional Subject. Accordingly, the religions do not conceive God as both in-itself and for-itself; they conceive God neither as in-itself nor as for-itself, in the Sartrian sense of these terms. Sartre, then, denies something entirely different from what the religious man affirms.

Man as Project to Be God

The way Sartre makes the idea of God a contradiction is heavy with consequences for his view of man. The existence of an in-itself-for-itself is a contradiction, but it cannot be denied that the in-itself and the for-itself meet in man. For man is the oppositional unity of subjectivity and facticity or, in Sartre's terminology, of the in-itself and the for-itself. The in-itself is wholly contingent, it "just" is, without necessity, without ground, without reason, for ground and reason refer to the for-itself or consciousness, and the in-itself has no consciousness. Man, then, must be conceived as the emergence of conscious-

---

[77]"Cette présence à soi, on l'a prise souvent pour une plénitude d'existence et un préjugé fort répandu parmi les philosophes fait attribuer à la conscience la plus haute dignité d'être." *EN*, p. 119.

ness in the compact density of a contingent and groundless in-itself. It is as if the in-itself, which "of itself" is without ground, "decompresses itself," [78] breaks through its density and pro-duces a certain distance with respect to itself, that is, it gives itself the modification of the for-itself in order to find a ground for its groundlessness.[79] This "adventure" is called man.

Man, then, is a project of grounding. Sartre conceives this project as the attempt of the for-itself to eliminate the distance separating it from the in-itself. The for-itself would like to be what it *is*; as not being what it *is* and being what it is *not,* the for-itself would like to be what it *is*.[80] The for-itself would like to give itself the fullness, the massivity and density of the in-itself and, nonetheless, maintain itself as for-itself. If man were to succeed in identifying in himself the for-itself and the in-itself, then man's contingence would have been overcome: man would have grounded his existence by elevating himself to the dignity of the "Being which is Its own Cause" *(Ens causa sui),* he would have become his own cause.[81] But this self-caused being, this identity of the in-itself and the for-itself is precisely the definition of God. Thus the project of ground which man is, is the desire to be God.[82]

In his transcendence, man tries to execute this project. As not being what he *is* and being what he is *not*—as oppositional unity of facticity and potentiality—man, in his actions, tries to seize the possibilities anchored in his facticity. Once realized, the newly established meaning remains as an in-itself which, however, is again "nihilated" by the for-itself. In this way new possibilities arise and these, in their turn, are realized and re-main as an in-itself to be "nihilated" again by the for-itself. The for-itself, which is a "nothing" (no-thing), continually fol-lows close on the heels of the in-itself,[83] which "of itself" is

---

[78]"L'ontologie nous fournit deux renseignements . . . ; c'est d'abord, que tout processus de fondement de soi est rupture de l'être-identique de l'en-soi, recul de l'être par rapport à lui-même et apparition de la présence à soi ou conscience." *EN,* p. 714.

[79]"L'ontologie se bornera donc à déclarer que tout se passe comme si l'en-soi, dans un projet pour se fonder lui-même, se donnait la modification du pour-soi." *EN,* p. 715.

[80]*EN,* p. 653.

[81]*EN,* p. 708.

[82]"Ainsi peut-on dire que ce qui rend le mieux concevable le projet fondamental de la réalité humaine, c'est que l'homme est l'être qui projette d'être Dieu." *EN,* p. 653.

[83]*EN,* p. 47.

fullness of being, without, however, ever being able to identify itself with the in-itself. Man is essentially a "hole," a breach, a tear in being, and this "hole" cannot be annulled by his transcendence. Man is essentially a "disease of being."

What else does this mean but that the execution of the self-grounding project which man is, is doomed to failure? For the for-itself is an invincible "nihilation" of the in-itself, so that there is and remains an infinite distance between the in-itself and the for-itself.[84] By means of his transcendence man tries to overcome precisely this distance in order to give a ground to his existence. Obviously, this attempt cannot succeed. "Human reality," as a project of self-grounding, is absurd. This is not surprising at all, for the attempt to make the for-itself identical with the in-itself is an attempt to realize the definition of God, a definition which implies a contradiction.[85]

If man were to succeed in reaching his ideal, he would lose himself. There would no longer be any distance between for-itself and in-itself, and what else could this mean but that man is no longer man? [86] Human consciousness, therefore, is an "unhappy consciousness," and there is no remedy for this unhappiness. Man never succeeds in being more than a mere abortive God.[87] Thus man's "passion" is just the opposite of Christ's passion, for man would wish to lose himself as man in order that God be born. But the idea of God is a contradiction: man loses himself for nothing. Man is a useless passion.[88]

Man, an Abortive God?

For Sartre, however, the uselessness of the passion which human *existence* is does not give any reason to despair.[89] The authentic man is not a nihilist,[90] but renounces even despair,[91]

---

[84]*EN*, p. 714.

[85]"Sans doute, cet *ens causa sui* est impossible et son concept, nous l'avons vu, enveloppe une contradiction." *EN*, p. 717.

[86]*EN*, p. 134.

[87]"Tout se passe comme si le monde, l'homme et l'homme-dans-le-monde n'arrivaient à réaliser qu'un Dieu manqué." *EN*, p. 717.

[88]*EN*, p. 708.

[89]"La vie humaine commence de l'autre côté du désespoir." Sartre, *"Les Mouches," Théâtre*, Paris, 1947, p. 114.

[90]"Le nihiliste est proche de l'esprit de sérieux, car au lieu de réaliser sa négativité comme mouvement vivant, il conçoit son anéantissement d'une manière substantielle; il veut n'être rien et ce néant qu'il rêve est encore une sorte d'être, exactement l'antithèse hégélienne de l'être, un donné immobile." S. de Beauvoir, *Pour une morale de l'ambiguïté*, p. 75.

[91]"Mais dans la mesure où cette tentative participe encore de l'esprit de

for he who despairs shows by his attitude that he still lives on the contradictory ideal of identifying the for-itself and the in-itself in his *existence*. The authentic man accepts himself as a "lack of being," for the negativity of his subjectivity-as-*volo* is invincible. Sartre does not call God back.

In its transcendence the for-itself tries to identify itself with the in-itself to find a ground for its groundlessness. The for-itself, says Sartre, would indeed have found a ground for itself, even *be* its own ground, if the identification of the for-itself with the in-itself could be attained, in other words, if man in his *existence* could realize the contradictory definition of God. As we have shown, however, God cannot be conceived as the identity of the in-itself and the for-itself. A consequence of this is that man also, as the oppositional unity of for-itself and in-itself, cannot be conceived as a project to be God.

Nevertheless, man is a search for ground. This is what Sartre did "see" and which leads him where he does not wish to go. The question is now to discover what this search for ground really means if it is not man's desire to deify himself. That man is an attempted self-deification is for Sartre the result of what he calls an "existential psychoanalysis." [92] Such an analysis does not consist in dressing up a list of human forms of behavior, tendencies, and inclinations, but is an attempt to decipher all this. [93] On the basis of a pre-ontological understanding of what man as man is, on the basis of man's unreflected presence to his own essence, it is possible to decipher individual forms of behavior and tendencies as manifestations of what man is in his inmost essence. The result of Sartre's investigation is: "Man is a useless passion." He is an attempt to make the for-itself and the in-itself coincide, an impossible attempt because the for-itself is nothing but "nihilation," the creation of distance between the in-itself and the for-itself.

One who rejects the result of Sartre's existential psychoanalysis, his way of deciphering man, could try to "re-interpret"

---

sérieux et où ils peuvent croire encore que leur mission de faire exister l'en-soi-pour-soi est écrite dans les choses, ils sont condamnés au désespoir, car ils découvrent en même temps que toutes les activités humaines sont équivalentes - car elles tendent toutes à sacrifier l'homme pour faire surgir la cause de soi - et que toutes sont vouées par principe à l'échec." *EN*, p. 721.

[92]"La psychanalyse existentielle va lui découvrir le but réel de sa recherche qui est l'être comme fusion synthétique de l'en-soi avec le pour-soi." *Ibid.*

[93]*EN*, p. 656.

man's behavior, his tendencies and inclinations, as manifestations of man's deepest essence. This would not require that he doubt the real content of Sartre's phenomenological descriptions of man as transcendence in which man's project of self-grounding is executed; it does require, however, that he try to "read between the lines" in order to see what Sartre really did "see" when he described man as a search for ground. We must add that another approach is possible, one which perhaps throws more light on what man is in his inmost essence, on what Sartre did "see," an approach which is an investigation of what Sartre really rejects when he thinks that he denies God.

Sartre calls the man who adheres to God a "grave man." The grave man is a coward because he conceals his own absolute freedom from himself.[94] The grave man interprets his own being as the being of a thing-in-the-midst-of things, he renounces his manhood in favor of the world.[95] He ascribes to himself the mode of being of a rock, the firmness, inertia and density of a thing-in-the-world.[96] Marx is a typical example of a grave man, for he affirms the priority of the object over the subject: man is "grave" when he considers himself as an object.[97] Because he buries his consciousness of his freedom, the grave man is "in bad faith." [98]

Sartre's analysis of bad faith brings us further. Strange as it seems, according to him, anyone who tries to be sincere is in bad faith. For what else is the attempt to be sincere but an attempt to be for oneself what one is? [99] Being what one is—that is exactly the definition of the in-itself, the thing.[100] Such an attempt, therefore, is always and of necessity hypocritical, for man is a being for whom, in his being, "this being itself is an issue," and this means that man "nihilates" what he is.[101] Man of necessity escapes from what he is; hence the ideal of sincerity is an impossible task, for it means a contradiction with

---

[94]Sartre, *EH*, p. 84.
[95]*EN*, p. 669.
[96]"Il s'est donné à lui-même le type d'existence du rocher, la consistance, l'inertie, l'opacité de l'être-au-milieu-du-monde." *Ibid.*
[97]*Ibid.*
[98]"Il va de soi que l'homme sérieux enfouit au fond de lui-même la conscience de sa liberté, il est de mauvaise foi. . . ." *Ibid.*
[99]"Or quel est l'idéal à atteindre en ce cas? Il faut que l'homme ne soit pour lui-même que ce qu'il est, en un mot qu'il soit pleinement et uniquement ce qu'il est." *EN*, p. 98.
[100]*Ibid.*
[101]*EN*, p. 83.

the "nihilating" structure of the for-itself.[102] The desire, then, to be sincere is an attempt to be like a thing.[103]

Accordingly, the grave man is in bad faith because he ascribes to himself the mode of being of a thing. According to Sartre, this is exactly what is done by the man who accepts God. Let us see what this means. Man's giving himself the mode of being of a thing implies that he depreciates his freedom as distance. This is precisely the reason why he is in bad faith. As we saw, the distance, inherent in subjectivity's involvement in facticity, must be conceived in a twofold way. It contains not only "nihilation" on the cognitive level, but also on the affective level. The distance of the subject-as-*volo* with respect to facticity is essential for being-man. It is wholly impossible for man fully and unreservedly to consent to any worldly facticity whatsoever; hence, all fullness is permeated with emptiness, all fulfillment and satisfaction are affected by unfulfillment and dissatisfaction, all rest, peace, and happiness are mixed with unrest, trouble and unhappiness. When man fails to do justice to his non-being, he fails to do justice to his manhood; therefore, he is in bad faith.

This is the kind of man rejected by Sartre, and justly so. Man cannot be satisfied with any form of his being-in-the-world; he cannot definitively and fully say "yes" to any worldly reality. And this is precisely what the grave man does.[104] Thus he buries the affective distance of the subject-as-*volo* with respect to facticity: he gives himself a thing's mode of being, for a thing is compact density and lies "crushed upon itself." For this reason Sartre says that the grave man renounces his manhood in favor of the *world* and that he "belongs to the world." [105] Simone de Beauvoir, the most slavish follower of Sartre, alluding to Nietzsche's Superman, significantly calls the grave man a "subman." The subman loses himself in the object,[106] he clings to his facticity and, consequently, blocks the

---

102"Que signifie, dans ces conditions, l'idéal de sincérité sinon une tâche impossible à remplir et dont le sens même est en contradiction avec la structure de ma conscience. Etre sincère, disions-nous, c'est être ce qu'on est." *EN*, p. 102.

103*EN*, p. 103.

104"L'homme sérieux, s'il existe, est l'homme d'une seule chose à laquelle il dit oui." *EP*, p. 79.

105*EN*, p. 669.

106"L'attitude de sous-homme passe logiquement dans celle de l'homme sérieux: il s'efforce d'engloutir sa liberté dans le contenu que celiu-ci accepte

enlargement of man's domain, the unfolding of freedom.[107] But the subman is bored and experiences the world as a desert.[108]   He is in bad faith.[109]

It should be clear now what Sartre really rejects when he thinks that he is rejecting God. The man who accepts God is "grave," but the grave man is one who renounces his manhood in favor of the *world.* God, then, is conceived as a worldly reality, to which man gives his unreserved consent. Such a God must, of course, be unconditionally rejected, for he is not God. Simone de Beauvoir gives some unambiguous examples of the gravity—i.e., the acceptance of God—which she and Sartre despise so much: the soldier for whom the Army is everything, the colonist who sacrifices the natives to the building of the Road, the revolutionary who is blind to everything but the Revolution—all these are grave men because they are servants of divinities.[110]   But what are these divinities? Worldly realities to which an absolute value is assigned.   He who unreservedly consents to them, disregards the negativity affecting his *existence,* he crushes his freedom to death.   But life will necessarily disappoint him, for his gravity is the impossible attempt to realize in himself "the contradictory synthesis of the in-itself and the for-itself." [111]   Simone de Beauvoir returns to this Sartrian definition of God immediately after giving the examples of "gravity."

The matter, then, is evident: God is conceived as a reality within the world, and the man who adheres to God appears to us as one who absolutizes his own relativity.   In such conditions one need not hesitate to affirm the truth that man's authentic being dies when he comes in contact with *that* kind of absolute.[112]

It should hardly be necessary to point out that all this has nothing to do with the true God and the authentic affirmation

---

de sa société, il se perd dans l'objet afin d'anéantir sa subjectivité." de Beauvoir, *Pour une morale de l'ambiguïté,* pp. 65-66.

[107]de Beauvoir, *op. cit.,* p. 64.

[108]de Beauvoir, *op. cit.,* p. 65.

[109]"La mauvaise foi de l'homme sérieux provient de ce qu'il est obligé de sans cesse renouveler le reniement de cette liberté." de Beauvoir, *op. cit.,* p. 68.

[110]de Beauvoir, *op. cit.,* pp. 70-73.

[111]"Le sérieux est une des manières de chercher à réaliser l'impossible synthèse de l'en-soi et du pour-soi." de Beauvoir, *op. cit.,* p. 74.

[112]"La conscience métaphysique et morale meurt au contact de l'absolu." Merleau-Ponty, *SNS,* p. 191.

of God. One must even say that, for Christian religions, the acceptance of the Sartrian God is a sin. Sin, in the strict sense of the term, is precisely the absolutizing of a worldly reality, an affirmation *à la* "grave man," and man's struggle against evil is precisely a struggle against the temptation offered by the world to make such an affirmation.

Sartre's way of rejecting the subject's massive affirmation of the world, his "belonging to the world" is so penetrating that his insight into this matter may be called a permanent acquisition of philosophy. The deepest ground of the "having to be" which characterizes man has perhaps never been as clearly exposed as it is done in Sartre's philosophy. This ground is the negativity, which is essential to manhood. Perhaps no one else has ever thrown so much light on the fact that "having to be" constitutes the *inmost essence* of man. This insight results from what Sartre calls an "existential psychoanalysis," which starts from a pre-ontological and fundamental understanding of, and insight into the essence of the human person, and then tries to conceptualize this essence, expressing it in clear concepts.[113] The result of all this is that man is the desire to be God.[114] True, Sartre can say this only because of a wrong concept of God, but our rejection of Sartre's *interpretation* of man's inmost essence does not mean that we cannot accept the real value which his *description* of man's inmost essence has. For that description is very penetrating. The subject-as-*desidero* (I desire) is such that no worldly reality can give him fulfillment. As long as man lives locked up in the world, it is impossible for him definitively to consent to his subjectivity as "having to be," for all consent to himself stands in function of the fulfillment which subjectivity as "having to be" finds. Searching for a ground of his existence, man searches for the possibility of being able to give a definitive consent to his subjectivity as "having to be."

Within the dimension of the world this is impossible. The grave man, the subman, eloquently shows this. He is in bad

---

113*EN*, p. 656.
114"La valeur fondamentale, qui préside à ce projet est justement l'en-soi-pour-soi, c'est-à-dire l'idéal d'une conscience qui serait fondement de son propre être-en-soi par la pure conscience qu'elle prendrait d'elle-même. C'est cet idéal qu'on peut nommer Dieu. Ainsi peut-on dire que ce qui rend le mieux concevable le projet fondamental de la réalité humaine, c'est que l'homme est l'être qui projette d'être Dieu." *EN*, p. 653.

faith. He is bored in a world which for him is a desert. This boredom has a metaphysical dimension. It reveals to him the true character of subjectivity-in-the-world, understood as "natural desire"; it reveals that the "desire" which subjectivity-in-the-world is must be understood as "desiring much more than worldly reality," as "really desiring something entirely other" than the world. This "entirely Other" Christianity calls the Transcendent God. God, however, is not a "reality" in the way the world is a reality. For this reason God can *never* be "affirmed" just as the world is affirmed. Any attempt to do this degrades God's transcendence and fails to do justice to the true dimension of the human subject-as-*desidero*.

Man's being is indeed a project of self-grounding, a search of the subject for the possibility of definitively consenting to himself. On the basis of his "yes" to the world, it is not possible for the subject definitively to consent to himself, for this "yes" is essentially and, therefore, invincibly affected by a "no." But, one could ask, would a "yes" to God be able to function as the foundation for man's definitive consent to his own subjectivity?

Within the perspective of Sartre's own *explicit* theories, this question is meaningless, for he rejects God; therefore, any definitive "yes" is for Sartre nothing but a form of estrangement. If, however, one *radically* distinguishes God from the world— and failure to do this would be a failure to do justice to God, and therefore also to the human subject-as-*desidero*—it will at least be impossible to claim that a definitive "yes" to God implies "gravity." The grave man, it should be recalled, unreservedly affirms the *world*. The grave man's affirmation does not give any meaning to life but makes the latter a useless passion. Once man is convinced of this, his asking about the meaning of life, and the subject's attempt to find a ground for his groundlessness, enter into their proper dimension. With respect to *this* question and searching, Sartre does not give any answer because the possibility of such a question did not even arise in his field of vision. Perhaps, however, it would not be too much to say that Sartre's *implicit* doctrine is a theology without God.[115]

---

[115]E. Vietta, *Theologie ohne Gott. Versuch über die menschliche Existenz in der modernen französischen Philosophie*, Zürich, 1946.

We must now see whether the same must be said of Heidegger's philosophy.

4. HEIDEGGER'S "BEING TOWARD DEATH"

In his book BEING AND TIME Heidegger wishes to re-open the road to a right understanding of Being (*Sein*).[116] This is the first thing which needs to be done because, in Heidegger's opinion, the philosophers themselves have blocked this road in the history of thought.[117]

The Road to "Being"

To make it possible to ultimately understand being-in-general, Heidegger begins by asking about the being of man, for man is the being who raises the question about being.[118] Asking about the being of man must be the right approach to the concept of being-in-general, for man is the being for whom, in his being, this being itself is at issue;[119] man is a being who can reflect upon his own being; moreover, the question about being-in-general is a mode of man's own being.[120]

Reflection upon man's own being, however, will only then open the road to understanding being-in-general when reflection supplies a view of man in his totality. This view is given to man in his experience of dread *(Angst)*.[121] Dread, however, is a rare phenomenon,[122] for everyday man is continually fleeing from himself—that is, from the proper meaning of his being-himself—from his dread.[123]

Heidegger calls this flight from oneself "falling away" *(Verfallen)*.[124] He first speaks of this mode of being-man when he asks himself who really is the subject of man's every-

---

[116]Heidegger, *SZ*, p. 15.

[117]*SZ*, pp. 2-3.

[118]"Hinsehen auf, Verstehen und Begreifen von, wählen, Zugang zu sind konstitutive Verhaltungen des Fragens und so selbst Seinsmodi eines bestimmten Seienden, des Seienden, das wir, die Fragenden, je selbst sind." *SZ*, p. 7.

[119]*SZ*, p. 12.

[120]"Wenn die Interpretation des Sinnes von Sein Aufgabe wird, ist das Dasein nicht nur das primär zu befragende Seiende, es ist überdies das Seiende, das sich je schon in seinem Sein zu dem verhält, wonach in dieser Frage gefragt wird. Die Seinsfrage ist dann aber nichts anderes als die Radikalisierung einer zum Dasein selbst gehörigen wesenhaften Seinstendenz, des vorontologischen Seinsverständnisses." *SZ*, p. 15.

[121]*SZ*, p. 182.

[122]*SZ*, p. 190.

[123]*SZ*, p. 184.

[124]*SZ*, pp. 166-180.

day mode of being.[125]   This subject, he says, is the anonymous everybody or "they" (*das Man*), and not the *I*, the *I myself*.[126]   The others have robbed the *I* of its being.   "They" are not even particular others, for any "other" can replace and represent any "other."   The others exercise an unobtrusive control and dictatorship, but no one can be pointed to as the dictator.[127]   In using the means of transportation, in reading the newspaper, everyday man behaves like every other man.   We enjoy things and rejoice just like "they" rejoice and enjoy; we read, see, and judge just like "they" read, see, and judge; we find shocking what "they" find shocking.[128]   The "everybody," the anonymous "nobody" allows no exceptions, has no secrets. Its possibilities have been channeled and limited to well-determined tracks.   The "they" can justify everything, for no one in particular is responsible for anything.[129]

What remains in this state of the *I*'s selfhood?   The selfhood of the everyday mode of being-man is the selfhood of the anonymous "they," but this selfhood constitutes the inauthentic, non-genuine man.[130]   The inauthentic man is absorbed by the things in which "they" are absorbed; he ends up by being no longer capable of interpreting himself in any other way than as a thing among things.[131]

To clarify the inauthentic character of being-man, Heidegger undertakes a very detailed analysis of "talk," "curiosity" and "ambiguity" in which everyday man is absorbed.   This analysis shows that everydayness is a positive mode of being-in-the-world,[132] but in this mode the *I* is no longer *it-self*,[133] and its possibilities are no longer *its own*.[134]   For this reason this mode of being-man must be called a "falling away." [135]

Because man in his everydayness has fallen victim to the dictatorship of the anonymous "they," he only rarely experi-

---

[125]"Wer ist es denn, der das Sein als alltägliches Miteinandersein übernommen hat?" *SZ*, p. 125.
[126]"Das 'Wer' ist das Neutrum, das Man." *SZ*, p. 126.
[127]*SZ*, p. 126.
[128]*SZ*, pp. 126-127.
[129]*SZ*, p. 127.
[130]"Das Selbst des alltäglichen Daseins ist das Man-selbst, das wir von dem eigentlichen, d.h. eigens ergriffenen Selbst unterscheiden." *SZ*, p. 129.
[131]*SZ*, p. 130.
[132]*SZ*, pp. 175-176.
[133]"Von ihm selbst als faktischem In-der-Welt-sein ist das Dasein als verfallendes schon abgefallen." *SZ*, p. 176.
[134]*SZ*, p. 178.
[135]*SZ*, p. 175.

ences himself in his authenticity. Thus it should be clear why dread is a rare phenomenon, for it is dread which constitutes the proper, genuine, authentic meaning of the *I*. If, then, one wishes to acquire a view of man in his totality, and if the road to this view lies in understanding man as dread, there seems to be no possibility of ever acquiring such a view, because everyday man in his "falling away" always has avoided dread.

The difficulty, however, is merely apparent. For "falling away" evidently is a *flight* from being authentically human, from man's authentic selfhood, from dread.[136] But this flight betrays the unconcealedness of that from which man flees.[137] Man's flight from the genuine meaning of being-himself is only possible insofar as man as dread is unconcealed from himself.[138]

The flight of inauthentic man should not at all be conceived as a shrinking away or drawing back from *fear*. Fear is entirely different from dread.[139] What is feared is always a definite thing or a definite person.[140] A particular being approaches me in a threatening but not fatal way, its threat can be averted.[141] What approaches me threateningly as something definite coming from a determined region of being makes me fear *for* myself. Only the being for whom, in his being, this being itself is an issue, can fear.[142] What is feared and that for the sake of which I fear, then, are correlated: a certain worldly being threatens my being-in-the-world.[143] In fearing a determined worldly being, I am concerned with my own being-in-the-world as threatened.

In his inauthenticity man does not flee from fear but from

---

[136]"Das Aufgehen im Man und bei der besorgten 'Welt' offenbart so etwas wie eine Flucht des Daseins vor ihm selbst als eigentlichem Selbst-sein-können." *SZ*, p. 184.

[137]"Nur sofern Dasein ontologisch wesenhaft durch die ihm zugehörende Erschlossenheit überhaupt vor es selbst gebracht ist, kann es vor ihm fliehen." *SZ*, p. 184.

[138]*SZ*, p. 185.

[139]*Ibid*.

[140]"Das Wovor der Furcht, das 'Furchtbare', ist jeweils ein innerweltlich Begegnendes von der Seinsart des Zuhandenen, des Vorhandenen oder des Mitdaseins." *SZ*, p. 140.

[141]*SZ*, pp. 140-141.

[142]"Das Worum die Furcht fürchtet ist das sich fürchtende Seiende selbst, das Dasein. Nur Seiendes, dem es in seinem Sein um dieses selbst geht, kann sich fürchten." *SZ*, p. 141.

[143]"Das Fürchten um als Sichfürchten vor erschliesst immer . . . gleichursprünglich das innerweltliche Seiende in seiner Bedrohlichkeit und das In-Sein hinsichtlich seiner Bedrohlichkeit." *Ibid*.

dread.[144] Unlike the object of fear, that of dread is wholly indeterminate.[145] It is never a well-defined object of my world which makes me dread. What makes me dread is even wholly undeterminable: it cannot be pointed out. What threatens me does not approach me here or there: the dreadful is not really anywhere, yet it is so close that it takes my breath away.[146]

In dread, the world in which I am involved collapses. In dread, the world as totality reveals itself as unimportant, insignificant, null. What I dread is not a determined worldly being, but *the world as such*. In dread, the world as world imposes itself on me in all its nothingness.[147] In dread, the world reveals itself as nothing.[148]

This is not yet the most important point, however. With respect to *fear*, I am afraid *of* a certain thing but *for* or on behalf of myself. Regarding *dread*, we must say the same: I am in dread *of* my world but *for* myself, for my being-in-the-world as such.[149] For the world is a system of meanings correlated with my factical and possible modes of being-man as being-in-the-world. The world belongs essentially to being-man as *existence*.[150] If, then, the world as such reveals itself as unimportant, insignificant, null, the implication is that being-in-the-world-as-such is experienced as null. This is the reason why man does not "feel at home" in the world.[151] In dread man stands face to face with the hard, invincible, and inexorable fact that he is thrown into a state of not "being at home." [152]

Inauthentic man tries to flee from this hard fact. He takes refuge in being one-like-many (*das Man*), the peaceful and trusted world of the impersonal and anonymous. His flight is an escape from the not-being-at-home implied in his "thrownness" into the world.[153] In his falling-away man closes himself

---

[144]*SZ*, p. 186.
[145]"Das Wovor der Angst ist völlig unbestimmt." *Ibid.*
[146]*SZ*, p. 186.
[147]*SZ*, pp. 186-187.
[148]*SZ*, p. 187.
[149]"Worum sich die Angst ängstet, ist das In-der-Welt-sein selbst." *Ibid.*
[150]"Diese (die Welt) jedoch gehört ontologisch wesenhaft zum Sein des Daseins als In-der-Welt-sein." *Ibid.*
[151]"Das In-Sein kommt in den existentialen 'Modus' des Un-zuhause. Nichts anderes meint die Rede von der Unheimlichkeit." *SZ*, p. 189.
[152]"Die Angst ängstet sich um das nackte Dasein als in die Unheimlichkeit geworfenes. Sie bringt zurück auf das pure Dass der eigensten, vereinzelten Geworfenheit." *SZ*, p. 343.
[153]*SZ*, p. 189.

to the disclosure of the world-as-such and his being-in-the-world-as-such, in order to lose himself in "caring" for a particular well-defined world in which he feels at home, even though he thus sacrifices the authentic meaning of his being-himself. But his peace is fragile: in the most unexpected situations, dread can suddenly appear. If this happens, the impersonal man has only one escape, viz., fear. By interpreting dread as fear, the terror of unconcealing dread can be kept concealed.[154]

"Toward Death"

Why is it that in dread the world-as-world is experienced as unimportant, insignificant, and null, and that being-in-the-world-as-such reveals itself as being-not-at-home? It is an effect, if we may use this term, of the fact that in dread man faces the mysterious presence of the utmost possibility implied in his being as project.[155] As project, man is the oppositional unity of facticity and potentiality, of determinedness and possibility.[156] Dread discloses the utmost possibility of man as project, and this possibility is death. All dread, therefore, is dread of death.[157]

An adequate understanding of death is indispensable if one wishes to acquire a vision of the whole man. For how could anyone claim to have such a vision if man as project always contains an aspect of potentiality and, therefore, is never "finished"?[158] This difficulty can only be overcome by the explicitation of man's being as being-toward-death.[159] For as long as man is man, one or the other form of potential being always remains open to him. Among these forms, however, is also the end of his being-in-the-world, and this is death. The end of man as potential being limits and determines the possible totality of his being.[160]

---

[154]"Furcht ist an die 'Welt' verfallene, uneigentliche und ihr selbst als solche verborgene Angst." *SZ*, p. 189.
[155]*SZ*, pp. 265-266.
[156]*SZ*, p. 145.
[157]"Das Sein zum Tode ist wesenhaft Angst." *SZ*, p. 266.
[158]"Und wenn die Existenz das Sein des Daseins bestimmt und ihr Wesen mitkonstituiert wird durch das Seinkönnen, dann muss das Dasein, solange es existiert, seinkönnend je etwas noch nicht sein. Seiendes, dessen Essenz die Existenz ausmacht, widersetzt sich wesenhaft der möglichen Erfassung seiner als ganzes Seiendes." *SZ*, p. 233.
[159]*SZ*, p. 234.
[160]"Dieses Ende, zum Seinkönnen, d.h. zur Existenz gehörig, begrenzt und bestimmt die je mögliche Ganzheit des Daseins." *Ibid.*

Is not all this, one could ask, merely the postponement of a difficulty? The aim is a total vision of man; [161] but as long as man is—i.e., until his end—man has possibilities: his being includes a being-able-to-be, is unfinished, and, consequently, cannot be grasped as a totality. [162] On the other hand, as soon as being-man no longer includes any possibilities, is finished, man is "no longer there," his being is no longer an issue for him, he can no longer experience himself. [163]

This line of thought, however, reveals a fundamentally wrong view of man as being-able-to-be. [164] As potential being, being-man is not like the being of a thing "to which something can happen." [165] Man's being-unfinished is not like the being-not-yet-full of the moon or the not-yet-being-ripe of an apple. [166] Similarly, man's end, his death, is not like the end of a shower or the end of a road. [167] Such a way of thinking about death does not conceive man's death as the death of *man*. Death is only conceived as the death of *man* when man's being is understood as being-toward-death. [168]

Accordingly, when death is said to be the end of life, this expression means that life is a "being-toward-the-end," not a "being *at* the end" but a "being-*toward*-the-end." [169] Life is doomed to death: as soon as man comes to life, he is old enough to die. Death is not an external event which happens to man, [170] but is intrinsic to life; hence, man's being must be called a being-toward-death. Just as the facticity of human *existence* is not what it is without man's potential being, so also human life is not what it is without death. Because death is inherent to life,

---

161*SZ*, p. 236.
162" 'Solange es (das Dasein) ist' bis zu seinem Ende verhält es sich zu seinem Seinkönnen." *Ibid.*
163"Sobald jedoch das Dasein so 'existiert', dass an ihm schlechthin nichts mehr aussteht, dann ist es auch schon in eins damit zum Nicht-mehr-da-sein geworden. . . . Als Seiendes wird es dann nie mehr erfahrbar." *Ibid.*
164*SZ*, p. 237.
165*SZ*, p. 143.
166*SZ*, pp. 243-244.
167*SZ*, p.244.
168"Daseinsmässig aber ist der Tod nur in einem existenziellen Sein zum Tode." *SZ*, p. 234.
169"So wie das Dasein vielmehr ständig, solange es ist, schon sein Noch-nicht ist, so ist es auch schon immer sein Ende. Das mit dem Tod gemeinte Enden bedeutet kein Zu-Ende-sein des Daseins, sondern ein Sein zum Ende dieses Seienden. Der Tod ist eine Weise zu sein, die das Dasein übernimmt, sobald es ist. Sobald ein Mensch zum Leben kommt, sogleich ist er alt genug zu sterben." *SZ*, p. 245.
170*SZ*, p. 254.

death has to be understood in terms of the fundamental structure of man's being.[171] Heidegger characterized this fundamental structure as "care," [172] as the organic unity of *existence* (the "not yet"), facticity (the "already"), and "fallenness." [173] If death belongs to being-man, then death must be definable in terms of the fundamental structure of man's being.[174]

As a matter of fact, this can be done.[175] First of all, death is the mode of potential being which is most proper to man; it is the mode in which he, alone, is confronted with the possibility most proper to him—the invincible possibility of his impossibility.[176] In the most original way man's being "ahead of himself" becomes concrete in being-toward-death.[177] Death is the ultimate "not yet" of man's being as potential. This possibility, however, is not incidentally procured for himself by man in the course of his life. The extreme possibility of his *existence,* as a possibility, is also "already" present: [178] as soon as man comes to life, he is old enough to die. Finally, death reveals also the third characteristic of man's being as "care," viz., his "falling away." [179]

In his everydayness man is absorbed in the anonymity of the "they" and its impersonal, anonymous world. He flees from the most proper possibility of his existence, from dread and not being "at home." This flight from dread is an escape from the dread of death.[180]

The anonymous "they" is not ignorant of death, but its knowledge consists in a very special way of explicitating being-toward-death. The anonymous man knows death as an item

---

171*SZ*, p. 249.
172*SZ*, pp. 191-196.
173"Als Grundverfassung des Daseins wurde die Sorge Sichtbar gemacht, Die ontologische Bedeutung dieses Ausdrucks drückte sich in der 'Definition' aus: Sich-vorweg-schon-sein-in (der Welt) als Sein-bei (innerweltlich) begegnendem Seienden. Damit sind die fundamentalen Charaktere des Seins des Daseins ausgedrückt: im Sich-vorweg die Existenz, im Schon-sein-in. . . . die Faktizität, im Sein-bei . . . das Verfallen." *SZ*, pp. 249-250.
174*SZ*, p. 250.
175*SZ*, p. 252.
176"In dieser Möglichkeit geht es dem Dasein um sein In-der-Weltsein schlechthin. Sein Tod ist die Möglichkeit des Nicht-mehr-dasein-könnens. . . . Der Tod ist die Möglichkeit der schlechthinnigen Daseinsunmöglichkeit." *SZ*, p. 250.
177*SZ*, p. 251.
178"Sondern, wenn Dasein existiert, ist es auch schon in diese Möglichkeit geworfen." *SZ*, p. 251.
179"Das Dasein stirbt faktisch, solange es existiert, aber zunächst und zumeist in der Weise des Verfallens." *SZ*, p. 252.
180*Ibid.*

in the obituary column.[181] For the everyday man death is a
trivial event which befalls man from without: "one" will die
some day, of course, but right now "one" is spared.[182] "One
dies" does not mean: "I die," but "everybody dies" that is, nobody dies. In this way dying is explicitated as a "happening,"
while death itself does not *belong* to anyone. Everydayness is
the covering-up of death as the possibility which is *mine par
excellence*.[183] Even the way in which the dying are consoled
betrays the same inauthenticity: one tries to make him believe
that he will not die, that he will return to the trusted old everydayness. One tries to conceal to the dying man his *own* most
proper possibility.[184] The anonymous "they" simply does not
allow the courage to dread death to arise,[185] but only knows *fear*
for death-as-a-happening, a fear to which the self-assured man
may not give in.[186]

Evidently, then, the being of the impersonal "they" is a being estranged, estranged from itself and its ownmost possibility.
Death is conceived as a happening which strikes the anonymous
one. Thus the proper meaning of death, its being-already-
present-as-a-possibility, its possibility as a possibility of *me*, of
me *alone*, is not recognized but concealed. The impersonal
one is interested only in the certainty that *he himself is still
alive*.[187] He does not want to accept that the very being of
man is a being-toward-death, that life itself is affected by death
as an ever-present possibility.

In spite of this, the being of the anonymous "they" is still a
being-toward-death. We may even say that in his everydayness
man is concerned with his ownmost and invincible possibility,
albeit only by nurturing an undisturbed indifference toward his
possible impossibility.[188] The impersonal one is also quite cer-

181"Die Oeffenlichkeit des alltäglichen Miteinander 'kennt' den Tod als
ständig vorkommendes Begegnis, als 'Todesfall.'" *Ibid.*
182*SZ*, p. 253.
183"Das Man gibt Recht und steigert die Versuchung, das eigenste Sein
zum Tode sich zu verdecken." *Ibid.*
184*Ibid.*
185"Das Man lässt den Mut zur Angst vor dem Tode nicht aufkommen."
SZ, p. 254.
186*SZ*, p. 254.
187"Dass das je eigene Dasein faktisch immer schon stirbt, d.h. in seinem
Sein zu seinem Ende ist, dieses Faktum verbirgt es sich dadurch, dass es den
Tod umz alltäglich vorkommenden Todesfall bei Anderen umprägt, des allen-
falls uns noch deutlicher versichert, dass 'man selbst' ja noch 'lebt.'" *Ibid.*
188*SZ*, p. 255.

tain of death. Although this certainty does not seem to be more than a kind of empirical certainty, derived from the occurrence of death as an item in the obituary column, as merely a happening,[189] the impersonal one really knows better.[190] Insofar as he tries to hide, conceal and banish the proper meaning of death, the impersonal one really derives his certainty about death from an awareness that being-man is a being-toward-death.[191] Death is certain, for it is present in the being of man as being-toward-his-end.[192]

We are now perhaps in a position to determine the correct attitude of man toward death. This determination must be possible on the basis of the fact that the true meaning of death has been unveiled and the improper, inauthentic being-toward death unmasked.[193]

Man's proper response to his realization that his being is a being-toward-death demands at least that he do not try to escape from his ownmost possibility, conceal it, or give a false meaning to it.[194] This does not mean that man must put himself to death. Man's being is a "having to be," but in obedience to the unconcealedness of his essence. Man's essence lies in his *existence*;[195] consequently, his response to his consciousness of being-toward-death may not destroy his whole potential being. But by committing suicide, man would demolish all his potentialities.[196]

In his being-toward-death man must apprehend the possibility of death as a possibility without minimizing it; he must culture it as a possibility, "endure" it as a possibilty.[197] The authentic response to the consciousness of being-toward-death is "expectation" *(Erwarten)*, not in the way one expects a

---

189*SZ*, p. 257.
190"Wenngleich das Dasein in der Oeffentlichkeit des Man scheinbar nur von dieser 'empirischen' Gewissheit des Todes 'redet', so hält es sich im Grunde doch nicht ausschliesslich und primär an die vorkommenden Todesfälle. Seinem Tode ausweichend ist auch das alltägliche Sein zum Ende des Todes doch anders gewiss, als es selbst in rein theoretischer Besinnung wahrhaben möchte." *SZ*, pp. 257-258.
191"Das verdeckende Ausweichen vor dem Tode vermag seinem Sinne nach des Todes nicht eigentlich 'gewiss' zu sein und ist es doch." *SZ*, p. 256.
192"Der Tod ist als Ende des Daseins im Sein dieses Seienden zu seinem Ende." *SZ*, p. 259.
193*SZ*, p. 260.
194*Ibid.*
195*SZ*, p. 42.
196"Damit entzöge sich aber das Dasein gerade den Boden für ein existierendes Sein zum Tode." *SZ*, p. 261.
197*Ibid.*

rain shower, but by "running forward in thought" on its possible impossibility, in the realization that in the light of this extreme, yet present, possibility, it is futile to busy oneself with
things and with the company of fellowmen.[198]   Nevertheless,
this realization may not induce man to abandon his busy-ness
with things and his togetherness with fellowmen in a kind of
apathetic surrender.   For this busy-ness and togetherness belong to the essential structure of man's being: he must take up
all of this, but in the light of his ownmost possible impossibility.[199]   Man's proper being is an "ahead of himself" becoming-
free for the extreme possibility of his self-realizing essence; a
being free from losing himself in the particular possibilities
which happen to present themselves; it is an understanding and
choosing of these possibilities in the light of the extreme possibility; it is the impossibility of being "benumbed" by what has
already been attained.[200]

Thus it does not matter that the "when" of death, which itself is certain, is not determined.[201]   The continual "threat" of
death does not arise from death as a happening-at-a-certain-
moment.   The threat springs from man's unconcealedness to
himself as "running ahead of himself."   Man is certain of his
being-in-the-world and, consequently, of his extreme, "already"
present possibility.[202]   All this becomes disclosed in dread, for
all understanding is equiprimordially a being-affected (*befindliches*).[203]   The tonality or mood of being-man, through
which man continually and without qualification is faced with
the threat arising from his ownmost and isolated being, is nothing other than dread.[204]   In dread man stands face to face with
the nothingness of the possible impossibility of his *existence* as
self-realizing being; in dread, he stands face to face with death,
for dread is dread of death.[205]   The freedom to be authenti-

---

[198]*SZ,* pp. 262-263.
[199]"Das Dasein ist eigentlich es selbst nur, sofern es sich als besorgendes
Sein bei . . . und fürsorgendes Sein mit . . . primär auf sein eigenstes Seinkönnen, nicht aber auf die Möglichkeit des Man-selbst entwirft." *SZ,* pp.
263-264.
[200]*SZ,* p. 264.
[201]*SZ,* p. 265.
[202]"Im Vorlaufen zum unbestimmt gewissen Tode öffnet sich das Dasein
für eine aus seinem Da selbst entspringende ständige Bedrohung." *Ibid.*
[203]"Alles Verstehen ist befindliches." *Ibid.*
[204]*SZ,* pp. 265-266.
[205]*SZ,* p. 266.

cally himself which reveals itself in dread appears to be freedom-toward-death.

Conscience and Guilt

Finally, Heidegger seeks a confirmation of his theory about man's ownmost being in the testimony of conscience.[206] As Alphonse de Waelhens points out, looking for such a confirmation cannot mean much more than making an effort to approach the same question again from a different angle—that is, the question of the meaning of man's ownmost being.[207] Ultimately, then, that is, if we abstract from Heidegger's theory about the character of moral consciousness, the analysis of the testimony of conscience does not offer any important new perspective. Although he has lapsed into losing himself in the anonymity of the impersonal, man has sometimes privileged moments in which the voice of his conscience speaks to him.[208] The one thus addressed is man, insofar as he has become lost in the impersonal anonymity of the "they." But this being spoken to by his conscience is a call upon man, a call to his ownmost potential being-himself.[209]

How must this "voice" be understood? Who calls him? Undoubtedly, it is man himself who calls,[210] but not man as lost in impersonal anonymity. The voice of conscience is man in his not-being-at-home, in his original thrownness-into-the-world, into his "nullity."[211] Man calls himself from his inauthenticity to his ownmost potential being.

The origin of the call is not the main point, however. Before one can say that he really understands the call of conscience, it is necessary to clarify the relationship which evidently exists between conscience and guilt.[212] Here also, however, the anonymous "they" has done its nefarious work: it has cou-

[206]*SZ*, pp. 267-301.
[207]A. De Waelhens, *La philosophie de Martin Heidegger*, pp. 150-151.
[208]*SZ*, pp. 270-271.
[209]"Der Ruf stellt, seiner Ruftendenz entsprechend, das angerufene Selbst nicht zu einer 'Verhandlung', sondern als Aufruf zum eigensten Selbstseinkönnen ist er ein Vor-(nach 'vorne'-)Rufen des Daseins in seine eigensten Möglichkeiten." *SZ*, p. 273.
[210]"Das Dasein ruft im Gewissen sich selbst. . . . Der Ruf kommt aus mir und doch über mich." *SZ*, p. 275.
[211]*SZ*, pp. 276-277.
[212]*SZ*, pp. 280-281.

pled conscience of guilt to certain evil deeds.[213] This is wrong, for guilt is not the result of evil deeds, but evil deeds are only possible on the basis of an original being-guilty.[214] What, then, is this original guilt?

This guilt is constituted by thrownness. Man's being as care is always also a being-already-thrown-into-the-world. Man is a "having to be," but as "already embarked": he has to undertake his being without having chosen it himself; man belongs to himself, but without being his own gift to himself; man is the ground of his potential being, his possibilities, but he himself has not established this ground.[215] Man, whose task it is to be himself, can never be *himself* to such an extent that he overcomes his "already." [216] Man undertakes his own being, he realizes himself, without ever acquiring perfect power over himself. He is a thrown project and, therefore, null, and this radical and invincible nullity constitutes his guilt.[217]

The call of conscience is an invitation by man himself to recognize his guilt,[218] but at the same time, it is a call to take his guilt, his nullity, upon himself—that is, as null—and to project himself to his ownmost possibility, his end, his death.[219] Man is the null-like ground of his nullity, the thrown project of his death, and it is as such that he "has to be." [220] The authentic answer to the call of conscience is the resolve (*Entschlossenheit*) [221] with which man, as an *I myself*, takes the nullity of his being-thrown-into-the-world upon himself, and in anguished silence projects himself forward to the nothingness of his own death.

"Being Toward God"?

Heidegger's commentators used to be uncertain whether,

---

[213]*SZ*, pp. 281-282.
[214]"Das Schuldigsein resultiert nicht erst aus einer Verschuldung, sondern umgekehrt: diese wird erst möglich 'auf Grund' eines ursprünglichen Schuldigseins." *SZ*, p. 284.
[215]*SZ*, pp. 284-285.
[216]"Das Selbst, das als solches den Grund seiner selbst zu legen hat, kann dessen nie mächtig werden und hat doch existierend das Grundsein zu übernehmen." *SZ*, p. 284.
[217]*SZ*, p. 285.
[218]*SZ*, p. 287.
[219]"Die Entschlossenheit wird eigentlich das, was sie sein kann, als verstehendes Sein zum Ende, d.h. als Vorlaufen in den Tod." *SZ*, p. 305.
[220]*SZ*, pp. 305-306.
[221]". . . das verschwiegene, angstbereite Sichentwerfen auf das eigenste Schuldigsein. . . ." *SZ*, p. 297.

judged by his philosophy, he should be called an atheist or not. Sartre says that Heidegger is a representative of atheistic existentialism, but he fails to tell us on what basis he "resolved" this question.[222] Heidegger's work published after BEING AND TIME, however, show that Sartre is wrong.

In this matter Heidegger had to defend himself against the grossest misconceptions. Because he called the essence of man *existence,* some critics imagined that he wished to substitute man for God; [223] for traditional metaphysics conceived God's essence as *existentia,* and Heidegger called man's essence *existence.*[224] The critics did not see, or did not wish to see, that in Heidegger the term *existence* expresses man's specific mode of being, as distinct from that of God or things. Heidegger's intention was precisely to indicate that in our thinking we may not divinize man, for man's being is a being-in-the-world, which could never be affirmed of God. "God is, but He does not *exist.*" [225]

For some representatives of existentialism and phenomenology, however, the *way* in which they call man *existence* constitutes the direct foundation of their atheism. As we have mentioned, those who define man's being as nothing but being-in-the-world make it *a priori* impossible for themselves to say that man's being is *also* a being-toward-God.[226] It is striking, however, that Heidegger, who also says that man's being is a being-in-the-world, has never claimed that man's being is *nothing but* a being-in-the-world. On the contrary. According to Heidegger, the interpretation of man as being-in-the-world neither positively nor negatively decides anything about the possibility of man's being-toward-God. What this interpretation does is open up the possibility of asking the question whether man has perhaps a relationship to God.[227]

---

[222]Sartre, *EH,* p. 17.

[223]Takatura Ando, *Metaphysics, A Critical Survey of Its Meanings,* The Hague, 1963, p. 107.

[224]"Die letzte Verirrung wäre jedoch, wollte man den Satz über das eksisente Wesen des Menschen so erklären, als sei er die säkularisierte Übertragung eines von der christlichen Theologie über Gott ausgesagten Gedankens (Deus est suum esse) auf den Menschen." Heidegger, *Über den Humanismus,* pp. 16-17.

[225]Heidegger, *Was ist Metaphysik?,* p. 15.

[226]"Mais si nous retrouvons le temps sous le sujet et si nous rattachons au paradoxe du temps ceux du corps, du monde, de la chose et d'autrui, nous comprendrons qu'il n'y a rien à comprendre au-delà." Merleau-Ponty, *PP,* p. 419.

[227]"Durch die ontologische Interpretation des Daseins als In-der-Welt-sein ist weder positiv noch negativ über ein mögliches Sein zu Gott entschieden.

But, one may ask, does not such a relationship become illusory if it is supposed to be certain that being-in-the-world does not have any "higher instance" above itself than death? [228] For K.- Roessing, Heidegger's theory of death is an indication that he does not recognize any "higher world." [229] This conclusion, however, does not follow. One can readily concede to Heidegger that death is the "highest instance" of being-in-the-world. But the question is whether man is encompassed by his being-in-the-world. If man's being would also have to be called a "being over and beyond the world," death would still remain the "highest instance" for his being-in-the-world, but not for his integral being-man. Nowhere does Heidegger suggest that man's being is encompassed by being-in-the-world. Nowhere, therefore, does he exclude that the subject as "functioning intentionality" is the "affirmation" of the Transcendent Absolute. Heidegger has never considered this aspect of the *existent* subject because he first wanted to renew the only ground on which all authentic affirmations are possible.

Because thinking must first renew the ground on which alone all authentic affirmations are possible, Heidegger considers it very difficult—but not impossible—to reflect upon the "way" to God. This way will not be found until thinking recovers its proper dimension, develops as a thinking of the "truth of Being." From the truth of Being it will then be possible to think the "coming to pass" of the holy; only from the "coming to pass" of the holy it is possible to think the "coming to pass" of the "divinity"; and in the light of the "divinity's" "coming to pass" it is possible to think and say what the term "God" means.[230] To bring about the "coming to pass" of Being "thinking" must prepare a "place" where man is sensitive for the "call of Being"; in other words, man must first rediscover

---

Wohl aber wird durch die Erhellung der Transzendenz allererst ein zureichender Begriff des Daseins gewonnen, mit Rücksicht auf welches Seiende nunmehr gefragt werden kann, wie es mit dem Gottesverhältnis des Daseins ontologisch bestellt ist." Heidegger, *Vom Wesen des Grundes*, Frankfurt a.M., 1949, p. 39, note 56.

[228]*SZ*, p. 313.

[229]K. H. Roessing, *Martin Heidegger als Godsdienstwijsgeer*, Assen, 1956, p. 149.

[230]"Erst aus der Wahrheit des Seins lässt sich das Wesen des Heiligen denken. Erst aus dem Wesen des Heiligen ist das Wesen von Gottheit zu denken. Erst im Lichte des Wesens von Gottheit kann gedacht und gesagt werden, was das Wort 'Gott' nennen soll." Heidegger, *Ueber den Humanismus*, pp. 36-37.

the scope of his own essence, so that the truth of Being can "come to pass." In the same way, man must first enter the dimension of the holy's "coming to pass" before he may expect that he can think and express what the term "God" means. Heidegger suspects that reflection on religiousness could perhaps be the road to God.

For Heidegger, however, the holy has nothing to do with virtues in the traditional sense of the term. It is primarily nature that is called holy. "Nature 'educates' the poets," [231] and the poets are called to give expression to the holy.[232] Poets are seized by the mighty power, the divine beauty, the omnipresence of nature; [233] they celebrate that which most of all "concerns" the sons of the earth when they have to be able to "dwell." Poets express the holy which rules over gods and men. Through the poets' expression, the gods become aware of themselves as gods and induce themselves to appear in the dwelling place of men on earth. Poets stand midway between the gods and men as pointers.[234] The blooming of a tree contains the unmerited fortune of the fruit, the saving holy which favors mortal man. The openness of the holy is the "wholeness," the integrity of authentic "dwelling."

The fundamental feature of "dwelling" is "tending" (*Schonen*), that is, respecting, saving, and keeping in good order.[235] This feature shows us that being-man lies in "dwelling," in the sense of the mortals' sojourn on earth. "On earth"—that means "under heaven." Earth and heaven refer to the gods and the "together" of the mortals. Earth and heaven, the gods and the mortals belong together in an original unity.[236] The earth is

---

[231]M. Heidegger, *Erläuterungen zu Hölderlins Dichtung*, 3rd ed., Frankfurt, a.M., 1963, p. 51.

[232]"Der Dichter denkt das Heilige." *Was ist Metaphysik?*, p. 51.

[233]Heidegger, *Erläuterungen zu Hölderlins Dichtung*, p. 53.

[234]"Aber soll der Dichter nicht gerade das Heilige denken, das über den Göttern und den Menschen ist? Gewiss. Doch muss er das Heilige darstellen, damit durch sein Sagen die Götter sich selbst fühlen und so sich selbst zum Erscheinen bringen in der Wohnstatt der Menschen auf dieser Erde. Der Dichter muss an das denken, was die Erdensöhne zuerst angeht, wenn sie sollen wohnen können in ihrem Heimischen. . . . Der Dichter steht als der Zeigende zwischen den Menschen und den Göttern." Heidegger, *op. cit.*, p. 116.

[235]Heidegger, *Vorträge und Aufsätze*, p. 149.

[236]"Doch 'auf der Erde' heisst schon 'unter dem Himmel'. Beides meint mit 'Bleiben vor den Göttlichen' und schliesst ein 'gehörend in das Miteinander der Menschen.' Aus einer *ursprünglichen* Einheit gehören die Vier: Erde und Himmel, die Göttlichen und die Sterblichen in eins." Heidegger, *op. cit.*, p. 149.

what serves and bears, blooms and gives fruit, what extends itself in water and rocks, what grows and flourishes as plant and animal. Heaven in the vaulting course of the sun and the moon, the brilliance of the stars, the seasons, the light and darkness of the day, the darkness and light of the night, the clemency and inclemency of the weather, the drifting-by of the clouds, the blue depth of the ether. The gods are the bidding messengers of the divinity. The mortals are men, who are called mortals because they have the power of death as death. Heidegger calls the original belonging together of these four "the four-some" [237] ("quadrate"—*Geviert*).

"Dwelling," then, implies four aspects. Mortals "dwell" insofar as they "save" the earth—that is, do not overpower and subdue it; they "dwell" insofar as they receive heaven as heaven, that is, let the sun and the moon have their course, the seasons their blessing or their rawness, and do not make the night into day and the day into night by their restless pursuits; they "dwell" insofar as they expect the gods, hoping for the unhoped-for, while still afflicted by the unwholesome, waiting for the wholesome that has gone; they "dwell" insofar as they accompany the mortals in order that death be a good death. In the "saving" of the earth, the receiving of heaven, the expectation of the gods, and the accompanying of the mortals, "dwelling" "comes to pass" as the fourfold "tending" of the "foursome." To "tend" means to shepherd the "foursome" in its "coming to pass." [238]

Man, however, has totally unlearned authentic "dwelling." He has let the "wholeness" of his *Dasein* shrink and shrivel away. The "real 'dwelling famine' does not consist in a housing shortage," [239] but in the homelessness of man. This means that not only the holy, as pointing to the Divinity, is concealed but also "wholeness" itself is dislocated, so that even the pointing to the holy is erased.[240] The gods are gone. Only when he becomes again sensitive to the "coming to pass" of the holy will

---

[237]Heidegger, *op. cit.*, p. 150.
[238]Heidegger, *op. cit.*, pp. 150-151.
[239]Heidegger, *op. cit.*, p. 162.
[240]"Das Heile entzieht sich. Die Welt wird heil-los. Dadurch bleibt nicht nur das Heilige als die Spur zur Gottheit verborgen, sondern sogar die Spur zum Heiligen, das Heile, scheint ausgelöscht zu sein." Heidegger, *Holzwege*, p. 272.

it be possible for man to hope that he will again be able to think and express what the term "God" means.

Heidegger sees Hölderlin as *the* poet of God's absence.[241] The poets, however, are also called to re-express the holy and prepare the coming of God. In his poetical "naming," the poet lets the High One Himself appear.[242] God's appearance comes to pass in a disclosure which makes visible that which conceals itself. But this disclosure does not let us see by tearing the concealed from its concealment, but by "shepherding" the concealed in its self-concealment.[243] The unknown God appears as the Unknown.[244]

Conclusion

"We must often remain silent for lack of holy 'names,'" said Hölderlin in reference to man's efforts to speak of God. Others go further and think that, at least provisionally, we must keep entirely silent about God. But even the Death-of-God theologians cannot execute this "program" and, as long as they continue to speak so loudly and write so much, their firm resolve to keep silent about God remains somewhat ambiguous. It appears impossible to remain silent about God as long as man cannot cease speaking authentically about himself. This authenticity, however, imposes the condition that man does not call "halt" at the very moment when he realizes that he must speak although he cannot use the "simple" word "is" as he has always used it hitherto. God *is* not as beings are. Man, however, is not merely the "saying"-of-"is"-in-the-world. The "is"-"saying"-in-the-world—which man himself is as "functioning intentionality"—reveals itself as embedded in an "affirmation" whose correlate *is* not, but at the same time, is not *is-not*. This reciprocal implication of "affirmation" and "negation" is the being of man himself as "being over and beyond the world."

241"Indem Hölderlin das Wesen der Dichtung neu stiftet, bestimmt er erst eine neue Zeit. Es ist die Zeit der entflohenden Götter und des kommenden Gottes. Das ist die dürftige Zeit, weil sie in einem gedoppelten Mangel und Nicht steht: im Nichtmehr der entflohenen Götter und im Nochnicht des Kommenden." Heidegger, *Erläuterungen zu Hölderlins Dichtung,* p. 44.

242"Dichtend nennen bedeutet: im Wort den Hohen selbst erscheinen lassen." Heidegger, *op. cit.* p. 26.

243Heidegger, *Vorträge und Aufsätze,* p. 197.

244"So erscheint der unbekannte Gott als der Unbekannte durch die Offenbarkeit des Himmels." Heidegger, *ibid.*

In the past, metaphysics in its second phase tried to express this "affirmation" and "negation" on the level of the *cogito*. In Sartre one can find an unwilled attempt to do the same on the level of the *volo*. Heidegger very decidedly makes a "step back" in order to first seek the dimension of man's essence in which the self-revelation of the Unknown God as the Unknown can come about. "We must often remain silent." At the same time, however, it is certain that man may not let himself be seduced to an absolute silence, for anything of which man preserves an absolute silence dies for him. But if God had really died for him, modern man would now be in his death agony.

INDEX OF NAMES

INDEX OF SUBJECT MATTER